Building a Better Mouse Trap: A Programmer's Guide to the Mouse

Disk Contents

The 3.5-inch 720Kb disk that accompanies this book contains the complete listings for all of the programs found in the book. The disk is divided into the following subdirectories:

Subdirectory	Contents of Subdirectory
DOSCODE	Source code for all DOS programming examples
WINCODE	Source code for all Windows programming examples
BOBJ	Precompiled object files for Borland users
MOBJ	Precompiled object files for Microsoft users

The precompiled object files are for the DOS programming examples that require an assembler. If you do not have an assembler, use the file(s) located in these subdirectories.

The root directory also contains a README file that provides additional help and last-minute notices.

You will need a 3.5-inch 720Kb disk drive to read the disk.

Requirements for DOS Programming

The DOS programming examples in this book require the following:

- An Intel 8086, 8088, 80286, 80386, 80486 (or compatible) computer with DOS 2.0 or later. You will also need a mouse (Microsoft or 100-percent compatible), and the appropriate mouse driver (MOUSE.COM or MOUSE.SYS).

- The examples found in Chapters 1 through 16 require a CGA, EGA, or VGA video system. The examples found in Chapters 18 through 21 require an EGA or VGA video system.

- Borland programmers need Turbo C version 2.0 or Borland C++ version 1.0 or later. Microsoft programmers need Microsoft C version 6.0, or Microsoft QuickC version 2.5 or later.

- It is recommended that you have Borland TASM.EXE 1.0, BASM.EXE, or Microsoft MASM.EXE 5.0 or later. However, it is not required.

Requirements for Windows Programming

The Windows programming examples in this book require the following:

- Windows 3.1 running on an Intel 80286, 80386, or 80486 (or compatible) computer with DOS 3.1 or later. You will also need a mouse and monitor that Windows supports.

- Borland programmers need Turbo C++ for Windows version 3.1, or Borland C++ 3.1 or later. Microsoft programmers need Microsoft C/C++ 7.0 or later.

WARNING: BEFORE OPENING THE DISK PACKAGE OPPOSITE, CAREFULLY READ THE TERMS AND CONDITIONS OF THE DISK WARRANTY FOUND ON THE BACK OF THIS PAGE.

DISK WARRANTY

This software is protected by both United States copyright law and international copyright treaty provision. You must treat this software just like a book, except that you may copy it into a computer to be used and you may make archival copies of the software for the sole purpose of backing up our software and protecting your investment from loss.

By saying, "just like a book," Osborne/McGraw-Hill means, for example, that this software may be used by any number of people and may be freely moved from one computer location to another, so long as there is no possibility of its being used at one location or on one computer while it is being used at another. Just as a book cannot be read by two different people in two different places at the same time, neither can the software be used by two different people in two different places at the same time (unless, of course, Osborne's copyright is being violated).

LIMITED WARRANTY

Osborne/McGraw-Hill warrants the physical diskette(s) enclosed herein to be free of defects in materials and workmanship for a period of sixty days from the purchase date. If Osborne/McGraw-Hill receives written notification within the warranty period of defects in materials or workmanship, and such notification is determined by Osborne/McGraw-Hill to be correct, Osborne/McGraw-Hill will replace the defective diskette(s).

The entire and exclusive liability and remedy for breach of this Limited Warranty shall be limited to replacement of defective diskettes(s) and shall not include or extend to any claim for or right to cover any other damages, including but not limited to, loss of profit, data, or use of the software, or special, incidental, or consequential damages or other similar claims, even if Osborne/McGraw-Hill has been specifically advised of the possibility of such damages. In no event will Osborne/McGraw-Hill's liability for any damages to you or any other person ever exceed the lower of the suggested list price or actual price paid for the license to use the software, regardless of any form of the claim.

OSBORNE, A DIVISION OF McGRAW-HILLL, INC., SPECIFICALLY DISCLAIM ALL OTHER WARRANTIES, EXPRESS OR IMPLIED, INCLUDING BUT NOT LIMITED TO, ANY IMPLIED WARRANTY OF MERCHANTABILITY OR FITNESS FOR A PARTICULAR PURPOSE. Specifically, Osborne/McGraw-Hill make no representation or warranty that the software is fit for any particular purpose and any implied warranty of merchantability is limited to the sixty-day duration of the Limited Warranty covering the physical diskette(s) only (and not the software) and is otherwise expressly and specifically disclaimed.

This limited warranty gives you specific legal rights; you may have others which may vary from state to state. Some states do not allow the exclusion of incidental or consequential damages, or the limitation on how long an implied warranty lasts, so some of the above may not apply to you.

Building a Better Mouse Trap: A Programmer's Guide to the Mouse

Jeffrey S. Donovan

Osborne **McGraw-Hill**

Berkeley New York St. Louis San Francisco
Auckland Bogotá Hamburg London Madrid
Mexico City Milan Montreal New Delhi Panama City
Paris São Paulo Singapore Sydney
Tokyo Toronto

Osborne McGraw-Hill
2600 Tenth Street
Berkeley, California 94710
U.S.A.

For information on software, translations, or book distributors outside of the U.S.A.,
please write to Osborne **McGraw-Hill** at the above address.

Building a Better Mouse Trap: A Programmer's Guide to the Mouse

1234567890 DOC 99876543

ISBN 0-07-881930-X

To my most wonderful parents, Charles and Doris Donovan,
my lovely wife Anne Brown,
and the late George Brown, whom we all miss very much.

Acquisitions Editor ————————————
Frances Stack

Associate Editor ————————————
Jill Pisoni

Technical Editor ————————————
Herbert Schildt

Project Editor ————————————
Vicki Van Ausdall

Copy Editor ————————————
Paul Medoff

Proofreaders ————————————
Peter K. Vacek

Indexer ————————————
Jeffrey S. Donovan

Computer Designers ————————————
Stefany Otis

Illustrator ————————————
Marla Shelasky

Cover Design ————————————
Compass Marketing

Contents

Foreword   xv
Acknowledgments   xvii
Introduction   xix

Part I
Interfacing with the Mouse

1

How To Communicate with
the Mouse: Interrupt 33 Hex   3

The Mouse Driver   3
Interrupt 33 Hex   4
  Interrupt Service Functions   4
  The Working Registers   5
  Declarations   5
  The General Registers   6
  Making a Function Call to the
    Mouse Driver   6
Borland and Microsoft Compiler
  Compatibility   7
  Modifying COMPILER.H   9
  Graphics and Text I/O   10

2

The Video Function Library   11

Introduction to the Video Function
  Library   11
  Using the Same Format for
    Graphics and Text Modes   11
  Inner Workings of the Video
    Function Library   12
Source Code for the Video
  Function Library   15
  The Borland Video Function
    Library   15
  The Microsoft Video Function
    Library   21
Notes on the Video Function
  Library   28
Testing the Video Function Library   29
  Compiling the Test Program   29
Running the Test Program   30

3

The Ten Necessary Mouse
Functions   33

Mouse Buttons   33
The Mouse Functions   34
Global Variables   35
About Graphics and Text Modes   36

The Mouse Function Library 36
Mouse Function 0: Reset and Status 44
   Determining Mouse Presence 45
   Number of Buttons 46
   Text Cell Sizes 46
   Mouse Cursor Size 47
Your First Mouse Program 47
The Invisible Mouse Cursor 49
   Limiting the Range Based on
     Mouse Cursor Size 51
   Warning: Mouse Function 38 52

4

How To Keep A Mouse
from Turning into a Rat   53

The Golden Rule 53
The Problem 54
The Solutions 57
   Method 1: Hiding and Showing
     the Mouse Cursor 58
   Method 2: Setting an Exclusion
     Area 62
EGA Registers, Compatibility, and
   OEM Mice 66
   EGA.SYS 68
   The EGA_REG_READ Variable 68
   EGA Workaround 69

5

Tracking the Mouse Cursor
and Emulating Cursor
Movement with the
Keyboard   71

Tracking Mouse Coordinates 71
Tracking Text Coordinates in a
   Graphics Mode 74
Emulating Mouse Cursor
   Movement with the Keyboard 76
   Moving the Mouse Cursor 77

6

Determining the Button
Status and Limiting the
Range of Movement   81

The Button Functions 81

Trapping Single Button Presses and
   Releases 83
   The Reverse Trap 86
Double-Clicking Mouse Buttons 86
   Timing a Double-Click 86
   Determining a Double-Click 87
Limiting Range in Sequential
   Applications 90

7

Creating an Event Handler   95

The Problems with Polling 95
What is an Event Handler? 96
Installing an Event Handler 96
   The Call Mask 96
   Event Handler Address 97
   Mouse Functions Used to Install
     an Event Handler 97
Mouse Function 12: Set Event
   Handler 98
   Limitations 100
   Overcoming the Limitations in
     Assembler 100
Compiling the Event Handler 107
   Different Memory Models 108
   If You Don't Have the Assembler 108

8

Using the Event Handler   111

Compiling a Program that Uses the
   Event Handler 111
   File Order 112
   Stack Checking 112
   Integrated Environment
     Compiling 112
   Command-Line Compiling 113
   The New Header File 115
Your First Program Using the Event
   Handler 115
   Terminating the Application and
     Event Handler 117
   Reseting the Global Status
     Variables 118
The Full-Blown Event
   Handler/Processor 118
   Revisiting the touch_cursor()
     Function 122

Using the Mouse Cursor
   Coordinates 123
Other Event Handler Functions 123
   Mouse Function 20: Swap Event
   Handlers 123
   Mouse Function 24: Set
   Alternate Event Handler 124
The spawn() and exec() Functions 124
Terminate-and-Stay-Resident
   Applications (TSRs) 125
Moving Forward 125

9

Handling Menus 127

Floating Menus 127
   Keeping It Simple 128
Horizontal Menu Considerations 128
Vertical Menu Considerations 130
Combined Menu Considerations 131
The Floating Menu Program 131
Finer Points and Details 143
   Restoring the Range 143
   Restoring the Mouse Cursor
   Position 143
   Resetting Event Status Variables 145
Keyboard Input 146

10

Using the Mouse as a
Crosshair 151

Defining the Crosshair 151
Interacting with the Mouse Cursor 153
The Crosshair Algorithm 153
Crosshair Restriction 154
Crosshair Example 155
Program Details 160
   Defining the Crosshair 160
   Turning the Mouse Cursor Off 161
   Turning the Mouse Cursor On 161
   Defining the Chart Coordinates 162
Why a Crosshair? 164

11

Using the Mouse in
CAD-Type Operations 165

Stretching or Dragging? 165

Stretching a Graphics Object 166
   Dropping the Anchors 166
   The Undo Option 167
   XOR and COPY_PUT Drawing
   Modes 167
   Line Stretching Example 168
   Rectangle Stretching Example 171
   Ellipse Stretching Example 172

12

The Optional Mouse
Functions 179

Six New Mouse Functions 179
Using the Optional Functions 184
About the Information 186
   Mouse Type and IRQ Number 186
   CRT Page 187
   Major and Minor Version
   Numbers 187

13

Setting the Speed: Mickeys
and Pixels 189

Mickeys 189
   Mickey-to-Pixel Ratio 190
   Multiplication Factor 190
   Double-Speed Threshold 190
Changing the Speed 190
   Speed Sensitivity Rates 191
   Speed Sensitivity Example 192
   Double-Speed Threshold
   Example 194
   Maximum Speed 198

14

Changing and Managing the
Graphics Mouse Cursor 199

Graphics Mouse Cursor Mechanics 200
   The Screen and Cursor Masks 200
   Bit Expansion 201
   The Hot Spot 203
Setting the Mouse Cursor Shape 203
Windows-Style Cursor Management
   in DOS 208
   Sizing Arrows on Borders 208
   The Default Mouse Cursor Shape 209

15

The Mouse's Text Cursor 229

The Two Types of Text Cursors 229
  The Software Text Cursor 230
  The Hardware Text Cursor 230
Using the set_text_cursor()
Function 231
  Modifying the Software Text
  Cursor 231
  Modifying the Hardware Text
  Cursor 234

16

Combining the Functions into One Library 239

A Real Mouse Function Library 239
  Library Files 240
  Creating the Library File 240
Using the Library 245
  Using the Library with Your
  Own Applications 248

Part II
Building Your Own Mouse Cursor and the Elusive 800 × 600 16-Color Mode

17

Building Your Own Mouse Cursor 253

The Reason for Building Your Own
Mouse Cursor 253
  The 800 × 600 16-Color Super
  VGA Mode 254
  Existing Solutions 256
  A Universal Solution 257

18

Building the Sprite Driver 259

The Graphics Mouse Cursor 260

EGA/VGA Read/Write Mode 0 260
Cursor/Sprite Mechanics 262
The Sprite Driver 263
  Low-Level Graphics Functions 264
  Sprite Functions 265
  The Sprite Driver Source Code 266
  Compiling SPRITELL.C 288
  On to the New Mouse Function
  Library 290

19

The New Mouse Function Library and Sprite Cursor 291

Modifying the Mouse Function
Library 291
  Show and Hide Functions 291
  Setting an Exclusion Area 292
  Event Processor 292
  Cursor Position 292
The New Mouse Function Library 293
  Compiling MOUSEDRV.C 304
Combining the Event Handler,
Mouse Function Library, and
Sprite Driver 306
  The New Library Header File 306
Using the Sprite Cursor 310
  Initializing the Sprite Cursor 313
  Destroying the Sprite Cursor 316
  The Default Mouse Cursor 316

20

The Sprite Cursor in the 800 × 600 16-Color Mode 317

New Video Functions 317
Running in Any 16-Color Mode 322
Setting the 800 × 600 16-Color Mode 326
Verifying Proper Behavior 326

21

Sprite Usage Rules and Features 333

Sprite Cursor Usage Rules 333
  Global Variables 333
  Valid Ranges 334
  Display Boundaries 334
  Hiding the Sprite Cursor 334

Switching Cursors	335
Keeping the Event Handler Active	335
Destroying the Sprite Cursor	336
Sprite Features	336
Modifying the Sprite Color and Write Mode	337
Changing the Sprite Cursor Mask	342
Using Other Sprites	348
Dual Sprite Cursors	348
The Dual Cursor CAD Mirror Program	350

Part III
Interfacing with the Mouse in Windows

22

The Generic Windows Program 367

Windows, the Big Event Processor	368
Communicating with the Mouse in Windows	368
The Fundamental Windows Program	369
The Module Definition File	371
Compiling GENERIC.C	371
Running GENERIC.EXE	374
Understanding GENERIC.C	376
Understanding GENERIC.DEF	380

23

Windows Mouse Button Messages 383

Button Press and Release Messages	383
Additional Information from Button Messages	390
Detailed Information in the Client Area	391
Detailed Information in the Nonclient Area	398
Double-Click Time	405

24

Changing the Windows Cursor 413

The Standard Windows Cursors	414
Setting the Default Registered Cursor	414
Loading Windows Cursors on the Fly	414
WM_MOUSEMOVE	420
WM_SETCURSOR	420
Creating and Using Your Own Cursors	426
Resource Cursors	427
Dynamic Cursors	434

25

Additional Windows Mouse-Related Topics 445

Tracking Cursor Coordinates in Windows	445
Emulating Mouse Movement with the Keyboard	450
Determining Mouse Presence	452
Moving the Cursor with the Keyboard	452
The Internal Display Count	452
Limiting Range of Movement	454
Keyboard Mouse-Emulation Program	455
Scope	461
WM_NCHITTEST	462

Part IV
Appendixes

A

The 50 Documented Mouse Functions 465

Conventions	465
Mouse Function 0: Mouse Reset and Status	466

Mouse Function 1: Show Cursor 468
Mouse Function 2: Hide Cursor 468
Mouse Function 3: Get Button
  Status and Cursor Position 469
Mouse Function 4: Set Mouse
  Cursor Position 470
Mouse Function 5: Get Button Press
  Information 471
Mouse Function 6: Get Button
  Release Information 472
Mouse Function 7: Set Min/Max
  Horizontal Cursor Position 473
Mouse Function 8: Set Min/Max
  Vertical Cursor Position 474
Mouse Function 9: Set Graphics
  Cursor 475
Mouse Function 10: Set Text Cursor 476
Mouse Function 11: Read Mouse
  Motion Counters 477
Mouse Function 12: Set Event
  Handler 478
Mouse Function 13: Light-Pen
  Emulation Mode On 479
Mouse Function 14: Light-Pen
  Emulation Mode Off 480
Mouse Function 15: Set
  Mickey-to-Pixel Ratio 480
Mouse Function 16: Set Exclusion
  Area 481
Mouse Functions 17 and 18:
  Undocumented 482
Mouse Function 19: Set
  Double-Speed Threshold 482
Mouse Function 20: Swap Event
  Handlers 483
Mouse Function 21: Get Mouse
  Driver State Buffer Size 485
Mouse Function 22: Save Mouse
  Driver State 485
Mouse Function 23: Restore Mouse
  Driver State 486
Mouse Function 24: Set Alternate
  Event Handler 487
Mouse Function 25: Get Alternate
  Event Handler 489
Mouse Function 26: Set Sensitivity
  Rate 490
Mouse Function 27: Get Sensitivity
  Rate 491

Mouse Function 28: Set Mouse
  Interrupt Rate 491
Mouse Function 29: Set CRT Page
  Number 492
Mouse Function 30: Get CRT Page
  Number 493
Mouse Function 31: Disable Mouse
  Driver 494
Mouse Function 32: Enable Mouse
  Driver 494
Mouse Function 33: Software Reset 495
Mouse Function 34: Set Language
  for Messages 496
Mouse Function 35: Get Language
  Number 497
Mouse Function 36: Get Driver
  Version, Type, and IRQ # 498
Mouse Function 37: Get General
  Driver Information 500
Mouse Function 38: Get Maximum
  Virtual Coordinates 501
Mouse Function 39: Get Screen and
  Cursor Mask Values and Mickey
  Count 502
Mouse Function 40: Set Video Mode 503
Mouse Function 41: Enumerate
  Video Modes 504
Mouse Function 42: Get Cursor Hot
  Spot 505
Mouse Function 43: Load
  Acceleration Curves 506
Mouse Function 44: Read
  Acceleration Curves 508
Mouse Function 45: Set/Get
  Acceleration Curve 509
Mouse Function 46:
  Undocumented 510
Mouse Function 47: Mouse
  Hardware Reset 510
Mouse Function 48: Set/Get
  BallPoint Information 511
Mouse Function 49: Get Min/Max
  Virtual Coordinates 512
Mouse Function 50: Get Active
  Advanced Function 513
Mouse Function 51: Get Switch
  Settings 514
Mouse Function 52: Get
  MOUSE.INI 516

B

Windows Mouse and Cursor Functions 517

ClipCursor	518
CreateCursor	519
DestroyCursor	519
GetCapture	520
GetClipCursor	520
GetCursorPos	521
GetDoubleClickTime	521
LoadCursor	521
ReleaseCapture	523
SetCapture	523
SetCursor	523
SetCursorPos	524
SetDoubleClickTime	524
ShowCursor	525
SwapMouseButton	525

C

Windows Mouse Messages 527

HIWORD( ) and LOWORD( )	527
Client Area Button Messages	527
Nonclient Area Button Messages	528
WM_MOUSEACTIVATE	529
WM_MOUSEMOVE	530
WM_NCHITTEST	531
WM_NCMOUSEMOVE	532
WM_SETCURSOR	532

Foreword

Building a Better Mouse Trap is, in a word, delightful! Jeff Donovan has succeeded in transforming the rather dry (and sometimes daunting) task of mouse interfacing into an interesting exploration of both the mouse and its software drivers. What makes this book so unique is that it not only covers the fundamentals of mouse interfacing but also adds several tips and techniques that even a seasoned pro will find new and useful.

I am familiar with this book because of a happy accident. When my editor at Osborne/McGraw-Hill, Frances Stack, was considering this book for publication, she asked me if I could take a brief look at it and give her my impression. Upon first glance and then supported by a complete reading, I enthusiastically recommended the book for publication because it was well written and offered a much needed reference to the increasingly important topic of the mouse. Further, I was so interested by the material in this book that I volunteered to be the technical editor on the project. Because of my busy schedule, I do few editing jobs, but this is one that I couldn't pass up. As such, I am sure that you will find the material in this book as accurate as it is interesting.

Building a Better Mouse Trap begins in the traditional way, by describing the basics of mouse interfacing in the DOS environment. It then describes how to build your own custom mouse-interfacing library. While many other books would have stopped at this point, Jeff continues with a complete discussion of interfacing to the mouse when writing Windows programs. Because mouse support is built into Windows, you might at first think that there is little to say about it, but this is wrong. Jeff shows you how to avoid several pitfalls and suggests creative solutions to typical mouse troubles encountered when programming for Windows.

It has almost become cliché to say this, but this book is for both beginners and experienced programmers. Although it contains a complete discussion of the fundamentals, it goes far beyond them. Simply put, you will find information in this book that you won't find anywhere else. So, if the mouse is important to you and your programming efforts, this book is one that you will want on your shelf.

Herbert Schildt
Mahomet, IL
Dec. 1, 1992

Acknowledgments

First and foremost, thanks to everyone at Osborne/McGraw-Hill. To say that their help has been enormous would be an understatement. Special thanks to Frances Stack for her infinite wisdom and superb guidance—also to Jill Pisoni, Vicki Van Ausdall, Judy Kleppe, and Paul Medoff for their professionalism and attention to detail, and to Tom Sheldon for introducing me to Osborne.

Herbert Schildt, Osborne author and programmer extraordinare, has been writing top-notch programming books for many years, several of which are in my personal library. It was both a privilege and an honor to work with him. The experience is one I shall not soon forget.

James McCarthy, engineer, developer relations at Logitech Inc., provided me with clear details regarding many "fuzzy" or poorly documented technical aspects of the mouse. Jim pulled my rear out of the wringer many times, and his technical expertise and knowledge of mouse hardware and software is unsurpassed.

Eric Hanson, support engineer and mouse-support lead for Microsoft Inc., helped me find the answers to many questions and went to the trouble of writing code that duplicated some of my concerns. It just goes to show that Microsoft still holds their technical support departments in the highest regard.

To Reed E. Slatkin, Richard D. McMullin, Steve Hammer, and Richard J. Greenstone: better partners and colleagues there never were.

To Richard Bonati who forced me to deal with the Super VGA problems and continuously asked me when it would be done.

Frank and Tracy Still, Craig and Jackie Minor, Mike and Melanie Feeley—thanks for understanding why I could never get out of the basement.

To anyone who ever told me something was impossible.

Introduction

In today's computer world, the mouse is as commonly used as the keyboard, and has been integrated increasingly into new computer applications. As a programmer, I have often found myself frustrated with the lack of source material specific to mouse programming. The purpose of this book is to provide a higher level of understanding to enable you to successfully integrate mouse functions into your own applications. Whether you are a novice programmer or a seasoned veteran, the information, step-by-step instructions and source code presented in this book will help to make all your mouse programming endeavors rich and rewarding.

Brief History of the Mouse

The mouse you use as a pointing device on the computer was invented by Douglas Engelbart at Stanford Research Institute in 1963. Engelbart is a computer visionary without whom the personal computer, GUIs, virtual reality, and many other technologies might not exist as we know them today or will know them in the future. His first mouse was designed to be used on the ARC (Augmentation Research Center) computer and was basically an analog device in a wooden box with two metal wheels on the bottom and a single button on top.

In the early seventies, Xerox Corporation's Palo Alto Research Center commissioned Jack S. Hawley to build a digital mouse for their new Alto computer. After Hawley finished his work for Xerox, he opened The Mouse House in Berkeley, California, to continue designing and fabricating mice.

While several mouse designs and standards exist today, they have all in some way been influenced by the work of Engelbart and Hawley.

Microsoft introduced their first generation bus mouse in June of 1983. A year later the serial mouse was introduced. Since that time, Microsoft has continuously brought forth new generations of mice, all the while improving and streamlining their design and functionality. With the development of the Enhanced Graphics Adapter (EGA) in 1984, and the Video Graphics Array (VGA) in 1987, the mouse's popularity exploded as new generations of high-performance graphics applications began to surface. By the summer of 1988, Microsoft had sold one million mice. Aside from the keyboard, the mouse has become the most commonly used input device available.

About This Book

In this book you will learn the mechanics and techniques of mouse programming in the most straightforward manner possible. All coding is simple and to the point, and with the exception of Chapter 18, no objects or complex structures are defined.

There are four parts that make up this book. Each part serves a distinctive goal in teaching you mouse programming. The following is a brief outline.

Part I   Part I teaches you all the techniques required to successfully interface with the mouse. This encompasses Chapters 1 through 16. When you have completed these chapters, you will have learned all the fundamental aspects of mouse programming, and will have mastered techniques based on realistic programming issues such as event processing, menu handling, CAD systems, cursor-shape management, and more. You can consider yourself a full-fledged mouse programmer. Additionally, in Chapter 16 you will combine everything created in previous chapters into one complete mouse function library, ready to use in your own applications.

Part II   Part II teaches you how to create your own graphics mouse cursor capable of many new and exciting features. This encompasses Chapters 17 through 21. You learn about sprite animation, cursor mechanics, and the problems associated with Super VGA mouse programming, specifically the 800×600 16-color graphics mode. When you have completed these chapters, you will truly feel as though you know the inner workings of the graphics mouse cursor, and will possess a new advanced mouse function library ready to use in your own applications. This library allows you to utilize either the default graphics mouse cursor, or your own sprite/mouse cursor, which operates in the EGA 640×200 16-color, EGA 640×350 16-color and monochrome, VGA 640×480 16-color and monochrome, and the Super VGA 800×600 16-color graphics modes.

Part III   Part III teaches you how to properly interface with the mouse in Windows. This encompasses Chapters 22 through 26. Proper Windows mouse techniques, rules, and guidelines are discussed and explored in detail.

Part IV   Part IV, the appendixes, provides you with a detailed reference to all 50 documented MS-DOS mouse functions, all Windows mouse and cursor functions, and all Windows mouse-related messages.

Guidelines For the DOS Chapters

If this is your first attempt to interface with the mouse in DOS-based applications, I suggest you start at Chapter 1 and continue forward. You will learn mouse programming step by step through each successive chapter, and nothing will take you by surprise. Whether you are a novice, intermediate, or expert mouse programmer, the following chapters contain information you should not overlook, or may have special interest in.

The table of contents and index are also excellent references to specific mouse related topics.

Chapter 1   In Chapter 1, you learn about the mouse driver, interrupt services, registers, and how to communicate with the mouse through interrupt 0x33. Additionally, the Borland and Microsoft compiler differences are discussed, and you create a file called COMPILER.H to handle most of the differences.

Chapter 2   In this chapter, you create the Video Function Library, which is used in every DOS programming example except those in Chapter 20. This is the only code found in this book that is located in separate files for the Borland and Microsoft compilers.

Chapter 3   This is where you create the initial mouse function library. You should at least browse this chapter to become familiar with the functions and how they are implemented.

Chapter 7 and Chapter 8   It is *absolutely essential* that you read and understand Chapters 7 and 8. In Chapter 7, you create an event handler and event processor. In Chapter 8, you learn how to use them. All programming examples following Chapter 7 use the event handler and event processor, and you *must* understand the underlying mechanics of both. There are also specific rules and guidelines you must adhere to when using the event handler and event processor.

Chapter 12   Chapter 12 introduces mouse functions that are not considered necessary, but optional. Although you can control the mouse without these functions, utilizing them will add that extra touch of professionalism to all your applications.

In addition to Chapter 12, the lessons and programming examples in Chapters 13, 14, and 15 are based on the optional functions.

Chapter 16   All mouse functions are combined in one file and compiled to an actual library (.LIB) file. A master header file is made for the library, and it becomes a completely reusable resource ready to utilize in your own applications.

Chapter 17   This chapter serves as an introduction to Chapters 18, 19, 20, and 21. You'll learn about the problems associated with Super VGA mouse programming (specifically the 800×600 16-color VGA/Super VGA graphics mode), why the 800×600 16-color mode should be considered a standard, and the Super VGA work-arounds developed by various video card and mouse manufacturers. Then, in Chapter 18, you'll start to work on a universal solution; building a sprite driver to generate your own graphics mouse cursor.

Guidelines For the Windows Chapters

If you are a novice Windows programmer or new to Windows 3.1 programming, I suggest you first read and understand Chapter 22, where you will create a generic Windows program and learn how the program interacts with Windows.

If you are an intermediate or experienced Windows programmer familiar with Windows 3.1 standards, you can start virtually anywhere you desire in the Windows section.

 The table of contents and index are also excellent references to specific mouse related topics.

OEM Mice

The DOS mouse-function library you create in this book is designed to be a commercial-grade resource. As such, mice other than the Microsoft mouse must be considered in the overall design.

When you write commercial applications, you must maintain compatibility with all OEM mice to ensure that your application operates properly under any circumstance. The majority of OEM mouse manufacturers have not implemented Microsoft's advanced mouse functions, even though they claim their mice are 100-percent Microsoft compatible. These advanced functions began to be released in Microsoft's mouse driver version 6.26. Since then, Microsoft has continued to release more advanced functions in newer versions, and to date they range from mouse function 37 to mouse function 52. To the best of my knowledge, the only OEM manufacturers to implement them all are Logitech, with their mouse driver version 6.1 and later, and Kraft with their mouse driver version 8.2 and later.

Therefore, in order to maintain compatibility with the majority of OEM mice, this book focuses on mouse functions below function number 37. Appendix A provides a complete reference to all 50 documented mouse functions, along with code fragments to demonstrate their implementation.

Requirements

Requirements for the MS-DOS and Windows chapters differ significantly. The MS-DOS requirements will be listed first, followed by the Windows requirements.

MS-DOS Resources

For the MS-DOS programming examples, the following hardware and software is required:

Hardware

The MS-DOS hardware requirements are as follows:

- An IBM 8086, 8088, 80286, 80386, 80486 or 100-percent compatible computer.
- MS-DOS or PC-DOS version 2.0 or later.
- A mouse (Microsoft or 100-percent compatible) and the appropriate mouse driver (MOUSE.COM or MOUSE.SYS).
- The examples found in Chapters 1 through 16 will operate on a CGA, EGA, or VGA video system.
- The examples found in Chapters 18 through 21 require an EGA or VGA video system.

Software

The MS-DOS software requirements are as follows:

- Borland programmers need Turbo C version 2.0 or Borland C++ version 1.0 or later.
- Microsoft programmers need Microsoft C version 6.0 or Microsoft QuickC version 2.5 or later.

- Two source files require compiling with an assembler. However, you are not required to have an assembler, as the object files for the code are provided on the companion disk supplied with this book. If you wish to make changes to the assembly code, you will need either Borland's Turbo Assembler version 1.0, or Microsoft's Macro Assembler version 5.0, or later. Borland has bundled Turbo Assembler with various releases of their C and C++ compilers, and you should see your Borland documentation regarding availability. The Microsoft Macro Assembler is not included with Microsoft C or C++ compilers, and must be purchased separately.

Windows Resources

For the Windows programming examples, the following hardware and software is required:

Hardware

The Windows hardware requirements are as follows:

- An IBM 80286, 80386, 80486, or 100-percent compatible machine.
- MS-DOS or PC-DOS version 3.1 or later.
- A mouse that Windows supports.
- A monitor that Windows supports.

Software

The Windows software requirements are as follows:

- The Window's programming examples are written specifically for the new standards found in Windows 3.1, and therefore require Windows 3.1 to run.
- Borland programmers need Turbo C++ for Windows version 3.1, or Borland C++ 3.1 or later.
- Microsoft programmers need the Microsoft C/C++ 7.0 Windows 3.1 SDK compiler or later.
- The Windows code will port directly from the Borland compiler to the Microsoft compiler. No Turbo OWL libraries or Microsoft Class libraries are used, and only straight C code is presented. Therefore, the Windows code should port to any compiler maintaining Windows 3.1 SDK compatibility.

Testing

Due to the complexities involved with mouse programming, the number of OEM mice available, video monitor configuration and compatibility, and supported compilers, every programming example presented in this book has been tested thoroughly to ensure it's functionality and reliability. The following section details the testing performed.

MS-DOS Testing

For the DOS chapters, the following testing was performed for every programming example:

- Compiled and run with Borland's Turbo C 2.0, Borland C/C++ 2.0, Microsoft C/C++ 7.0, and Microsoft QuickC 2.5. The assemblers used were Borland's Turbo Assembler 1.0, and Microsoft's Macro Assembler 5.0.

- Compiled and run in the SMALL, MEDIUM, COMPACT, LARGE, and HUGE memory models, with each previously mentioned compiler.

- Compiled and run in both graphics mode and text modes, where text modes are applicable.

- Run on EGA and VGA color monitors in both color and monochrome modes. CGA modes were emulated on the EGA monitor.

- Run under MS-DOS versions 3.2, 4.0, and 5.0, on 80286, 80386, and 80486 machines.

- Run in Windows as a DOS-based application, using Windows 3.1 running under MS-DOS 5.0 on an 80?86 machine.

- Examples in Chapters 18 through 21 run only on pure EGA, VGA, and Super VGA systems, and were tested in the 640×200, 640×350, 640×480, and 800×600 16-color graphics modes. Additional testing included the 640×350 and 640×480 monochrome graphics modes.

The equipment used for testing included:

- The Microsoft mouse with driver versions 7.0, 7.04, 8.16, and 8.20a. Also tested were the Logitech mouse and driver versions 4.0 and 6.1, Kraft Trackball and driver version 3.0, IMSI mouse and driver version 3.03, SUN Crystal Mouse and driver version 3.81, and the ATI InPort mouse and driver version 2.00.

- The graphics cards used include the Everex EGA card, Compaq EGA card, Everex VGA card, ATI Wonder Plus 16 VGA card, Paradise Plus 16 VGA card, Video-7 VRAM II ERGO card, and the ATI Graphics Ultra Accelerator card.

- The monitors used include the NEC Multisynch 5FG, Multisynch 3-D, Multisynch II, Hyuandai VGA, Compaq VGA, and Compaq EGA.

Windows Testing

All Windows programming examples were compiled and run in Windows 3.1, with both the Borland C/C++ 3.1 compiler and the Microsoft 7.0 C/C++ compiler. Examples were tested in DOS 5.0 running on an 80486 machine.

Part I

Interfacing with the Mouse

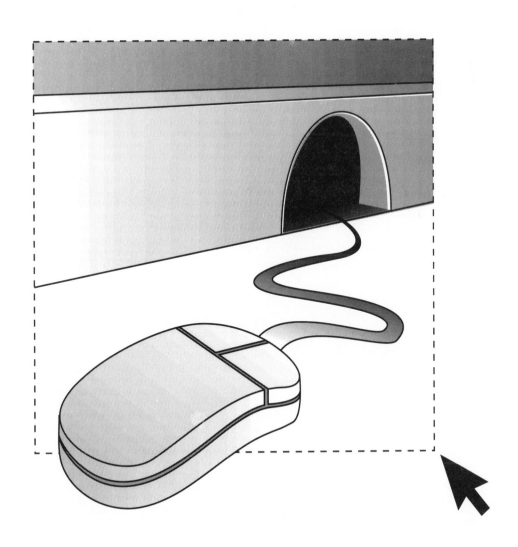

Chapter *1*

How To Communicate with the Mouse: Interrupt 33 Hex

If this is your first attempt at communicating with the mouse you may think you're in for a nightmare of elusive, complex code. You couldn't be further from the truth. Microsoft and ensuing OEM manufacturers have made it extremely easy for you to interface with the little rodent. How you act upon the information you send or receive is where things get a bit involved, but actually communicating with the mouse is not a complex task, and I think you will be quite relieved.

The Mouse Driver

The Microsoft mouse allows you to communicate with it through a program called a *device driver.* There are usually two device drivers included with the mouse's software package, the first being MOUSE.SYS and the second being MOUSE.COM. You *must* load one of these drivers before any communications to the mouse can be performed.

To load the device driver(s), copy either MOUSE.SYS or MOUSE.COM to the computer's boot disk, in the root directory. If you are using MOUSE.SYS, add the line:

DEVICE=MOUSE.SYS

to the CONFIG.SYS file, located in the boot disk's root directory. To load MOUSE.COM, add the statement:

    MOUSE

to the AUTOEXEC.BAT file, located in the boot disk's root directory. Once MOUSE.SYS is added to CONFIG.SYS, or MOUSE.COM is added to AU-TOEXEC.BAT, the mouse driver is installed whenever the computer is turned on or rebooted.

Alternatively, if MOUSE.COM is being used, you can just type **MOUSE** and press ENTER at the DOS command line. This allows you to load the mouse driver only when you need it.

The installation manuals supplied with your mouse contain valuable information regarding advanced installation, available options, switches, and so on. A setup program may also be available to install the mouse driver for you. Consult your manual for further details.

Interrupt 33 Hex

To send and retrieve information to and from the mouse driver, use interrupt 33 hex exclusively. Interrupt 33 hex is installed when the mouse driver is initially loaded. If you have ever programmed using interrupt services, and specifically interrupt 33 hex, the following discussion will be old hat, and you may skip to the section, "Borland and Microsoft Compiler Compatibility." If you have never programmed using inter-rupt services, read on.

Interrupt Service Functions

Interrupt services are easy to understand when they are taken for what they are: function calls made to ROM BIOS, DOS, and external device drivers.

To access the interrupt services, Borland and Microsoft have given you number of high-level functions. It should be pointed out that almost all high- and low-level DOS compilers have interrupt service functions, and are usually implemented similar to the way they are here.

You will be using two of the interrupt service functions. Both of the function prototypes and associated type definitions are found in the header file DOS.H, which comes with your compiler. These are

    int86(int *INTNO*,union REGS **inregs*,union REGS **outregs*) and

int86x(int *INTNO*,union REGS **inregs*,union REGS
        *outregs,struct SREGS **segregs*)

where:

- *INTNO* is the interrupt number.

- **inregs* is a pointer to a REGS union. You pass arguments to the interrupt function by loading values into the union **inregs* points to.

- **outregs* is a pointer to a REGS union. Arguments are sent from the interrupt function by loading values into the union **outregs* points to. In most cases, the union **outregs* points to can be the same union **inregs* points to.

- **segregs* is a pointer to an SREGS structure. Arguments are sent to or received from the interrupt function by loading values into the structure **segregs* points to. The SREGS structure components (registers) are usually used for special addressing purposes.

The interrupt number for mouse functions is 0x33, or 33 hexadecimal. With one exception, this is the only interrupt number you will use until Part II of this book.

The Working Registers

Consider the REGS union and SREGS structure the interrupt service variables. The component variables defined within the union and structure are called the *working registers*. Working registers are registers you have access to and can modify.

Declarations

Before you can make calls to the interrupt service functions, you must declare the working registers. To declare a REGS union variable, follow this example:

union REGS mregs;

To declare an SREGS structure variable, follow this example:

struct SREGS segregs;

(See your C manual for complete reference to the union and structure definitions.)

The General Registers

There are four main working registers you will use. These four registers are contained within the REGS union components, and are the AX, BX, CX, and DX registers. These registers are called the *general registers*. General registers are registers that can be used for a number of different purposes. Most can be used as a whole integer value, or broken up into two one-byte values. The structure components that represent these registers are:

Integer Component	High Byte	Low Byte
mregs.x.ax	mregs.h.ah	mregs.h.al
mregs.x.bx	mregs.h.bh	mregs.h.bl
mregs.x.cx	mregs.h.ch	mregs.h.cl
mregs.x.dx	mregs.h.dh	mregs.h.dl

There are other registers you will use, but these four are the most common. Registers other than the general registers (such as those in the SREGS structure) can only be used as whole 16-bit integer values.

Making a Function Call to the Mouse Driver

As an example of using an interrupt service function to interface with the mouse driver, the following code fragment demonstrates how to load a register with a value, use an interrupt service to reset the mouse and determine the mouse status (int 33 hex, mouse function 0), and use a value sent back in a register to determine whether the mouse is installed or not.

```
unsigned char reset_mouse(void)
   {
   union REGS mregs;

   mregs.x.ax = 0;    /* AX always equals mouse function number*/
                      /* Function 0 used to reset the mouse    */

   int86(0x33,&mregs,&mregs);  /* Interrupt number 33 hex      */

   if (mregs.x.ax!=0)          /* If AX not 0, mouse is there */
      MOUSE_THERE=1;
   else
      MOUSE_THERE=0;           /* Otherwise no mouse           */
   }
```

By studying this example, you should know the following:

- How to load the registers with values

- How to use the interrupt service function to communicate with the mouse driver

- How to use the values sent back to you from the interrupt function

Every mouse function available is called in the same manner as the previous code fragment. The AX register is always loaded with the function number you are calling, and the other register meanings vary from function to function. Appendix A contains a complete reference guide to all 50 documented mouse functions and register definitions.

Actually communicating with the mouse does not get much more complex than this. For further details regarding registers and interrupt services, the Borland and Microsoft compiler manuals contain excellent reference material.

Before you begin programming and interfacing with the mouse, some differences between the Borland and Microsoft compilers must be dealt with, and a library of video functions must be created.

Borland and Microsoft Compiler Compatibility

Every programming example found in this book can be compiled with both the Borland and Microsoft C compilers. Many of the graphics functions, interrupt services, and inline assembly macros used in the source code are not defined by ANSI C standards and are named or implemented differently in each compiler. Therefore, some initial adjustments must be made to accommodate each compiler.

Many of the compiler differences can be accommodated with a file containing specific compiler macro definitions (#define statements). This file is named COM-PILER.H, and will be included in *all* programming examples. COMPILER.H also contains many header files used by both the Borland and Microsoft compiler—you should familiarize yourself with this file, no matter which compiler you are using.

The source code in this book was initially written for the Borland compilers and then imported to the Microsoft compilers. Therefore, the majority of statements in COM-PILER.H are to accommodate the Microsoft compilers.

Here is the compiler definition file, COMPILER.H:

```
/*-------------------------------------------------------*/
/* COMPILER.H                                            */
/* Use BORLAND for Turbo & Borland C                     */
/* Use MICROSOFT for Microsoft C                         */
/* If using Microsoft 6.0 or QuickC 2.5, issue the       */
/* statement "#define OLDC" as well.                     */
/*-------------------------------------------------------*/
#define BORLAND


/*-------------------------------------------------------*/
/* Standard #include files needed and used by both       */
/* Borland and Microsoft compilers.                      */
/*-------------------------------------------------------*/
#include <stdio.h>
#include <dos.h>
#include <conio.h>


/*-------------------------------------------------------*/
/* For BORLAND Compilers. Notice evp_type MUST be        */
/* huge. Defines appropriate #include files.             */
/*-------------------------------------------------------*/
#ifdef BORLAND
    #define evp_type huge
    #define graphics <graphics.h>
    #define videolib "tcvidlib.inc"
    #define allocate <alloc.h>
#endif


/*-------------------------------------------------------*/
/* For MICROSOFT Compilers. Notice evp_type MUST be      */
/* far. Microsoft does not allow functions to be of      */
/* type huge. Defines appropriate #include files, and    */
/* also redefines some Borland graphics functions        */
/* and DOS interrupt service types and functions.        */
/*-------------------------------------------------------*/
#ifdef MICROSOFT
    #define evp_type far
    #define graphics <graph.h>
    #define videolib "msvidlib.inc"
    #define allocate <malloc.h>

    #ifdef OLDC                     /* C 6.0, QC 2.5    */
```

```
    #define _videoconfig videoconfig
    #define asm _asm
    #define getvect _dos_getvect
#else                               /* Else C/C++ 7.0   */
    #define asm _asm                /* DOS Services     */
    #define REGS _REGS
    #define SREGS _SREGS
    #define int86 _int86
    #define int86x _int86x
    #define outp _outp
    #define getvect _dos_getvect
#endif

#define XOR_PUT _GXOR               /* Graph constants  */
#define COPY_PUT _GAND
#define DASHED_LINE 0xF0F0
#define SOLID_LINE 0xFFFF
                                    /* Graph functions  */
#define setwritemode _setwritemode
#define setlinestyle(linestyle,up,width) _setlinestyle
(linestyle)
#define line(x1,y1,x2,y2) {_moveto(x1,y1);_lineto(x2,y2);}
#define ellipse(x1,y1,sa,ea,rx,ry) _ellipse(_GBORDER,x1-
rx,y1-ry,x1+rx,y1+ry)
#endif
```

Modifying COMPILER.H

If you are using a Borland compiler, you can leave COMPILER.H as is. If you are using a Microsoft compiler, you need to modify the file to match the compiler. Here's how:

1. Change the statement #define BORLAND to #define MICROSOFT.

2. Save the file.

If you are using Microsoft C 6.0, or QuickC 2.5:

1. Add the statement #define OLDC on the line immediately following the #define MICROSOFT statement.

2. Save the file.

Graphics and Text I/O

The differences between the graphics libraries and text I/O functions in each compiler represent the biggest compatibility problems. Although some of these differences can be resolved in the file COMPILER.H, many cannot. Look at these statements in COMPILER.H:

```
#define videolib "tcvidlib.inc"
#define videolib "msvidlib.inc"
```

To manage the graphics and text I/O, a video function library is presented in the following chapter. The video function library is specific to either the Borland or Microsoft compiler and is the only source code in this book replicated for each compiler.

Chapter 2

The Video Function
Library

Throughout this book, you will be learning to interface with the mouse in both graphics and text modes, so some basic graphics and text functions are required. These functions are included in all DOS programming examples, with one exception in Chapter 20. The functions are located in one file, which is called "The Video Function Library". For the Borland compiler, this file is named TCVIDLIB.INC, and for the Microsoft compiler, this file is named MSVIDLIB.INC.

Introduction to the Video Function Library

Because the examples presented in this book demonstrate realistic programming topics, they need a realistic, professional-looking interface to illustrate the subject matter properly. While the video function library presented in this chapter is not intended to be commercial grade, it does provide a collection of clean, good-looking, easy-to-implement functions for you to use in both graphics and text modes. As such, the video function library is a bit involved, and there's a fair amount of code to brew over.

Using the Same Format for Graphics and Text Modes

A good set of video functions should allow you to implement graphics- and text-mode functions in the same calling format whenever possible. Most standard graphics functions, and their text-mode equivalent functions (if any), do not use the same calling format. Here is an example. To write the string "Hello World." in a text mode at display location (5,5) in Turbo C would require the following code:

```
gotoxy(5,5);
cprintf("Hello World.");
```

To write the same string in a graphics mode, at the same location, would require the following code:

```
outtextxy((5*HFONT_SIZE)-HFONT_SIZE,
          (5*VFONT_SIZE)-VFONT_SIZE,"Hello World.");
```

As you can see, writing text to the display requires different methods for graphics and text modes. Look at the following line of code:

```
out_text_xy(5,5,"Hello World.");
```

This is an actual function from the video function library you create in this chapter. It works *exactly* the same in either graphics or text mode. Inside the function, a determination is made about what video mode the system is in, and the appropriate choice is made about how and where to write the string. The key is that it becomes transparent to you, the programmer, and no recoding is required when switching between graphics and text modes.

The entire video function library is set up in this dual-mode fashion. With very few exceptions, you only need to change a mode constant to switch from graphics, install_video(GMODE), to text mode, install_video(TMODE).

 Microsoft does have special functions that write text to the display in either mode. However, the logical operations these functions perform against the background while in graphics mode make them unsuitable for the video function library. Only the Microsoft registered font functions are used (see your compiler's reference manual) in the video function library.

Of course, certain functions are relevant only in graphics or text modes, and can only be implemented in one or the other. The ellipse() function is one example. Ellipses cannot be drawn in text modes and are only used when in graphic modes.

Inner Workings of the Video Function Library

As little time as possible is taken to explain the inner workings of the video function library. The source code in the library is heavily documented, and you will probably grasp it all very quickly. If you're new to graphics programming, or programming entirely, don't worry if you don't understand everything right off the bat. The only requirment is for you to enter the code and use it as instructed. If you want to learn more about graphics- and text-mode programming, the source code presented here is a great starting point. However, you can do this anytime, and at your own pace. Your Borland and Microsoft reference manuals can provide you with details regarding the specific graphics and text I/O routines called within the video function library.

The video function library contains 14 functions. The following is a list of the function names, calling parameters, and a brief description of what each individual function does.

install_video(int *mode***)**   This function installs and sets up the video card to the highest available graphics mode or the 80 × 25 16-color text mode.

shut_down_video(void)   This function deactivates the video system and returns to the previous text mode.

out_text_xy(int *x***,int** *y***,char** **str***)**   This function writes text to the display using text coordinates.

out_int_xy(int *x***,int** *y***,int** *number***)**   This function writes integers to the display using text coordinates.

clear_line_from(int *linenum***,int** *from***,**
            int *how_many***,int** *color***)**   This function clears a line of text on the display using a background color of *color.*

change_color(int *color***)**   This function changes the current drawing color.

change_background(int *color***)**   This function changes the current background color. In graphics modes, the background is not actually changed, but the fill color used to clear lines. This emulates changing the background color of text in text modes.

draw_rectangle(int *x1***,int** *y1***,int** *x2***,int** *y2***)**   This function draws a rectangle in either text or graphics mode. Do not confuse this function with the Borland or the Microsoft rectangle functions. The functions operate differently.

header(void)   This function draws a rectangle around the perimeter of the display and writes a string of text in the upper-left corner telling the user if the system is in graphics or text modes. This function is only applicable to the examples found in this book, and is used to save coding.

mouse_error(int *x***,int** *y***)**   This function writes an error message to the display at location *x,y.* This is used when a user does not have the mouse. Again, this function is only applicable to the examples found in this book and is used to save coding.

The other four functions are standard Borland or Microsoft graphics functions and are defined similarly in almost all graphics platforms. The functions listed next use Borland's calling format and are duplicated for the Microsoft compiler in the file COMPILER.H, which you created in Chapter 1. The four functions are used only in pure graphics mode examples. They are:

line(int *x1,***int** *y1,***int** *x2,***int** *y2*)   This function draws line on the display.

setwritemode(int *mode*)   This function sets the current drawing mode to COPYPUT, AND, or XOR.

setlinestyle(int *linestyle,***unsigned** *pattern,***int** *thickness*)   This function sets the line style to solid, dashed, dotted, and so on.

ellipse(int *x,***int** *y,***int** *stangle,***int** *endangle,*
　　　　int *xrad,***int** *yrad*)   This function draws an ellipse on the display.

Global Variables

The video function library will also need a few global variables, as follows:

- Two integers to hold the maximum display coordinates. These are named VID_MAXX and VID_MAXY.

- Two integers to hold the horizontal and vertical font size when in graphics mode. These are named HFONT_SIZE and VFONT_SIZE.

- One integer to hold the maximum color allowed. This is named MAX_COLOR.

- An unsigned char variable to determine if the system is running in graphics or text mode, called IN_GMODE. IN_GMODE is set to 1 when running in graphics mode and 0 when running in text mode. IN_GMODE will be formally declared in Chapter 3, in the mouse function library header file, but it is used here.

The video function library is the only source code found in this book needing separate copies for the Borland and Microsoft compilers, and both files are listed here. You can import the file you need from the companion disk to eliminate typing errors, or you can type it in yourself for practice.

Source Code for the Video Function Library

Finally, here is the actual source code for the video function library.

The Borland Video Function Library

If you use a Borland compiler, the file is called TCVIDLIB.INC. Here it is:

```
/*------------------------------------------------------------*/
/*                    TCVIDLIB.INC                      */
/*                                                      */
/* Borland C text/graphics functions for use with MS-DOS    */
/* examples. Operates in both text and graphics modes.      */
/*------------------------------------------------------------*/

#define GMODE 1            /* Define graphics mode constant */
#define TMODE 0            /* Define text mode constant    */

int HFONT_SIZE,VFONT_SIZE;  /* Font sizes in graphics mode  */
int VID_MAXX,VID_MAXY;      /* Maximum display coordinates  */
int MAX_COLOR;             /* Maximum color allowed        */


/* MODULE : INSTALL VIDEO                                */
/*------------------------------------------------------------*/
/* Install the video system to highest available mode.      */
/* Also get/set the maximum coordinates, maximum color and   */
/* font size.                                           */
/* Input parameters                                      */
/*     mode - use GMODE or 1 for graphics mode, TMODE or 0   */
/*            for text mode                             */
/*                                                      */
void pascal install_video(int mode)
    {
    int graphics_adapter,graphics_mode;
    struct text_info tinfo;
```

```
    if (mode==GMODE)                     /* If graphics mode    */
      {
      graphics_adapter=DETECT;           /* Reqst Auto-Detect   */
      detectgraph(&graphics_adapter,&graphics_mode);
      initgraph(&graphics_adapter,&graphics_mode,"");

      settextstyle(DEFAULT_FONT,0,1);    /* Load 8 x 8 font     */
      setbkcolor(0);                     /* Background black     */
      setfillstyle(1,0);                 /* Set fill type        */
      VID_MAXX=getmaxx();                /* Get max horz coord  */
      VID_MAXY=getmaxy();                /* Get max vert coord  */
      VFONT_SIZE=textheight("X");        /* Get font height     */
      HFONT_SIZE=textwidth("X");         /* Get font width       */
      MAX_COLOR=getmaxcolor();           /* Get max color        */
      IN_GMODE=1;                        /* Set in graf mode     */
      }
    else                                 /* If text mode         */
      {                                  /* Mode 3, 80 x 25 16  */
      textmode(3);                       /* Mono users change    */
                                         /* to text mode(7)      */
      textbackground(0);                 /* Background black     */
      clrscr();                          /* Clear display        */
      gettextinfo(&tinfo);               /* Get text settings    */
      VID_MAXX=tinfo.screenwidth;        /* Get max horz coord  */
      VID_MAXY=tinfo.screenheight;       /* Get max vert coord  */

      if ((tinfo.currmode==BW40)||       /* If mono, 1 color    */
          (tinfo.currmode==BW80)) MAX_COLOR=1;
      else MAX_COLOR=15;

      IN_GMODE=0;                        /* In TEXT mode         */
      }
    }

/* MODULE : SHUT DOWN VIDEO                                        */
/*--------------------------------------------------------------*/
/* Shuts down the video system, returns it to last text mode. */
/*                                                              */
void shut_down_video(void)
  {
  if (IN_GMODE) closegraph();            /* Shut down graf sys  */
  textmode(-1);                          /* Return to last mode */
  clrscr();                              /* Clear the display    */
  }
```

```
/* MODULE : OUT TEXT XY                                     */
/*---------------------------------------------------------*/
/* Outputs a string of text at TEXT coordinates x,y         */
/* Input parameters                                         */
/*     x,y - Text coordinates to start drawing at           */
/*     *str- address of string                              */
/*                                                          */

void pascal out_text_xy(int x,int y,char *str)
    {
    if (IN_GMODE)                       /* If graphics mode    */
       {
       x=(x*HFONT_SIZE)-HFONT_SIZE;     /* Make x graphics pos */
       y=(y*VFONT_SIZE)-VFONT_SIZE;     /* Make y graphics pos */
       outtextxy(x,y,str);             /* Output the string    */
       }
    else
       {                                /* If text mode        */
       gotoxy(x,y);cprintf("%s",str);
       }
    }


/* MODULE : OUT INT XY                                      */
/*---------------------------------------------------------*/
/* Outputs an integer at TEXT coordinates x,y               */
/* Input parameters                                         */
/*     x,y    - Text coordinates to start drawing at        */
/*     number - number to print                             */
/*                                                          */
void pascal out_int_xy(int x,int y,int number)
    {
    char numstr[15];                    /* Need convrsn string */

    if (IN_GMODE)                       /* If graphics mode    */
       {
       sprintf(numstr,"%d",number);     /* Convert numb to str */
       x=(x*HFONT_SIZE)-HFONT_SIZE;     /* Make x graphics pos */
       y=(y*VFONT_SIZE)-VFONT_SIZE;     /* Make y graphics pos */
       outtextxy(x,y,numstr);          /* Output str(number)   */
       }
    else                                /* If text mode        */
       {
       gotoxy(x,y);cprintf("%d",number);
       }
    }
```

```
/* MODULE : CLEAR LINE FROM                                    */
/*------------------------------------------------------------*/
/* Clears a line of text from a starting position out to how  */
/* many pos., in color.                                       */
/* Input parameters                                           */
/*     linenum  - Line number to clear                        */
/*     from     - Start the clear from what TEXT x coordinate */
/*     how_many - How many spaces to clear                    */
/*     color    - color to clear line as                      */
/*                                                            */
void pascal clear_line_from(int linenum,int from,
                            int how_many,int color)
    {
    int x1,x2,y1,y2,loop;                /* Graphic coordinates */

    if (IN_GMODE)                        /* If graphics mode    */
        {                                /* Convert to graphics */
        x1=(from*HFONT_SIZE)-HFONT_SIZE;
        x2=((from+how_many)*HFONT_SIZE)-HFONT_SIZE;
        y1=(linenum*VFONT_SIZE)-VFONT_SIZE;
        y2=((linenum*VFONT_SIZE)-1);
        setfillstyle(1,color);           /* Set fill color      */
        bar(x1,y1,x2,y2);                /* Clear rect region   */
        setfillstyle(1,0);
        }
    else                                 /* If text mode        */
        {                                /* Clear by writing    */
        textbackground(color);
        for (loop=from;loop<from+how_many;loop++)
            {gotoxy(loop,linenum);cprintf("%c",255);}
        }
    }


/* MODULE : CHANGE COLOR                                       */
/*------------------------------------------------------------*/
/* Change the current drawing color.                          */
/* Input parameters                                           */
/*     color - color to change to                             */
/*                                                            */
void pascal change_color(int color)
    {                                        /* Check for past max */
    if (color>MAX_COLOR) color=MAX_COLOR;
    if (IN_GMODE)
        setcolor(color);                     /* Set graf mode color */
```

```
      else
         textcolor(color);                 /* Set text mode color */
      }



/* MODULE : CHANGE BACKGROUND                                    */
/*-------------------------------------------------------------*/
/* Change the current background color.                         */
/* Input parameters                                             */
/*    color - color to change to                                */
/*                                                              */
void pascal change_background(int color)
      {                                  /* Check for past max  */
      if (color>MAX_COLOR) color=MAX_COLOR;
      if (IN_GMODE)
         setfillstyle(1,color);            /* Set graf mode color */
      else
         textbackground(color);            /* Set text mode color */
      }



/* MODULE : DRAW RECTANGLE                                       */
/*-------------------------------------------------------------*/
/* Draws a rectangle on the screen regardless of text or        */
/* graphics mode.                                               */
/* NOTE: When calling in graphics modes, use graphic coords.    */
/*        In text modes use text coords.                        */
/* Input parameters                                             */
/*     x1,y1 - Upper-left corner of rectangle                   */
/*     x2,y2 - Lower-right corner of rectangle                  */
/*                                                              */
void pascal draw_rectangle(int x1,int y1,int x2,int y2)
      {
      int loop;
      if (IN_GMODE)                        /* If in graphics mode */
         {
         setfillstyle(1,0);                /* Border only,no fill */
         rectangle(x1,y1,x2,y2);           /* Call Turbo rect func*/
         }
      else                                 /* Else in text mode   */
         {
         textbackground(0);
         for (loop=x1+1;loop<x2;loop++)    /* Upper horiz line    */
             {gotoxy(loop,y1);cprintf("%c",196);}
```

```
      for (loop=x1+1;loop<x2;loop++)    /* Lower horiz line    */
          {gotoxy(loop,y2);cprintf("%c",196);}

      for (loop=y1+1;loop<y2;loop++)    /* Left vert line      */
          {gotoxy(x1,loop);cprintf("%c",179);}

      for (loop=y1+1;loop<y2;loop++)    /* Right vert line     */
          {gotoxy(x2,loop);cprintf("%c",179);}

      gotoxy(x1,y1);cprintf("%c",218); /* Four corners        */
      gotoxy(x2,y1);cprintf("%c",191);
      gotoxy(x1,y2);cprintf("%c",192);
      gotoxy(x2,y2);cprintf("%c",217);
      }
  }


/* MODULE : HEADER                                             */
/*-----------------------------------------------------------*/
/* Draws a rectangle around the screen and tells user if in   */
/* graphics or text modes.                                    */
/*                                                            */
void header(void)
  {
  change_color(4);                      /* Color to RED        */

  if (IN_GMODE)                         /* If in graphics mode */
     {                                  /* Border at MAX edges */
     draw_rectangle(1,1,VID_MAXX,VID_MAXY);
     change_color(15);
     out_text_xy(2,2,"Graphics Mode");
     }
  else                                  /* Else if in text mode*/
     {                                  /* Border at MAX edges */
                                        /* Can't write to last */
                                        /* row; it will scroll.*/
     draw_rectangle(1,1,VID_MAXX,VID_MAXY-1);
     change_color(15);
     out_text_xy(2,2,"Text Mode");
     }
  }
```

```
/* MODULE : MOUSE ERROR                                         */
/*-------------------------------------------------------------*/
/* Prints an error message when mouse driver is not installed.*/
/* Input parameters                                            */
/*    x,y - coordinates to write message at                    */
/*                                                             */
/*                   .                                         */
void mouse_error(int x,int y)
   {
   change_color(10);
   out_text_xy(x,y,"No Mouse Is Installed!");
   out_text_xy(x,y+1,"Please Install The Mouse Driver Before
                   Continuing...");
   printf("%c",7);
   change_color(15);
   }
```

The Microsoft Video Function Library

If you use a Microsoft compiler, the file is called MSVIDLIB.INC. Here it is:

```
/*-------------------------------------------------------------*/
/*                    MSVIDLIB.INC                             */
/*                                                             */
/* Microsoft C text/graphics functions for use with MS-DOS    */
/* examples. Operates in both text and graphics modes.        */
/*-------------------------------------------------------------*/


#include <time.h>            /* For c_clock type def          */

#define GMODE 1              /* Define graphics mode constant */
#define TMODE 0              /* Define text mode constant     */

int HFONT_SIZE,VFONT_SIZE;   /* Font sizes in graphics mode   */
int VID_MAXX,VID_MAXY;       /* Maximum display coordinates   */
int MAX_COLOR;               /* Maximum color allowed         */

int FCOLOR=15;               /* Need because MSC sets fill    */
                             /* color to draw color. Need SUB.*/

/* MODULE : INSTALL VIDEO                                       */
/*-------------------------------------------------------------*/
/* Install the video system to highest available mode.         */
/* Also get/set the maximum coordinates, maximum color and     */
```

```
/* font size.                                       */
/* Input parameters                                 */
/*     mode - use GMODE or 1 for graphics mode, TMODE or 0  */
/*            for text mode                          */
/*                                                   */
void pascal install_video(int mode)
   {
   struct _videoconfig tinfo;
   struct _fontinfo fi;

   if (mode==GMODE)                      /* If graphics mode   */
      {                                  /* Reqst Auto-Detect  */
      _setvideomoderows(_MAXRESMODE,_MAXTEXTROWS);

      _registerfonts("OEM08.FON");       /* Load OEM font      */
      _setfont("t'Courier'h8w8fb");      /* Load 8 x 8 font    */
                                         /* Select 'best fit'  */

      _setbkcolor(0);                    /* Background black    */
      _setfillmask(NULL);                /* Set fill type       */
      _getvideoconfig(&tinfo);           /* Get configuration   */
      VID_MAXX=tinfo.numxpixels-1;       /* Get max horz coord  */
      VID_MAXY=tinfo.numypixels-1;       /* Get max vert coord  */
      MAX_COLOR=tinfo.numcolors;         /* Get max color       */

      _getfontinfo(&fi);                 /* Get font sizes      */
      VFONT_SIZE=fi.pixheight;           /* Get font height     */
      HFONT_SIZE=fi.pixwidth;            /* Get font width      */

      IN_GMODE=1;                        /* Set in graf mode    */
      }
   else                                  /* If text mode        */
      {                                  /* Mode 3, 80 x 25 16  */
      _setvideomode(_TEXTC80);           /* Mono users change   */
                                         /* to _TEXTBW80        */
      _setbkcolor(0);                    /* Background black    */
      _clearscreen(_GCLEARSCREEN);       /* Clear display       */
      _getvideoconfig(&tinfo);           /* Get text settings   */
      VID_MAXX=tinfo.numtextcols;        /* Set max horz coord  */
      VID_MAXY=tinfo.numtextrows;        /* Set max vert coord  */
      MAX_COLOR=tinfo.numcolors;

      IN_GMODE=0;                        /* In TEXT mode        */
      }
   }
```

```
/* MODULE : SHUT DOWN VIDEO                                      */
/*-------------------------------------------------------------*/
/* Shuts down the video system, returns it to last text mode. */
/*                                                             */
void shut_down_video(void)
   {
   _setvideomode(_DEFAULTMODE);        /* Return to last mode */
   _setbkcolor(0);                     /* Background black    */
   _clearscreen(_GCLEARSCREEN);        /* Clear the display   */
   }


/* MODULE : OUT TEXT XY                                          */
/*-------------------------------------------------------------*/
/* Outputs a string of text at TEXT coordinates x,y            */
/* Input parameters                                            */
/*     x,y - Text coordinates to start drawing at              */
/*     *str- address of string                                 */
/*                                                             */
void pascal out_text_xy(int x,int y,char *str)
   {
   if (IN_GMODE)                       /* If graphics mode    */
      {
      x=(x*HFONT_SIZE)-HFONT_SIZE;     /* Make x graphics pos */
      y=(y*VFONT_SIZE)-VFONT_SIZE;     /* Make y graphics pos */
      _moveto(x,y);
      _outgtext(str);                  /* Output the string   */
      }
   else                                /* If text mode        */
      {
      _settextposition(y,x);
      _outtext(str);
      }
   }


/* MODULE : OUT INT XY                                           */
/*-------------------------------------------------------------*/
/* Outputs an integer at TEXT coordinates x,y                  */
/* Input parameters                                            */
/*     x,y   - Text coordinates to start drawing at            */
/*     number - number to print                                */
/*                                                             */
void pascal out_int_xy(int x,int y,int number)
   {
   char numstr[15];                    /* Need convrsn string */
```

```c
        sprintf(numstr,"%d",number);            /* Convert numb to str */
        if (IN_GMODE)                           /* If graphics mode    */
          {
          x=(x*HFONT_SIZE)-HFONT_SIZE;          /* Make x graphics pos */
          y=(y*VFONT_SIZE)-VFONT_SIZE;          /* Make y graphics pos */
          _moveto(x,y);
          _outgtext(numstr);                    /* Output str(number)  */
          }
        else                                    /* If text mode        */
          {
          _settextposition(y,x);
          _outtext(numstr);                     /* Output the string   */
          }
        }


/* MODULE : CLEAR LINE FROM                                          */
/*-----------------------------------------------------------------*/
/* Clears a line of text from a starting position out to how        */
/* many pos., in color                                              */
/* Input parameters                                                 */
/*     linenum  - Line number to clear                              */
/*     from     - Start the clear from what TEXT x coordinate       */
/*     how_many - How many spaces to clear                          */
/*     color    - color to clear line as                            */
/*                                                                  */
void pascal clear_line_from(int linenum,int from,
                            int how_many,int color)
    {
    unsigned char blank[3]={255,0};      /* Blank str constant  */
    int x1,x2,y1,y2,loop;                /* Graphics coordinates*/

    if (IN_GMODE)                        /* If graphics mode    */
      {                                  /* Convert to graphics */
      x1=(from*HFONT_SIZE)-HFONT_SIZE;
      x2=((from+how_many)*HFONT_SIZE)-HFONT_SIZE;
      y1=(linenum*VFONT_SIZE)-VFONT_SIZE;
      y2=((linenum*VFONT_SIZE)-1);
      _setcolor(color);                  /* Set fill color      */
                                         /* Clear rect region   */
      _rectangle(_GFILLINTERIOR,x1,y1,x2,y2);

      _setcolor(FCOLOR);                 /* Set color back to    */
                                         /* previous color      */
      }
```

```
    else                                /* If text mode        */
       {                                /* Clear by writing    */
       _setbkcolor(color);
       for (loop=from;loop<from+how_many;loop++)
           {_settextposition(linenum,loop);_outtext(blank);}
       }
    }


/* MODULE : CHANGE COLOR                                       */
/*-----------------------------------------------------------*/
/* Change the current drawing color.                          */
/* Input parameters                                           */
/*    color - color to change to                              */
/*                                                            */
void pascal change_color(int color)
    {                                   /* Check for past max  */
    if (color>MAX_COLOR) color=MAX_COLOR;
    if (IN_GMODE)
       _setcolor(color);               /* Set graf mode color */
    else
       _settextcolor(color);           /* Set text mode color */
    FCOLOR=color;
    }


/* MODULE : CHANGE BACKGROUND                                  */
/*-----------------------------------------------------------*/
/* Change the current background color.                       */
/* Input parameters                                           */
/*    color - color to change to                              */
/*                                                            */
void pascal change_background(int color)
    {                                   /* Check for past max  */
    if (color>MAX_COLOR) color=MAX_COLOR;
    if (IN_GMODE)
       {
       _setfillmask(NULL);
       _setcolor(color);               /* Set graf mode color */
       }
    else
       _setbkcolor(color);             /* Set text mode color */
    }


/* MODULE : DRAW RECTANGLE                                     */
/*-----------------------------------------------------------*/
/* Draws a rectangle on the screen regardless of text or      */
```

```c
/* graphics mode.                                        */
/* NOTE: When calling in graphics modes, use graphic coords.  */
/*       In text modes use text coords.                  */
/* Input parameters                                      */
/*     x1,y1 - Upper-left corner of rectangle            */
/*     x2,y2 - Lower-right corner of rectangle           */
/*                                                       */
void pascal draw_rectangle(int x1,int y1,int x2,int y2)
   {
   int loop;
   unsigned char hline[2]={196,0};       /* Horiz text line chr */
   unsigned char vline[2]={179,0};       /* Vert text line chr  */
   unsigned char luc[2]={218,0};         /* Left Up Corner chr  */
   unsigned char llc[2]={192,0};         /* Left Lw Corner chr  */
   unsigned char ruc[2]={191,0};         /* Right Up Corner chr */
   unsigned char rlc[2]={217,0};         /* Right Lw Corner chr */

   if (IN_GMODE)                         /* If in graphics mode */
                                         /* Border only,no fill */
      _rectangle(_GBORDER,x1,y1,x2,y2);/* call MSC rect func. */

   else                               . /* Else in text mode   */
      {
      for (loop=x1+1;loop<x2;loop++)     /* Upper horiz line    */
         {_settextposition(y1,loop);_outtext(hline);}

      for (loop=x1+1;loop<x2;loop++)     /* Lower horiz line    */
         {_settextposition(y2,loop);_outtext(hline);}

      for (loop=y1+1;loop<y2;loop++)     /* Left vert line      */
         {_settextposition(loop,x1);_outtext(vline);}

      for (loop=y1+1;loop<y2;loop++)     /* Right vert line     */
         {_settextposition(loop,x2);_outtext(vline);}

                                         /* Four corners        */
      _settextposition(y1,x1);_outtext(luc);
      _settextposition(y1,x2);_outtext(ruc);
      _settextposition(y2,x1);_outtext(llc);
      _settextposition(y2,x2);_outtext(rlc);
      }
   }
```

```
/* MODULE : HEADER                                                */
/*--------------------------------------------------------------*/
/* Draws a rectangle around the screen and tells user if in     */
/* graphics or text modes.                                      */
/*                                                              */
void header(void)
  {
  change_color(4);                      /* Color to RED         */

  if (IN_GMODE)                         /* If in graphics mode */
     {                                  /* Border at MAX edges */
     draw_rectangle(1,1,VID_MAXX,VID_MAXY);
     change_color(15);
     out_text_xy(2,2,"Graphics Mode");
     }
  else                                  /* Else if in text mode*/
     {                                  /* Border at MAX edges */
                                        /* Can't write to last */
                                        /* row, it will scroll.*/
     draw_rectangle(1,1,VID_MAXX,VID_MAXY-1);
     change_color(15);
     out_text_xy(2,2,"Text Mode");
     }
  }


/* MODULE : MOUSE ERROR                                           */
/*--------------------------------------------------------------*/
/* Prints an error message when mouse driver is not installed.*/
/* Input parameters                                             */
/*    x,y - coordinates to write message at                     */
/*                                                              */
void mouse_error(int x,int y)
   {
   change_color(10);
   out_text_xy(x,y,"No Mouse Is Installed!");
   out_text_xy(x,y+1,"Please Install The Mouse Driver Before
                      Continuing...");
   printf("%c",7);
   change_color(15);
   }


/* MODULE : DELAY                                                 */
/*--------------------------------------------------------------*/
/* Microsoft Replacement for Borland 'delay(microsecs)' func. */
/* Input parameters                                             */
```

```
/*    microsecs - microseconds to delay system.            */
/*                                                         */
void delay(int microsecs)
   {
   clock_t elapse;
   elapse=(clock_t)microsecs+clock();
   while (elapse>clock());
   }
```

The last function in MSVIDLIB.INC is not a video function. Borland's delay(microsecs) function had to be duplicated because there is no similar function in the Microsoft compiler.

Notes on the Video Function Library

There are some features in the video function library that deserve a little explanation. This is to avoid programming pitfalls and to help you understand the video function library a bit more thoroughly.

- In graphics modes, the *origin*, the upper-left corner of the display, is 0,0, so if you are working on an EGA 640 × 350 system, the graphics coordinates range from 0–639 and 0–349. In text modes the origin is 1,1, so, when you are working in an 80 × 25 text mode, the text locations range from 1–80, and 1–25.

- When running in text modes, even though the coordinate system is 80 × 25, the rectangle drawn around the perimeter of the display will assume 24 is the maximum vertical coordinate and draw the rectangle around the 80 × 24 region. This is because if any character is written to text location 80,25 , the display will scroll up one line.

- All functions in the video library use text coordinates in both graphics and text modes, with one exception. The rectangle(*x1,y1,x2,y2*) function uses graphics coordinates in graphics mode and text coordinates in text modes.

- The standard graphics functions such as the ellipse(*x,y,stangle,endangle,xrad,yrad*) function, will of course use only graphics coordinates. Functions such as this are used in examples that run in graphics modes only.

- In the text drawing routines, you may notice that when in graphics mode, the x coordinate is multiplied by HFONT_SIZE, and the y coordinate by VFONT_SIZE. The reason for this is because while you are in graphics modes, text cannot be positioned on the display using text coordinates. You must use graphics coordinates. Since the video functions are expecting text coordinates, they are converted into graphics coordinates within the functions themselves.

Depending on your display, four different font sizes are available: 8×8, 8×14, 8×16, and 9×16. The font size represents the number of horizontal pixels and the number of vertical pixels required to draw a letter on the display. Since the number of x pixels can vary from 8 to 9, the x coordinate passed into the functions is multiplied by HFONT_SIZE to convert it to graphics coordinates. Since the number of y pixels can vary between 8, 14, and 16, the y coordinate passed into the function is multiplied by VFONT_SIZE. Both HFONT_SIZE and VFONT_SIZE are set in the video library function install_video().

You might notice that the font sizes are actually set to 8×8 when in graphics mode using the defined compiler constants. However, HFONT_SIZE and VFONT_SIZE are still determined at run time, so the function will determine the correct font sizes, should you decide to change font style.

- In text modes, the font sizes will be 0. They are irrelevant to the video function library in text modes and are not set.

- Microsoft users, you might need to change the OEM08.FON filename found in the install_video() function. OEM08.FON comes bundled with the Microsoft C/C++ 7.0 compiler and is located in the C:\C700\BIN directory. If the font is not available to you, try using COURB.FON, or see your Microsoft reference manual for available fonts. The font file(s) should be located in the same directory you are running the programming examples in.

- If you change the font type in the install_video() function, use only fixed bitmap fonts for the video function library. See your Borland or Microsoft reference manuals regarding fixed bitmap fonts.

Testing the Video Function Library

Now you should test the video functions quickly before moving ahead. This is to make sure your compiler is set correctly, and to get a "feel" for how to use the video function library.

Compiling the Test Program

When you compile the following test program, follow these guidelines.

Borland Compilers

If you are compiling from the integrated environment, you must set the Graphics Library linker option to ON. If compiling from the command line, GRAPHICS.LIB must be included in the library file(s) argument. Additionally, the correct ".BGI" graphics file must be in the same directory you are running the program from. This is regardless of whether the ".BGI" file is in a directory in the environment path.

Consult the Borland reference manual regarding available ".BGI" files, and their default location.

Microsoft Compilers

If you are using Microsoft C 6.0 or C/C++ 7.0, you must include the GRAPHICS.LIB file in the Additional Global Libraries. If you are compiling from the command line, be sure to include GRAPHICS.LIB in the library file(s) argument.

If you are using Microsoft QuickC, the graphics libraries are installed when you initially set up QuickC. If you did not install the graphics libraries, you will not be able to compile the program. See your Microsoft QuickC Toolkit reference for information about linking libraries.

Additionally, the correct .FON file must be in the same directory you are running the program from. This is regardless of whether the .FON files are in a directory in the environment path. Consult the Microsoft reference manual regarding available .FON files and their default locations.

Running the Test Program

The following test program sets the display to the highest available graphics mode, draws a border around the entire display, informs you of the video mode, maximum display coordinates, font sizes, and maximum color available. The program then asks you to press a key to test the clear line function. After pressing a key, the words "Maximum" and "Font" are erased by the function clear_line_from(). Press another key to exit the program.

Since the variable IN_GMODE has not been defined yet, it will be declared temporarily in the following test program. Notice that the filenames for the #include files are defined in COMPILER.H and are set appropriately according to the compiler being used.

Remember to set the compiler definition file, COMPILER.H, to match your compiler!

```
/*-------------------------------------------------------------*/
/*                        VIDTEST.C                            */
/*                                                             */
/* Program to test TCVIDLIB.INC, or MSVIDLIB.INC file.         */
/*-------------------------------------------------------------*/

unsigned char IN_GMODE;          /* Define here for vidtest.c  */
```

```
#include "compiler.h"           /* Borland Microsoft defines  */
#include graphics              /* Graphics library header    */
#include videolib              /* Video functions            */

void main()
   {
   install_video(GMODE);        /* Install video in 'mode'    */

   header();                    /* Do header                  */
   change_color(15);
   out_text_xy(17,2,"Video System Installed");

                                /* Write Max Coords           */
   out_text_xy(2,4,"Maximum X Coordinate  =");
   out_int_xy(26,4,VID_MAXX);
   out_text_xy(2,5,"Maximum Y Coordinate  =");
   out_int_xy(26,5,VID_MAXY);
                                /* Font width (graphics mode) */
   out_text_xy(2,6,"Font Width In Pixels  =");
   if (IN_GMODE) out_int_xy(26,6,HFONT_SIZE);
   else out_text_xy(26,6,"N/A");
                                /* Font height (graphics mode)*/
   out_text_xy(2,7,"Font Height In Pixels =");
   if (IN_GMODE) out_int_xy(26,7,VFONT_SIZE);
   else out_text_xy(26,7,"N/A");
                                /* Max color available        */
   out_text_xy(2,8,"Maximum Color Value   =");
   out_int_xy(26,8,MAX_COLOR);
   out_text_xy(2,10,
            "Press Any Key To Test Clear Line function.");

   getch();                     /* Wait for keypress          */

   clear_line_from(4,2,7,0);    /* Clear 'Maximum' from 4th   */
   clear_line_from(6,2,4,0);    /* Clear 'Font' from 6th      */
   clear_line_from(10,2,45,0);  /* Clear line 10              */

   out_text_xy(2,10,"The first 'Maximum' should now be blank.");
   out_text_xy(2,11,"The word 'Font' should now be blank.");
   out_text_xy(2,15,"Press Any Key To End...");

   getch();                     /* Wait for keypress          */
```

```
shut_down_video();                /* Shut down video system    */
}
```

When you run VIDTEST.EXE, the display shown here appears:

```
Graphics Mode   Video System Installed
Maximum X Coordinate   = 639
Maximum Y Coordinate   = 479
Font Width In Pixels   = 8
Font Height In Pixels  = 8
Maximum Color Value    = 15

Press Any Key To Test Clear Line function.
```

After pressing a key, the display will appear as shown here:

```
Graphics Mode   Video System Installed
        X Coordinate   = 639
Maximum Y Coordinate   = 479
        Width In Pixels  = 8
Font Height In Pixels  = 8
Maximum Color Value    = 15

The first 'Maximum' should now be blank.
The word 'Font' should now be blank.

Press Any Key To End...
```

You should also try the program in a text mode. To change from graphics mode to text mode, change the line

install_video(GMODE)

to

install_video(TMODE)

in VIDTEST.C, recompile the program, and run it. That's all you need to do; the video function library will handle the rest. The program runs exactly the same, only in text mode.

This wraps up the video function library. Now you are ready to begin the real task, interfacing with the mouse.

Chapter *3*

The Ten Necessary
Mouse Functions

Now that you know how to communicate with the mouse through interrupt 0x33 and
have the video functions ready to use, it's time to move ahead to the real topic:
programming and interfacing with the mouse. First, a brief discussion about mouse
buttons.

Mouse Buttons

While Microsoft's mouse has only two buttons, there are several OEM manufacturers
building three-button mice. However, using the third (middle) button is usually
equivalent to using both left and right buttons simultaneously. Therefore, while the
source code presented in this book does determine if a three-button mouse is
present, the functions and programming examples assume the mouse has either
two buttons, or three buttons with the middle button acting as a simultaneous left
and right button. When you write commercial applications, you can never be
positive what type of mouse the end user has, but since the most popular mouse
(Microsoft) has two buttons, you can consider this the standard. More information
regarding three-button mice can be found in Appendix A. The Logitech standards
are used in the reference.

If you have a three-button mouse, consult the manufacturer's installation manual regarding the middle-button setup. Many OEMs allow you to change the middle button to either act independently or as a simultaneous left and right button.

The Mouse Functions

While there are 50 documented mouse functions, only ten are needed for everyday mouse programming. Some programmers argue that you don't even need that many, but if you want to be a true mouse programmer, you do. With these ten functions, you can manage mouse applications of any size. They are the mainstay of mouse programming.

Before proceeding, some terminology is needed to avoid confusion in the following chapters. The functions you create in this book are called *mouse library functions*. The functions they call internally via interrupt 0x33 are called *mouse functions*. It is important to understand that the two terms refer to different levels of mouse programming.

The following is a list of the ten mouse library functions, calling parameters, the mouse function numbers called via interrupt 0x33, and a brief description of what each function does.

reset_mouse(void)   This function calls mouse function 0, which resets the mouse software and is used to determine whether a mouse is present and the software installed.

show_mouse_cursor(void)   This function calls mouse function 1, which makes the mouse cursor visible.

hide_mouse_cursor(void)   This function calls mouse function 2, which hides the mouse cursor, or makes it invisible.

set_hide_bounds(int *x1*,int *y1*,int *x2*,int *y2*)   This function calls mouse function 16, which hides the mouse cursor if it moves into a predefined region.

set_mouse_position(int *x*,int *y*)   This function calls mouse function 4, which moves the mouse cursor to a desired display location.

set_mouse_hlimits(int *x1*,int *x2*)   This function calls mouse function 7, which sets the horizontal display limits that the mouse cursor can move in.

set_mouse_vlimits(int *y1*,int *y2*)   This function calls mouse function 8, which sets the vertical display limits that the mouse cursor can move in.

get_mouse_button(unsigned char *lbutton1,\
                unsigned char *rbutton2,\
                int *x,int *y)   This function calls mouse function 3, which determines if mouse buttons have been pressed and gets the current mouse cursor location.

get_button_rls_info(int *butt_no*,\
              int *count*,\
              int *x,int *y)   This function calls mouse function 6, which determines if mouse buttons have been released and gets the mouse cursor location, at the time of the last button release.

set_event_handler(int *call_mask*,
              void (far *location*)(void))   This function calls mouse function 12, which sets an event handler.

Global Variables

Along with the previous ten functions, some global constants and variables are used in the mouse function library. These are:

- Three constant macro definitions for button status comparisons used during event processing. These constants are called MV_LBUTTON, MV_RBUTTON, and MV_BBUTTON.

- Two integers to hold the mouse text cell sizes. These are called HCELL_SIZE and VCELL_SIZE.

- One integer to hold the size of the mouse cursor. This is called MOUSE_SIZE.

- Three unsigned chars (used as Boolean variables) to determine

  - Which video mode the system is in. This is called IN_GMODE.

  - If the mouse is present or not. This is called MOUSE_THERE.

  - If the mouse is visible or not. This is called MOUSE_VISIBLE.

- Seven unsigned chars (used as Boolean variables) for event processing. These are called LBUTTON_DOWN, RBUTTON_DOWN, BBUTTON_DOWN, LBUTTON_UP, RBUTTON_UP, BBUTTON_UP, and CURSOR_MOVED.

- Two integers to hold mouse coordinates during event processing. These are called CMX and CMY.

- One integer to hold the value of the button state during event processing. This is called BSTATE.

- Two register variables for the mouse function calls. (If you don't know what register variables are, please read Chapter 1.) These are called mregs and msegregs.

- One Boolean variable for EGA register status. This is called EGA_REG_READ.

About Graphics and Text Modes

Ninety-five percent of mouse functions called via interrupt 0x33 are used for the same purpose in both graphics and text modes. There is one drawback; in text modes, the coordinates used by the mouse functions are graphics coordinates. This is just fine if all you do is program in graphics mode, but it becomes very cumbersome when programming in text modes. This is because you are required to think in graphics coordinates, not the text coordinates used in your program. It's much more natural for you to use text coordinates in text modes, and graphics coordinates in graphics modes. Therefore, conversions are performed inside the mouse library functions based upon the variable IN_GMODE. If IN_GMODE is 1, the system is in a graphic mode and no conversions are necessary. If IN_GMODE is 0, the system is in a text mode, and all coordinates are converted inside the mouse library functions, freeing you from this tedious process.

IN_GMODE is initially set in the function install_video(), located in the video function library you created in Chapter 2 .

The actual overhead for the coordinate conversions is very small. By studying the source code for the mouse function library and running the programming examples in both graphics and text mode (when applicable), you should be able to determine how, when, and why the coordinate conversions take place.

The Mouse Function Library

The following two files represent the mouse function library for the time being. In Chapter 7 and Chapter 12, more mouse library functions are created using new mouse functions called via interrupt 0x33.

It's not necessary to understand every mouse library function or variable meaning just yet. They are covered in detail throughout this book. If you're new to programming, some of the technical discussions following the code listings may seem like an alien language. Don't be discouraged, these things take time. As you develop your programming vocabulary, you will appreciate the discussions more and more.

The global variables are located in a file called MOUSE.H. Here it is:

```
/*-----------------------------------------------------------*/
/*                      MOUSE.H                              */
/*                                                          */
/* Header file for the mouse function library.              */
/*-----------------------------------------------------------*/

#define MV_LBUTTON 1          /* For event driver button    */
#define MV_RBUTTON 2          /* status when CURSOR_MOVED    */
#define MV_BBUTTON 3          /* message is trapped.         */

int NUMBER_BUTTONS=2;         /* Number of mouse buttons     */

int HCELL_SIZE=8,             /* Cursor cell sizes - text mode */
    VCELL_SIZE=8;

int MOUSE_SIZE=16;            /* Mouse cursor size - use 16 in */
                             /* graphics mode, 1 in text.   */

unsigned char IN_GMODE;       /* 1 in graphics mode, 0 in text */

unsigned char MOUSE_THERE;    /* 1 if mouse present, 0 if not */
unsigned char MOUSE_VISIBLE;  /* Internal for HIDE_CURSOR and */
                             /* SHOW_CURSOR functions - 1 if */
                             /* mouse currently visable, 0 if */
                             /* not.                        */

unsigned char LBUTTON_DOWN,   /* Boolean vars or 'messages'  */
              RBUTTON_DOWN,   /* set by event processor.     */
              BBUTTON_DOWN,
              LBUTTON_UP,
              RBUTTON_UP,
              BBUTTON_UP,
              CURSOR_MOVED;

int CMX=0,CMY=0;              /* Mouse coords set by event   */
int BSTATE=0;                 /* handler; Also button state. */
```

```
union  REGS  mregs;            /* DOS/Mouse registers        */
struct SREGS msegregs;         /* DOS/Mouse segment register */

unsigned char EGA_REG_READ=1;/* EGA regs handled properly?   */
                             /* Default YES, see Chapter 4   */
```

The ten mouse library functions are located in a file named MOUSE.INC. Here it is:

```
/*-----------------------------------------------------------*/
/*                    MOUSE.INC                              */
/*                                                           */
/*          The Ten Necessary Mouse Functions                */
/*                                                           */
/* The minimum functions needed to interface successfully    */
/* with and operate the mouse.                               */
/*                                                           */
/* In graphics modes these functions use and return graphics */
/* coordinates. In text modes they use and return text       */
/* coordinates.                                              */
/*                                                           */
/*-----------------------------------------------------------*/


/* MODULE : RESET MOUSE                                      */
/*-----------------------------------------------------------*/
/* Reset mouse and get status.                               */
/* Output parameters                                         */
/*      None. Global variables set inside function.          */
/*                                                           */
void reset_mouse(void)
   {

   MOUSE_THERE=0;                    /* Default NOT there   */
   MOUSE_SIZE=16;                    /* Default graphic size*/
   HCELL_SIZE=8;VCELL_SIZE=8;        /* Default text cell sz*/
   MOUSE_VISIBLE=0;                  /* Default not visible */

   if (getvect(0x33)!=0L)            /* If Int 33 installed */
      {
      mregs.x.ax=0;                  /* Mouse function  0   */
      int86(0x33,&mregs,&mregs);     /* Reset mouse         */

      if (mregs.x.ax!=0)             /* If AX=0, no mouse   */
         {                           /* If mouse is present */
```

```
          MOUSE_THERE=1;                  /* Set global variable */

          NUMBER_BUTTONS=mregs.x.bx;    /* Number buttons in BX*/

       if (!IN_GMODE)                  /* If in text mode     */
          {
          mregs.h.ah=0x0F;              /* NON mouse function  */
          int86(0x10,&mregs,&mregs);  /* Int 10h, func 0Fh   */
          switch(mregs.h.al)            /* Get video mode      */
             {
             case 0:                    /* If 40 char mode     */
             case 1:                    /* Adjust cell size    */
                   HCELL_SIZE=16;break;
             }
          MOUSE_SIZE=1;                 /* Text cursor=one char*/
          }

       LBUTTON_DOWN=0;                  /* Reset Status vars   */
       RBUTTON_DOWN=0;                  /* used in event prcess*/
       BBUTTON_DOWN=0;
       }
     }
   }


/* MODULE : SHOW MOUSE CURSOR                                   */
/*-----------------------------------------------------------*/
/* Make mouse cursor visible.                                  */
/*                                                             */
void pascal show_mouse_cursor(void)
   {
   if (MOUSE_THERE)
      {
      mregs.x.ax=1;                     /* Mouse function  1   */
      int86(0x33,&mregs,&mregs);      /* Show the cursor     */
      MOUSE_VISIBLE=1;                  /* Set flag to 1 - ON  */
      }
   }


/* MODULE : HIDE MOUSE CURSOR                                   */
/*-----------------------------------------------------------*/
/* Hide the mouse cursor.                                      */
/*                                                             */
void pascal hide_mouse_cursor(void)
   {
   if ((MOUSE_VISIBLE)&&(MOUSE_THERE)) /* If mouse not hidden */
```

```
        {
     mregs.x.ax=2;                        /* Mouse function 2   */
     int86(0x33,&mregs,&mregs);           /* Hide the cursor    */
     MOUSE_VISIBLE=0;                     /* Set flag to 0      */
        }
   }


/* MODULE : SET HIDE BOUNDS                                       */
/*--------------------------------------------------------------*/
/* Set a rectangular region of the display that the mouse        */
/* cursor is to be hidden in.                                     */
/* Input parameters                                              */
/*      x1 - left horizontal bound of region                     */
/*      y1 - upper vertical bound of region                      */
/*      x2 - right horizontal bound of region                    */
/*      y2 - bottom vertical bound of region                     */
/*                                                               */
void pascal set_hide_bounds(int x1,int y1,int x2,int y2)
   {
   if ((EGA_REG_READ)&&(MOUSE_THERE))  /* EGA regs in tact?  */
      {
      if (!IN_GMODE)                    /* If in text mode    */
         {
         x1=(x1*HCELL_SIZE)-HCELL_SIZE;/* x1 to graf coord   */
         x2=(x2*HCELL_SIZE)-HCELL_SIZE;/* x2 to graf coord   */
         y1=(y1*VCELL_SIZE)-VCELL_SIZE;/* y1 to graf coord   */
         y2=(y2*VCELL_SIZE)-VCELL_SIZE;/* y2 to graf coord   */
         }
      mregs.x.ax=16;                       /* Mouse function 16  */
      mregs.x.cx=x1;                       /* Set exclusion area */
      mregs.x.dx=y1;
      mregs.x.si=x2;
      mregs.x.di=y2;
      int86(0x33,&mregs,&mregs);
      }
   else hide_mouse_cursor();             /* EGA regs not intact */
   }                                     /* hide cursor instead.*/


/* MODULE : SET MOUSE POSITION                                    */
/*--------------------------------------------------------------*/
/* Set the current mouse cursor position.                        */
/* Input parameters                                              */
/*      x,y - coordinates of where to place mouse cursor          */
/*                                                               */
void pascal set_mouse_position(int x,int y)
```

```
   {
 if (MOUSE_THERE)
    {
    if (!IN_GMODE)                      /* If in text mode     */
       {
       x=(x*HCELL_SIZE)-HCELL_SIZE;  /* x to graf coord     */
       y=(y*VCELL_SIZE)-VCELL_SIZE;  /* y to graf coord     */
       }

    mregs.x.ax=4;                       /* Mouse function 4    */
    mregs.x.cx=x;                       /* Load reg cx with x  */
    mregs.x.dx=y;                       /* Load reg dx with y  */
    int86(0x33,&mregs,&mregs);          /* Change cursor pos   */
    }
 }

/* MODULE : SET MOUSE HLIMITS                                    */
/*-------------------------------------------------------------*/
/* Set the maximum horizontal mouse cursor display region.      */
/* Input parameters                                             */
/*     x1,x2 - Horizontal mouse cursor display boundary         */
/*                                                              */
void pascal set_mouse_hlimits(int x1,int x2)
 {
 if (MOUSE_THERE)
    {
    if (!IN_GMODE)                      /* If in text mode     */
       {
       x1=(x1*HCELL_SIZE)-HCELL_SIZE;/* x1 to graf coord     */
       x2=(x2*HCELL_SIZE)-HCELL_SIZE;/* x2 to graf coord     */
       }

    mregs.x.ax=7;                       /* Mouse function 7    */
    mregs.x.cx=x1;                      /* Reg cx = start x    */
    mregs.x.dx=x2;                      /* Reg dx = end x      */
    int86(0x33,&mregs,&mregs);          /* Set horiz limits    */
    }
 }

/* MODULE : SET MOUSE VLIMITS                                    */
/*-------------------------------------------------------------*/
/* Set the maximum vertical mouse cursor display region.        */
/* Input parameters                                             */
/*     y1,y2 - Vertical mouse cursor display boundary           */
/*                                                              */
```

```
void pascal set_mouse_vlimits(int y1,int y2)
    {
    if (MOUSE_THERE)
        {
        if (!IN_GMODE)                         /* If in text mode     */
            {
            y1=(y1*VCELL_SIZE)-VCELL_SIZE;/* y1 to graf coord     */
            y2=(y2*VCELL_SIZE)-VCELL_SIZE;/* y2 to graf coord     */
            }

        mregs.x.ax=8;                          /* Mouse function 8    */
        mregs.x.cx=y1;                         /* Reg cx = start y    */
        mregs.x.dx=y2;                         /* Reg dx = end y      */
        int86(0x33,&mregs,&mregs);             /* Set vertical limits */
        }
    }


/* MODULE : GET MOUSE BUTTON                                          */
/*------------------------------------------------------------------*/
/* Get the status of the mouse buttons and the current               */
/* location of the mouse cursor.                                     */
/* Input parameters                                                  */
/*      *lbutton - address to left button status var                 */
/*      *rbutton - address to right button status var                */
/*      *x       - address to x coordinate var                       */
/*      *y       - address to y coordinate var                       */
/* Output parameters                                                 */
/*      button status vars = 1 if button pressed, o if not           */
/*      x,y variables contain current mouse cursor location          */
/*                                                                   */
void pascal get_mouse_button(unsigned char *lbutton,
                             unsigned char *rbutton,
                             int *x,int *y)
    {
    if (MOUSE_THERE)
        {
        mregs.x.ax=3;                          /* Mouse function 3    */
        int86(0x33,&mregs,&mregs);             /* Button & coord stats*/

        *lbutton =(mregs.x.bx == 1) ? 1 : 0; /* Button1 pressed?*/
        *rbutton =(mregs.x.bx == 2) ? 1 : 0; /* Button2 pressed?*/
```

```
        if (mregs.x.bx==3)                  /* Both buttons pressd?*/
          {*lbutton=1;*rbutton=1;}

        if (IN_GMODE)                       /* If in graphics mode */
          {
          *x=mregs.x.cx;                    /* Reg cx = x coord    */
          *y=mregs.x.dx;                    /* Reg dx = y coord    */
          }
        else                                /* If in text mode     */
          {                                 /* Convert to text crds*/
          *x=(mregs.x.cx+HCELL_SIZE)/HCELL_SIZE;
          *y=(mregs.x.dx+VCELL_SIZE)/VCELL_SIZE;
          }
        }
      }


/* MODULE : GET BUTTON RLS INFO                                    */
/*---------------------------------------------------------------*/
/* Get information about button releases since last call to        */
/* function.                                                       */
/* Input parameters                                                */
/*      butt_no - which button? 0=left, 1=right                    */
/*      *count  - Address of var-how many times butt released      */
/*      *x,*y   - Address of new coordinate variables              */
/* Output parameters                                               */
/*      If butt_no =0 and left button released, returns 1          */
/*      If butt_no =0 and left button not released, returns 0      */
/*      If butt_no =1 and right button released, returns 1         */
/*      If butt_no =1 and right button not released, returns 0     */
/*                                                                 */
/*                                                                 */
unsigned char pascal get_button_rls_info(int butt_no,
                                         int *count,
                                         int *x,int *y)
    {
    if (MOUSE_THERE)
       {
       mregs.x.ax=6;                        /* Mouse function 6    */
       mregs.x.bx=butt_no;                  /* Which button,       */
                                            /* 0=left, 1=right     */
       int86(0x33,&mregs,&mregs);           /* Retrieve information*/
```

```
        *count=mregs.x.bx;                      /* bx = number releases*/
        *x=mregs.x.cx;                          /* cx = horiz coord     */
        *y=mregs.x.dx;                          /* dx = vert coord      */

                                                /* Bit 1 in ax contain */
                                                /* left butt status     */
                                                /* Released or not?     */
        if (butt_no==0) return(!(mregs.x.ax & 1));

                                                /* Bit 2 in ax contains*/
                                                /* right butt status    */
        else return(!((mregs.x.ax & 2) >> 1));
        }
    return(0);
    }


/* MODULE : SET EVENT HANDLER                                          */
/*-------------------------------------------------------------------*/
/* Function sets the EVENT handler subroutine to be called by */
/* the mouse driver.                                          */
/* Input parameters                                           */
/*    call_mask - action that causes event handler to be called*/
/*    location  - pass in actual function name                 */
/*                                                             */
void pascal set_event_handler(int call_mask,
                        void (far *location)(void))
    {
    if (MOUSE_THERE)
        {
        mregs.x.ax=12;                      /* Mouse function 12    */
        mregs.x.cx=call_mask;               /* Call mask-action     */
        mregs.x.dx=FP_OFF(location);        /* Offset of e-handler */
        msegregs.es=FP_SEG(location);       /* Segment of e-handler*/
        int86x(0x33,&mregs,&mregs,&msegregs);
        }
    }
```

Mouse Function 0: Reset and Status

In any mouse application, your first order of business is determining if a mouse is present in the system. To do this, you use the mouse library function reset_mouse(), which in turn calls mouse function 0, reset and status.

Take a look inside the function reset_mouse(). Notice the following items.

Determining Mouse Presence

To tell a program whether a mouse is present and installed, mouse function 0 returns a status value in the AX register (mregs.x.ax). If a mouse is not present in the system, the AX register is 0. A nonzero value indicates the mouse hardware is present and the software installed. However, before mouse function 0 can be used, the following precautions must be taken.

Determining a Valid Interrupt Vector

Although mouse function 0 is used to determine if a mouse is present in the system, you must first determine if the interrupt 0x33 vector is valid. You do this with the function getvect(0x33). The reason for this is some DOS versions prior to 3.0 initially set the interrupt 0x33 vector to 0000:0000. If this is the case and you call interrupt 0x33, mouse function 0, the system will crash. Therefore, you must first check to make sure the interrupt 0x33 vector points to valid code before you make any calls to interrupt 0x33. Only then can you use mouse function 0 to determine if the mouse is present and the software installed.

Additionally, the interrupt vector might point to an IRET(interrupt return) instruction, indicating no mouse is present. However, the IRET instruction will not crash the system, and the register values are not modified. Since the AX register is set to 0 when calling mouse function 0, it is not necessary to determine if interrupt 0x33 points to an IRET instruction, because the AX register is still 0 when control returns from interrupt 0x33, which is the correct value when no mouse is present.

Handling the Status

If mouse function 0 determines the mouse is present and the software installed, the global variable MOUSE_THERE is set to 1. Notice that every other function in the mouse function library uses MOUSE_THERE upon entry to the function. If MOUSE_THERE is 1, a function continues with operations. If MOUSE_THERE is 0, no operations are performed, and control is passed back to the calling routine. This is because when you write applications that interface with the mouse, the application should still operate properly, even if a mouse is not installed.

If the status is handled outside of the mouse library functions, then every call made to a mouse library function must be preceded with the statement

```
if (MOUSE_THERE) do_mouse_function();
```

Compound statements require even more coding, such as the following:

```
if (MOUSE_THERE)
   {
   do_mouse_function1();
```

```
do_mouse_function2();
  }
```

By using the MOUSE_THERE variable inside the actual mouse library functions, you are free to write the code as if the mouse existed all the time. It becomes transparent, and you can write code such as

```
do_mouse_function1();
do_mouse_function2();
```

without having to worry if the mouse is actually present or not, because it is handled internally, inside the mouse library functions.

There are many instances when you don't want routines in your application to execute if the mouse is not present. In these instances, using the variable MOUSE_THERE before entering the routines is appropriate. This is demonstrated in several programming examples throughout the book.

Number of Buttons

Mouse function 0 also returns the number of buttons on a mouse in the BX register (mregs.x.bx).

Text Cell Sizes

Look at the following code fragment:

```
if (!IN_GMODE)
    {
    mregs.h.ah=0x0F;
    int86(0x10,&mregs,&mregs);
    switch(mregs.h.al)
        {
        case 0:
        case 1:
                HCELL_SIZE=16;break;
        }
    MOUSE_SIZE=1;
    }
```

This is the only *non*mouse function call in the mouse function library. If the current video mode is a text mode, a call to interrupt 0x10 function 0x0F is made to determine if the text mode is a 40-column mode. Here's why:

When in text modes, the mouse cursor uses its own cell size to determine the location. The location is not based on the systems font size, as with text processing, because the mouse driver may be using a *virtual screen* different from the actual video system. A virtual screen can be thought of as a screen using different coordinates than the actual physical coordinates of the display. The cell size is 8 × 8 in 80-column text modes, and 16 × 8 in 40-column text modes.

So, while the 40-character text mode is rarely used, if you wish to remain compatible with *all* text modes, the cell size adjustment is necessary to ensure correct display coordinates are used.

Mouse Cursor Size

Take a look at the variable MOUSE_SIZE. This variable is used to hold the mouse cursor's physical size. In graphics mode, the mouse cursor is 16 bits high and 16 bits (pixels) wide. In text modes the mouse cursor is one character high and one character wide. MOUSE_SIZE is used to set appropriate display range boundaries, which are used to keep the mouse cursor visibly on the display.

Your First Mouse Program

If you have never programmed the mouse before, I bet you're just "itching" to display that mouse cursor! There's just one more item to take care of first.

Instead of having several #include "*filename*" statements in the programming examples, it is better to build one header file that contains all the macros, as shown here. The header file is used throughout the following three chapters and is called HEADER1.H. It contains all the necessary #include files.

```
/*                      HEADER1.H                        */
/*-----------------------------------------------------*/

#include "compiler.h"  /* Compiler directives            */
#include "mouse.h"     /* Mouse global header file        */
#include "mouse.inc"   /* 10 mouse functions              */
#include graphics      /* Graphics library header         */
#include videolib      /* Video function library          */
```

Now for your first program using the mouse function library. The following program sets up the display, makes the mouse cursor visible, and waits for you to press a key. During this time, move the mouse around and watch the mouse cursor mimic mouse movement. Press any key to exit the program.

Here is MOUSE1.C:

```
/*-------------------------------------------------------------*/
/*                        MOUSE1.C                             */
/*                                                             */
/* Demonstrate how to show the mouse cursor.                   */
/*-------------------------------------------------------------*/

#include "header1.h"        /* Directives, headers, includes */

void main()
   {
   install_video(GMODE);    /* Install video system          */
   header();                /* Draw header                   */
   reset_mouse();           /* Reset mouse                   */

                            /* If no mouse, print error mssg */
   if (!MOUSE_THERE) mouse_error(10,4);

   out_text_xy(25, 7,"Mouse cursor should now be visible.");
   out_text_xy(25, 8,"Move it around with the mouse!");
   out_text_xy(25,10,"Press a key when finished.");

   show_mouse_cursor();     /* Make the cursor visible        */

   getch();                 /* Wait for keypress              */

   hide_mouse_cursor();     /* Hide the cursor                */

   shut_down_video();       /* Shut down video system         */
   }
```

When you run the program in graphics mode, the mouse cursor "pops" up in the center of the display, as shown in Figure 3-1.

If you have never interfaced with the mouse before, you may be suprised at how easy it is to display the mouse cursor. Try running the program again, only this time in text mode. Change the line

install_video(GMODE)

to

install_video(TMODE)

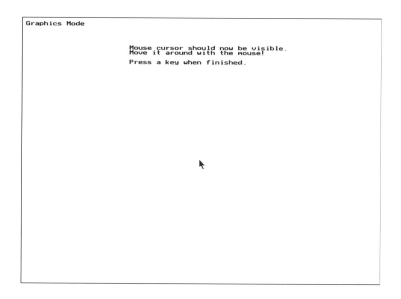

```
Graphics Mode


                        Mouse cursor should now be visible.
                        Move it around with the mouse!
                        Press a key when finished.
```

Figure 3-1.   *The graphics mouse cursor*

Recompile and run. This time you should see a box cursor instead of the arrow cursor. This is the mouse's text cursor.

If perhaps you own a Video-7 VRAM II Ergo Super VGA card, you will still see the graphics arrow. That because the folks at Video-7 implement the graphics mouse cursor in hardware, and the graphics arrow is used in both text and graphic modes.

The Invisible Mouse Cursor

When the program was running in graphics mode, you probably noticed something odd. You were able to move the mouse cursor clear of the display to the right and lower regions. This rendered the mouse cursor invisible. In real-time applications, you cannot allow this to happen. The end user who mistakenly moves the mouse off the display might not know this and might simply assume the mouse is not functioning. All the while, the mouse cursor is hidden off to the side. What you must do is limit the amount of display region the mouse can access. You do this with the mouse library functions set_mouse_hlimits() and set_mouse_vlimits(). In turn, set_mouse_hlimits() calls mouse function 7, set minimum and maximum horizontal cursor position, and set_mouse_vlimits() calls mouse function 8, set minimum and maximum vertical cursor position.

In the following example, MOUSE2.C, the mouse cursor is allowed to move only on and inside the rectangle border:

```
/*------------------------------------------------------------*/
/*                      MOUSE2.C                           */
/*                                                         */
/* Demonstrate how to show the mouse cursor and limit its  */
/* movement to on or inside the header rectangle.          */
/*------------------------------------------------------------*/

#include "header1.h"          /* Directives, headers, includes */

void main()
   {
   install_video(GMODE);     /* Install video system          */
   header();                 /* Draw header                   */
   reset_mouse();            /* Reset mouse                   */

                             /* If no mouse, print error mssg */
   if (!MOUSE_THERE) mouse_error(10,4);

                             /* Set mouse horiz & vert limits */
   set_mouse_hlimits(1,VID_MAXX-MOUSE_SIZE+1);
   set_mouse_vlimits(1,VID_MAXY-MOUSE_SIZE);

   out_text_xy(25, 7,"Mouse cursor should now be visible.");
   out_text_xy(25, 8,"Motion limited to on/inside rectangle.");
   out_text_xy(25, 9,"Move it around with the mouse!");
   out_text_xy(25,11,"Press a key when finished.");

   show_mouse_cursor();      /* Make the cursor visible        */

   getch();                  /* Wait for keypress              */

   hide_mouse_cursor();      /* Hide the cursor                */

   shut_down_video();        /* Shut down graphics system      */
   }
```

The mouse cursor should not be able to move off the display, as Figure 3-2 illustrates.

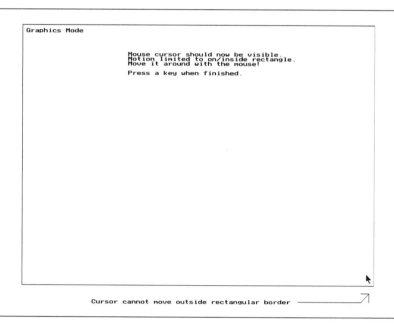

Figure 3-2.   *Keeping the mouse cursor on the display*

After you run the program in graphics mode, try it in text mode. Again, change the line

install_video(GMODE)

to

install_video(TMODE)

Limiting the Range Based on Mouse Cursor Size

Remember that the graphics mouse cursor is 16 bits (pixels) wide, and the text mouse cursor is one character wide. When you are running in a graphics mode, the whole mouse cursor should remain visible on the display. That is where the MOUSE_SIZE variable comes in. When setting the limits on a 640-pixel-wide graphics display, the statement

```
set_mouse_hlimits(1,VID_MAXX-MOUSE_SIZE+1)
```

will set the horizontal limit to 639–16+1, or 624. This will contain the mouse cursor inside the entire display region. Although the +1 adjustment is not necessary in graphics modes, it is for running in text modes. This is because in a text mode, say the 80 × 25 column text mode, MOUSE_SIZE is 1. So, 80–1+1 limits the mouse cursor to the 80th column. If the +1 adjustment is eliminated, the limit becomes 80–1, or 79. This is one column less than the desired amount.

Warning: Mouse Function 38

If, by chance, you use mouse function 38, get maximum virtual coordinates, *do not* use the coordinates returned to set the display limits, unless you know precisely what you are doing and what mouse driver you are using. The reason is twofold:

- Mouse function 38 is not available in many OEM mouse drivers, and unpredictable values will be returned. (Usually the values are 0, and the mouse cursor gets trapped in the upper-left corner of the display.)

- The mouse driver might be using a virtual screen size different from the actual display size, and you would limit the mouse cursor to the wrong coordinates. Always use display coordinates. If the mouse driver is using a different virtual screen, it will make the adjustment internally on its own.

  The virtual screen sizes are different from the display in 320 × 200 graphics modes and might be different in all text modes, depending on the display type. They might also be different in some super-high-resolution modes (800 × 600 and higher), depending on the mouse driver and function availability.

Chapter *4*

How To Keep A Mouse from Turning into a Rat

This chapter is an important one. You will not be able to write successful mouse applications until you understand the principles discussed. So please, keep a tight watch.

The Golden Rule

The most fundamental rule the mouse cursor must follow is not to disturb any portion of the display it is moving over. To accomplish this, the mouse driver saves the background image the mouse cursor is moving over and restores the background image when the mouse cursor moves to a new location. These operations occur whenever the mouse cursor is visible and moving.

When the display is not being updated, you never need to worry about the mouse cursor disturbing it. However, when the mouse cursor is visible and moving, and you update the display in any manner (write text, draw graphs, and so on), there exists the possibility of seriously disrupting what is currently on the display, what is being written to the display, and the mouse cursor itself.

The Problem

Since the person using your application controls the physical mouse, he can move the mouse cursor whenever, and wherever desired. When you update the display, you are never sure if the area you are updating is currently under modification by the mouse driver. Therefore, if the mouse cursor is visible and you are updating a display region where the mouse cursor is located, the background image operations the mouse driver performs can disrupt whatever you are writing to the display.

For instance, suppose you are drawing a small circle at graphics location 100,100. If the mouse cursor is visible and moving over location 100,100, the following sequence of events is one way the circle can be disrupted:

1. The mouse driver saves the background image the mouse cursor is moving over at location 100,100.

2. You draw the circle at location 100,100.

3. As the mouse cursor moves past location 100,100, the previous background image is restored, which does not contain the circle you just drew at that location.

Additionally, the same logic applies to any background image operations you perform. Suppose you design a graphics object to use in some type of animation sequence. To properly manage the animation sequence, you must save the background image at the location the object is to be drawn and then draw the object. Before the object moves, you restore the background image where the object is currently located, save the background image where the object is moving to, and draw the object again at the new location. If the mouse cursor is visible while these operations occur, the following sequence of events shows one way the mouse cursor could disrupt the background. Assume you are drawing the object at display location 100,100.

1. The mouse cursor moves to location 100,100.

2. You save the background image at location 100,100 in preparation to draw the graphics object. The background image you save now contains the mouse cursor.

3. You write the graphics object to the display.

4. The mouse cursor moves to location 50,50.

5. You restore the background image where the graphics object is located in preparation for the next animation sequence.

6. The background image you restore contains a mouse cursor, and there are now *two* mouse cursors on the display: the actual mouse cursor, which is still

operational, and a "dead" mouse cursor, which was contained in the background image you saved.

Because a picture is worth a thousand words, the following program demonstrates the bad effects that occur when updating the display while the mouse cursor is visible and moving. The program will display the mouse cursor and go into a routine that draws a string of text on the display in different colors, at different locations. While the text is being drawn, move the mouse cursor around, and watch the text as it gets disrupted.

Try and keep the mouse cursor in front of the text as it cycles through the drawing loop. This will generally leave portions of the text on the display after it gets erased. Also, try leaving the mouse cursor stationary, and watch it get erased as text writes over it.

Here is MOUSE3.C, the "Mouse to Rat" demonstration:

```
/*------------------------------------------------------------*/
/*                    MOUSE3.C                                */
/*                                                            */
/* Demonstrate the effect that occurs when writing to the    */
/* display without hiding the mouse cursor. This is the      */
/* "Mouse to Rat" effect.                                    */
/*------------------------------------------------------------*/

#include "header1.h"        /* Directives, headers, includes */

void main()
   {
   int loop1,loop2,cloop;   /* Misc. loops, color loop        */

   install_video(GMODE);    /* Install video system           */
   header();                /* Draw header                    */
   reset_mouse();           /* Reset mouse                    */

   if (MOUSE_THERE)
      {
      out_text_xy(10,5,"Move the mouse around while the text
                  draws on the display");

                           /* Set horiz & vert limits         */
      set_mouse_hlimits(1,VID_MAXX-MOUSE_SIZE+1);
      set_mouse_vlimits(1,VID_MAXY-MOUSE_SIZE);

      show_mouse_cursor();  /* Show the mouse cursor           */
```

```
/* This next loop will draw the text "MOUSETORAT" on the*/
/* display at different locations in different colors.  */
/* It delays for a bit, then erases the last text drawn.*/
/* It will continue to cycle through text and colors as */
/* it goes along. Press any key to exit the loop.       */
/*-----------------------------------------------------*/

cloop=1;
while (!kbhit())         /* Draw text on the display    */
    {                    /* until user presses a key.   */
    loop1=8;             /* Start at row 8              */
    while ((loop1<=20)&&(!kbhit()))
        {
        loop2=5;         /* Start at 5th column         */
        while ((loop2<=66)&&(!kbhit()))
            {
                         /* Change color & write text   */
            change_color(cloop);
            out_text_xy(loop2,loop1,"MOUSETORAT");

                         /* Delay, then clear line       */
            delay(100);
            clear_line_from(loop1,loop2,10,0);

                         /* Update loops                */
            ++cloop;loop2+=12;
            if (cloop==16) cloop=1;
            }
        ++loop1;
        }
    }
else mouse_error(10,4);

getch();                      /* Get char in keyboard buffer  */

hide_mouse_cursor();
shut_down_video();
}
```

See the strange results? Figure 4-1 shows some of the bad effects that can occur.
Try it in text mode. Don't forget to change the line

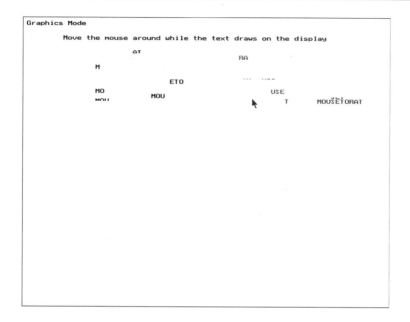

Figure 4-1. *Bad effects caused by the mouse cursor*

install_video(GMODE)

to

install_video(TMODE)

In text modes, these bad effects are less obvious. In text modes, the image saving and restoring does not occur. A single character block is XORed against the current character and attribute (a further discussion of XOR, AND, REVERSE, and COPY/PUT modes follows in Chapters 14 and 15). You'll see by running the program in text modes though, that bad effects do occur, and the damage to your programming reputation from just one character being "glitched" could be disastrous.

The Solutions

There are two methods to solving the problem of display disruption. The first method is to hide the mouse cursor before any display updating takes place and show it again immediately after. The second method is to set an *exclusion area*, which defines a rectangular region the mouse cursor will be hidden in, should the mouse cursor move into the region. Both methods have advantages and disadvantages, and both have other problems associated with them. These two methods will be discussed in detail, starting with method 1.

Method 1: Hiding and Showing the Mouse Cursor

To avoid the problems associated with display updating, you must hide the mouse cursor before any display update occurs and redisplay the mouse cursor after the display update is complete. Since the mouse cursor is not visible during the update, the mouse driver is not performing any background image operations while the update takes place, and no disruption occurs. This method is fine for times when one quick screen write is desired—hide it, write it, and show it.

To hide the mouse cursor, use the mouse library function hide_mouse_cursor(). This function calls mouse function 2, hide cursor. To make the mouse cursor visible, use the mouse library function show_mouse_cursor(). This function calls mouse function 1, show cursor.

Hide-and-Show Programming Example

The following example cures the disruption problem by calling hide_mouse_cursor() before display updating, and show_mouse_cursor() immediately after. The program writes text to the upper-right portion of the display, in the same manner as the previous example. The reason for leaving a portion of the display blank is so you will understand the concepts yet to come in method 2, setting an exclusion area.

Here is MOUSE4.C:

```
/*-------------------------------------------------------------*/
/*                        MOUSE4.C                             */
/*                                                             */
/* Demonstrate hiding and showing the mouse cursor during      */
/* display updating. Example will flicker as a result of       */
/* constant hide-shows.                                        */
/*-------------------------------------------------------------*/

#include "header1.h"          /* Directives, headers, includes */

void main()
    {
    int loop1,loop2,cloop;    /* Misc. loops, color loop        */

    install_video(GMODE);     /* Install video system           */
```

```
header();                      /* Draw header                */
reset_mouse();                 /* Reset mouse                */

if (MOUSE_THERE)
   {
   out_text_xy(10,5,"Hide/Show Cursor During Display
                    Writes/Updates");

                               /* Set horiz & vert limits    */
   set_mouse_hlimits(1,VID_MAXX-MOUSE_SIZE+1);
   set_mouse_vlimits(1,VID_MAXY-MOUSE_SIZE);

   show_mouse_cursor();    /* Show the mouse cursor          */

   cloop=1;                /* Start the 'MOUSETORAT' loop    */
   while (!kbhit())        /* Draw text on the display       */
      {                    /* until user presses a key.      */
      loop1=8;             /* Start at 8th row               */
      while ((loop1<=20)&&(!kbhit()))
         {
         loop2=40;         /* Start at 40th column           */
         while ((loop2<=66)&&(!kbhit()))
            {
            change_color(cloop);

                           /* Hide cursor, write the text,   */
                           /* then show the cursor.          */
            hide_mouse_cursor();
            out_text_xy(loop2,loop1,"MOUSETORAT");
            show_mouse_cursor();

            delay(100);
                           /* Hide cursor, write the text,   */
                           /* then show the cursor.          */
            hide_mouse_cursor();
            clear_line_from(loop1,loop2,10,0);
            show_mouse_cursor();

                           /* Update loops                   */
            ++cloop;loop2+=12;
            if (cloop==16) cloop=1;
            }
         ++loop1;
         }
      }
```

```
        }
    else mouse_error(10,4);

    getch();                        /* Get char in keyboard buffer    */

    hide_mouse_cursor();
    shut_down_video();
    }
```

Now there is no graphics disruption! Try it in text mode. Don't forget to change the line

install_video(GMODE)

to

install_video(TMODE)

You may have noticed that the mouse cursor is flickering quite a bit. That's because the program is hiding and showing the mouse cursor for every single write to the display. For many applications, this is not a good method. Here's a more realistic situation that's appropriate for using this method. Suppose a user makes a menu choice in an application that alters some values used in a graphics formula. When the values change, it causes a graph to redraw. You only need to hide the mouse cursor once before the entire display update and then show the mouse cursor once after the display update. The mouse cursor does *not* need to be visible during any portion of display writing, unless that is what you desire.

The method of hiding and showing is also suitable for menu updates. Suppose you have a floating type of menu system where options highlight and dehighlight as the mouse cursor passes over them (this technique is presented in Chapter 9). Since you know the mouse cursor is in the update region, you know it must be hidden before any highlighting operations take place. It's a fast hide-write-show routine. The flicker doesn't matter because the user's attention is on the menu option highlighting.

Before proceeding any further, mouse function 2, hide cursor, has a glitch you must be aware of.

The Internal Cursor Flag Glitch   The internal cursor flag is what determines if the mouse cursor is visible or invisible (hidden). This flag is internal to the mouse driver, and you have no direct access to its value.

Mouse function 42, get cursor hot spot, does return the internal cursor flag. However, it is unavailable in most OEM mouse drivers. See Appendix A regarding mouse function 42.

Here's how the internal cursor flag works:

- If the cursor flag is 0, the mouse cursor is visible. Any value below 0 means the mouse cursor is invisible, or hidden. The value will never be greater than 0, but it may be less than −1, as in −2, −3, −4, −5, and so on.

- Any calls to mouse functions 0 or 33, to reset the mouse, will set the cursor flag to −1 and make the mouse cursor invisible.

- Any call to mouse function 1, show cursor, will increment the cursor flag. If the value of the cursor flag is −1 and a call is made to mouse function 1, the cursor flag is incremented to 0, and the mouse cursor becomes visible.

- Any call to mouse function 2, hide cursor, will decrement the cursor flag. If the value of the cursor flag is 0 and a call is made to mouse function 2, the cursor flag is decremented to −1, and the mouse cursor becomes invisible.

The glitch is this: any calls to mouse function 1, show cursor, will increment the cursor flag, but the value will *never* go higher than 0. You can call the show cursor function as many times as you like, and only one hide cursor function call is needed to make the mouse cursor invisible. However, any calls to mouse function 2, hide cursor, decrement the cursor flag and continue to subtract 1 from the cursor flag as each subsequent call is made (bringing the value well below −1). This means that if you call mouse function 2, hide cursor, a number of times in a row, you *must* call mouse function 1, show cursor, the same number of times before the mouse cursor becomes visible again.

This might not sound like much of a problem, but I can assure you from personal experience debugging deeply embedded applications to find one extra "hide cursor" call, it can be. The only reason I can think of for this logic is some type of recursive hide and show routines. However, that would be the exception, and not the rule. For normal programming tasks, any value below −1 is meaningless.

Alternatively, you could call mouse function 0 or 33 to reset the mouse and then make one call to mouse function 1, show cursor. However, this will reset the mouse cursor's position to the center of the display and is not a good approach.

Fixing the Glitch   The mouse library functions hide_mouse_cursor() and show_mouse_cursor() correct this glitch. Here's how:

When the mouse library function reset_mouse() is called, it sets the global variable MOUSE_VISIBLE, found in MOUSE.H, to 0. The reason is because the mouse cursor is initially invisible, and any call to reset_mouse() or mouse function 0, reset and status, will hide the mouse cursor if it is currently visible.

Every time the function show_mouse_cursor() is called, it calls mouse function 1, show cursor, and the variable MOUSE_VISIBLE is set to 1, meaning the mouse cursor is visible.

When the function hide_mouse_cursor() is called, it checks the value of MOUSE_VISIBLE. If MOUSE_VISIBLE is 1, the mouse cursor is currently visible, and mouse function 2, hide cursor, is called to make the mouse cursor invisible. If MOUSE_VISIBLE is 0, the mouse cursor is currently invisible, and the function exits without further processing.

This small bit of additional logic effectively solves the glitch associated with the internal cursor flag and mouse function 2, hide cursor. If you make a small mistake and program two hide_mouse_cursor() calls in a row, you will still be able to reenable the mouse cursor with only one call to show_mouse_cursor(), as it should be.

Method 2: Setting an Exclusion Area

In the previous example, MOUSE4.C, the right-hand portion of the display was completely blank, but the mouse cursor still flickered in that area, even though no display writing occurred there. If the mouse cursor's movement range was limited to the right-hand portion of the display, the function hide_mouse_cursor() would never need to be called, since the mouse cursor would never be in the display updating region. However, there is a method to eliminate the hiding (and associated flicker) while the cursor is not in the display region and allow the mouse cursor to move into the display updating region safely.

The mouse library function set_hide_bounds() allows you to define a rectangular region of the display used for updating called an *exclusion area*. The function set_hide_bounds() calls mouse function 16, set exclusion area. The function is used just like hide_mouse_cursor(), with one exception. Instead of simply hiding the mouse cursor, you pass in coordinates defining a rectangular region of the display updating is to occur in. From that point on, the mouse driver constantly checks to see if the mouse cursor moves into the region. If it does, the mouse cursor is hidden. If the mouse cursor does not venture into the region, it remains visible.

Even if the mouse cursor does not venture into the exclusion area, you must still use the function show_mouse_cursor() directly after display updating occurs, just as if you were using the function hide_mouse_cursor() instead of set_hide_bounds(). This is because there is no way to determine (through mouse functions) whether or not the mouse cursor went into the region and became invisible. Therefore, you must always assume it did, and show the mouse cursor after the display update. If the mouse cursor is already visible, an extra call to show_mouse_cursor() causes no harm or flickering, because internally the driver knows it's already visible and takes no action. Also, any call to show_mouse_cursor(), or mouse function 0, show cursor, will destroy the exclusion-area boundaries specified with set_hide_bounds(), or mouse function 16, set exclusion area. Therefore, the boundaries must be reset every time show_mouse_cursor() is called.

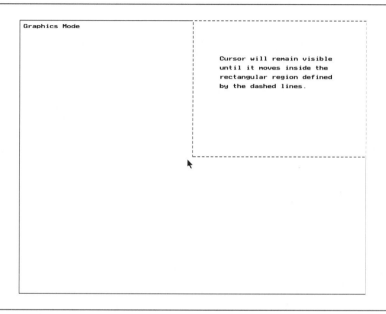

Figure 4-2.   *The defined exclusion area*

Exclusion Hide-and-Show Programming Example

The following example demonstrates the use of the mouse library function set_hide_bounds(). It sets an exclusion area instead of using the function hide_mouse_cursor(). The exclusion area is defined approximately the same as the dashed rectangle in Figure 4-2 indicates.

Here is MOUSE5.C:

```
/*-----------------------------------------------------------*/
/*                      MOUSE5.C                             */
/*                                                           */
/* Demonstrate hiding the cursor only when it moves into a   */
/* predefined region, called the exclusion area.             */
/* With this method, flicker is eliminated when the cursor is */
/* not in display update region.                             */
/*-----------------------------------------------------------*/

#include "header1.h"          /* Directives, headers, includes */
```

```c
void main()
   {
   int loop1,loop2,cloop,max;/* Misc. loops, max rows         */

   install_video(GMODE);      /* Install video system         */
   header();                  /* Draw header                  */
   reset_mouse();             /* Reset mouse                  */

   if (MOUSE_THERE)
      {
      out_text_xy(10,5,"Exclusion/Hide And Show Cursor During
                      Display Writes/Updates");

                              /* Set horiz & vert limits      */
      set_mouse_hlimits(1,VID_MAXX-MOUSE_SIZE+1);
      set_mouse_vlimits(1,VID_MAXY-MOUSE_SIZE);
                              /* Set cursor upper-left         */
      set_mouse_position(1,1);

      show_mouse_cursor();    /* Show the mouse cursor         */

      if (IN_GMODE)           /* If in graphics mode           */
         max=((VID_MAXY/2)/VFONT_SIZE)-1;
      else                    /* Else if in text mode          */
         max=(VID_MAXY/2)-2;

      cloop=1;
      while (!kbhit())        /* Draw text on the display until*/
         {                    /* user presses key.             */
         loop1=8;
         while ((loop1<=max)&&(!kbhit()))
            {
            loop2=40;         /* Start write halfway over      */

            while ((loop2<=66)&&(!kbhit()))
               {
               change_color(cloop);

                              /* Set exclusion, write text and */
                              /* show cursor.                  */
               set_hide_bounds(VID_MAXX/2,0,VID_MAXX,VID_MAXY/2);
               out_text_xy(loop2,loop1,"MOUSETORAT");

                              /* Show cursor                   */
               show_mouse_cursor();
```

```
            delay(100);
                          /* Set exclusion, clear text and */
                          /* show cursor.                   */
            set_hide_bounds(VID_MAXX/2,0,VID_MAXX,VID_MAXY/2);
            clear_line_from(loop1,loop2,10,0);

                          /* Show cursor                    */
            show_mouse_cursor();

                          /* Update loops                   */
            ++cloop;loop2+=12;
            if (cloop==16) cloop=1;
            }
        ++loop1;
        }
    }
}

else mouse_error(10,4);

getch();                  /* Get char in buff or keyboard  */

hide_mouse_cursor();
shut_down_video();
}
```

The flicker is gone, at least when the mouse cursor is not in the display update region. Move the mouse into the region and the flicker returns as the mouse cursor hides and shows itself.

You could also choose to set the exclusion area once, do a complete display update, and then show the mouse cursor after the update. This method is great when pop-up windows are being created. If the mouse cursor doesn't venture into the pop-up window while it is being created, it will never become invisible.

When running the program, if you move the mouse cursor into the exclusion area and then leave it stationary, does it disappear? If it does, you are using a mouse driver that contains a "buggy" feature.

A Possible Bug in the Exclusion Area   Recent minor versions of the Microsoft mouse driver, and some OEM mouse drivers, may contain a "buggy" feature when using an exclusion area. Here's what the "bug" is:

The mouse library function show_cursor(), which calls mouse function 1, show cursor, should make the mouse cursor visible and destroy any exclusion area specified with set_hide_bounds(). This it does, but some type of logic error occurs and the mouse cursor remains invisible if it is stationary, and in the exclusion area when show_cursor() is called. The next time the mouse driver detects mouse movement, the mouse cursor does become visible, but while stationary, it remains invisible. This "bug" is very problematical, and the precise cause has not been determined. However, a solution has been worked out.

If you have experienced the visibility problem, here's a quick fix to clear it up. Look at the following function, touch_cursor():

```
void touch_cursor(void)
    {
    unsigned char lbutton,rbutton;
    int x,y;
    get_mouse_button(&lbutton,&rbutton,&x,&y);
    set_mouse_position(x,y);
    }
```

The function touch_cursor() simulates (fakes) a mouse move by retrieving the current mouse cursor coordinates and setting the mouse cursor's position using those coordinates.

In the previous example, MOUSE5.C, add the function touch_cursor() before main(), and add the statement touch_cursor() immediately following every show_cursor() statement, as in

```
show_mouse_cursor();
touch_cursor();
```

This effectively solves the visibility problem (if it exists) when using an exclusion area. No noticeable performance is lost, and it ensures that the mouse cursor becomes visible when show_cursor() is called. If you experience the problem, you need to add the function touch_cursor() to the following examples: MOUSE6.C, and MOUSE13.C. Be sure to call the function immediately after every show_cursor() statement.

It's up to you as to whether to make the function touch_cursor() a permanent addition to your mouse function library. It will depend on your needs, commercial viability, and what type of hiding techniques you choose to implement. The function touch_cursor() is included with the supplemental disk supplied with this book, and is called TOUCH.INC.

EGA Registers, Compatibility, and OEM Mice

There is a another possible problem associated with setting an exclusion area to hide the mouse cursor during display updating. To see if the problem exists on your system, take out the statement

```
clear_line_from(loop1,loop2,10,0);
```

from the previous example, MOUSE5.C, and recompile the program. When you run the program, the text will not be erased, and the upper-left portion of the display will fill up with the "MOUSETORAT" statements. While the display writing is occurring, move the mouse cursor around, away from the text. If graphics garbage in the text similar to Figure 4-3 appears, even though the mouse cursor is *nowhere near* the text as it was being written, you have hit upon a major issue regarding EGA registers, older driver versions, and OEM mice.

Even though the problem might not exist on your system, if you are writing commercial applications for resale, you must plan for the worst, as the problem does exist on many systems.

Prior to VGA graphics systems, the EGA system ruled supreme. The EGA standard is what truly brought the mouse to life (for IBM compatibles), as graphics-oriented programs started becoming very sophisticated. A major drawback of *pure* EGA graphics systems is the inability to read the EGA registers. For the most part, they are write-only registers. Since the mouse driver uses the EGA registers for its cursor-drawing routines, any EGA graphics routine that modifies the EGA registers will disrupt the mouse's cursor-drawing routines, and vice-versa. This is because they are modifying the same registers. This will cause unpredictable graphics results.

```
Graphics Mode

    Exclusion/Hide And Show Cursor During Display Writes/Updates

                             MOUSETORAT   MOUSETORAT   MOUSETORAT
                             MOUSETORAT   MOUSETORAT   MOUSETORAT
                             MOUSETORAT   MOUSETORAT   MOUSETORAT
                             MOUSETORAT   MOUSETORAT   MOUSETORAT
                             MOUSETORAT   MOUSETORAT   MOUSETORAT

                             MOUSETORAT   MOUSETORAT   MOUSETORAT
                             MOUSETORAT   MOUSETORAT   MOUSETORAT
                             MOUSETORAT   MOUSETORAT   MOUSETORAT

                ▸            MOUSETORAT   MOUSETORAT   MOUSETORAT
                             MOUSETORAT   MOUSETORAT   MOUSETORAT
                             MOUSETORAT   MOUSETORAT   MOUSETORAT

                             MOUSETORAT   MOUSETORAT   MOUSETORAT
                             MOUSETORAT   MOUSETORAT   MOUSETORAT
```

Figure 4-3.   *Garbage associated with EGA registers*

EGA.SYS

A solution to this came in the form of EGA.SYS. EGA.SYS is a device driver that makes a backup copy of the EGA registers. The mouse driver can read the registers from EGA.SYS, thus allowing a working copy of the EGA registers, called a *shadow map*. This technique is required for *pure* EGA systems using interrupt-driven graphics routines such as the mouse cursor.

If EGA.SYS is not available, the programmer using a pure EGA system is forced to use hide-and-show routines whenever *any* display updating is performed, no matter where the mouse cursor is located.

 EGA.SYS first became available in DOS 3.3

With the implementation of VGA graphics systems, programmers could finally read what were once write-only registers. However, Microsoft didn't start implementing new methods of reading the registers in the mouse driver until version 7.04, released in May of 1990. So, even if you have a VGA graphics system, if you are using a mouse driver previous to version 7.04, you must still use EGA.SYS to fix the problem or use the hide-and-show routines exclusively. Also, quite a few OEM mouses have not implemented the new standards either, and the problem exists with them as well.

The EGA_REG_READ Variable

The EGA_REG_READ variable, found in MOUSE.H, is used by the mouse function library to determine if the EGA registers can be read. A value of 1 means that the EGA registers can be read, and a value of 0 indicates they cannot be read. EGA_REG_READ is initialized to 1. EGA_REG_READ is only used in one mouse library function, that being set_hide_bounds(). If EGA_REG_READ is 0, the function assumes the EGA registers cannot be read and calls the mouse library function hide_mouse_cursor() instead of setting an exclusion area. This is because if the registers can't be read, it won't make any difference if the mouse cursor is in the display update region or not; it must be hidden first. If EGA_REG_READ is set to 1, the function library assumes that the EGA registers can be read and sets the exclusion area as normal.

It's up to you to determine the state of EGA_REG_READ in your applications. This is because there are so many factors involved that there would not be room to talk about much else. First, you must determine if you have a mouse driver version capable of reading the registers directly. This would be Microsoft versions 7.04 or later, Logitech versions 6.1 or later, Kraft versions 3.0 or later, and so on. You can determine the version number, as will be demonstrated in Chapter 12, but you will need to keep tables of all OEM version numbers you wish to be compatible with. Then, if you have a driver capable of reading the registers, you need to identify the graphics adapter. If it is a pure EGA system, you must *then* determine if EGA.SYS has been loaded.

EGA Workaround

If you do not want to go through the process of determining all this information, here's a possible scenario to work around the problem. Assume the EGA registers can be read. Somewhere in the application's documentation (if it's a commercial application), place a note about loading EGA.SYS from the CONFIG.SYS file at bootup if you are using a pure EGA system, an older mouse driver version, or an OEM mouse not implementing the new graphics standard. As a last resort, if the users do not have EGA.SYS, instruct them to pass in the command-line argument NOREGS. Capture the argument and set the variable EGA_REG_READ to 0.

Hopefully, every OEM mouse manufacturer will have caught up to the new standards soon. However, many users will still be using their old mice for quite a while, so the previous problems are very important to keep in mind.

Chapter **5**

Tracking the Mouse Cursor and Emulating Cursor Movement with the Keyboard

Now the fun begins. In the previous chapters, a solid foundation was built on which to begin your mouse programming endeavors. You know how DOS interrupt service 0x33 is used to communicate with the mouse. You have entered the ten necessary mouse functions. You know how to make the mouse cursor visible, and keep it on the display. I have warned you of the dangers involved in display writing while the mouse is visible. You're ready to get on to the good stuff—here goes.

Tracking Mouse Coordinates

One of the most fundamental aspects of mouse programming is determining the mouse cursor's location on the display. To track the mouse cursor's current display coordinates use the mouse library function get_mouse_button(), which calls mouse function 3, get button press information. The function returns the status of the mouse buttons and the current display coordinates of the mouse cursor. For now, don't worry about the button variables. They are covered in Chapter 6.

In the following example, mouse cursor coordinates are written to the display as the mouse moves. Here's how it works. There are two pairs of coordinates, x, y, oldx,

and oldy. When the program starts, they are all initialized to 0. Next the program
enters a continuous loop and waits for a keypress. During the keypress loop, the
function get_mouse_button() is constantly called to retrieve the current mouse
cursor coordinates. If the new coordinates do not match the old coordinates, the
mouse cursor has moved, and the coordinates are written to the display. The old
coordinates are then set to the new coordinates, and the keypress loop continues.
The coordinates are graphics coordinates in graphics mode and text coordinates in
text mode. Run the example, move the mouse around and watch the coordinates
change as you do so.

 *The "keypress loop" referred to in the previous paragraph is used throughout most of the
remaining programming examples. Whenever you want to exit a program, simply press a key.*

Here is MOUSE6.C:

```
/*-------------------------------------------------------------*/
/*                        MOUSE6.C                          */
/*                                                          */
/* Demonstrate how to track the mouse coordinates.         */
/*-------------------------------------------------------------*/

#include "header1.h"          /* Directives, headers, includes */

void main()
    {                         /* Coords and button vars(dummys)*/
    int x=0,y=0,oldx=0,oldy=0;
    unsigned char lbutton,rbutton;

    install_video(GMODE);     /* Install video system          */
    header();                 /* Draw header                   */
    reset_mouse();            /* Reset mouse                   */

    if (!MOUSE_THERE) mouse_error(10,4);

    out_text_xy(15,7,"Move The Mouse Around To See
                   The Coordinates..");
    out_text_xy(25,20,"X - ");
    out_text_xy(45,20,"Y - ");

                              /* Set display limits            */
    set_mouse_hlimits(1,VID_MAXX-MOUSE_SIZE+1);
    set_mouse_vlimits(1,VID_MAXY-MOUSE_SIZE);
```

```
    show_mouse_cursor();        /* Show the mouse cursor       */

while (!kbhit())                /* Do until user presses a key */
   {
                                /* Get the current coordinates */
                                /* from button status function. */
    get_mouse_button(&lbutton,&rbutton,&x,&y);

                                /* If current <> last coords    */
    if ((x != oldx) || (y !=oldy))
       {
                                /* Hide with exlusion area      */
        if (IN_GMODE)
           set_hide_bounds(24*HFONT_SIZE,19*VFONT_SIZE,
                           55*HFONT_SIZE,21*VFONT_SIZE);
        else
           set_hide_bounds(24,19,55,21);

        clear_line_from(20,30,4,0);   /* Clear the old coords*/
        clear_line_from(20,50,4,0);
        out_int_xy(30,20,x);          /* Write the new coords*/
        out_int_xy(50,20,y);
        oldx=x;                       /* Old coords=new coord*/
        oldy=y;
        show_mouse_cursor();          /* Show the cursor     */
       }
   }

getch();                       /* Get char in key buffer       */

hide_mouse_cursor();
shut_down_video();
}
```

When the program is run, it should resemble Figure 5-1. Try it in text mode. Remember to change the line

    install_video(GMODE)

to

    install_video(TMODE)

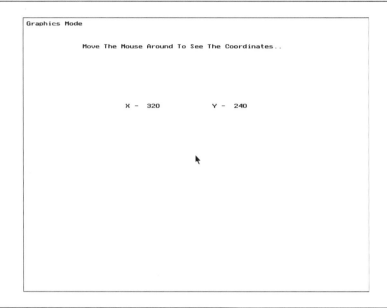

Figure 5-1.   *Tracking mouse cursor display coordinates*

Tracking Text Coordinates in a Graphics Mode

Now, suppose you are in graphics mode but you wish to track the mouse using text coordinates. In today's graphics environments this is a fairly common practice. What's required is converting the graphics coordinates inside the application. You may be wondering why I didn't include two additional global variables and track text coordinates in graphics mode internally. My decision was based on personal experience. Throughout my years of mouse programming, I have found that the most common use of text coordinates in graphics mode is during menu processing. Most other operations in graphics mode are biased to graphics coordinates (when using the mouse). The conversion algorithm, when needed, is extremely easy to implement and should be managed inside the application.

This is not true of text modes. Since the mouse driver uses graphics coordinates in both graphics and text modes, text-to-graphics coordinate conversions are done inside the mouse function library, so you can use coordinates naturally suited to text modes, namely text coordinates.

The following example tracks graphics coordinates, converts them to text coordinates, and writes them to the display.

Run this program in graphics mode only!

Here is MOUSE7.C:

```
/*------------------------------------------------------------*/
/*                       MOUSE7.C                             */
/*                                                            */
/* Demonstrate how to track graphic mouse coordinates and    */
/* and display using text mode coordinates.                  */
/* RUN THIS ONLY IN GRAPHICS MODE!                           */
/*------------------------------------------------------------*/

#include "header1.h"         /* Directives, headers, includes */

void main()
    {                        /* Coords and button vars(dummys)*/
    int x=0,y=0,oldx=0,oldy=0;
    unsigned char lbutton,rbutton;

    install_video(GMODE);    /* Install video system          */
    header();                /* Draw header                   */
    reset_mouse();           /* Reset mouse                   */

    if (!MOUSE_THERE) mouse_error(10,4);

    out_text_xy(15,7,"Tracking graphic coordinates as
                 text coordinates...");

    out_text_xy(25,20,"X - ");
    out_text_xy(45,20,"Y - ");

                             /* Set display limits            */
    set_mouse_hlimits(1,VID_MAXX-MOUSE_SIZE+1);
    set_mouse_vlimits(1,VID_MAXY-MOUSE_SIZE);

    show_mouse_cursor();     /* Show the mouse cursor         */

    while (!kbhit())         /* Do until user presses a key   */
        {
                             /* Get the current coordinates   */
                             /* from button status function.  */
```

```
        get_mouse_button(&lbutton,&rbutton,&x,&y);

                                /* If current <> last coords    */
        if ((x != oldx) || (y !=oldy))
          {
                                /* Hide with exclusion area      */
          set_hide_bounds(24*HFONT_SIZE,19*VFONT_SIZE,
                          55*HFONT_SIZE,21*VFONT_SIZE);

          clear_line_from(20,30,4,0);    /* Clear the old coords*/
          clear_line_from(20,50,4,0);
                                        /* Write graph coords   */
                                        /* as text coordinates.*/
          out_int_xy(30,20,x / HFONT_SIZE + 1);
          out_int_xy(50,20,y / VFONT_SIZE + 1);

          oldx=x;                        /* Old coords=new coord*/
          oldy=y;
          show_mouse_cursor();           /* Show the cursor      */
          }
        }

    getch();                    /* Get char in keyboard buffer   */

    hide_mouse_cursor();
    shut_down_video();
    }
```

In this example, the coordinate conversions are done within the arguments passed to the function out_int_xy().

 HFONT_SIZE and VFONT_SIZE represent the current horizontal and vertical font sizes. They are fully explained in Chapter 2.

Emulating Mouse Cursor Movement with the Keyboard

In many commercial applications, even if a mouse is present and installed, mouse cursor movement can be duplicated with the keyboard. This supplies the user with an alternative input device while still maintaining the mouse cursor for visual guidance. This task can be accomplished easily.

Moving the Mouse Cursor

So far, you've only used the function set_mouse_position() once, to move the mouse cursor to the upper-left corner of the display in MOUSE5.C, which is in Chapter 4. Here's a small example of how powerful this function can really be. The following program allows the user to move the mouse cursor with the keyboard. The arrow keys on the numeric keypad are used so make sure you have NUMLOCK off when running the example (or if you're using a keyboard with a separate arrow keypad, use those).

Here's how the program works: When an arrow key is pressed, the current position of the mouse cursor is determined by using the mouse library function get_button_status(). Depending on what arrow key is pressed, a value of 5 is added or subtracted to the x or y coordinates, and the mouse cursor's position is changed using the mouse library function set_mouse_position(), which calls mouse function 4, set cursor position. The mouse cursor moves in the direction of the arrow key pressed.

Here is MOUSE8.C:

```
/*------------------------------------------------------------*/
/*                      MOUSE8.C                              */
/*                                                            */
/* Demonstrate how to emulate mouse cursor movement with the  */
/* keyboard. Use the Right, Left, Up, and Down arrows on the  */
/* numeric keypad or equivalent. (NUMLOCK must be OFF).       */
/* The cursor will move 5 pixels or text locations for each   */
/* keypress and will move in the direction of the arrow used. */
/*------------------------------------------------------------*/

#include "header1.h"        /* Directives, headers, includes */

void main()
    {                       /* Keychar, button & prgrm stats */
    char keychar;
    unsigned char lbutton,rbutton,end_program=0;
    int x,y;

    install_video(GMODE);   /* Install video system          */
    header();               /* Draw header                   */
    reset_mouse();          /* Reset mouse                   */

    if (!MOUSE_THERE) mouse_error(10,4);

                            /* Set display limits            */
    set_mouse_hlimits(1,VID_MAXX-MOUSE_SIZE+1);
    set_mouse_vlimits(1,VID_MAXY-MOUSE_SIZE);
```

```
out_text_xy(15,5,"Use KeyPad Arrow Keys To Emulate
                  Cursor Movement");
out_text_xy(15,7,"Press <Esc> to exit..");

out_text_xy(15,5,"Press any key to stop and exit..");

show_mouse_cursor();        /* Show the mouse cursor         */

while (!end_program)        /* While end program not 1       */
   {
   keychar=getch();         /* Get a keypress                */
                            /* if char=0 and buff not empty, */
                            /* a function key was pressed.   */
   if ((keychar==0)&&(kbhit()))
      {
      keychar=getch();      /* Get the extended key code     */
      switch(keychar)
         {                  /* Right Arrow pressed           */
        case 77:get_mouse_button(&lbutton,&rbutton,&x,&y);
                set_mouse_position(x+5,y);
                break;
                            /* Left Arrow pressed            */
        case 75:get_mouse_button(&lbutton,&rbutton,&x,&y);
                set_mouse_position(x-5,y);
                break;
                            /* Down Arrow pressed            */
        case 72:get_mouse_button(&lbutton,&rbutton,&x,&y);
                set_mouse_position(x,y-5);
                break;
                            /* Up Arrow pressed              */
        case 80:get_mouse_button(&lbutton,&rbutton,&x,&y);
                set_mouse_position(x,y+5);
                break;
         }
      }
   else                     /* If <Esc> pressed, end program */
      if (keychar==27) end_program=1;

   }

hide_mouse_cursor();
shut_down_video();
}
```

Try it in text mode. Don't forget to change the line

install_video(GMODE)

to

install_video(TMODE)

Now your applications can use the keyboard, as well as the mouse, to move the mouse cursor. There is an incredible number of end users who will use this option if it's available, and keeping everybody happy should be a goal in your commercial applications.

Chapter **6**

Determining the Button Status and Limiting the Range of Movement

The mouse wouldn't be of much good if you couldn't use it to make choices and take some action based on those choices. With the mouse, this is accomplished by pressing buttons. There are two buttons, left and right, and some OEMs have a middle button. Each button has a status variable associated with it so you can determine when a button has been pressed or released.

This book assumes that three-button OEM mice use the middle button to generate simultaneous left and right button presses and releases. For information regarding true middle-button detection, see Appendix A in reference to the following three mouse functions.

The Button Functions

There are three mouse functions that retrieve information about the mouse buttons. Mouse function 3 informs you if one (or both) of the buttons has been pressed. Mouse function 5 tells you how many times a button has been pressed since the last time the function was called, and mouse function 6 tells you how many times a button has been released since the last call to the function. Here's a more detailed look at how each function works.

Mouse function 3, get button status and cursor position, determines if a button has been pressed or not. When called, it returns the status of both buttons and the mouse cursor's current display location. Mouse function 3 is located in the mouse library function get_mouse_button(). You have already used this function in Chapter 5 to retrieve the mouse cursor's display location. Along with the cursor coordinates, get_mouse_button() receives two Boolean type variables to record the button status. In the following examples, these variables are called lbutton and rbutton. If the left button has been pressed, get_mouse_button() sets lbutton to 1; otherwise it is set to 0. If the right button has been pressed, rbutton is set to 1; otherwise it is set to 0.

Mouse function 6, get button release information, determines how many times a button has been released since the last time the function was called. Additionally, the function returns the mouse cursor's display location at the time of the last release. Mouse function 6 is located in the mouse library function get_button_rls_info(). This function works much differently than get_mouse_button(), as there are no button status variables sent to the function. Instead, you send an index number of 0 or 1 representing the button (left or right) you want information about. The function then returns a counter indicating the number of times the specified button has been released since the last time the function was called. If the counter is 0, the button has not been released. If the counter is 2, the button has been released twice, and so on.

Mouse function 5, get button press information, works identically to mouse function 6, except button presses are determined instead of button releases. Mouse function 5 is not included in the mouse function library. Here's why:

- Mouse function 3 returns the mouse cursor's current display location, regardless of whether a button was pressed or not. Therefore, mouse function 3 can be used for two purposes: determining button presses *and* determining the mouse cursor's current location at any given time. This is not true with mouse function 5, which returns the mouse cursor's location at the time of the last button press.

- Mouse function 6 can be used equally as well as mouse function 5 to determine double button clicks, or more if desired. This is the main purpose of both mouse function 5 and mouse function 6.

- Because mouse function 6 and mouse function 5 are nearly identical, once you know how to use one, you know how to use the other. Feel free to incorporate mouse function 5 into your own mouse function library.

Trapping Single Button Presses and Releases

The following example writes a string of text informing you if a button has been pressed, which button, and if a button has been released. Only single presses and releases (clicks) are trapped.

Here is MOUSE9.C:

```
/*-------------------------------------------------------------*/
/*                      MOUSE9.C                              */
/*                                                           */
/* Determine if a button(s) have been pressed or released.   */
/*-------------------------------------------------------------*/

#include "header1.h"          /* Directives, headers, includes */

void main()
    {
    int x,y;                  /* Coords and button status vars */
    unsigned char lbutton=0,rbutton=0,lrelease=0,rrelease=0;
    int count;

    install_video(GMODE);     /* Install video system          */
    header();                 /* Draw header                   */
    reset_mouse();            /* Reset mouse                   */

    if (!MOUSE_THERE) mouse_error(10,4);

    out_text_xy(30,7,"Press and release a mouse button....");

                              /* Set display limits            */
    set_mouse_hlimits(1,VID_MAXX-MOUSE_SIZE+1);
    set_mouse_vlimits(1,VID_MAXY-MOUSE_SIZE);

    show_mouse_cursor();      /* Show the mouse cursor         */

    while (!kbhit())          /* Do until user presses a key   */
        {
                              /* Get the current button        */
                              /* status.                       */
        get_mouse_button(&lbutton,&rbutton,&x,&y);
```

```
                                    /* Left button pressed only    */
        if ((lbutton)&&(!rbutton))
           {
           hide_mouse_cursor();
           clear_line_from(20,30,20,0);
           out_text_xy(30,20,"Left button Pressed");
           show_mouse_cursor();
           }
                                    /* Right button pressed only   */
        if ((rbutton)&&(!lbutton))
           {
           hide_mouse_cursor();
           clear_line_from(20,30,20,0);
           out_text_xy(30,20,"Right Button Pressed ");
           show_mouse_cursor();
           }
                                    /* Both buttons pressed        */
        if ((lbutton)&&(rbutton))
           {
           hide_mouse_cursor();
           clear_line_from(20,30,20,0);
           out_text_xy(30,20,"Both Buttons Pressed ");
           show_mouse_cursor();
           }
                                    /* Vars to 0, get release info */
        lrelease=0;rrelease=0;
        if ((get_button_rls_info(0,&count,&x,&y))&&(count>0))
           lrelease=1;
        if ((get_button_rls_info(1,&count,&x,&y))&&(count>0))
           rrelease=1;

                                    /* Left button released only   */
        if ((lrelease)&&(!rrelease))
           {
           hide_mouse_cursor();
           clear_line_from(22,30,25,0);
           out_text_xy(30,22,"Left Button Released");
           show_mouse_cursor();
           }
                                    /* Right button released only  */
        if ((!lrelease)&&(rrelease))
           {
           hide_mouse_cursor();
           clear_line_from(22,30,25,0);
           out_text_xy(30,22,"Right Button Released");
```

```
    show_mouse_cursor();
    }
                        /* Both buttons released        */
if ((lrelease)&&(rrelease))
    {
    hide_mouse_cursor();
    clear_line_from(22,30,25,0);
    out_text_xy(30,22,"Both Buttons Released");
    show_mouse_cursor();
    }
                        /* Clear button status          */
while ((lbutton)||(rbutton))
    get_mouse_button(&lbutton,&rbutton,&x,&y);
    }

getch();                    /* Get char in buff or keyboard  */

hide_mouse_cursor();
shut_down_video();
}
```

If you run the program and press the left mouse button, a message appears, as in Figure 6-1. Try it in text mode. Again, change the line:

install_video(GMODE)

to

install_video(TMODE)

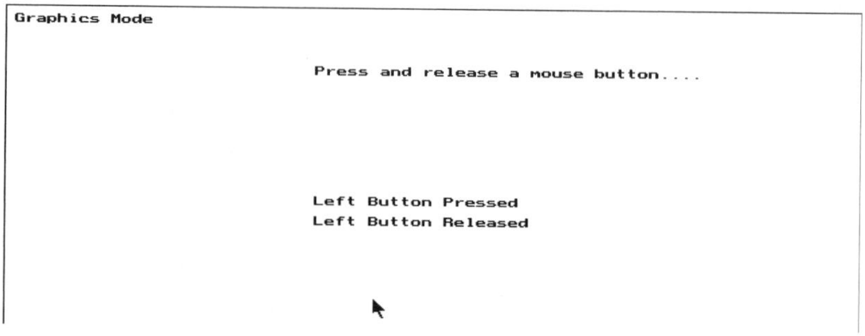

Figure 6-1.   *Determining a left-button press*

The Reverse Trap

If you study the code in MOUSE9.C you might wonder about the statement:

```
                        /* Clear button status           */
while((lbutton)||(rbutton))
    get_mouse_button(&lbutton,&rbutton,&x,&y);
```

This is called a reverse trap, and is used to ensure that the button states are cleared to 0, meaning no buttons have been pressed, before the next cycle in the loop. Here's why:

- When a user presses a mouse button, the time spent holding the button down might be longer than the time it takes to record the button press and execute the appropriate routines. For instance, if the user takes 1/4 of a second to press and release a button, but the routine executed when the button press is trapped only takes 1/8 of a second, a duplicate button press is recorded when the button status is examined again.

- When the routine executed after a button trap does a good deal of work, chances are that the status is reset by the time the button is examined again (assuming the user released the button), and more than likely, button presses are missed. (The solution to missed button presses is covered in Chapters 7 and 8). However, when the routine is very quick, as the previous example is, a reverse trap is required to accommodate for human delay time.

Double-Clicking Mouse Buttons

Double-clicking the mouse buttons is a common event in Windows and Windows-based applications. It is much less frequent in DOS-based applications. For instance, Microsoft Word 5.5 for DOS uses single-clicks to choose menu options, whereas Microsoft Word for Windows 2.0 uses double-clicks to choose menu options. Although single clicks are the status quo in DOS applications, there's no reason to limit your application to using them exclusively, as double-click traps can be implemented in any application.

Timing a Double-Click

Double-clicking is the process of recording two consecutive button presses (or releases) within a given amount of time. As the amount of time delay grows, the more time a user has to pause between clicks. As the amount of time delay shrinks, the less time a user has to pause between clicks.

Clock Speed

Most timing mechanisms are based on the clock speed of the computer. As this varies from machine to machine, and because other factors are involved as well, it's a bit difficult to precisely process the amount of pause time needed to determine double-clicks. Borland's delay() function works fairly well, but is sometimes a little quirky. The Microsoft equivalent you created in the video function library is also based on the clock time and works fairly well. For the following demonstration, these functions adequately serve the purpose. The timer itself has lots of room for improvement, should you desire further precision.

Determining a Double-Click

The counter used to determine button releases in the previous example, MOUSE9.C, can be used to determine if a mouse button has been double clicked, or released. If the counter is 1, the mouse button has been released one time, but if the counter is two, the mouse button has been released twice, and a double-click is recorded.

The counter can also be used to determine triple-clicks, quad-clicks, and so on. The counter's range is 0 to 65,535.

In the following example, a double-click is defined as a button press, button release, button press, and button release. The delay time is defined in the macro definition DBL_CLICK_TIME as 500 milliseconds.

The process to record a double-click for the left mouse button is as follows:

1. Determine if the left button has been pressed.

2. If it has, pause the specified number of milliseconds.

3. Determine if the left button was released twice.

4. If it was, a left-button double-click occurred.

5. If not, a left-button single-click occurred.

The following example traps single and double mouse clicks in this manner and writes a string of text informing you of the action that occurred. Notice that the release status is cleared with a dummy call at the end of the main loop. This is to avoid noncurrent status variables.

Here is MOUSE10.C:

```
/*-------------------------------------------------------------*/
/*                        MOUSE10.C                            */
/*                                                             */
/* Determine Double-Clicks.                                    */
/* NOTE : Heavily based on computer clock time, so adjustment  */
/*        may need to be made. 500 mllsecs seem to work on     */
/*        even the fastest 486.                                */
/*-------------------------------------------------------------*/

#define DBL_CLICK_TIME 500    /* Delay time user has for dblclk*/

#include "header1.h"          /* Directives, headers, includes */

void main()
   {
   int x,y;                   /* Coords and button status vars */
   unsigned char lbutton=0,rbutton=0;
   int count;

   install_video(GMODE);    /* Install video system         */
   header();                /* Draw header                  */
   reset_mouse();           /* Reset mouse                  */

   if (!MOUSE_THERE) mouse_error(10,4);

   out_text_xy(30,7,"Double click a mouse button....");

                            /* Set display limits           */
   set_mouse_hlimits(1,VID_MAXX-MOUSE_SIZE+1);
   set_mouse_vlimits(1,VID_MAXY-MOUSE_SIZE);

   show_mouse_cursor();     /* Show the mouse cursor        */

   while (!kbhit())         /* Do until user presses a key  */
      {
                            /* Get the current button       */
                            /* status.                      */
      get_mouse_button(&lbutton,&rbutton,&x,&y);

                            /* Left button pressed only     */
      if ((lbutton)&&(!rbutton))
         {
```

```
                              /* Delay DBL_CLICK_TIME mllsecs   */
      delay(DBL_CLICK_TIME);
      hide_mouse_cursor();
      clear_line_from(20,30,30,0);

                              /* Button released twice?        */
      if ((get_button_rls_info(0,&count,&x,&y))&&(count==2))
         out_text_xy(30,20,"Left Button Double Clicked");

      else               /* No, only one time               */
         out_text_xy(30,20,"Left Button Pressed");

      show_mouse_cursor();
      }
                              /* Right button pressed only     */
   if ((rbutton)&&(!lbutton))
      {
                              /* Delay DBL_CLICK_TIME mllsecs  */
      delay(DBL_CLICK_TIME);
      hide_mouse_cursor();
      clear_line_from(20,30,30,0);

                              /* Button released twice?        */
      if ((get_button_rls_info(1,&count,&x,&y))&&(count==2))
         out_text_xy(30,20,"Right Button Double Clicked");

      else               /* No, only one time               */
         out_text_xy(30,20,"Right Button Pressed ");

      show_mouse_cursor();
      }
                              /* Clear release count to 0      */
   get_button_rls_info(0,&count,&x,&y);

                              /* Clear button status           */
   while((lbutton)||(rbutton))
      get_mouse_button(&lbutton,&rbutton,&x,&y);
   }

getch();                      /* Get char in buff or keyboard  */

hide_mouse_cursor();
shut_down_video();
}
```

To determine triple-clicks, change the comparison (count==2) to (count==3). To define a double-click as button down, button up, button down, see Appendix A regarding mouse function 5, get button press information.

After running the program and examining the code, can you see how DBL_CLICK_TIME could be used to duplicate the way Windows allows the double-click speed to be modified by the user? This would be a nifty feature for you to work on.

Change DBL_CLICK_TIME to an integer that can be modified during program execution.

Limiting Range in Sequential Applications

The following example illustrates a concept frequently used in MS-DOS based applications and also serves as an example of taking action based on button presses. Look again at the mouse library functions set_mouse_hlimit(), and set_mouse_vlimit(). So far, you have only used the functions to limit the mouse cursor's range of movement to whole or half portions of the display. In many applications, users often make a choice that pops up a menu, or moves them to a different display region. After the choice is made, it is often desirable for the application to limit the mouse cursor's range of movement to the new menu or display region. When the pop-up menu or function is terminated, the mouse cursor's range is reset to the original menu or display region.

When programming in DOS-based platforms, the flow of programming *and* of user interaction is generally done in a sequential fashion (as opposed to Windows, which is an event-driven platform, requiring a different approach to user interaction and control flow). In sequential applications, this method of mouse cursor range limitation forces users to make choices from the available menu or display region only, and they do not become confused as to what section of the application they are using. This method would not be applicable for Windows-type event-driven platforms, but for sequentially structured applications it is one giant step forward in "idiot-proofing" a program.

The following example draws four boxes on the display. These boxes represent independent regions of the display. Each box can be on or off. If a box is on, the outline color is yellow and the mouse cursor is limited to moving within the box or region. If the box is off, the outline color is red and the mouse cursor is somewhere else.

At startup, box #1 is on, and all others are off. While running, the program continuously examines the state of the mouse buttons for a button press. If the right button is pressed, the program turns the current on box off and rotates in a clockwise direction to turn the next box on. If the left button is pressed, the program turns the current on box off and rotates in a counterclockwise direction to turn the next box on.

Here is MOUSE11.C:

```
/*---------------------------------------------------------------*/
/*                       MOUSE11.C                               */
/*                                                               */
/* Determine if buttons are pressed, limit range of movement     */
/* corresponding to rectangular region and button presses.       */
/*---------------------------------------------------------------*/

#include "header1.h"          /* Directives, headers, includes */

#define ON 1                  /* Define ON/OFF to 1 and 0       */
#define OFF 0

int x1[4],x2[4],y1[4],y2[4]; /* Four box coordinates            */


/* MODULE : INIT BOXES                                          */
/*---------------------------------------------------------------*/
/* Initialize the four box coordinates.                          */
/*                                                               */
void init_boxes(void)
   {
   x1[0]=VID_MAXX/8;x2[0]=VID_MAXX/8*3;   /* Upper left box #1 */
   y1[0]=VID_MAXY/8*2;y2[0]=VID_MAXY/8*4;

   x1[1]=VID_MAXX/8*5;x2[1]=VID_MAXX/8*7;/* Upper right box #2*/
   y1[1]=VID_MAXY/8*2;y2[1]=VID_MAXY/8*4;

   x1[2]=VID_MAXX/8*5;x2[2]=VID_MAXX/8*7;/* Lower right box #3*/
   y1[2]=VID_MAXY/8*5;y2[2]=VID_MAXY/8*7;

   x1[3]=VID_MAXX/8;x2[3]=VID_MAXX/8*3;   /* Lower left box #4 */
   y1[3]=VID_MAXY/8*5;y2[3]=VID_MAXY/8*7;
   }


/* MODULE : BOX                                                 */
/*---------------------------------------------------------------*/
/* Draw a rectangle and tell user what box.                      */
/* Input parameters                                              */
/*      number - box number to turn on or off. Range is 1 to 4 */
```

```
/*     on_off - 1 if box turned on, 0 if turned off          */
/*                                                            */
void box(int number,unsigned char on_off)
   {
   int texty;                 /* Y coordinate for text        */

   —number;                   /* Array starts at 0            */
   hide_mouse_cursor();       /* Hide mouse cursor            */

                              /* If box on, color = 14,       */
                              /* else color = 4.              */
   if (on_off) change_color(14);else change_color(4);

                              /* Draw the box                 */
   draw_rectangle(x1[number],y1[number],x2[number],y2[number]);

   if (on_off)                /* If the box is being turned on */
      {
                              /* Set limits to box            */
      set_mouse_hlimits(x1[number],x2[number]);
      set_mouse_vlimits(y1[number],y2[number]);

                              /* Figure text coord            */
      if (IN_GMODE) texty=VID_MAXY/VFONT_SIZE;else texty=23;

                              /* Tell user what box           */
      clear_line_from(texty,35,15,0);
      out_text_xy(35,texty,"Box #");
      out_int_xy(40,texty,number+1);
      out_text_xy(42,texty,"Chosen");
      }

   show_mouse_cursor();       /* Show mouse cursor            */
   }

void main()
   {
   int box_count=1,x,y;       /* Box count, what box now in?  */
   unsigned char lbutton=0,rbutton=0;

   install_video(GMODE);      /* Install video system         */
   header();                  /* Draw header                  */
   reset_mouse();             /* Reset mouse                  */
```

```
if (MOUSE_THERE)
   {
   out_text_xy(10,4,"Press LEFT  button to move in a
                     counter-clockwise direction");
   out_text_xy(10,5,"Press RIGHT button to move in a
                     clockwise direction");

   show_mouse_cursor();    /* Show the mouse cursor        */

   init_boxes();           /* Init coordinates             */
                           /* Box #1 on, all others off    */
   box(2,OFF);box(3,OFF);box(4,OFF);
   box(1,ON);

   while (!kbhit())        /* Do until user presses a key  */
      {
                          /* Get the button status        */
      get_mouse_button(&lbutton,&rbutton,&x,&y);

      if (rbutton)        /* If right button pressed.      */
         {                /* Turn last box off, inc count  */
                          /* and turn new box on.          */
         box(box_count,OFF);
         ++box_count;
         if (box_count==5) box_count=1;
         box(box_count,ON);
         }

      if (lbutton)        /* If left button pressed.       */
         {                /* Turn last box off, dec count  */
                          /* and turn new box on.          */
         box(box_count,OFF);
         —box_count;
         if (box_count==0) box_count=4;
         box(box_count,ON);
         }
                          /* Clear button status           */
      while((lbutton)||(rbutton))
         get_mouse_button(&lbutton,&rbutton,&x,&y);

      }
   }
```

```
else mouse_error(10,4);

getch();                        /* Get char in buff or keyboard  */

hide_mouse_cursor();
shut_down_video();
}
```

After pressing the left mouse button four times, the program will look like Figure 6-2. Try it in text mode. Again, change the line:

install_video(GMODE)

to

install_video(TMODE)

In some applications, this method is very appropriate, and in some it is not. Artistic license will let you decide. This concept is used in Chapter 9, so you might want to take a look there, as well.

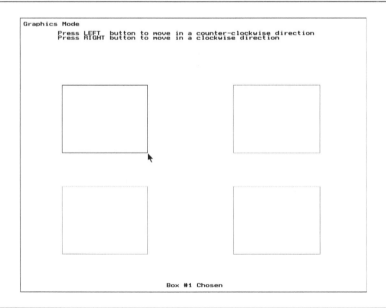

Figure 6-2.   *Results of the program limiting the range to various display regions*

Chapter **7**

Creating an Event Handler

In the previous chapter, you learned how to determine button presses and releases by constantly polling the state of the mouse buttons. In this chapter, you learn a much more efficient method of determining button presses, button releases, and mouse cursor movement.

The Problems with Polling

Polling is the act of constantly requesting information from the mouse driver regarding mouse buttons, mouse movement, or mouse cursor location. The problem with polling methods is that information can easily be lost. Although it's not too apparent from the examples in this book, when an application starts using more system resources such as disk drives, printers, the keyboard, and serial and parallel port services, it is likely that activities such as button presses are missed. This is because a button press (or other mouse activity) might occur while another system resource is being accessed, and the information about the button press is lost by the time your application examines the button status. Even a simple display write is capable of causing a missed button press or release.

If you are writing a commercial application that interfaces with the mouse, keep this thought in mind: nothing annoys end users more than a missed button press, and they might stop using the mouse altogether if the problem exists throughout the application. What a waste of a great resource (and programming effort) that would be.

A better method to determine the state of mouse buttons, mouse cursor movement, and mouse cursor location, is to stop retrieving information from the mouse driver (polling) and force the mouse driver to start sending information directly to the application, regardless of any other activity occurring in the system. This is accomplished by creating an *event handler.*

What is an Event Handler?

Exactly what an event handler does is defined by its name. It handles events. An *event* is some type of action occurring in the system. When relating events to the mouse, an event would be defined as a button press, button release, or mouse movement.

The mouse driver can be told to call an external function, not part of its own code, when specific mouse events occur. When the mouse driver calls the external function, it sends along information regarding the mouse buttons, mouse movement, and the mouse cursor's display location. This external function is known as the event handler.

Although you create the event handler's code, once it is installed, it becomes transparent to you and your application, as if you had created a new function within the mouse driver itself. However, it is you who determines what happens inside the event handler, and when the event handler is called by the mouse driver.

Installing an Event Handler

To install and activate an event handler properly, you must first give the mouse driver some specific information regarding the event handler. This information includes the following:

The Call Mask

The *call mask* is a 16-bit integer whose individual bits specify which action(s) cause the mouse driver to call the event handler. You set the call mask to match your needs when initializing the event handler. One or all of the bits in the call mask can be set at any given time. The call mask's bit meanings are as follows:

Bit Number	Action
0	Mouse movement
1	Left-button press
2	Left-button release

Bit Number	Action
3	Right-button press
4	Right-button release
5	OEM middle-button press
6	OEM middle-button release
5-15	Not used by Microsoft and other two-button mice
7-15	Not used by three-button mice

Event Handler Address

You must also inform the mouse driver of the address where the event handler function is located. Since the event handler is not part of the mouse driver's code, it has no idea where the event handler resides in memory unless you provide it with that information.

To inform the mouse driver of where the event handler is located, the segment and offset of the function are needed. This information is determined with the functions **FP_OFF**(*function*) and **FP_SEG**(*function*), with the argument being the event handler function itself. The address is sent to the mouse driver when the event handler is installed.

Mouse Functions Used to Install an Event Handler

There are three mouse functions available to install an event handler. They are listed here:

Mouse Function Number	Name
12	Set event handler
20	Swap event handlers
24	Set alternate event handler

This book concentrates on mouse function 12, which is the most common function used to install an event handler. Mouse function 20 is used primarily with TSRs and child processes needing to temporarily substitute a new event handler for the current event handler. Mouse function 24 is used in conjunction with either mouse function 12 or mouse function 20, to call an alternate event handler when specific keyboard control keys (such as ALT, CTRL, and SHIFT) are down, in conjunction with other mouse events. A brief summary of mouse functions 20 and 24 can be found in Chapter 8.

Mouse Function 12: Set Event Handler

Mouse function 12, set event handler, is located in the mouse library function set_event_handler(). Take a quick look.

```
void pascal set_event_handler(int call_mask,
                              void (far *location)(void))
   {
   if (MOUSE_THERE)
      {
      mregs.x.ax=12;                      /* Mouse function 12   */
      mregs.x.cx=call_mask;               /* Call mask-action    */
      mregs.x.dx=FP_OFF(location);        /* Offset of e-handler */
      msegregs.es=FP_SEG(location);       /* Segment of e-handler*/
      int86x(0x33,&mregs,&mregs,&msegregs);
      }
   }
```

This function is used to *install* the event handler. It is *not* the event handler itself, but merely informs the mouse driver of the call mask and address used for the event handler. Look at the following code fragment:

```
void far event_handler(void)
   {
   do_something();
   }
```

Assuming this represents the actual event handler, then to install the event handler and make the mouse driver call the function every time the mouse is moved requires the following statement:

```
set_event_handler(1,event_handler);
```

The function event_handler() is now transparent to you and your application. From the time the event handler is installed, every time the mouse moves, the function event_handler() is called by the *mouse driver*, not your application. This is *regardless* of any other activity occurring within the application.

Here's another small example to get you going. Do *not* try to enter this code and run it, or your system may lock up, or crash entirely. The following is used for illustration only:

```
unsigned char LBUTTON_DOWN,RBUTTON_DOWN;
```

```
void far event_handler(void)
   {
   unsigned char int lbutton,rbutton;
   int x,y;

   get_mouse_button(&lbutton,&rbutton,&x,&y)
   if (lbutton) LBUTTON_DOWN=1
   if (rbutton) RBUTTON_DOWN=1
   }

void main()
   {
   reset_mouse();
   set_event_handler(10,event_handler);

   while (!kbhit())
      {

      if (LBUTTON_DOWN)
         {
         LBUTTON_DOWN=0;
         do_some_long_sorting_algorithm();
         }

      if (RBUTTON_DOWN)
         {
         RBUTTON_DOWN=0;
         do_something_else();
         }


      }
   }
```

See how the main program loop *never* polls the mouse driver for button presses, but instead traps status variables sent by the event handler. When a button is pressed, the event handler is called by the mouse driver. Inside the event handler, the function get_mouse_button() is called to determine what buttons have been pressed. The global variables LBUTTON_DOWN and RBUTTON_DOWN are set accordingly, and are trapped by the main program. This method ensures that the program never misses a button press.

While this concept may set your mind on fire, there are some limitations that make the previous example impossible (well, not impossible, just incorrect, and subject to failure of the highest degree).

Limitations

There are two major limitations that render the previous example unusable.

The Data Segment

Since the event handler is called by the mouse driver, not your application, the mouse driver considers it part of its own code. Upon entry to the event handler, the data segment may be that of the mouse driver, not your application. This means that the data segment must be saved upon entry to the event handler and loaded with the data segment used by your application. When the event handler has finished, it must restore the previous data segment used by the mouse driver.

With the Borland compiler, you can force the data segment to be saved, modified, and restored automatically upon entry and exit from a function by declaring it to be a huge function. With the Microsoft compiler, functions cannot be of type huge, and the easiest way to make sure the data segment is handled properly is to use the /Au compiler option.

But there is yet another limitation to consider.

Interrupt Services

Although the event handler itself is not an interrupt function (it contains no **IRET** instruction), it is a subroutine called by an interrupt function. As such, the event handler *cannot* use any DOS or BIOS interrupts, because interrupts cannot call instances of themselves, they are non-reentrant.

This means that you cannot use any interrupt 0x33 services within the event handler to determine the status of the mouse. Another method of retrieving the mouse's button and cursor status is required.

Overcoming the Limitations in Assembler

The easiest way to accommodate the previous limitations is to write the event handler in assembly language, where you can control the data segment. Additionally, before the mouse driver calls the event handler, the event status, button status, and current mouse cursor coordinates are loaded in the general registers, and the event handler has easy access to them by managing the stack. No interrupt 0x33 calls are necessary.

C Event Processing

As long as the data segment and stack are maintained, the assembly language event handler can call an external C function from within, and the C function can process the event data. The C function called by the event handler is called the *event processor.*

Function Rules

In addition to maintaining the data segment and stack, the assembly language event handler and the C event processor must adhere to the following rules:

- The assembly language event handler must be a FAR function. This is to ensure an intersegment return to the mouse driver.

- The C event processor must be a NEAR function. This is because the C event processor must use the same code segment as the assembly language event handler. Declaring it as a near function is the only way to ensure that this is true.

- Again, neither the event handler or the event processor can use any DOS or BIOS interrupt services.

The Actual Event Handler

Without further adieu, here is the assembly language event handler. It's small, tight, and fast. The file is called EVENT.ASM.

Don't worry about compiling just yet, some additional reading is required first.

```
; EVENT.ASM
; -----------------------------------------------------------
; Event handler called by the mouse driver. In turn calls the
; C event processor. Function can be compiled with TASM or
; MASM.
;
; MASM - MASM /MX EVENT
; TASM - TASM /MX EVENT
;-----------------------------------------------------------

.MODEL HUGE                 ; Change model to match C cmplr
.DATA                       ; Data directive
.CODE                       ; Code directive

PUBLIC _event_handler       ; Handler is public for C code
EXTRN  _event_processor:near ; The C event processor

eactive db 0                ; EventActive flag so recursion
                            ; will not occur.
```

```
;Module : EVENT HANDLER
;---------------------------
;
_event_handler PROC FAR           ; MUST be FAR procedure

                                  ; STACK MAINTENANCE
                                  ;------------------------
    push    bp                    ; Push BP register
    mov     bp,sp                 ; Assign SP to BP, stacks base
    sub     sp,8                  ; Subtract 8 from stack pointer
                                  ; so args are available.

                                  ; DATA SEG MAINTENANCE
                                  ;------------------------
    push    ds                    ; Push driver data seg
    push    ax                    ; Push AX
    mov     ax,DGROUP             ; Move correct segment
    mov     ds,ax                 ; Assign new segment

                                  ; RECURSION CHECK
                                  ;------------------------
    cmp     eactive,0             ; Is event active now?
    jne     norecurse             ; YES - Go to end
                                  ;------------------------
    mov     eactive,1             ; Event is now active

                                  ; EVENTS AND STATUS
                                  ;------------------------
                                  ; Since AX was pushed already
    pop     ax                    ; pop it for event status.
    push    dx                    ; Push Y coordinate
    push    cx                    ; Push X coordinate
    push    bx                    ; Push Button Status
    push    ax                    ; Push Event Status


                                  ;------------------------
    call    _event_processor      ; CALL C EVENT PROCESSOR!!
                                  ;------------------------
    add     sp,8                  ; Update stack pointer
                                  ; Arguments OFF stack


    mov     eactive,0             ; Event not active now
    jmp     normend               ; Goto normal end label
```

```
                             ; CLEANUP AND LEAVE
                             ;-------------------------
     norecurse:              ; Recursive jump label
     pop    ax               ; AX didn't get popped if
                             ; event was already active.

     normend:                ; Normal end, AX already popped
     pop    ds               ; Pop data segment
     mov    sp,bp            ; Update stack pointer
     pop    bp               ; Pop BP register

     ret                     ; Exit

_event_handler ENDP          ; End event handler
END                          ; End code
```

When the event handler is called by the mouse driver, the following sequence of operations is performed:

1. Stack maintenance is performed.

2. Data segment maintenance is performed.

3. The status registers are pushed unto the stack.

4. The C event processor is called. The status registers are on the stack and are sent to the C event processor.

5. The stack pointer is updated.

6. The original data segment and stack are restored for the mouse driver.

7. The function returns control to the mouse driver.

Recursive Check   Within EVENT.ASM, notice the internal variable eactive. eactive is used by the event handler so a recursive call cannot occur. If an event takes place while the event handler is currently active, it must exit and wait until the current event has been processed. Therefore, if no event is currently being processed when the event handler is called, eactive is set to 1 to indicate the event handler *is* currently active. If the event handler is called again while active, eactive is 1, and the function exits without any further operations. Upon exiting normally, eactive is set to 0 so the event handler can be used again.

Recursion rarely occurs (if ever) in the event handler. However, the check should still be made for safety.

The C Event Processor

The C event processor and two additional functions, to install the event handler and reset the status variables, are located in the file MEVENT.INC. Here it is:

```
/*-----------------------------------------------------------*/
/*                      MEVENT.INC                          */
/* Global mouse event handler message processor.            */
/*-----------------------------------------------------------*/


void far event_handler(void); /* Declaration for assembly   */
                              /* language event handler.     */


/* MODULE : EVENT PROCESSOR                                  */
/*-----------------------------------------------------------*/
/* This routine is FULLY internal and is ONLY called by the  */
/* assembly function Event_Handler.                          */
/* Event_Handler automatically calls this routine, at which  */
/* time it can take control based on the activity.           */
/*                                                           */
/*                                                           */
void near event_processor(int event_status,int button_status,
                          int x,int y)
   {
   if ((CMX!=x)||(CMY!=y))    /* Cursor moved?               */
      {
      if (!IN_GMODE)          /* If in text mode             */
         {                    /* convert coordinates.        */
         x=(x+HCELL_SIZE)/HCELL_SIZE;
         y=(y+VCELL_SIZE)/VCELL_SIZE;
         }
      CURSOR_MOVED=1;         /* Set cursor moved to 1       */
      CMX=x;CMY=y;            /* Assign global vars          */
      }

   BSTATE=button_status;      /* Set BSTATE every call       */

   if (event_status & 2)      /* Left button down            */
      LBUTTON_DOWN=1;

   if (event_status & 8)      /* Right button down           */
      RBUTTON_DOWN=1;
                              /* Both buttons down           */
   if (((event_status & 2)||(event_status & 8))
```

```
                  &&(button_status==3))
         BBUTTON_DOWN=1;
                              /* If 3-button, check for down   */
      if ((NUMBER_BUTTONS==3)&&(event_status & 32))
         BBUTTON_DOWN=1;

      if (event_status & 4)     /* Left button up              */
         LBUTTON_UP=1;

      if (event_status & 16)    /* Right button up             */
         RBUTTON_UP=1;
                              /* Both buttons up               */
      if ((LBUTTON_UP)&&(RBUTTON_UP))
         BBUTTON_UP=1;
                              /* If 3-button, check for up     */
      if ((NUMBER_BUTTONS==3)&&(event_status & 64))
         BBUTTON_UP=1;
      }

/* MODULE : INSTALL EVENT HANDLER                              */
/*-----------------------------------------------------------*/
/* Installs the global mouse event handler. Sets the mask so  */
/* all first five bits are on with two-button mice, and first */
/* seven bits are on with three-button mice.                  */
/*                                                            */
void install_event_handler(void)
   {
   if (NUMBER_BUTTONS==3)                  /* Set for 3-button*/
      set_event_handler(127,event_handler);
   else                                    /* Set for 2-button*/
      set_event_handler(31,event_handler);
   }

/* MODULE : RESET EVENT STATUS                                 */
/*-----------------------------------------------------------*/
/* Resets all event status variables to 0.                    */
/*                                                            */
void reset_event_status(void)
   {
   CURSOR_MOVED=0;
   LBUTTON_DOWN=0;LBUTTON_UP=0;
   RBUTTON_DOWN=0;RBUTTON_UP=0;
   BBUTTON_DOWN=0;BBUTTON_UP=0;
   }
```

Notice the function prototype for the assembly function event_handler() in MEVENT.INC:

```
void far event_handler(void); /* Declaration for assembly    */
                              /* language event handler.     */
```

The C compiler must know the assembly function exists somewhere, so a function prototype is required.

How the Event Handler and Processor Work Together

To understand how the event handler and event processor interface with one another, take a look at the following code fragment from the assembly function event_handler():

```
push    dx              ; Push Y coordinate
push    cx              ; Push X coordinate
push    bx              ; Push Button Status
push    ax              ; Push Event Status


                        ;-------------------------
call    _event_processor ; CALL C EVENT PROCESSOR!!
```

Next look at the argument list in the function event_processor():

```
void near event_processor(int event_status,int button_status,
                          int x,int y)
```

The registers containing the mouse status information are pushed unto the stack in the assembly function event_handler(), and the C function event_processor() takes them off in its argument list. Mouse status information is now available in the C event processor, which examines the status variables to determine which mouse events have taken place. Here's what the variables in the argument list mean.

Event Status   The variable event_status is a 16-bit integer representing the event that occurred. The bits used to determine which event occurred are defined exactly the same as the call mask used to install the event handler (see "The Call Mask"). The only difference between the variable event_status and the call mask is that the individual bits in event_status are turned on according to what type of event occurred.

Determining Button Presses and Releases   To determine if a button has been pressed or released, the appropriate bit in event_status is examined, and the appropriate global button variable is set. For instance, to determine if the left button was pressed, the comparison

```
if (event_status & 2)
```

is made. If the bit is on, LBUTTON_DOWN is set to 1, meaning the left button was pressed.

In the function event_processor(), notice that if the mouse is a three-button mouse, the status is located in the higher bits of event_status. These bits (5 and 6) are meaningless to a two-button mouse, so a determination is first made to see if the bits even need to be examined. When the event handler is installed with the function install_event_handler(), the same determination is made regarding a three-button mouse, and the call mask is set accordingly.

Button Status   The variable button_status does not indicate that an event has taken place. The button status is used to determine if buttons are down when any other event takes place. The button status can be 1, 2, or 3, indicating the left, right, or middle (OEM) button is down when an event occurred. The global variable BSTATE is always set to button_status, so it can always be used to determine whether a button is currently down.

Mouse Cursor Coordinates   The coordinates x and y are the mouse cursor's current display coordinates. These coordinates are used to determine whether the mouse cursor has moved, and its current location. You might wonder why the variable event_status is not used to determine when the mouse cursor has moved. The reason is because the mouse driver does not base movement on pixels, but mickeys (mickeys are discussed in Chapter 13). To make a long story short, when mouse movement generates an event, it might not mean that the mouse cursor's display coordinates have changed. To accommodate this, the global variables CMX and CMY are used to compare against the actual mouse cursor coordinates sent from the event handler. If they are different, the mouse cursor has moved, and CMX and CMY are set to the new coordinates. This also means the mouse cursor's position *never* needs to be polled again. The global variables CMX and CMY are updated every time the mouse cursor makes a valid move, so these variables *always* contain the mouse cursor's current display coordinates.

Compiling the Event Handler

To compile the event handler, you need Borland's Turbo Assembler 1.0 or later, or Microsoft's Macro Assembler 5.0 or later. Follow these instructions:

1. In the file EVENT.ASM, change the line

.MODEL HUGE

to

.MODEL *XXX*

where *XXX* represents the memory model you are compiling the programming examples in. This is either the HUGE, LARGE, COMPACT, MEDIUM, or SMALL memory model. The only memory model the event handler does not operate with is the TINY model.

2. Type **TASM /MX EVENT** to compile EVENT.ASM using Borland's Turbo Assembler, or type **MASM /MX EVENT** to compile EVENT.ASM using Microsoft's Macro Assembler, to EVENT.OBJ.

The MX compiler option specifies that all global names are case sensitive. Do not leave this option out. Furthermore, if you insert additional compiler options when compiling EVENT.ASM, be sure you know exactly what you are doing; otherwise unpredictable results may occur.

Different Memory Models

A word of warning: the biggest problem you will encounter with the event handler is when it is compiled in a different memory model than the C application code is compiled in. Some memory models will allow mixed-model compiling, but usually this generates _TEXT fixup linker errors and does not compile to an .EXE file. In any case, the safest method is to compile using the same memory model throughout.

If You Don't Have the Assembler

If you do not have either the Borland or Microsoft assembly language compiler, the object code is provided with the companion disks for each memory model. EVENT.ASM compiles to EVENT.OBJ, but on the companion disk the file names represent the memory model they were compiled in, as shown here:

Filename	Memory Model
EVENTH.OBJ	Huge memory model
EVENTL.OBJ	Large memory model
EVENTC.OBJ	Compact memory model
EVENTM.OBJ	Medium memory model
EVENTS.OBJ	Small memory model

You can use the exact filename when compiling a program or rename a specific model's filename to EVENT.OBJ. The remaining examples in this book assume the file is named EVENT.OBJ.

That wraps up the specifics regarding the event handler. In the next chapter, you learn how to use the event handler, and you may be quite surprised at how powerful it really is.

Chapter **8**

Using the Event Handler

The time has come for you to exterminate the possibility of lost mouse activity, such as button presses, and learn to use the event handler and event processor created in Chapter 7. Additionally, this chapter discusses other mouse functions used to install an event handler and special programming considerations, such as TSR applications.

The first order of business is compiling a program that uses the event handler.

Before continuing, it is strongly recommended that you read Chapter 7. At the very least, read the section "Compiling the Event Handler," since detailed instructions are provided regarding EVENT.ASM and how it is compiled to EVENT.OBJ.

Compiling a Program that Uses the Event Handler

Compiling a C program that uses the assembly language event handler is a bit more complex than compiling programs containing only C source code, and so detailed compiling instructions are given for both the Borland and Microsoft compilers.

The first programming example presented in this chapter is called MOUSE12.C. The following instructions use MOUSE12.C for the compiling guidelines. When compiling other programs, just change MOUSE12.C to the name of the current program you are compiling.

File Order

When compiling an application using the event handler, the file EVENT.OBJ must precede the application source file. This is due to the way files are linked and because the assembly language event handler must be close to the C event processor when the application is compiled. In the following instructions, do not change the order of files in the project file, or the command-line options.

Stack Checking

Microsoft compiler users must turn stack checking off when compiling an application that uses the event handler *regardless* of the environment you are compiling in. If you do not, the application generates a run-time error R6000. See your compiler's reference manual for instructions about turning off stack checking in the integrated environment. Instructions are presented here for the command-line compiler. Borland compiler users can leave stack checking on or turn it off as desired.

Integrated Environment Compiling

If you are compiling within the Borland or Microsoft QuickC integrated environment, or the Microsoft Programmer's Workbench, you need a project file for the remaining DOS programming examples presented in this book.

Microsoft C users can stop using project files in Chapter 16, where the mouse functions, event handler, and event processor are combined into one complete library (.LIB) file. Borland users still need a project file for additional libraries.

The Project File

A *project file* is used to manage individual files that an application is composed of. These files can be source files or precompiled object and library files.

Since the assembly language event handler, EVENT.ASM, cannot be compiled within the C compiler(s), it must be compiled to EVENT.OBJ with an assembler and included in a project file along with the C program's source file. The compiler then compiles the C source file and links it with EVENT.OBJ, forming one complete .EXE file.

File names of project files end with the extension .PRJ if using a Borland compiler, or .MAK if using a Microsoft compiler. Both types are included on the companion disk supplied with this book. However, throughout the remainder of the book, the project files are specified with a .PRJ file extension. See your compiler's reference manual for a more detailed explanation of project files and how to use them.

The project file for MOUSE12.C is

```
EVENT.OBJ
MOUSE12.C
```

The Graphics Library

If you are compiling with a Borland compiler, you must turn the Graphics Library linker option to On. With the Microsoft C 6.0 or C/C++ 7.0 compiler, you must include GRAPHICS.LIB in the Additional Libraries Linker option. Microsoft QuickC installs the graphics library when it is initially set up. If you did not install the library, the programs will not compile. Consult your QuickC reference manual for details regarding the graphics library.

Microsoft QuickC users must also set the Build flags to Release when compiling in the integrated environment.

Command-Line Compiling

If you prefer compiling with command-line compilers, use the following instructions.

The following sections regarding command-line compiling are case sensitive. Be careful— the compiler will not function properly unless the commands are entered correctly.

Borland Compilers

From the DOS command line, issue the command

> TCC –IC:\TC\INCLUDE –LC:\TC\LIB –mh –eMOUSE12.EXE EVENT.OBJ
> MOUSE12.C C:\TC\LIB\GRAPHICS.LIB

where

- *TCC* is the the Borland Turbo C command-line compiler. If you are using the Borland C/C++ compiler, use BCC instead.

- *–IC:\TC\INCLUDE* is the directory where your standard #include files are located.

- *–LC:\TC\LIB* is the directory where your standard libraries are located.

- *–mh* means compile using the huge memory model. Change this to match the memory model you compiled EVENT.OBJ with. ms=SMALL, mm=MEDIUM, mc=COMPACT, ml=LARGE, mh=HUGE.

- *–eMOUSE12.EXE* is the name of the .EXE file generated.
- *EVENT.OBJ* is the event handler's object file.
- *MOUSE12.C* is the name of the applications source file.
- *C:\TC\LIB\GRAPHICS.LIB* is the graphics library.

Microsoft C 6.0 and C/C++ 7.0 Compilers

From the DOS command line, issue the command

CL /AH /Gs /Oe /FeMOUSE12.EXE EVENT.OBJ MOUSE12.C –link GRAPH-ICS.LIB

where

- *CL* is the Microsoft command-line compiler.
- */AH* means compile using the huge model. Change this to match the memory model you compiled EVENT.OBJ with. AS=SMALL, AM=MEDIUM, AC=COMPACT, AL=LARGE, AH=HUGE.
- */Gs* means remove stack-check calls.
- */Oe* means enable register allocation (this command is not necessary, but advisable).
- */FeMOUSE12.EXE* is the name .EXE file generated.
- *EVENT.OBJ* is the event handler object file.
- *MOUSE12.C* is the name of the applications source file.
- *–link GRAPHICS.LIB* tells the linker to include the graphics library.

Microsoft QuickC Compilers

From the DOS command line, issue the command

QCL /AH /Gs /Oe /FeMOUSE12.EXE EVENT.OBJ MOUSE12.C

The compiler options are identical to those in the Microsoft C 6.0 or C/C++ 7.0 compiler. However, no graphics library is included in the link option. QuickC installs the graphics library when it is initially set up. If you did not install the library, the programs will not compile. Consult your QuickC reference manual for details regarding the graphics library.

The New Header File

Since the C event processor is located in the file MEVENT.INC, a new header file is needed to incorporate the file into the application. The header file for the next three chapters is called HEADER2.H. Here it is:

```
#include "compiler.h"         /* Compiler directives        */
#include "mouse.h"            /* Include global header file */
#include "mouse.inc"          /* Include 10 mouse functions */
#include "mevent.inc"         /* Event processor            */
#include graphics
#include videolib             /* Include tiny video library */
```

Your First Program Using the Event Handler

The following is the first example using the event handler and processor. In order to not overwhelm you with the full capacity of the event handler and processor just yet, the first example traps only mouse cursor movement and left or right button presses.

If compiling from the integrated environment, the project file is MOUSE12.PRJ. Here it is:

```
EVENT.OBJ
MOUSE12.OBJ
```

and here is MOUSE12.C:

```
/*-------------------------------------------------------------*/
/*                      MOUSE12.C                              */
/*                                                             */
/* First example using the event handler and processor.       */
/* Cursor movement, left and right button presses are trapped.*/
/*-------------------------------------------------------------*/

#include "header2.h"          /* New header with e-handlers    */

void main()
   {
   install_video(TMODE);      /* Install video system          */
   header();                  /* Draw header                   */
   reset_mouse();             /* Reset mouse                   */

   if (MOUSE_THERE)
      {
```

```
out_text_xy(25, 2,"Event Handler/Processor");
out_text_xy(20, 5,"Press buttons and move the mouse around.");
out_text_xy(30, 10,"X -    , Y - ");

                        /* Set mouse horiz & vert limits */
set_mouse_hlimits(1,VID_MAXX-MOUSE_SIZE+1);
set_mouse_vlimits(1,VID_MAXY-MOUSE_SIZE);


                        /* Install event handler        */
install_event_handler();
show_mouse_cursor();

while (!kbhit())        /* Do until keypressed          */
   {

   if (CURSOR_MOVED)    /* If cursor moved              */
      {
      CURSOR_MOVED=0;
                        /* Clear last coords, write new */
      change_color(14);
      hide_mouse_cursor();
      clear_line_from(10,34,3,0);
      clear_line_from(10,43,3,0);
      out_int_xy(34,10,CMX);
      out_int_xy(43,10,CMY);
      show_mouse_cursor();
      }

   if (LBUTTON_DOWN)    /* Left button pressed          */
      {
      LBUTTON_DOWN=0;
      change_color(11);
      hide_mouse_cursor();
      clear_line_from(15,28,22,0);
      out_text_xy(28,15,"Left Button Pressed");
      show_mouse_cursor();
      }

   if (RBUTTON_DOWN)    /* Right button pressed         */
      {
      RBUTTON_DOWN=0;
      change_color(11);
```

```
                hide_mouse_cursor();
                clear_line_from(15,28,22,0);
                out_text_xy(28,15,"Right Button Pressed");
                show_mouse_cursor();
                }
            }
        }

    else mouse_error(5,4);

    getch();
                                /* Need to reset,no event handler*/
    if (MOUSE_THERE) reset_mouse();

    shut_down_video();
    }
```

When running the program, if you press the left mouse button, the following message appears:

```
Graphics Mode           Event Handler/Processor
                   Press buttons and move the mouse around.


                        X - 314, Y - 144


                   Left Button Pressed

                              ▶
```

Terminating the Application and Event Handler

In the previous example, notice the call to reset_mouse() when the program terminates. If the mouse driver is not reset with mouse function 0 or 33, the event handler remains in affect even after the program terminates. If the event handler is not disabled at program termination, the system crashes the next time the user moves the mouse or presses a button. This is because the mouse driver is looking for the event handler, which no longer exists.

Another quick and easy way to deactivate the event handler is to use the mouse library function set_event_handler() with NULL arguments, as in set_event_handler(0,0). This is recommended when you do not desire to reset the mouse entirely.

Reseting the Global Status Variables

In the previous example, notice that when each status variable is trapped, it is immediately reset to 0, as in

```
if (LBUTTON_DOWN)
    {
    LBUTTON_DOWN=0;
```

The reason is that the event processor does not reset the status variables to 0; they are either set to 1 or left at their current setting. This is in order to not lose one event due to another. To better explain this, suppose the following events occur:

1. The user presses the left mouse button, triggering the event handler and processor, which sets LBUTTON_DOWN to 1.

2. The user moves the mouse *before* your application processes LBUTTON_DOWN. This triggers the event handler and processor, which sets CURSOR_MOVED to 1.

If LBUTTON_DOWN is reset to 0 inside the event processor, then mouse movement triggering the event handler would reset LBUTTON_DOWN to 0, even though your application might not have processed LBUTTON_DOWN. The result is a missed left button press. Therefore, status variables are not reset to 0 upon entry to the event processor.

It is your responsibility to reset a status variable to 0 after it is trapped. If you do not, the status variable is always 1 after the first occurrence of a specific event and is continuously trapped, even though no subsequent events may occur.

There are times when you want to reset all the event status variables at one time. The function reset_event_status() was created for just this purpose, and is demonstrated in Chapter 9.

The Full-Blown Event Handler/Processor

After studying the code from the previous example, you are ready for the full Event Handler/Processor Debugger. The following program captures every possible status variable and button state.

The project file, shown here, is MOUSE13.PRJ:

```
EVENT.OBJ
MOUSE13.C
```

Here is MOUSE13.C:

```
/*------------------------------------------------------------*/
/*                     MOUSE13.C                          */
/*                                                        */
/* Event Handler/Processor Debugger. Every event and status   */
/* variable is trapped as it occurs and sends a message to the*/
/* display.                                               */
/*------------------------------------------------------------*/

#include "header2.h"          /* New header with e-handlers   */

/* MODULE : MENU                                          */
/*------------------------------------------------------------*/
void menu(void)
   {
   change_color(15);
   out_text_xy(25, 2,"Event Handler/Processor Debugger");
   out_text_xy( 2, 5,"Cursor Coordinates    :");
   out_text_xy(30, 5,"X -     , Y - ");
   out_text_xy(50, 5,"BSTATE - ");
   out_text_xy( 2, 9,"Last Button Pressed  :");
   out_text_xy( 2,11,"Last Button Released :");
   out_text_xy(30,20,"Press Any Key To Exit");
   }

void main()
   {
   install_video(GMODE);     /* Install video system        */
   header();                 /* Draw header                 */
   reset_mouse();            /* Reset mouse                 */

   if (MOUSE_THERE)
      {
      menu();                     /* Draw menu               */
                            /* Set mouse horiz & vert limits */
      set_mouse_hlimits(1,VID_MAXX-MOUSE_SIZE+1);
      set_mouse_vlimits(1,VID_MAXY-MOUSE_SIZE);

                            /* Install event handler         */
      install_event_handler();
      show_mouse_cursor();

      while (!kbhit())      /* Do until keypressed          */
```

```
{

if (CURSOR_MOVED)     /* If cursor moved              */
   {
   CURSOR_MOVED=0;
                      /* Clear last coords, write new */
   change_color(14);
                      /* Set exclusion area           */
   if (IN_GMODE)
      set_hide_bounds(33*HFONT_SIZE,4*VFONT_SIZE,
                         78*HFONT_SIZE,6*VFONT_SIZE);
   else
      set_hide_bounds(33,4,78,6);

   clear_line_from(5,34,3,0);
   clear_line_from(5,43,3,0);
   out_int_xy(34,5,CMX);
   out_int_xy(43,5,CMY);

   change_color(10);
   clear_line_from(5,60,18,0);

   switch(BSTATE)    /* What's the state of the bttns?*/
      {
      case MV_LBUTTON:out_text_xy(60,5,
                                  "Left Button Down");
                 break;
      case MV_RBUTTON:out_text_xy(60,5,
                                  "Right Button Down");
                 break;
      case MV_BBUTTON:out_text_xy(60,5,
                                  "Both Buttons Down");
                 break;
      }
                     /* Show the cursor              */
   show_mouse_cursor();
   }

change_color(11);    /* Now check for current button */
                     /* presses and releases.        */


if (LBUTTON_DOWN)
   {
   hide_mouse_cursor();
```

```
     LBUTTON_DOWN=0;
     clear_line_from(9,25,22,0);
     out_text_xy(25,9,"Left Button Pressed");
     show_mouse_cursor();
     }

 if (LBUTTON_UP)
     {
     hide_mouse_cursor();
     LBUTTON_UP=0;
     clear_line_from(11,25,23,0);
     out_text_xy(25,11,"Left Button Released");
     show_mouse_cursor();
     }

 if (RBUTTON_DOWN)
     {
     hide_mouse_cursor();
     RBUTTON_DOWN=0;
     clear_line_from(9,25,22,0);
     out_text_xy(25,9,"Right Button Pressed");
     show_mouse_cursor();
     }

 if (RBUTTON_UP)
     {
     hide_mouse_cursor();
     RBUTTON_UP=0;
     clear_line_from(11,25,23,0);
     out_text_xy(25,11,"Right Button Released");
     show_mouse_cursor();
     }

 if (BBUTTON_DOWN)
     {
     hide_mouse_cursor();
     BBUTTON_DOWN=0;
     clear_line_from(9,25,22,0);
     out_text_xy(25,9,"Both Buttons Pressed");
     show_mouse_cursor();
     }

 if (BBUTTON_UP)
     {
     hide_mouse_cursor();
```

```
                    BBUTTON_UP=0;
                    clear_line_from(11,25,23,0);
                    out_text_xy(25,11,"Both Button Released");
                    show_mouse_cursor();
                    }


                }
            }

    else mouse_error(5,4);

    getch();                        /* Need to reset,no event handler*/

    if (MOUSE_THERE) reset_mouse();
    shut_down_video();
    }
```

When the program is running, if you press the right mouse button and release it, press the left mouse button and hold it down, and then move the mouse cursor while holding the button down, the following is generated:

```
Graphics Mode           Event Handler/Processor Debugger

Cursor Coordinates   :      X - 484, Y - 82      BSTATE - Left Button Down

Last Button Pressed  : Left Button Pressed
Last Button Released : Right Button Released                 ▶



                        Press Any Key To Exit
```

Revisiting the touch_cursor() Function

The function touch_cursor() was introduced in Chapter 4. It is used to work around a possible bug when using an exclusion area to hide the mouse cursor. In the previous example, look inside the CURSOR_MOVED status trap. An exclusion area is set using the mouse library function set_hide_bounds(). If you experienced the visibility problem discussed in Chapter 4, add the statement

```
set_mouse_position(CMX,CMY);
```

immediately after the call to show_cursor() in the CURSOR_MOVED status trap. When using the event handler and processor, the variables CMX and CMY always represent the mouse cursor's current location, and this one line of code replaces the entire function touch_cursor() presented in Chapter 4.

Using the Mouse Cursor Coordinates

Some caution must be exercised when using the global coordinate variables CMX and CMY. For instance, suppose you have a function to draw a rectangle based on the mouse cursor coordinates. You might think you could use CMX and CMY like this:

```
line(CMX,CMY,CMX+50,CMY);
line(CMX+50,CMY,CMX+50,CMY+50)
line(CMX+50,CMY+50,CMX,CMY+50)
line(CMX,CMY+50,CMX,CMY);
```

This might work and it might not. You see, if a user moves the mouse during the line-drawing functions, the coordinates CMX and/or CMY are modified by the event handler as the rectangle is being drawn.

The event handler is always processing events.

The proper method is to "anchor" the current position, and use the anchor in the drawing routines like this:

```
x=CMX;y=CMY;
line(x,y,x+50,y);
line(x+50,y,x+50,y+50)
line(x+50,y+50,x,y+50)
line(x,y+50,x,y);
```

Other Event Handler Functions

In this book, mouse function 12, set event handler, is used exclusively. However, you should be aware of the other two similar mouse functions and what situations you would use them in.

Mouse Function 20: Swap Event Handlers

Mouse function 20, swap event handlers, is very similar to mouse function 12, set event handler. The only difference is that after loading the registers with the necessary information and calling mouse function 20 to install the event handler, mouse function 20 returns the call mask and function address of the previously installed event handler. If the returned call mask is 0, there was no event handler previously installed. This allows an application to swap a new event handler with the current event handler and restore the previous event handler upon termination. See the following section regarding terminate-and-stay-resident applications and Appendix A for details regarding this function.

Mouse Function 24: Set Alternate Event Handler

Mouse function 24 can be used in conjunction with mouse function 12, or mouse function 20, or independently if desired. The main purpose of mouse function 24 is to allow an alternate event handler, called by the mouse driver when specific keyboard control keys, the CTRL, ALT, and SHIFT keys, are down, in conjunction with other mouse events. Mouse function 24 will not call the alternate event handler unless one of these keys is down and the appropriate key was set in the call mask.

Mouse function 24 also differs from mouse function 12 in the following ways:

- It provides a wider range of call mask definitions. This allows you to specify which keyboard control key (ALT, CTRL, or SHIFT) must be down for the mouse driver to call the alternate event handler.

- It allows up to three alternate event handlers to be installed at one time.

- It allows DOS and BIOS interrupt services to be used inside the alternate event handler. However, use extreme caution and do plenty of testing when using interrupts inside the alternate event handler.

- The only way to clear the call mask used by mouse function 24 is to reset it to 0. Thus, mouse function 24 must be called again upon termination, with the call mask set to 0. Mouse function 12 and mouse function 20 can each be deactivated by calling mouse function 0 or 33.

See Appendix A for details regarding this function, and the extended call mask bit meanings used to set the alternate event handler(s).

The spawn() and exec() Functions

If you use the Borland or Microsoft functions spawn() or exec() to shell to DOS, run a child process, or execute another application, always deactivate the event handler first. This ensures the mouse driver is not looking for the event handler's code. If you are running a child process, reactivate the event handler when the parent program is reentered.

Terminate-and-Stay-Resident Applications (TSRs)

TSR programming requires some special considerations from the mouse programmer. Since the underlying program being used when the TSR is activated may be mouse driven and use event handlers, the possibility of serious mishap exists.
    If you are writing a TSR that utilizes the mouse, follow these guidelines:

- Use mouse function 20 instead of mouse function 12 to set the event handler in the mouse library function set_event_handler(). Mouse function 20 returns the previous call mask and event handler address after the new event handler is installed.

- Before the program terminates, use the values that mouse function 20 returned to reset the event handler to the previous call mask and address. This ensures that the underlying program's event handler (if any) is restored.

- You might want to use polling methods only in the TSR. What if another TSR pops up on top of your TSR and doesn't check the mouse status and event handlers? The answer is the system more than likely crashes. So, to ensure proper operation in TSRs, you might want to use polling methods exclusively. However, you must still be sure to first deactivate the event handler (if any) the underlying program is using and reactivate it upon termination.

- When writing TSRs, the video modes the underlying program is using and the TSRs might be different. See Appendix A regarding mouse functions 21, 22, and 23. These functions allow saving and restoring of the current mouse state. Save the current state upon entry to the TSR and restore it upon termination.

Moving Forward

All programming examples from this point forward use the event handler and processor to determine button presses, button releases, and mouse cursor movement. The polling methods presented in Chapters 5 and 6 are important, since you need understand the basic mechanics of trapping mouse button presses and determining the mouse cursor's location. Additionally, there are certain conditions when you want to use polling instead of event processing. However, under normal circumstances, using the event handler and processor is a method far superior to polling.

Always deactivate the event handler upon termination of the program.

Chapter *9*

Handling Menus

By far the heaviest use of the mouse in today's applications is in menus. You move the mouse cursor to a menu choice, press a button, and the application calls the appropriate routine for that choice. Anybody who has run Windows or other popular applications utilizing the mouse knows how to pick menu choices with the mouse. Menus can be horizontal, vertical, or both.

Floating Menus

Since the mouse and menus interact so often, the subject deserves a great deal of attention. The programming examples presented in this chapter use what I have termed *floating menus*. Floating menus are the most tedious type of menu to manage, and require a good deal of programming effort. However, they are by far the most rewarding in DOS-based applications, both for you and your end users. Here's how they work:

- As you move the mouse cursor over a menu option, the option is highlighted.

- When you move the mouse cursor to a new menu option, the previous option is deactivated (background normal), and the new option is highlighted.

- If the mouse cursor is currently over a menu option when you press a mouse button, action is taken based on the specific choice.

The reason this type of menu is termed a floating menu is because, as you move mouse cursor from menu option to menu option, the highlighting of the options seems to "float" along with the mouse cursor. Users of your application will let you know how much they appreciate this type of menuing system, and my experience has been that, when offered a choice, users prefer it to other systems (such as those that highlight the options only when a button is pressed).

The programming examples presented in this chapter demonstrate this method using both horizontal and vertical menus.

Keeping It Simple

Because the techniques required to implement a floating menu are fairly involved, a few shortcuts have been taken to keep matters as simple as possible.

While the vertical menu presented in this chapter resembles a *pop-up* or *pull-down* menu, in reality it is not. By definition, a pop-up or pull-down menu saves the underlying background image before it is initiated, and restores the background image when it is terminated (removed from the display). The difference between a pop-up menu and a pull-down menu is that pop-up menus are only one level deep, while pull-down menus may have additional menus nested within.

Because the examples presented in this chapter do not have a background image to overwrite, no background image saving and restoring is performed. Therefore, the vertical menu cannot be considered a true pop-up or pull-down menu, and from this point forward is simply called a *submenu*.

 For information regarding true pop-up and pull-down menus, see The Art of C *by Herbert Schildt, Osborne/McGraw-Hill, 1991.*

Only one horizontal menu option will bring up a vertical submenu. The other horizontal options simply write a string of text informing you of the choice made.

The following sections examine the finer points of floating-menu processing.

Horizontal Menu Considerations

The horizontal main menu presented in this chapter has the following form:

(The Horizontal Menu)

If the mouse cursor is between the horizontal locations of Option #1 when the program is running, Option #1 will be highlighted. As the mouse cursor moves horizontally, it will eventually reach the border of Option #2. The border is approximately halfway between the end of Option #1 and the beginning of Option #2. When the mouse cursor moves into Option #2's region, Option #1 is deactivated (background normal), and Option #2 is highlighted. The same logic applies all the way across the menu in both left and right directions.

Consider the text coordinates of the menu option, as shown here:

Horizontal text coordinates menu options are located on.

To determine if the mouse cursor is on a menu option, two items must be determined:

- Is the mouse cursor's vertical coordinate equal to the vertical coordinate the menu options are located on?

- If yes, is the mouse cursor in a menu option's region?

The reason for using regions and not just one coordinate is that you want the option to remain highlighted when the mouse cursor is over the entire option, not just one character.

When the mouse cursor moves into a new menu option, two actions occur:

- The option the mouse cursor was previously on is deactivated (background returned to normal).

- The option where the mouse cursor is currently located is highlighted.

Limiting Range in Horizontal Menus

If the mouse cursor's movement range is limited to the vertical coordinate the horizontal menu options are located on, there is no need to determine the vertical coordinate when the mouse cursor is moving, because you already know what it is (since you limited movement to that coordinate). However, in most applications, the horizontal menu is usually the first, or main menu, and other choices exist about the entire display. Therefore, the range is usually never limited in a horizontal, or main menu. This of course is up to you, and different menus call for different implementation.

Vertical Menu Considerations

The vertical submenu presented in this chapter has the following form:

```
Sub-Menu Option#1
Sub-Menu Option#2
Sub-Menu Option#3
Sub-Menu Option#4
Exit
```
            (The Vertical Menu)

Consider the text coordinates of the vertical menu options, as shown here:

```
Sub-Menu Option#1    <- 5
Sub-Menu Option#2    <- 6
Sub-Menu Option#3    <- 7
Sub-Menu Option#4    <- 8
Exit                 <- 9
```

Vertical text coordinates menu options are located on.

Limiting Range in Vertical Menus

Ninety percent of vertical menus are of the pop-up or pull-down type. In a sharp DOS application, the mouse cursor's movement range is limited to the vertical menu's rectangular region. This way, the user is forced to choose from the available options in the current menu. As such, the horizontal menu coordinates are irrelevant, as each menu option is located on distinct vertical coordinates, and the mouse cursor cannot move outside the menu's region.

This only applies to sequentially structured programs, where the order of operations is determined by you, the programmer. Most DOS-based applications are sequentially structured.

After the vertical location has been determined, two actions occur:

- The option the mouse cursor was previously on is deactivated (background returned to normal).

- The option where the mouse cursor is currently located is highlighted.

Combined Menu Considerations

A *combined menu* is a menu that has choices in both horizontal and vertical regions (two-line horizontal menu). Both horizontal and vertical coordinates need to be determined and matched to menu options. All other logic remains the same.

The Floating Menu Program

Probably the easiest way to understand the methods previously discussed and how they are implemented is to run an example utilizing them.

The following example implements a horizontal, or "main" menu, and a vertical submenu. To pick menu options, move the mouse cursor over the option and press the left mouse button. Choose Option #1 to pull up the vertical submenu.

Become as familiar with the code and program operation as possible. More details of the menuing system are discussed following the example. There's a bit of code here, but it's worth the effort.

If you are compiling from inside the integrated environment, the project file shown here is MOUSE14.PRJ:

```
EVENT.OBJ
MOUSE14.C
```

Here is MOUSE14.C:

```
/*-------------------------------------------------------------*/
/*                      MOUSE14.C                          */
/*                                                         */
/* Demonstrate how to implement and use both horizontal and  */
/* vertical menus.                                         */
/*-------------------------------------------------------------*/

#include "header2.h"         /* New header with e-handlers    */


                /*----------------------------*/
                /*    VERTICAL MENU HANDLING   */
                /*----------------------------*/
```

```
/* MODULE : DRAW VMENU                                        */
/*-----------------------------------------------------------*/
/* Draw the vertical submenu, limit mouse to rectangular menu */
/* region.                                                    */
/*                                                            */
void draw_vmenu(void)
    {            .
    int x1,y1,x2,y2;

    hide_mouse_cursor();
    change_color(15);          /* Write the entire menu       */
    out_text_xy(5,5,"Sub-Menu Option#1");
    out_text_xy(5,6,"Sub-Menu Option#2");
    out_text_xy(5,7,"Sub-Menu Option#3");
    out_text_xy(5,8,"Sub-Menu Option#4");
    out_text_xy(5,9,"Exit              ");

    x1=4;x2=22;                /* Rectangle coordinates for   */
    y1=4;y2=10;                /* submenu box.                */

    if (IN_GMODE)              /* If in graphics mode convert to*/
       {                       /* graphic coords, also add a   */
       ++x2;++y2;              /* space and a line for padding. */
       x1=x1*HFONT_SIZE-HFONT_SIZE;
       x2=x2*HFONT_SIZE-HFONT_SIZE;
       y1=y1*VFONT_SIZE-VFONT_SIZE;
       y2=y2*VFONT_SIZE-VFONT_SIZE;
       }


    change_color(4);           /* Change color to red, do rect */
    draw_rectangle(x1,y1,x2,y2);
                               /* Set new limits to submenu    */
    set_mouse_hlimits(x1,x2);
    set_mouse_vlimits(y1,y2);
    show_mouse_cursor();
    }


/* MODULE : DRAW VCHOICE                                      */
/*-----------------------------------------------------------*/
/* Redraw a menu choice from the vertical submenu.            */
/* Input parameters                                           */
/*    number - choice to redraw                               */
/*                                                            */
```

```
void draw_vchoice(int number,int bcolor)
   {
   hide_mouse_cursor();
   switch(number)                /* Draw choice based on number   */
       {
      case 1:clear_line_from(5,5,17,bcolor);
             out_text_xy(5,5,"Sub-Menu Option#1");
             break;
      case 2:clear_line_from(6,5,17,bcolor);
             out_text_xy(5,6,"Sub-Menu Option#2");
             break;
      case 3:clear_line_from(7,5,17,bcolor);
             out_text_xy(5,7,"Sub-Menu Option#3");
             break;
      case 4:clear_line_from(8,5,17,bcolor);
             out_text_xy(5,8,"Sub-Menu Option#4");
             break;
      case 5:clear_line_from(9,5,17,bcolor);
             out_text_xy(5,9,"Exit              ");
             break;
       }
   show_mouse_cursor();
   }




/* MODULE : WHICH VCHOICE                                       */
/*------------------------------------------------------------*/
/* Vertical submenu menu handler.                              */
/* Input parameters                                            */
/*         x,y - current mouse location                        */
/*     *lastcode - address of last menu choice                 */
/* Output parameters                                           */
/*    Function returns the value of the current menu choice.   */
/*    Returns -1 if not on a choice                            */
/*    *lastcode - Adress contents are updated to current       */
/*               choice after change, or 0 if not on a choice*/
/*                                                             */
int which_vchoice(int x,int y,int *lastcode)
   {
   int code;

   if (IN_GMODE)                /* If in graphics mode, convert */
      {                         /* to text coordinates.         */
      x=(x+HFONT_SIZE)/HFONT_SIZE;
```

```
      y=(y+VFONT_SIZE)/VFONT_SIZE;
      }

  code=-1;                   /* Set code to -1, invalid     */

  switch(y)                  /* Which vertical line?        */
    {
    case 5:code=1;break;     /* If first choice             */
    case 6:code=2;break;     /* If second choice            */
    case 7:code=3;break;     /* If third choice             */
    case 8:code=4;break;     /* If fourth choice            */
    case 9:code=5;break;     /* If fifth choice             */
    }

  if (code!=*lastcode)       /* If this choice not equal to */
    {                        /* last choice then -          */
    if (code!=-1)            /* If this choice not invalid- */
      {                      /* Draw last choice normal     */

      change_color(15);draw_vchoice(*lastcode,0);

                             /* Draw new choice HIGHLIGHTED */
      change_color(0);draw_vchoice(code,15);
      change_background(0);
      *lastcode=code;        /* Update last choice to new   */
      }
    else                     /* Else if this choice invalid */
      {                      /* mouse out of range then -   */
      if (*lastcode!=0)
        {                    /* Draw last choice normal     */
        change_color(15);
                             /* Not in menu anymore         */
        draw_vchoice(*lastcode,0);
        *lastcode=0;         /* Set last code to zero       */
        }
      }
    }

  return(code);              /* Return this choice          */
  }
```

```
/* MODULE : EXIT SUBMENU                                      */
/*-----------------------------------------------------------*/
/* Exit the vertical submenu. Erase it and set mouse limits   */
/* back to full display area.                                 */
/* Input parameters                                           */
/*      old_mousex,                                           */
/*      old_mousey - mouse coordinates before function call   */
/*                                                            */
void exit_sub_menu(int old_mousex,int old_mousey)
   {
   int loop;
   hide_mouse_cursor();        /* Clear the submenu           */

   for (loop=4;loop<=11;loop++)
       clear_line_from(loop,2,50,0);

                              /* Set limits and position back */
                              /* to previous before submenu.  */
   set_mouse_hlimits(1,VID_MAXX-MOUSE_SIZE+1);
   set_mouse_vlimits(1,VID_MAXY-MOUSE_SIZE);
   set_mouse_position(old_mousex,old_mousey);
   show_mouse_cursor();
   }


/* MODULE : SUBMENU CHOICE                                    */
/*-----------------------------------------------------------*/
/* Choice from within submenu. Tell user what choice, delay   */
/* a bit, erase message and continue.                         */
/* Input parameters                                           */
/*      number     - choice                                   */
/*      old_mousex,                                           */
/*      old_mousey - mouse coordinates before function call   */
/*                                                            */
void submenu_choice(int number,int old_mousex,int old_mousey)
   {
   hide_mouse_cursor();       /* Tell user what choice        */
   change_color(14);
   out_text_xy(27,7,"Sub Option #");out_int_xy(39,7,number);
   out_text_xy(41,7,"Chosen.");
```

```
printf("%c",7);              /* Beep at user              */
delay(2000);
clear_line_from(7,27,22,0);
                             /* Set cursor position to    */
                             /* previous before option.   */
set_mouse_position(old_mousex,old_mousey);
show_mouse_cursor();
}




/* MODULE : SUBMENU                                        */
/*-------------------------------------------------------*/
/* Routine handler for the vertical submenu.              */
/*                                                         */
void sub_menu(int old_mousex,int old_mousey)
   {
   unsigned char exit=0;     /* Exit status, menu choices  */
   int newchoice=0,oldchoice=0;

   draw_vmenu();             /* Draw the vertical submenu  */

   reset_event_status();     /* Reset all status variables */

   while (!exit)             /* Do until exit chosen       */
      {
      if (CURSOR_MOVED)      /* If cursor moved . . .      */
         {
         CURSOR_MOVED=0;
                             /* Update/Find menu choice    */
         newchoice=which_vchoice(CMX,CMY,&oldchoice);
         }

       if (LBUTTON_DOWN)     /* If left button pressed     */
          {
          LBUTTON_DOWN=0;

          switch(newchoice)  /* Act upon menu choice       */
             {
             case -1:break;  /* No choice                  */

                             /* Exit subroutine            */
            case  5:exit_sub_menu(old_mousex,old_mousey);
                  exit=1;
```

```
                    break;

                            /* Any other choice           */
            default:submenu_choice(newchoice,CMX,CMY);
                    break;
            }
                            /* Reset events after any choice */
        reset_event_status();
        }
      }
    }


            /*---------------------------*/
            /*  HORIZONTAL MENU HANDLING  */
            /*---------------------------*/



/* MODULE : DRAW HMENU                                     */
/*---------------------------------------------------------*/
/* Draw the initial top-line horizontal menu.              */
/*                                                         */
void draw_hmenu(void)
    {
    clear_line_from(2,2,20,0);   /* Clear graphic/text message */
    change_color(15);            /* Write the entire menu      */
    out_text_xy( 5,2,"Option#1");
    out_text_xy(25,2,"Option#2");
    out_text_xy(45,2,"Option#3");
    out_text_xy(65,2,"Exit    ");
    }



/* MODULE : DRAW HCHOICE                                   */
/*---------------------------------------------------------*/
/* Redraw a menu choice from the top-line horizontal menu. */
/* Input parameters                                        */
/*    number - choice to redraw                            */
/*                                                         */
void draw_hchoice(int number,int bcolor)
    {
    hide_mouse_cursor();
    switch(number)          /* Draw choice based on number  */
        {
        case 1:clear_line_from(2,5,10,bcolor);
```

```
            out_text_xy( 5,2,"Option#1");
            break;
    case 2:clear_line_from(2,25,10,bcolor);
            out_text_xy(25,2,"Option#2");
            break;
    case 3:clear_line_from(2,45,10,bcolor);
            out_text_xy(45,2,"Option#3");
            break;
    case 4:clear_line_from(2,65,10,bcolor);
            out_text_xy(65,2,"Exit     ");
            break;
    }
  show_mouse_cursor();
  }


/* MODULE : WHICH HCHOICE                                     */
/*------------------------------------------------------------*/
/* Top-line horizontal menu handler.                         */
/* Input parameters                                          */
/*          x,y - current mouse location                     */
/*      *lastcode - address of last menu choice              */
/* Output parameters                                         */
/*    Function returns the value of the current menu choice. */
/*    Returns -1 if not on a choice.                         */
/*    *lastcode - address contents are updated to current    */
/*              choice after change, or 0 if not on a choice*/
/*                                                           */
int which_hchoice(int x,int y,int *lastcode)
    {
    int code;

    if (IN_GMODE)            /* If in graphics mode, convert  */
        {                    /* to text coordinates.          */
        x=(x+HFONT_SIZE)/HFONT_SIZE;
        y=(y+VFONT_SIZE)/VFONT_SIZE;
        }

    code=-1;                 /* Set code to -1, invalid       */

    if (y==2)                /* If cursor on line 2           */
        {
                             /* Code=which choice cursor is in*/
        if ((x>=2)&&(x<=19))  code=1;
        if ((x>=20)&&(x<=39)) code=2;
```

```
      if ((x>=40)&&(x<=59)) code=3;
      if ((x>=60)&&(x<=79)) code=4;
      }

   if (code!=*lastcode)        /* If this choice not equal to  */
      {                        /* last choice then -           */
      if (code!=-1)            /* If this choice not invalid-  */
         {                     /* Draw last choice normal      */

         change_color(15);draw_hchoice(*lastcode,0);

                              /* Draw new choice HIGHLIGHTED   */
         change_color(0);draw_hchoice(code,15);
         change_background(0);
         *lastcode=code;       /* Update last choice to new    */
         }
      else                     /* Else if this choice invalid  */
         {                     /* mouse out of range then -    */
         if (*lastcode!=0)
            {                  /* Draw last choice normal       */
            change_color(15);
            draw_hchoice(*lastcode,0);
            *lastcode=0;       /* Set last code to zero         */
            }
         }
      }

   return(code);               /* Return this choice            */
   }




/* MODULE : MENU CHOICE                                         */
/*------------------------------------------------------------*/
/* Menu choice for options 2, 3 and 4. Menu option 1 calls     */
/* vertical submenu. Tell user what choice, delay a bit,       */
/* erase message and continue.                                 */
/* Input parameters                                            */
/*      number    - choice                                     */
/*      old_mousex,                                            */
/*      old_mousey - mouse coordinates before function call    */
/*                                                             */
void menu_choice(int number,int old_mousex,int old_mousey)
   {
   hide_mouse_cursor();
```

```
        change_color(14);          /* Tell user option              */
        out_text_xy(32,4,"Option #");
        out_int_xy(40,4,number);
        out_text_xy(42,4,"Chosen");

        printf("%c",7);            /* Beep at user                  */
        delay(2000);
        clear_line_from(4,32,22,0);
                                    /* Set limits and position back  */
                                    /* to previous before choice.    */
        set_mouse_position(old_mousex,old_mousey);
        show_mouse_cursor();
        }


                /*---------------------------*/
                /*            MAIN           */
                /* Main Uses Horizontal Menu */
                /* Bar, and Calls Vertical   */
                /* PopUp Menu When Option #1 */
                /* is Chosen.                */
                /*---------------------------*/


void main()
   {
   unsigned char exit=0;      /* Exit status, menu choices     */
   int newchoice=0,oldchoice=0;

   install_video(GMODE);      /* Install video system          */
   header();                  /* Draw header                   */
   reset_mouse();             /* Reset mouse                   */

   if (MOUSE_THERE)
      {
      out_text_xy(5,23,"Move the mouse cursor to a menu option,
                     press left mouse button...");

                              /* Set mouse horiz & vert limits */
      set_mouse_hlimits(1,VID_MAXX-MOUSE_SIZE+1);
      set_mouse_vlimits(1,VID_MAXY-MOUSE_SIZE);

                              /* Install event handler         */
      install_event_handler();
```

```
draw_hmenu();                /* Draw horizontal menu        */
show_mouse_cursor();
                             /* Do until exit or keypress   */
while ((!exit)&&(!kbhit()))
   {

   if (CURSOR_MOVED)    /* If cursor was moved . . .    */
      {                 /* Update/Find menu choice      */
      CURSOR_MOVED=0;
                             /*---------------------------*/
                             /* Notice that CMX & CMY are   */
                             /* ALWAYS current due to event */
                             /* handler and processor.      */
                             /*---------------------------*/

      newchoice=which_hchoice(CMX,CMY,&oldchoice);
      }

   if (LBUTTON_DOWN)    /* If left button pressed       */
      {
      LBUTTON_DOWN=0;
                             /* Act upon choice             */
      switch(newchoice)
         {
                             /* Option #1 chosen            */
         case  1:sub_menu(CMX,CMY);
               break;

                             /* No choice                   */
         case -1:break;

                             /* Exit chosen. Exit program.  */
         case  4:exit=1;
               break;

                             /* Option #2, #3, and #4       */
         default:menu_choice(newchoice,CMX,CMY);
               break;
         }
                             /* Reset events after any choice */
      reset_event_status();
      }

   }
```

```
    reset_mouse();              /* Reset mouse,deactivate ehandlr*/
    }

else mouse_error(10,4);

shut_down_video();
}
```

When you are running the program, pull up the submenu and choose "Sub-Menu Option#1". The message in Figure 9-1 appears.

Try running the program in text mode. Remember to change the line

install_video(GMODE)

to

install_video(TMODE)

Figure 9-1.   Choosing menu options

Finer Points and Details

To illustrate the following topics and discussions better, you are going to modify MOUSE14.C several times, recompile the program, and run it.

Restoring the Range

Take a look at the following code fragment from the function exit_sub_menu():

```
                        /* Set limits and position back      */
                        /* to previous before submenu.       */
set_mouse_hlimits(1,VID_MAXX-MOUSE_SIZE+1);
set_mouse_vlimits(1,VID_MAXY-MOUSE_SIZE);
```

When the vertical submenu is terminated, these statements restore the mouse cursor's movement range to the entire display. If you do not do this, the mouse cursor remains bound to the vertical menu's rectangular region and cannot move to any horizontal menu options.

To verify this, remove (or simply remark out) the statements set_mouse_hlimits() and set_mouse_vlimits() in the function exit_sub_menu(), recompile it, and run it. While the program is running, pull up the vertical menu and choose Exit. Notice that the mouse cursor is still limited to the vertical menu's boundaries, as shown in Figure 9-2, and you cannot exit the program with the mouse.

Press a key to exit the program normally. Do not press CTRL-BREAK *if the program is running from the integrated environment, or the event handler will remain active.*

When you exit from a submenu that limits the mouse cursor's movement range, always restore the range to the values used before the submenu was called.

Restoring the Mouse Cursor Position

Look again at the code fragment found in the function exit_sub_menu().

```
                        /* Set limits and position back  */
                        /* to previous before submenu.   */
set_mouse_hlimits(1,VID_MAXX-MOUSE_SIZE+1);
set_mouse_vlimits(1,VID_MAXY-MOUSE_SIZE);
set_mouse_position(old_mousex,old_mousey);
show_mouse_cursor();
```

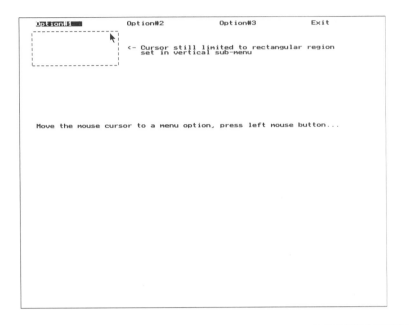

Figure 9-2.   Bad range management

In addition to restoring the mouse cursor's movement range, the mouse cursor's previous display location is also restored. The variables old_mousex and old_mousey are sent to the function exit_sub_menu() from sub_menu(), and sub_menu() receives the coordinates from main(), when the following line of code is executed:

```
        /* Option #1 chosen              */
case  1:sub_menu(CMX,CMY);
```

This is the mouse cursor's current location when the vertical submenu is initially activated. Try removing the statement set_mouse_position() from exit_sub_menu(), recompile the program, and run it. Pull up the vertical submenu and choose Exit. Notice the mouse cursor remains at the location of the vertical submenu's Exit option, as shown in Figure 9-3.

When exiting a submenu, always reposition the mouse cursor to its previous location before the submenu was activated.

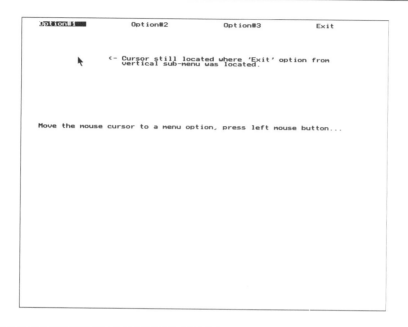

Figure 9-3.   *Bad location restoration*

Resetting Event Status Variables

Inside the main program loop, take a look at the following statement:

```
                /* Reset events after any choice */
reset_event_status();
```

The function reset_event_status() (created in Chapter 7) resets all event status variables to 0. The reason for doing this is that from the time the vertical submenu (or any other option) is terminated, there remains a brief instance that the user can move the mouse or press buttons when it is not desired. The function reset_event_status() ensures that no unwanted events are recorded during this time and subsequently trapped in the application. This function is also located before the menu loop is activated in the function sub_menu(). Again, it is to ensure no unwanted events are recorded and trapped.

To illustrate the effects that occur when status variables are not reset, remove the statements reset_event_status() from main(), and the function sub_menu().

Recompile the program and run it. Choose any menu option. From the time a choice is made to the time the mouse cursor returns to the menu option, move the mouse and press buttons. Quirky and unusual behavior occurs. You must remember, the event handler is *always* active.

Although it's only necessary to reset the status variables your application traps (LBUTTON_DOWN, RBUTTON_DOWN, and so on), you don't need to concern yourself with the individual status variables if you use the function reset_event_status(). The function reset_event_status() resets them all.

Keyboard Input

Within applications that utilize the mouse, keyboard input is usually handled in a normal fashion. However, in a sharp and lively application, using keystrokes will not only pull up choices, but also emulate mouse movement and option highlighting.

The following code fragment demonstrates using keyboard and mouse input to choose menu options. To use it, you must edit the previous example MOUSE14.C. Replace the entire contents of main() with the following code, which is also located on the companion disk and is called KBMENU.INC.

The new code fragment uses the keys 1, 2, 3, and E to represent the four menu options. E represents Exit in the main menu. The code fragment uses mouse and keyboard input in the main horizontal menu only.

Here is KBMENU.INC:

```
/*---------------------------*/
/*            MAIN           */
/* Main Uses Horizontal Menu */
/* Bar, and Calls Vertical   */
/* Pop-Up Menu When Option #1 */
/* is Chosen.                */
/*---------------------------*/
void main()
   {
   char keypress;
   unsigned char exit=0;       /* Exit status, menu choices   */
   int newchoice=0,oldchoice=0;
   unsigned char pb1,pb2;      /* Phony button 1 and 2        */

   install_video(GMODE);       /* Install video system        */
   header();                   /* Draw header                 */
   reset_mouse();              /* Reset mouse                 */
```

```
if (MOUSE_THERE)
   {
   out_text_xy(5,21,"Move the mouse cursor to a menu option,
                     press left mouse button...");

   out_text_xy(5,23,"Or use the keys '1', '2', '3', and 'E'
                     to choose options");

                         /* Set mouse horiz & vert limits */
   set_mouse_hlimits(1,VID_MAXX-MOUSE_SIZE+1);
   set_mouse_vlimits(1,VID_MAXY-MOUSE_SIZE);

                         /* Install event handler        */
   install_event_handler();

   draw_hmenu();          /* Draw horizontal menu          */
   show_mouse_cursor();
                         /* Do until exit or keypress     */
   while (!exit)
      {       (
      if (kbhit())        /* User pressed key             */
         {
         keypress=getch();
         switch(keypress) /* Was key a menu option?       */
            {
            case '1':if (IN_GMODE)
                       set_mouse_position(10*HFONT_SIZE,
                                 2*VFONT_SIZE-VFONT_SIZE);
                     else
                       set_mouse_position(10,2);

                     get_mouse_button(&pb1,&pb2,&CMX,&CMY);
                     newchoice=which_hchoice(CMX,CMY,
                                             &oldchoice);
                     sub_menu(CMX,CMY);
                     break;

            case '2':if (IN_GMODE)
                       set_mouse_position(30*HFONT_SIZE,
                                 2*VFONT_SIZE-VFONT_SIZE);
                     else
                       set_mouse_position(30,2);

                     get_mouse_button(&pb1,&pb2,&CMX,&CMY);
                     newchoice=which_hchoice(CMX,CMY,
```

```
                                        &oldchoice);
                menu_choice(newchoice,CMX,CMY);
                break;

        case '3':if (IN_GMODE)
                    set_mouse_position(50*HFONT_SIZE,
                            2*VFONT_SIZE-VFONT_SIZE);
                else
                    set_mouse_position(50,2);

                    get_mouse_button(&pb1,&pb2,&CMX,&CMY);
                    newchoice=which_hchoice(CMX,CMY,
                                        &oldchoice);
                    menu_choice(newchoice,CMX,CMY);
                    break;


        case 'e':
        case 'E':if (IN_GMODE)
                    set_mouse_position(70*HFONT_SIZE,
                            2*VFONT_SIZE-VFONT_SIZE);
                else
                    set_mouse_position(70,2);

                    get_mouse_button(&pb1,&pb2,&CMX,&CMY);
                    newchoice=which_hchoice(CMX,CMY,
                                        &oldchoice);
                    exit=1;
                    break;
        }
    }

    if (CURSOR_MOVED)     /* If cursor was moved . . .     */
        {                 /* Update/Find menu choice       */
        CURSOR_MOVED=0;
                            /*-----------------------------*/
                            /* Notice that CMX & CMY are    */
                            /* ALWAYS current due to event  */
                            /* handler and processor.       */
                            /*-----------------------------*/

        newchoice=which_hchoice(CMX,CMY,&oldchoice);
        }

    if (LBUTTON_DOWN)     /* If left button pressed        */
```

```
                    {
                    LBUTTON_DOWN=0;
                                    /* Act upon choice              */
                    switch(newchoice)
                        {
                                    /* Option #1 chosen             */
                        case   1:sub_menu(CMX,CMY);
                                break;

                                    /* No choice                    */
                        case -1:break;

                                    /* Exit chosen. Exit program.   */
                        case   4:exit=1;
                                break;

                                    /* Option #2, #3, and #4        */
                        default:menu_choice(newchoice,CMX,CMY);
                                break;
                        }
                                    /* Reset events after any choice */
                        reset_event_status();
                        }

                }

        reset_mouse();          /* Reset mouse,deactivate ehandlr*/
        }

else mouse_error(10,4);

shut_down_video();
}
```

Notice that the function set_mouse_position() is used to set the mouse cursor to the menu option location. However, setting the mouse cursor position does not create a mouse move event, and the global coordinates CMX and CMY are still set to the last coordinates. In normal routines this is OK, because the next mouse movement event sets CMX and CMY correctly, but for emulating menu choices, CMX and CMY must be updated first. To do this you can do one of these two things:

• Set CMX and CMY manually.

• Use the mouse library function get_button_status() and send CMX and CMY as the coordinate variables. They are then updated correctly.

That's it for menus. There's a lot of code to mull over, but it's worth mulling. Once you know how to implement this type of menuing system and understand the mechanics behind it, you'll be on the fast track to creating some very dynamic mouse-driven menus.

Chapter *10*

Using the Mouse as a Crosshair

In many scientific, stock market, simulation, and other applications, it becomes desirable to implement a crosshair. While many applications implement a crosshair by redefining the mouse cursor as a big + symbol, the crosshair presented in this chapter goes far beyond a simple cursor shape and offers a much more complex, interactive charting tool.

You learn how to redefine the mouse cursor in Chapter 14.

Defining the Crosshair

The crosshair presented in this chapter is a grid composed of a horizontal line and a vertical line, bound by a rectangular region, called the *crosshair region*. The horizontal crosshair line moves up or down in the region, and the vertical crosshair line moves from side to side. Where the two lines cross is called the *crosshair center*. The crosshair lines are represented by dashed lines, as shown in Figure 10-1.

The purpose of using a crosshair is generally to determine a numeric value of chart data at the crosshair center. Consider Figure 10-2.

The data in Figure 10-2 has values ranging from 0 to 20,000 vertically, and 0 to 10,000 horizontally. When users move the crosshair to a specific position on the chart, they see the values corresponding to the crosshair center.

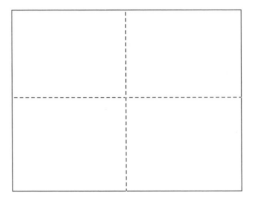

The Crosshair
Dashed Lines are Crosshair Lines
Solid Rectangle is Crosshair's Region

Figure 10-1.   *The crosshair*

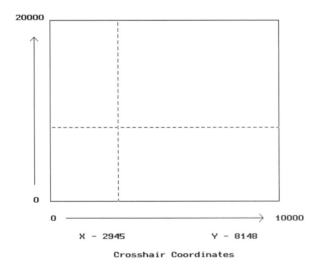

Figure 10-2.   *Crosshair chart coordinates*

Alternatively, some crosshairs use individual axes to represent different types of data. For instance, in stock market charts, the horizontal line is used to determine price levels, while the vertical line is used to represent time periods (dates). The two values are updated on the display as the crosshair moves.

Most applications implementing graphical charts do not define the entire display as the charting area (which is also the crosshair region), but instead use a rectangular area smaller than the actual display. This way, items such as menu choices can coexist on the display for other program functions.

Interacting with the Mouse Cursor

When an application using a crosshair is initialized, the mouse cursor is made visible and allowed to move about the display as normal, to pick menu choices or perform other operations. When the user moves the mouse cursor into the crosshair region, it is turned off (made invisible), and the crosshair is activated. While the crosshair is active, it literally becomes the operative mouse cursor, and the crosshair's center is used as the reference point. When the user moves the crosshair's center to one of the crosshair region's borders, it is deactivated and removed from the display, the mouse cursor is turned on (made visible), and mouse operations continue as normal.

In this manner, the mouse cursor and the crosshair work in unison to provide the user with a smooth flow of program operation, requiring no special commands to activate or deactivate the crosshair.

The Crosshair Algorithm

The algorithm to manage, update, draw, and figure chart coordinates for the crosshair routine is relatively simple, and in pseudocode would look something like this:

```
has mouse position changed?
if (yes)
   {
   is mouse cursor in crosshair region?
   if (yes)
      {
      is crosshair currently off?
      if (yes)
         {
         turn mouse cursor off
         turn crosshair on
```

```
        calculate chart values
        write chart values
        }
    else crosshair currently on
        {
        erase current crosshair
        draw crosshair using new coordinates
        calculate chart values
        write chart values
        }
    }
else
    {
    is crosshair exiting crosshair region?
    if (yes)
        {
        erase crosshair
        turn mouse cursor on
        }
    }
}
```

That's about all there is to it. In actuality, both the horizontal and the vertical coordinates are examined independently. This is because in many instances one crosshair line will be moving, and the other will not, depending on how the user is moving the mouse. As a result, it might not be necessary to redraw both crosshair lines for every mouse move, and the processing time used to draw a line is much more than an extra comparison to determine if the line should be drawn.

Crosshair Restriction

When the crosshair is active and moving, it *must* conform to one restriction. It *must not* disturb the background image it is moving over. To accomplish this, the crosshair's lines are drawn using the XOR drawing mode. This allows the crosshair to move over the background image without disturbing it (much like the mouse cursor moves over the background image without disturbing it). In the following example, look for the function setwritemode(XOR_PUT). This is where the line-drawing mode is changed to XOR.

Crosshair Example

Instead of going through the laborious task of actually developing a chart using actual data, the following example simply writes some text in the center of the crosshair region. This way, you will be able to determine that the XOR lines do not disturb the background image. Additionally, the program uses imaginary chart coordinates, hardcoded in the source file. The crosshair region is defined as a rectangular area located in the center of the display.

If compiling from the integrated environment, the project file is MOUSE15.PRJ. Here it is:

```
EVENT.OBJ
MOUSE15.C
```

Here is the example that implements a crosshair and manages chart coordinates, MOUSE15.C:

Run this example in graphics mode only!

```
/*------------------------------------------------------------*/
/*                    MOUSE15.C                           */
/*                                                        */
/* Demonstrate how to implement and use a crosshair and manage*/
/* chart coords.                                          */
/* RUN THIS ONLY IN GRAPHICS MODE !!!                     */
/*------------------------------------------------------------*/

#include "header2.h"

void main()
    {
    int newx=0,newy=0;,        /* Position when trapped       */
    unsigned char ch_on=0;     /* Crosshair on or off         */
    int x1,x2,y1,y2;           /* Crosshair's rect. region    */

    int max_chartx,max_charty;/* Max coords for imag. chart   */
    int min_chartx,min_charty;/* Min coords for imag. chart   */
    int x_divisor,y_divisor;  /* Crosshair/chart divisor      */
    int actual_number;        /* Actual num from imag. chart  */
```

```
    min_chartx=0;              /* Set minimum coords to 0    */
    min_charty=0;
    max_chartx=10000;          /* Max horiz for imag. chart  */
    max_charty=20000;          /* Max vert for imag. chart   */

    install_video(GMODE);      /* Install video system       */
    header();                  /* Draw header                */
    reset_mouse();             /* Reset mouse                */

if (MOUSE_THERE)
    {
    x1=VID_MAXX/4;             /* Set the crosshair's        */
    x2=VID_MAXX/4*3;           /* rectangular region.        */
    y1=VID_MAXY/4;
    y2=VID_MAXY/4*3;

                               /* Figure out what each coord */
                               /* move is in imag. chart     */
                               /* coordinates. Pixel = ?     */
    x_divisor=(max_chartx-min_chartx) / (x2-x1);
    y_divisor=(max_charty-min_charty) / (y2-y1);

    change_color(4);           /* Draw the imaginary chart brdr.*/
    draw_rectangle(x1,y1,x2,y2);

                               /* Label the chart with min   */
                               /* and max values.            */
    change_color(15);
    out_int_xy(x1/HFONT_SIZE-4,y1/VFONT_SIZE+1,max_charty);
    out_int_xy(x1/HFONT_SIZE-4,y2/VFONT_SIZE+1,min_charty);
    out_int_xy(x1/HFONT_SIZE+2,y2/VFONT_SIZE+4,min_chartx);
    out_int_xy(x2/HFONT_SIZE+1,y2/VFONT_SIZE+4,max_chartx);

                               /* Write a message in center  */
                               /* of crosshair region.       */
    change_color(10);
    out_text_xy(27,(y1+((y2-y1)/2))/VFONT_SIZE-2,
                " In Real Time, A Graph");

    out_text_xy(27,(y1+((y2-y1)/2))/VFONT_SIZE,
                "Representing Data Would Be");

    out_text_xy(27,(y1+((y2-y1)/2))/VFONT_SIZE+2,
                "       Written Here");
```

```
change_color(14);        /* Write out coord identifiers   */
out_text_xy(30,VID_MAXY/VFONT_SIZE,"X - ");
out_text_xy(50,VID_MAXY/VFONT_SIZE,"Y - ");

out_text_xy(5,4,"Move the cursor into the inner rectangle
               to see crosshair/chart coords.");
out_text_xy(5,6,"Press any key to exit demonstration...");

                         /* Limit cursor movement range   */
set_mouse_hlimits(1,VID_MAXX-MOUSE_SIZE+1);
set_mouse_vlimits(1,VID_MAXY-MOUSE_SIZE);

                         /* Install the event handler     */
install_event_handler();

set_mouse_position(5,5);/* Set mouse position to 5,5      */
newx=5;newy=5;,          /* Set coords                    */

                         /* Change color to white         */
                         /* SET WRITE MODE TO XOR !!!!     */
change_color(15);        /* SET LINESTYLE TO DASHED !      */
setwritemode(XOR_PUT);
setlinestyle(DASHED_LINE,0,NORM_WIDTH);

show_mouse_cursor();     /* Show the mouse cursor          */


while (!kbhit())         /* Do until user presses a key    */
   {
   if (CURSOR_MOVED)     /* If cursor moved                */
      {
      CURSOR_MOVED=0;
                         /* Is cursor in crosshair region?*/

      if ((CMX>=x1)&&(CMX<=x2)&&(CMY>=y1)&&(CMY<=y2))
         {

         if (!ch_on)    /* Is the crosshair currently      */
            {            /* off?                            */
            ch_on=1;    /* Then turn it on                  */
                         /* Trap coords, draw crosshair     */
            hide_mouse_cursor();
            newx=CMX;newy=CMY;
            change_color(15);
```

```
line(x1,newy,x2,newy);
line(newx,y1,newx,y2);

            /* Figure actual number based on */
            /* the crosshair/chart coords    */
            /* and write them.               */

change_color(11);
actual_number=(y2-newy)*y_divisor;
out_int_xy(54,VID_MAXY/VFONT_SIZE,actual_number);
actual_number=(newx-x1)*x_divisor;
out_int_xy(34,VID_MAXY/VFONT_SIZE,actual_number);
change_color(15);
}
else        /* Else crosshair is already on, */
{           /* so has vertical coord changed?*/
if (CMY!=newy)
    {
            /* Erase last horizontal line    */
    line(x1,newy,x2,newy);
    newy=CMY;
            /* Draw new horizontal line      */
    line(x1,newy,x2,newy);

            /* Figure actual number based on */
            /* the crosshair/chart coords    */
            /* and write them.               */
    change_color(11);
    actual_number=(y2-newy)*y_divisor;
    clear_line_from(VID_MAXY/VFONT_SIZE,
                54,5,0);
    out_int_xy(54,VID_MAXY/VFONT_SIZE,
                actual_number);

    change_color(15);
    }
            /* Has horiz coord changed?      */
if (CMX!=newx)
    {
            /* Erase last vertical line      */
    line(newx,y1,newx,y2);
    newx=CMX;
            /* Draw new vertical line        */
    line(newx,y1,newx,y2);
```

```
                          /* Figure actual number based on */
                          /* the crosshair/chart coords    */
                          /* and write them.               */
                change_color(11);
                actual_number=(newx-x1)*x_divisor;
                clear_line_from(VID_MAXY/VFONT_SIZE,
                            34,5,0);
                out_int_xy(34,VID_MAXY/VFONT_SIZE,
                            actual_number);
                change_color(15);
                }
            }


        }
    else                /* Else cursor is not in         */
        {               /* crosshair's region.           */

        if (ch_on)      /* Was cursor in crosshair regn? */
            {
                        /* If yes then -                 */
                        /* Erase last horiz/vert line    */
            line(x1,newy,x2,newy);
            line(newx,y1,newx,y2);

                        /* Clear the coords since out    */
            clear_line_from(VID_MAXY/VFONT_SIZE,54,5,0);
            clear_line_from(VID_MAXY/VFONT_SIZE,34,5,0);

            ch_on=0;    /* Turn crosshair var to off     */
            show_mouse_cursor();
            }
        }
        }
    }
    reset_mouse();
    }

else mouse_error(5,4);

getch();
shut_down_video();
}
```

When you run the program and move the mouse cursor into the crosshair region, the display resembles Figure 10-3.

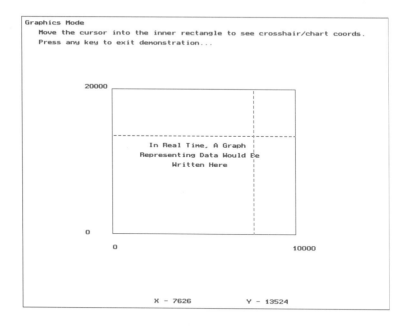

Figure 10-3. *Using the crosshair*

Program Details

In order for you better to understand some of the finer points of crosshair management, the following sections explore a few coding details from the previous example.

Defining the Crosshair

When MOUSE15.C is initialized, the crosshair's region is defined as a rectangular area occupying the center of the display. This is determined with the following code:

```
x1=VID_MAXX/4;         /* Set the crosshair's      */
x2=VID_MAXX/4*3;       /* rectangular region.      */
y1=VID_MAXY/4;
y2=VID_MAXY/4*3;
```

The variables x1, x2, y1, and y2 represent the crosshair's rectangular region. The region is 25 percent in from the display's left, right, top, and bottom borders.

Turning the Mouse Cursor Off

When the mouse cursor is not it the crosshair region, it is functioning as a normal mouse cursor. The instant you move it into the crosshair region, it is turned off (made invisible), and the crosshair is turned on. The mouse cursor's entry into the crosshair's region is determined like this:

```
if (CURSOR_MOVED)     /* If cursor moved              */
   {
   CURSOR_MOVED=0;
                       /* Is cursor in crosshair region?*/

   if ((CMX>=x1)&&(CMX<=x2)&&(CMY>=y1)&&(CMY<=y2))
      {
      if (!ch_on)    /* Is the crosshair currently   */
         {           /* off?                         */
         ch_on=1;    /* Then turn it on              */
                     /* Trap coords, draw crosshair  */
         hide_mouse_cursor();
         newx=CMX;newy=CMY;
         change_color(15);
         line(x1,newy,x2,newy);
         line(newx,y1,newx,y2);
```

When a CURSOR_MOVED event is trapped, the mouse cursor's current coordinates, CMX and CMY, are examined to determine if the mouse cursor is in the crosshair's region defined by x1, x2, y1, and y2. If it is, the variable ch_on is examined to determine if the crosshair is already on. If not, the mouse cursor is turned off using hide_mouse_cursor(), and the crosshair is activated by setting ch_on to 1 and drawing the crosshair.

Turning the Mouse Cursor On

When you move the crosshair's center to a border of the crosshair's rectangular region, the crosshair is deactivated, the crosshair lines erased, and the mouse cursor is turned on (made visible). This is accomplished with the following code:

```
else            /* Else cursor is not in        */
   {            /* crosshair's region.          */

   if (ch_on)   /* Was cursor in crosshair regn? */
```

```
{
                /* If yes then -              */
                /* Erase last horiz/vert line  */
        line(x1,newy,x2,newy);
        line(newx,y1,newx,y2);

                /* Clear the coords since out  */
        clear_line_from(VID_MAXY/VFONT_SIZE,54,5,0);
        clear_line_from(VID_MAXY/VFONT_SIZE,34,5,0);

        ch_on=0;    /* Turn crosshair var to off    */
        show_mouse_cursor();
        }
    }
```

If the cursor's current coordinates are not in the crosshair's region, the variable
ch_on is examined to determine if the cursor was previously in the region. If not, no
further action is taken, because the mouse cursor is already on and functioning in a
normal fashion. If the coordinates were previously in the region, the crosshair's lines
are erased, the crosshair is deactivated by setting ch_on to 0, and the mouse cursor
is turned on using show_mouse_cursor().

Defining the Chart Coordinates

The data the crosshair is tracking in the crosshair region must have minimum and
maximum numeric values; otherwise it is impossible to determine a numeric value
for the data the crosshair's center is on. To keep things simple, the previous example
uses imaginary chart data. The minimum and maximum values are defined as follows:

```
min_chartx=0;           /* Set minimum coords to 0      */
min_charty=0;
max_chartx=10000;       /* Max horiz for imag. chart    */
max_charty=20000;       /* Max vert for imag. chart     */
```

The variable max_chartx represents the maximum obtainable numeric value in the
horizontal direction, and min_chartx is the minimum numeric value. The variable
max_charty represents the maximum obtainable numeric value in the vertical direction, and min_charty is the minimum numeric value.

When you create your own charts using *real* data, be sure to set these values to
reflect *your* chart data.

Converting Display Coordinates to Chart Data

Determining where the crosshair's center is in relation to the chart data is a bit complex. Some conversions and a little mathematics are required.

Pixel and Data Values

Since the crosshair's location is determined in pixels, you must determine what value a pixel represents in the chart data. For instance, suppose a chart contains data with values ranging from 1,000 to 11,000. The maximum number of possible chart values is 10,000, or 11,000 − 1,000. If the physical chart is drawn from horizontal pixel location 200, to horizontal pixel location 300, the chart occupies 100 horizontal pixels, or 300 − 200. By dividing the chart data range by the pixel location range, the chart value each individual pixel represents is obtained. So, 10,000 / 100 = 100, meaning each pixel represents a chart value of 100. This value is called the *chart divisor*. If the chart has different maximum values for horizontal and vertical data, then two divisors are required: one for the horizontal data and one for the vertical data.

In the previous example, the chart's data divisors are obtained with the following two lines of code:

```
x_divisor=(max_chartx-min_chartx) / (x2-x1);
y_divisor=(max_charty-min_charty) / (y2-y1);
```

Anchoring the Coordinates

When you move the cursor, the actual crosshair's display coordinates are anchored using the coordinates CMX and CMY, which are set in the C event processor when the mouse moves. The anchors are set like this:

```
newx=CMX;newy=CMY;
```

The reason for this is to ensure that the values do not change (if you are still moving the mouse) while the chart values are being determined (see Chapter 8 in the section "Using the Mouse Cursor Coordinates").

Actual Chart Data Values

After the crosshair coordinate achors are set, the actual chart data value for the vertical location is determined and written to the display with the following two lines of code:

```
actual_number=(y2-newy)*y_divisor;
out_int_xy(54,VID_MAXY/VFONT_SIZE,actual_number);
```

Next the chart data value for the horizontal location is determined and written to the display:

```
actual_number=(newx-x1)*x_divisor;
out_int_xy(34,VID_MAXY/VFONT_SIZE,actual_number);
```

Why a Crosshair?

When you are determining whether to provide a crosshair in your application, consider the following: By implementing a crosshair, you allow users of your application to determine data levels in a chart without necessarily having to be at the exact chart location. Since the crosshair lines span the entire width or length of the chart, data levels are easily determined anywhere on the chart, simply by moving one crosshair line on the desired axis. If you are writing applications that use charts and data levels, your end users will be elated when they discover a crosshair implementation.

Chapter **11**

Using the Mouse in CAD-Type Operations

In this chapter, you learn mouse techniques used in CAD, painting, and other related applications. This chapter does not teach you how to build a full-fledged CAD or related application, but merely demonstrates the concepts relating to the mouse.

About the only technique needed for CAD-type applications that has not been discussed in the previous chapters is how to stretch graphics shapes, or objects, using the mouse. These objects might be lines, rectangles, ellipses, or a multitude of other graphics objects. This chapter teaches how to stretch lines, rectangles, and ellipses. After learning these techniques, you should be able to apply them to any other graphics shape or object.

Stretching or Dragging?

While the terms "stretching" and "dragging" are sometimes used synonymously, there is a fundamental difference you should be sure to understand before continuing:

- *Stretching* implies that a graphics shape, with a known starting location, has one end moved to a new location, using the mouse, leaving the other end in its starting location. The shape's size and possibly its proportions are changed.

- *Dragging* implies that a stationary graphics object, known in size, is "grabbed", and relocated to a new display location by dragging it with the mouse, retaining its original size and shape.

In this chapter, the graphics object being drawn starts at a location set by the user and is stretched to a new size or shape, ending at any desired location.

Stretching a Graphics Object

As an example of how a graphics object is stretched in a typical CAD-type application, consider the following sequence of events that occur when a line is drawn:

1. The user moves the mouse cursor to the location where the line is to be initiated.

2. The user presses a mouse button, which drops an *anchor*. Anchors are the starting and ending coordinates of a particular graphics shape or object.

3. While the mouse button is held down, the user moves the mouse cursor about the display. While doing so, the line is continuously updated and redrawn from the starting anchor to the current location of the mouse cursor.

4. When the user reaches the desired ending location, the mouse button is released, and a second anchor, or *endpoint*, is dropped. The line then remains fixed on the display, defined by the two anchors, or endpoints.

This should be a familiar process to those of you currently using CAD-type applications.

Dropping the Anchors

The variations of how to drop anchors, or endpoints, is as limitless as the human imagination. Some frequently seen techniques are:

- Using one button, with button presses only.

  a. The user presses a button to drop the first anchor.

  b. The user stretches the graphics object to desired location.

  c. The user presses the same button again to drop the second anchor.

- Using two buttons, with button presses only.

  a. The user presses the left button to drop the first anchor.

  b. The user stretches the graphics object to the desired location.

  c. The user presses the right button to drop the second anchor.

- Using one button, with button presses and releases.

  a. The user presses a button to drop the first anchor.

  b. While the button is held down, the user stretches the graphics object to the desired location.

  c. The user releases the button to drop the second anchor.

All three methods work just fine and are valid. However, the third method offers two advantages:

- The user is forced to hold the button down while drawing and stretching and is less likely to leave the computer in the middle of a drawing operation (which happens frequently in office environments).

- The left button can be used as the drawing and stretching tool, leaving the right button free for other tasks, such as an *undo* option.

If you wish, you could choose to use the right button as the drawing and stretching tool, and the left button for other tasks.

The Undo Option

Most commercial applications allow the user to undo the last operation performed, and many applications allow undo operations many levels deep. The term *undo* means to cancel the previous operation, and restore the state of the program to that prior to the operation. In CAD applications, the undo option is normally used to delete the last graphics object drawn or restore the last graphics object deleted.

To illustrate the undo feature, the following examples use the right mouse button as an undo option. However, to keep matters simple, the examples only allow the last graphics object drawn to be "undone," or deleted.

XOR and COPY_PUT Drawing Modes

Like the crosshair presented in Chapter 10, when a graphics object is being drawn and stretched on the display, it *must not* disturb the background image it is drawing over. To accomplish this, the graphics object is drawn using the XOR drawing mode, which allows the object to move over the background image without disturbing it.

To erase an object drawn in the XOR drawing mode, redraw the object at the same location in the XOR drawing mode.

After the user has completed drawing and stretching a graphics object, the drawing mode is switched back to the COPY_PUT mode (which is the default mode), so that items such as menus boxes are drawn in a normal fashion, replacing the underlying background. Although there are no program menus in the following example, the mode is changed to demonstrate how and when to switch drawing modes.

In the following example, MOUSE16.C, look for the statements set_write_mode(XOR_PUT) and set_write_mode(COPY_PUT). This is where the drawing mode is changed to XOR and COPY_PUT modes.

Line Stretching Example

The first CAD example is a line drawing and stretching program. You can draw as many lines as you like with the program. Press any key to quit.

Run this example in graphics mode only!

Here is the project file, MOUSE16.PRJ:

```
EVENT.OBJ
MOUSE16.C
```

And here is MOUSE16.C:

```
/*------------------------------------------------------------*/
/*                      MOUSE16.C                          */
/*                                                         */
/* CAD #1 DEMO, Line Manipulation. RUN ONLY IN GRAPHICS MODE!!*/
/*------------------------------------------------------------*/

#include "header2.h"          /* Directives, headers, includes */

void main()
    {
    int newx=0,newy=0;           /* Mouse cursor positions       */
    int anchorx=0,anchory=0;     /* Anchors, coords for last line */
    int lastx1=0,lasty1=0,lastx2=0,lasty2=0;
    unsigned char draw_on=0;

    install_video(GMODE);        /* Install video system         */
    header();                    /* Draw header                  */
    reset_mouse();               /* Reset mouse                  */

    if (MOUSE_THERE)
        {
```

```
clear_line_from(2,2,20,0);
out_text_xy(5,2,"CAD Demo #1, Line Manipulation.");

out_text_xy(5,4, "To stretch a line, press left button,");
out_text_xy(5,5, "hold down, and draw line by moving");
out_text_xy(5,6, "the mouse. To set line to permanent");
out_text_xy(5,7, "position, release left button.  ");
out_text_xy(5,9, "To erase (Undo) last line drawn, ");
out_text_xy(5,10,"press and release right button. ");
out_text_xy(5,12,"Draw as many lines as you like. ");
out_text_xy(5,14,"Press any key to exit...");

                        /* Set horiz & vert limits      */
set_mouse_hlimits(1,VID_MAXX-MOUSE_SIZE+1);
set_mouse_vlimits(1,VID_MAXY-MOUSE_SIZE);

                        /* Install the event handler    */
install_event_handler();
show_mouse_cursor();

while (!kbhit())        /* Do until user presses a key   */
   {
                        /* If cursor moved and draw on    */
   if ((CURSOR_MOVED)&&(draw_on))
      {
      CURSOR_MOVED=0;
      hide_mouse_cursor();
                        /* Erase last line, old coords   */
      line(anchorx,anchory,newx,newy);

                        /* Draw new line, new coords      */
      newx=CMX;newy=CMY;
      line(anchorx,anchory,newx,newy);
      show_mouse_cursor();
      }

   else if (!draw_on)  /* If not in drawing mode          */
      {
      if (LBUTTON_DOWN)
         {
         LBUTTON_DOWN=0;
         draw_on=1;    /* Start drawing, set to 1         */
         newx=CMX;
         newy=CMY;
         anchorx=newx; /* Set the anchors                 */
```

```
      anchory=newy;
      hide_mouse_cursor();
      change_color(10);

                        /* MODE TO XOR! Draw initial line*/
      setwritemode(XOR_PUT);
      line(anchorx,anchory,newx,newy);
      show_mouse_cursor();
      }
                        /* Erase last, Undo              */
  if (RBUTTON_DOWN)
     {
     RBUTTON_DOWN=0;
                        /* Make sure there is a line to  */
                        /* erase. IF SO-                 */
     if (lastx1!=0)
        {
        hide_mouse_cursor();

                        /* MODE TO XOR! Erase last line  */
        setwritemode(XOR_PUT);
        line(lastx1,lasty1,lastx2,lasty2);

                        /* Set mode back to COPY_PUT     */
        setwritemode(COPY_PUT);
        lastx1=0;

        show_mouse_cursor();
        }
     }
  }
                        /* Left button rlsd, in draw mode*/
  if ((LBUTTON_UP)&&(draw_on))
     {
     LBUTTON_UP=0;LBUTTON_DOWN=0;

     draw_on=0;         /* Stop drawing, set to 0        */

     lastx1=anchorx;    /* Set coords for last line      */
     lasty1=anchory;    /* drawn so it can be erased      */
     lastx2=newx;       /* with the Undo feature.        */
     lasty2=newy;
                        /* Set mode back to COPY_PUT     */
     setwritemode(COPY_PUT);
     }
```

```
    }
  reset_mouse();
  }


else mouse_error(10,4);


getch();


shut_down_video();
}
```

Using MOUSE16.C, the picture in Figure 11-1 was created.

Rectangle Stretching Example

The rectangle stretching example is an easy modification to the previous line drawing example, MOUSE16.C. Change *every* line() statement to a draw_rectangle() statement, recompile the program, and run it.

With this one conversion, the rectangles in Figure 11-2 were created.

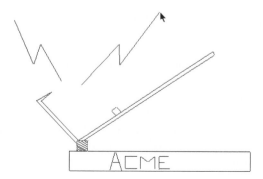

Figure 11-1.   *Drawing and stretching lines*

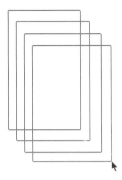

```
CAD Demo #1, Line Manipulation.
To stretch a line, press left button,
hold down, and draw line by moving
the mouse. To set line to permanent
position, release left button.
To erase (Undo) last line drawn,
press and release right button.
Draw as many lines as you like.
Press any key to exit...
```

Figure 11-2.　*Drawing and stretching rectangles*

Ellipse Stretching Example

The next example, which draws ellipses, is somewhat different than the previous example. Changing the write mode to XOR with the setwritemode() function does not affect an ellipse's drawing mode. It is always drawn in the COPY_PUT mode, meaning it will replace the background it is writing over. If you are an experienced low-level graphics programmer, you probably do not have this restriction with your own graphics library. Unfortunately, since the standard graphics libraries included with the Borland and Microsoft compilers are being used in this book, the limitation exists.

Due to the drawing-mode limitation, the ellipse cannot be stretched around in the same manner as the previous line and rectangle example. Here's how the limitation is dealt with: Since an ellipse can actually be defined by its rectangular borders, a rectangle is used as the stretching object. When the left button is released, the rectangle is converted into the appropriate ellipse. To highlight this feature, the rectangle is drawn using dashed lines.

Additionally, since the ellipse cannot be drawn in XOR mode, the only way to erase it with the undo option is to redraw it using the current background color. If you find a graphics library that allows you to XOR the ellipse, then the routines would follow the same erasing algorithm as the previous line and rectangle example.

　Run this example in graphics mode only!

Here is the project file, MOUSE17.PRJ:

```
EVENT.OBJ
MOUSE17.C
```

Here is MOUSE17.C:

```c
/*------------------------------------------------------------*/
/*                      MOUSE17.C                           */
/*                                                          */
/* CAD #2 DEMO.                                             */
/* Ellipse manipulation. Also demonstrates stretching a     */
/* rectangle.                                               */
/* RUN ONLY IN GRAPHICS MODE!!                              */
/*------------------------------------------------------------*/

#include "header2.h"          /* Directives, headers, includes */

void main()
    {
    int newx=0,newy=0;          /* Mouse cursor positions       */
    int anchorx=0,anchory=0;    /* Anchors, and ellipse coords  */
    int lastx=0,lasty=0,lastrx=0,lastry=0;
    int startex, startey, radex,radey;
    unsigned char draw_on=0;

    install_video(GMODE);       /* Install video system        */
    header();                   /* Draw header                 */
    reset_mouse();              /* Reset mouse                 */

    if (MOUSE_THERE)
       {
       clear_line_from(2,2,20,0);
       out_text_xy(5,2,"CAD Demo #2, Ellipse Manipulation.");

       out_text_xy(5,4, "To draw an ellipse, press left button");
       out_text_xy(5,5, "and hold down. Stretch the dashed    ");
       out_text_xy(5,6, "rectangle around until in a shape you");
       out_text_xy(5,7, "wish the ellipse to fill. To set and ");
       out_text_xy(5,8, "draw the actual ellipse, release the ");
       out_text_xy(5,9, "left button.                        ");
       out_text_xy(5,11,"To erase (Undo) last ellipse drawn, ");
       out_text_xy(5,12,"press and release right button.    ");
       out_text_xy(5,14,"Draw as many ellipses as you like. ");
```

```
        out_text_xy(5,16,"Press any key to exit...");

                            /* Set horiz & vert limits      */
        set_mouse_hlimits(1,VID_MAXX-MOUSE_SIZE+1);
        set_mouse_vlimits(1,VID_MAXY-MOUSE_SIZE);

                            /* Install the event handler     */
        install_event_handler();
        show_mouse_cursor();

        while (!kbhit())        /* Do until user presses a key   */
           {
                            /* If cursor moved and draw on    */
           if ((CURSOR_MOVED)&&(draw_on))
              {
              CURSOR_MOVED=0;
              hide_mouse_cursor();
                            /* Erase last rect., old coords  */
              draw_rectangle(anchorx,anchory,newx,newy);

                            /* Draw new rect., new coords     */
              newx=CMX;newy=CMY;
              draw_rectangle(anchorx,anchory,newx,newy);
              show_mouse_cursor();
              }

           else if (!draw_on)   /* If not in drawing mode        */
              {
              if (LBUTTON_DOWN)
                 {
                 LBUTTON_DOWN=0;
                 draw_on=1;    /* Start drawing, set to 1        */
                 newx=CMX;
                 newy=CMY;
                 anchorx=newx; /* Set the anchors                */
                 anchory=newy;
                 hide_mouse_cursor();
                 change_color(10);

                            /* MODE TO XOR! Also, linestyle  */
                            /* to dashed. Draw initial rect. */
                 setwritemode(XOR_PUT);
                 setlinestyle(DASHED_LINE,0,NORM_WIDTH);
                 draw_rectangle(anchorx,anchory,newx,newy);
                 show_mouse_cursor();
```

```
        }
                        /* Erase last, Undo        */
    if (RBUTTON_DOWN)
      {
      RBUTTON_DOWN=0;
                        /* Make sure there is a ellipse  */
                        /* to erase. IF SO-        */
      if (lastx!=0)
         {
         hide_mouse_cursor();

                        /* Erase last ellipse        */
         change_color(0);
         ellipse(lastx,lasty,
                0,360,
                lastrx,lastry);

         change_color(10);
         lastx=0;
         show_mouse_cursor();
         }
      }
   }
                        /* Left button rlsd, in draw mode*/
if ((LBUTTON_UP)&&(draw_on))
   {
   LBUTTON_UP=0;LBUTTON_DOWN=0;
   hide_mouse_cursor();

   draw_rectangle(anchorx,anchory,newx,newy);
   draw_on=0;       /* Stop drawing, set to 0        */

                     /* Check to see if horizontal    */
                     /* coords of rect are reversed   */
                     /* and figure ellipse.        */
   if (newx>=anchorx)
      {
      startex=anchorx+((newx-anchorx)/2);
      radex=(newx-anchorx)/2;
      }
   else
      {
      startex=newx+((anchorx-newx)/2);
      radex=(anchorx-newx)/2;
      }
```

```
                             /* Check to see if vertical    */
                             /* coords of rect are reversed  */
                             /* and figure ellipse.          */
         if (newy>=anchory)
            {
            startey=anchory+((newy-anchory)/2);
            radey=(newy-anchory)/2;
            }
         else
            {
            startey=newy+((anchory-newy)/2);
            radey=(anchory-newy)/2;
            }
                             /* Draw the new ellipse          */
         ellipse(startex,startey,
                 0,360,
                 radex,radey);

         lastx=startex;    /* Set coords for last ellipse   */
         lasty=startey;    /* drawn so it can be can erased.*/
         lastrx=radex;
         lastry=radey;

                             /* Set mode back to COPY_PUT     */
                             /* Linestyle back to solid       */
         setwritemode(COPY_PUT);
         setlinestyle(SOLID_LINE,0,NORM_WIDTH);
         show_mouse_cursor();
            }
         }
      reset_mouse();
      }

   else mouse_error(10,4);

   getch();

   shut_down_video();
   }
```

Figure 11-3 illustrates stretching the dashed rectangle on the display before it is converted into an ellipse.

When the left button is released, the rectangle converts to the ellipse, as shown in Figure 11-4.

```
CAD Demo #2, Ellipse Manipulation.

To draw an ellipse, press left button
and hold down. Stretch the dashed
rectangle around until in a shape you
wish the ellipse to fill. To set and
draw the actual ellipse, release the
left button.

To erase (Undo) last ellipse drawn,
press and release right button.

Draw as many ellipses as you like.

Press any key to exit...
```

Figure 11-3.   *Rectangular ellipse definition before button release*

```
CAD Demo #2, Ellipse Manipulation.

To draw an ellipse, press left button
and hold down. Stretch the dashed
rectangle around until in a shape you
wish the ellipse to fill. To set and
draw the actual ellipse, release the
left button.

To erase (Undo) last ellipse drawn,
press and release right button.

Draw as many ellipses as you like.

Press any key to exit...
```

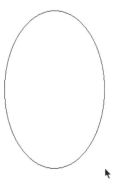

Figure 11-4.   *Ellipse after button is released*

That concludes the CAD-type programming examples. With the routines laid out in this chapter, you possess the necessary knowledge to utilize the mouse as a sophisticated drawing tool in any CAD-type application.

Chapter *12*

The Optional Mouse Functions

In Chapter 3, you created the ten necessary mouse functions. In Chapters 3 through 11, you learned all about using those ten functions. With them, you should be able to successfully interface with the mouse in every application you develop. However, there are many additional functions not considered necessary, but optional, whose utilization helps to add that touch of professionalism every programmer desires.

Six New Mouse Functions

In this chapter, six new functions are created for use in the mouse function library. The following list of the six new functions includes the function name, parameters, mouse function number called via interrupt 0x33, and a short description of what each function does.

get_mouse_type(int *maj_ver,int *min_ver,
        int *mtype,int *irq_num)   This function calls mouse function 36. It is used to determine the mouse type, version number, and IRQ number.

int get_crt_page(void)   This function calls mouse function 30. It is used to determine the current CRT page the mouse cursor is displayed on.

get_mouse_sensitivity(int **h_speed,*int **v_speed,*

int **threshold)*   This function calls mouse function 27. It returns the current speed sensitivity settings the mouse is using.

set_mouse_sensitivity(int *h_speed,*int *v_speed,*

int *threshold)*   This function calls mouse function 26. It is used to set the speed sensitivity settings for the mouse.

set_graphics_cursor(int far **cursor_mask,*

int *hotx,*int *hoty)*   This function calls mouse function 9. It sets the graphics mouse cursor shape to a new shape.

set_text_cursor(int *ctype,*

int *sm_or_sl,*int *cm_or_el)*   This function calls mouse function 10. It is used to modify the mouse text cursor.

Go ahead and look over the code for the optional functions, which are located in the file OPTIONAL.INC. Here it is:

```
/*--------------------------------------------------------------*/
/*                       OPTIONAL.INC                           */
/*                                                              */
/*            A Few Optional Mouse Functions                    */
/*                                                              */
/* These are functions considered optional. However, they can  */
/* be VERY useful, and add that extra touch of professionalism  */
/* to your applications.                                        */
/*--------------------------------------------------------------*/


/* MODULE : GET MOUSE TYPE                                      */
/*--------------------------------------------------------------*/
/* Function retrieves the mouse type, version number, and irq#  */
/* Input parameters                                             */
/*      Addresses of variables                                  */
/* Output parameters                                            */
/*      maj_ver - major version number                          */
/*      min_ver - minor version number                          */
/*      mtype   - type of mouse                                 */
/*      irq_num - irq_number                                    */
/*                                                              */
void pascal get_mouse_type(int *maj_ver,int *min_ver,
                           int *mtype,int *irq_num)
   {
```

```
   if (MOUSE_THERE)
      {
      mregs.x.ax=36;            /* Mouse function 36          */
      int86(0x33,&mregs,&mregs);

      *maj_ver=mregs.h.bh;    /* Major version number       */
      *min_ver=mregs.h.bl;    /* Minor version number       */
      *mtype  =mregs.h.ch;    /* Mouse type                 */
      *irq_num=mregs.h.cl;    /* Irq number                 */
      }
   }


/* MODULE : GET CRT PAGE                                          */
/*--------------------------------------------------------------*/
/* Function retrieves CRT page the current mouse cursor is       */
/* displayed on.                                                 */
/* Output parameters                                             */
/*    function returns page number                              */
int pascal get_crt_page(void)
   {
   if (MOUSE_THERE)
      {
      mregs.x.ax=30;            /* Mouse function 30          */
      int86(0x33,&mregs,&mregs);

      return(mregs.x.bx);     /* Return CRT page number     */
      }
   return(0);
   }


/* MODULE : GET MOUSE SENSITIVITY                                 */
/*--------------------------------------------------------------*/
/* Function gets the speed sensitivity level of the mouse.       */
/* Input parameters                                              */
/*    addresses of variables                                    */
/* Output parameters                                             */
/*    h_speed    = horizontal speed sensitivity (1 - 100)       */
/*    v_speed    = vertical speed sensitivity   (1 - 100)       */
/*    threshold = double speed threshold        (1 - 100)       */
/*                                                              */
void pascal get_mouse_sensitivity(int *h_speed,int *v_speed,
                                  int *threshold)
   {
   if (MOUSE_THERE)
      {
```

```
        mregs.x.ax=27;              /* Mouse function 27        */
        int86(0x33,&mregs,&mregs);

        *h_speed=mregs.x.bx;    /* Set horiz sensitivity       */
        *v_speed=mregs.x.cx;;   /* Set vert sensitivity        */
        *threshold=mregs.x.dx;  /* Set double speed threshld   */
        }
    }


/* MODULE : SET MOUSE SENSITIVITY                               */
/*------------------------------------------------------------*/
/* Function sets the speed sensitivity level of the mouse.     */
/* Input parameters                                            */
/*    h_speed   = horizontal speed sensitivity (1 - 100)       */
/*    v_speed   = vertical speed sensitivity   (1 - 100)       */
/*    threshold = double speed threshold       (1 - 100)       */
/*                                                             */
void pascal set_mouse_sensitivity(int h_speed,int v_speed,
                                  int threshold)
    {
    if (MOUSE_THERE)
        {                       /* Make check for some OEMs     */
        if (h_speed<=0) h_speed=1;
        if (v_speed<=0) v_speed=1;
        if (threshold<=0) threshold=1;

        mregs.x.ax=26;          /* Mouse function 26            */
        mregs.x.bx=h_speed;     /* Set horiz sensitivity        */
        mregs.x.cx=v_speed;     /* Set vert sensitivity         */
        mregs.x.dx=threshold;   /* Set double speed threshld    */
        int86(0x33,&mregs,&mregs);
        }
    }


/* MODULE : SET GRAPHICS CURSOR                                 */
/*------------------------------------------------------------*/
/* Function resets the graphics cursor mask to a new mask. The*/
/* hot spot of the cursor mask can also be redefined.          */
/* Input parameters -                                          */
/*    *cursor_mask  - address of new cursor mask               */
/*     hotx         - new horizontal hot spot                  */
/*     hoty         - new vertical hot spot                    */
/*                                                             */
void pascal set_graphics_cursor(int far *cursor_mask,
                                int hotx,int hoty)
```

```
   {
if (MOUSE_THERE)
   {
   mregs.x.ax = 9;          /* Mouse function 9           */
   mregs.x.bx = hotx;       /* Set horiz hot spot         */
   mregs.x.cx = hoty;       /* Set vert hot spot          */

                            /* Point to cursor mask       */
   mregs.x.dx = FP_OFF(cursor_mask);
   msegregs.es= FP_SEG(cursor_mask);

   int86x(0x33,&mregs,&mregs,&msegregs);
   }
}


/* MODULE : SET TEXT CURSOR                                 */
/*--------------------------------------------------------*/
/* Function resets the text cursor.                         */
/* Input parameters                                         */
/*     ctype    - cursor type. 0 for software cursor, 1 for */
/*                hardware cursor                            */
/*     dm_or_sl - if software cursor then display mask,      */
/*                otherwise start line                       */
/*     cm_or_sl - if software cursor then cursor mask,       */
/*                otherwise end line                         */
/*                                                          */
void pascal set_text_cursor(int ctype,int sm_or_sl,int cm_or_el)
   {
   if (MOUSE_THERE)
      {
      mregs.x.ax=10;        /* Mouse function 10          */
      mregs.x.bx=ctype;     /* Type of cursor             */
      mregs.x.cx=sm_or_sl;  /* Disp mask or start line     */
      mregs.x.dx=cm_or_el;  /* Cursor mask or end line     */
      int86(0x33,&mregs,&mregs);
      }
   }
```

A new header file is required to incorporate the optional mouse functions into the programming examples. The new header file is called HEADER3.H, and here it is:

```
#include "compiler.h"      /* Compiler directives        */
#include "mouse.h"         /* Include global header file  */
#include "mouse.inc",      /* Include 10 mouse functions  */
```

```
#include "mevent.inc"        /* Event processor              */
#include "optional.inc"      /* Optional mouse functions     */
#include graphics
#include videolib            /* Include tiny video library   */
```

Using the Optional Functions

As the first example of using the optional mouse functions, the following program retrieves all the information the mouse driver can provide about itself (using these functions). The output will be discussed after the example.

The project file is MOUSE18.PRJ:

```
EVENT.OBJ
MOUSE18.C
```

Here is MOUSE18.C:

```c
/*-------------------------------------------------------------*/
/*                      MOUSE18.C                        */
/*                                                       */
/* Demo to return valuable information about the mouse driver.*/
/*-------------------------------------------------------------*/

#include "header3.h"         /* New header with optional funcs */

void main()
    {
    int mouse_type=0,        /* Bus,Serial,InPort,PS/2,HP?     */
        irq_num=0,           /* IRQ number                     */
        maj_ver=0,min_ver=0, /* Version numbers                */
        crt_page=0,          /* Current mouse display page     */
        h_speed=0,v_speed=0, /* Speed sensitivity settings     */
        ds_threshold=0;      /* Double-speed threshold         */

    install_video(TMODE);    /* Install video system           */
    header();                /* Draw header                    */
    reset_mouse();           /* Reset mouse                    */

    if (!MOUSE_THERE) mouse_error(10,4);

                             /* Set horiz & vert limits        */
    set_mouse_hlimits(1,VID_MAXX-MOUSE_SIZE+1);
    set_mouse_vlimits(1,VID_MAXY-MOUSE_SIZE);
```

```
out_text_xy(10,5,"Default Mouse Settings");
out_text_xy(10,6,"---------------------");
out_text_xy(10,22,"Press any key to exit.");

                               /* Get type, version, IRQ      */
get_mouse_type(&maj_ver,&min_ver,&mouse_type,&irq_num);

                               /* Get mouse display page       */
crt_page=get_crt_page();

                               /* Get speed sensitivity        */
get_mouse_sensitivity(&h_speed,&v_speed,&ds_threshold);

                               /* Write out mouse type         */
out_text_xy(10,8,"Mouse Type        -");
switch(mouse_type)
   {
   case 1:out_text_xy(30,8,"Bus Mouse");break;
   case 2:out_text_xy(30,8,"Serial Mouse");break;
   case 3:out_text_xy(30,8,"InPort Mouse");break;
   case 4:out_text_xy(30,8,"PS/2 Mouse");break;
   case 5:out_text_xy(30,8,"Hewlett-Packard Mouse");break;
   default:out_text_xy(30,8,"Unknown Mouse Type");break;
   }

                               /* IRQ# , disp page, version    */
out_text_xy(10,10,"Irq Number         -");
out_int_xy(30,10,irq_num);

out_text_xy(10,12,"Display Page       -");
out_int_xy(30,12,crt_page);

out_text_xy(10,14,"Major Version #   -");
out_int_xy(30,14,maj_ver);
out_text_xy(10,15,"Minor Version #    -");
out_int_xy(30,15,min_ver);→

                               /* Speed sensitivity            */

out_text_xy(10,17,"Horiz Sensitivity -");
out_int_xy(30,17,h_speed);
out_text_xy(10,18,"Vert  Sensitivity -");
out_int_xy(30,18,v_speed);
out_text_xy(10,19,"Double Speed Thres-");
```

```
out_int_xy(30,19,ds_threshold);

show_mouse_cursor();

getch();

hide_mouse_cursor();
shut_down_video();
}
```

Figure 12-1 is the information returned from the Microsoft serial mouse and mouse driver version 8.16.

About the Information

The following discussions explain a few details about the information returned from the previous example and how to use the information in your own applications.

Mouse Type and IRQ Number

The mouse type and IRQ number are especially useful for communications applications that use the serial ports, because you can determine if the mouse driver is using the same serial port and IRQ number the application intends to use. If it is, operations should be halted, and the user should be told to deactivate the mouse or use a different serial port for either the mouse or the application before operations can continue.

```
Graphics Mode

        Default Mouse Settings
        ----------------------

        Mouse Type        - Serial Mouse

        Irq Number        - 4

        Display Page      - 0

        Major Version #   - 8
        Minor Version #   - 16

        Horiz Sensitivity - 50
        Vert  Sensitivity - 50
        Double Speed Thres- 50

        Press any key to exit.
```

Figure 12-1.   *Program results with Microsoft serial mouse and driver version 8.16*

The mouse type installed on the system can be a bus, serial, InPort, PS/2, or Hewlett-Packard type mouse. If the mouse is a PS/2 mouse, the IRQ number is 0, because the mouse interrupt is not routed through the system interrupt controller(s), and the program is free to use the serial port. If the mouse is a bus mouse, InPort mouse, or serial mouse, the IRQ number must be compared against the IRQ number the application uses. Serial mice use IRQ 4 for COM1, and IRQ 3 for COM2. The bus mouse and the InPort mouse may use IRQ 2, IRQ 3, IRQ 4, or IRQ 5.

CRT Page

Suppose you are writing an application that performs some type of animation sequence. Most animation on the PC is done using page flipping, and it is very desirable to determine what CRT page the mouse cursor is displayed on at any given time, so that it can be hidden, made visible, or modified if necessary.

The display page for the mouse cursor can be set using mouse function 29, set CRT display page. It is not included in the mouse function library because its use is rare. See Appendix A for details regarding mouse function 29.

Major and Minor Version Numbers

If you use any of the mouse functions above mouse function 37 and do not know beforehand which mouse driver is installed, determining the version number is a requirement, because you must check to see if the mouse driver supports the advanced functions. Appendix A contains information regarding the version numbers in which specific functions became available in the Microsoft mouse driver. The OEM mouse drivers known to support all of the advanced mouse functions are Logitech's mouse driver version 6.1 and later, and Kraft's mouse driver version 8.2 and later.

Mouse function 50, get active advanced functions, can be used to determine if a particular advanced function is active. However, it became available in Microsoft's mouse driver version 7.05, and many of the advanced functions became available before version 7.05.

The speed sensitivity settings returned in the previous example are covered in the next chapter.

Chapter 13

Setting the Speed: Mickeys and Pixels

Allowing end users to change the speed of mouse cursor movement is a great enhancement to any mouse application, since users can then customize the application to suit their own personal preferences. Windows users should be familiar with setting the Mouse Tracking Speed from within the Control Panel. With the right GUI and a little imagination, the speed sensitivity example presented in this chapter could be modified to duplicate this Windows feature in DOS applications.

While changing the speed of mouse cursor movement is really very easy, it is also the source of much confusion. In the following sections, mouse cursor speed is broken down step by step, to provide you with a complete understanding of how speed is determined.

Mickeys

The most fundamental aspect of mouse movement is in the mouse itself. The ball that rolls in the bottom of the mouse moves internal components that track the movement in both horizontal and vertical directions. The smallest amount of movement that can be determined by the mouse is called a *mickey*. A mickey is approximately 1/200 inch in 200 dpi mice and 1/400 inch in 400 dpi mice. When the mouse moves, it sends the mickey count to the mouse driver, which in turn moves the mouse cursor the appropriate number of pixels on the display.

Mickey-to-Pixel Ratio

The number of pixels the mouse cursor moves for each mickey count is determined by the *mickey-to-pixel ratios*. The default ratios are 8 mickeys to 8 pixels horizontally and 16 mickeys to 8 pixels vertically. If you set the mickey-to-pixel ratios at 4:8 horizontally, and 8:8 vertically, the mouse cursor would move twice as far on the display, given the same amount of physical movement from the mouse.

This is why the event processor sets the CURSOR_MOVED status variable based on pixel coordinates, not actual mouse movement events. A mouse move event does not necessarily mean the mouse cursor's location has changed, because movement events sent by the mouse driver are based on mickey movement, not pixel location.

Multiplication Factor

Along with the mickey-to-pixel ratios, the mouse driver keeps an internal mickey multiplication factor. The multiplication factor is applied to the mickey count *before* the mickey-to-pixel ratio is utilized. The default multiplication factor is 1.

Assuming the horizontal mickey-to-pixel ratio is set at the default of 8 mickeys to 8 pixels, and the multiplication factor is set to 3, a move of 10 mickeys translates into 30 pixel moves ((10×3) × (8/8)). If the horizontal mickey-to-pixel ratio is set at 4 mickeys to 8 pixels, and the multiplication factor is 3, the same move of 10 mickeys translates into 60 horizontal pixel moves, ((10×3) × (8/4)).

Double-Speed Threshold

Another factor that affects the mouse's speed is the *double-speed threshold*. The double-speed threshold is a value specifying the number of mickeys the mouse must move per second before the mouse driver starts doubling the number of pixels the mouse cursor traverses. The default threshold is 64 mickeys per second. If the mickey-to-pixel ratio is set to the default of 8 to 8 horizontally, and the mouse moves faster than 64 mickeys in one second, the speed factor is doubled to 8 pixels for every 4 mickeys horizontally. The same logic applies to vertical movement.

Changing the Speed

Mouse function 15, set mickey-to-pixel ratio, allows you to set the number of mickeys it takes to move one pixel. Values can range from 1 to 32,767.

Mouse function 19, set double-speed threshold, allows you to set the double-speed threshold, measured in mickeys. You can effectively disable this feature by setting the value to a number of mickeys that can never be obtained, such as 10,000 mickeys per second.

Speed Sensitivity Rates

Instead of using both mouse functions 15 and 16 to set the mickey-to-pixel ratios and double-speed threshold, mouse function 26, set sensitivity rate, allows you to set both at the same time. However, instead of changing the ratios directly, mouse function 26 changes the internal multiplication factors. Mouse function 26 is located in the optional library function set_mouse_sensitivity(). Here's how it works:

The multiplication factors used internally by the mouse driver are changed using a sensitivity rate with a range of 0 to 100. The default sensitivity rate, 50, specifies the default multiplication factor of 1. Any value above 50 increases the multiplication factor, and any value below 50 decreases the multiplication factor. The maximum sensitivity rate of 100 yields a multiplication factor of approximately 3.5, and a sensitivity rate of 5 yields a multiplication factor of approximately 0.03125. Changing the sensitivity rate to a value below 3 effectively disables any mouse cursor movement.

Setting the sensitivity rates offers a much more natural approach to changing the speed, as opposed to setting the mickey-to-pixel ratios directly. This is because the values range from 0 to 100, with 0 being the lowest setting, and 100 being the highest. You can think of the speed sensitivity rates as the mouse's speedometer.

Before proceeding, take a look at the code fragment found in the mouse library function set_mouse_sensitivity().

```
if (MOUSE_THERE)
    {                           /* Make check for some OEMs      */
    if (h_speed<=0) h_speed=1;
    if (v_speed<=0) v_speed=1;
    if (threshold<=0) threshold=1;
```

Although the values of the sensitivity rates can range from 0 to 100, many low-quality OEM mice generate divide by zero errors when a value of 0 is used. Clearly, these low-quality drivers implement the scaling methods in an unsuitable manner. To ensure that divide errors do not occur, an internal check is made first to make sure a value of 0 is never sent to the mouse driver. Since setting the speed sensitivity rates to 3, 2, or 1 effectively disables any mouse cursor movement, there's no reason to let the value decrement to 0.

In fact, some OEMs are of such poor quality that the speed sensitivity settings have absolutely no effect, even though the manufacturer might claim to be 100 percent Microsoft compatible.

Mouse function 27, get_sensitivity rates, retrieves the speed sensitivity rates and double-speed threshold. It is located in the optional library function get_mouse_sensitivity().

Speed Sensitivity Example

The following example allows you to experiment with the full range of speed sensitivity rates. Since setting the speed sensitivity rates produces the most obvious effects on mouse cursor speed, this example does not allow the double-speed threshold to be modified. Become familiar with the speed sensitivity factors first. Double-speed threshold is demonstrated in a separate example.

The project file is MOUSE19.PRJ. Here it is:

```
EVENT.OBJ
MOUSE19.C
```

Here is MOUSE19.C:

```
/*-----------------------------------------------------------*/
/*                      MOUSE19.C                          */
/*                                                         */
/* Demonstration of setting the horizontal and vertical speed */
/* sensitivity, (mickey-to-pixel multiplication factors).    */
/*-----------------------------------------------------------*/

#include "header3.h"          /* New header with optional funcs*/

void main()
    {                          /* Speed values at startup      */
    int sh_speed,sv_speed,sds_threshold;
                               /* Working speed values         */
    int h_speed,v_speed,ds_threshold;

    install_video(GMODE);     /* Install video system         */
    header();                 /* Draw header                  */
    reset_mouse();            /* Reset mouse                  */

    if (MOUSE_THERE)
       {
                               /* Get rates at startup         */
       get_mouse_sensitivity(&sh_speed,&sv_speed,&sds_threshold);

                               /* Copy to working rates        */
       h_speed=sh_speed;v_speed=sv_speed;
       ds_threshold=sds_threshold;
```

```
                              /* Set horiz & vert limits    */
set_mouse_hlimits(1,VID_MAXX-MOUSE_SIZE+1);
set_mouse_vlimits(1,VID_MAXY-MOUSE_SIZE);

                         /* Install the event handler    */
install_event_handler();

out_text_xy(10,4,"Demonstration of setting the
                 mouse speed.");
out_text_xy(10,5,"Both horizontal and vertical rates
                 are set simultaneously.");
out_text_xy(10,7,"Press LEFT  button to increase speed
                 by 5.");
out_text_xy(10,8,"Press RIGHT button to decrease speed
                 by 5.");
out_text_xy(10,10,"Sensitivity range is from 1 to 100. ");
out_text_xy(10,11,"Move the mouse to 'feel' the new
                  speeds.");

                         /* Output initial speed         */
out_text_xy(10,15,"Horizontal Sensitivity Rate  - ");
out_text_xy(10,16,"Vertical   Sensitivity Rate  - ");
change_color(14);
out_int_xy(45,15,h_speed);
out_int_xy(45,16,v_speed);

show_mouse_cursor();

while (!kbhit())        /* While key not pressed        */
   {
   if (LBUTTON_DOWN)
      {                 /* If speed is 1, set to 5,     */
                        /* otherwise increase by 5.     */
      if (h_speed==1) {h_speed=5;v_speed=5;}
      else {h_speed+=5;v_speed+=5;}

                        /* Set new speed sensitivity rate*/
      set_mouse_sensitivity(h_speed,v_speed,ds_threshold);
      }

   if (RBUTTON_DOWN)
```

```
                    {                    /* Decrease speed by 5           */
                    h_speed-=5;v_speed-=5;

                                         /* Set new speed sensitivity rate*/
                    set_mouse_sensitivity(h_speed,v_speed,ds_threshold);
                    }
                                         /* If EITHER button was pressed  */
        if ((LBUTTON_DOWN)||(RBUTTON_DOWN))
                    {
                                         /* Get new speed to verify set   */
                    get_mouse_sensitivity(&h_speed,&v_speed,
                                     &ds_threshold);
                    hide_mouse_cursor();

                                         /* Write new values to display   */
                    clear_line_from(15,45,5,0);
                    clear_line_from(16,45,5,0);
                    out_int_xy(45,15,h_speed);
                    out_int_xy(45,16,v_speed);
                    show_mouse_cursor();

                                         /* Reset all event status vars    */
                    reset_event_status();
                    }
            }
                                         /* Reset speed to startup rates  */
        set_mouse_sensitivity(sh_speed,sv_speed,sds_threshold);
        reset_mouse();
        }

    else mouse_error(10,4);

    getch();
    shut_down_video();
    }
```

When you run the program, try setting the rates to 10, as in Figure 13-1—oh, so slow. . . .

Next try setting the rates to 100, the max—wow! The blazing mouse cursor.

Double-Speed Threshold Example

The following example allows you to modify the double-speed threshold. The speed sensitivity levels remain constant at a low value of 25, so you can better observe the

```
Graphics Mode
        Demonstration of setting the mouse speed.
        Both horizontal and vertical rates are set simultaneously.

        Press LEFT  button to increase speed by 5.
        Press RIGHT button to decrease speed by 5.

        Sensitivity range is from 1 to 100.
        Move the mouse to 'feel' the new speeds.


        Horizontal Sensitivity Rate  -      10
        Vertical   Sensitivity Rate  -      10
```

Figure 13-1.   *Setting the speed sensitivity rates*

effects of the double-speed threshold. The effects on speed are far less obvious than changing the speed sensitivity factors, so pay close attention to how the mouse speed "feels" when changing the threshold.

Logitech's mouse driver versions 6.1 and later no longer use the double-speed threshold, and it is a meaningless value. Logitech now uses the acceleration curves (ballistic speed) found in the advanced mouse functions. See Appendix A regarding mouse functions 43, 44, and 45.

The project file is MOUSE20.PRJ. Here it is:

```
EVENT.OBJ
MOUSE20.C
```

Here is MOUSE20.C:

```
/*------------------------------------------------------------*/
/*                       MOUSE20.C                          */
/*                                                          */
/* Demonstration of setting the double-speed threshold.     */
/*------------------------------------------------------------*/

#include "header3.h"            /* New header with optional funcs*/

void main()
    {                           /* Speed values at startup      */
    int sh_speed,sv_speed,sds_threshold;
                                /* Working speed values         */
    int h_speed,v_speed,ds_threshold;

    install_video(TMODE);       /* Install video system         */
```

```
header();                     /* Draw header                */
reset_mouse();                /* Reset mouse                */

if (MOUSE_THERE)
   {
                             /* Get rates at startup        */
   get_mouse_sensitivity(&sh_speed,&sv_speed,&sds_threshold);

                             /* Copy to working rates       */
   h_speed=sh_speed;v_speed=sv_speed;
   ds_threshold=sds_threshold;

                             /* Set to low speed for demo   */
   set_mouse_sensitivity(25,25,sds_threshold);

                             /* Set horiz & vert limits      */
   set_mouse_hlimits(1,VID_MAXX-MOUSE_SIZE+1);
   set_mouse_vlimits(1,VID_MAXY-MOUSE_SIZE);

                             /* Install the event handler    */
   install_event_handler();

   out_text_xy(10,4,"Demonstration of setting the double
                    speed threshold");
   out_text_xy(10,6,"Press LEFT  button to increase
                    threshold by 5.");
   out_text_xy(10,7,"Press RIGHT button to decrease
                    threshold by 5.");
   out_text_xy(10,9,"Threshold range is from 1 to 100. ");
   out_text_xy(10,10,"Move the mouse to 'feel' the new
                     threshold(if you can).");

                             /* Output initial speed         */
   out_text_xy(10,13,"Horizontal Sensitivity Rate  - ");
   out_text_xy(10,14,"Vertical   Sensitivity Rate  - ");
   out_text_xy(10,16,"Double Speed Threshold       - ");
   change_color(14);
   out_int_xy(45,13,h_speed);
   out_int_xy(45,14,v_speed);
   out_int_xy(45,16,ds_threshold);

   show_mouse_cursor();
```

```
while (!kbhit())          /* While key not pressed       */
   {
   if (LBUTTON_DOWN)
      {                       /* If thres is 1, set to 5,    */
                              /* otherwise increase by 5.    */
      if (ds_threshold==1) ds_threshold=5;
      else ds_threshold+=5;


                              /* Set new thres sensitivity rate*/
      set_mouse_sensitivity(h_speed,v_speed,ds_threshold);
      }


   if (RBUTTON_DOWN)
      {                       /* Decrease thres by 5         */
      ds_threshold-=5;


                              /* If thres less than 5, set to 1*/
      if (ds_threshold<5) ds_threshold=1;


                              /* Set new thres sensitivity rate*/
      set_mouse_sensitivity(h_speed,v_speed,ds_threshold);
      }
                              /* If EITHER button was pressed  */
   if ((LBUTTON_DOWN)||(RBUTTON_DOWN))
      {
                              /* Get new thres to verify set   */
      get_mouse_sensitivity(&h_speed,&v_speed,&ds_threshold);
      hide_mouse_cursor();


                              /* Write new values to display   */
      clear_line_from(16,45,5,0);
      out_int_xy(45,16,ds_threshold);
      show_mouse_cursor();


                              /* Reset all event status vars   */
      reset_event_status();
      }
   }
                              /* Reset speed to startup rates  */
set_mouse_sensitivity(sh_speed,sv_speed,sds_threshold);
reset_mouse();
}
```

```
else mouse_error(10,4);

getch();
shut_down_video();
}
```

As you can see, the effects of the double-speed threshold are far less obvious than the speed sensitivity settings.

Maximum Speed

What's the maximum speed the mouse cursor can obtain? 56 pixels per one mickey. Here's how:

Since changing the multiplication factor does not actually change the mickey-to-pixel ratio, but rather multiplies the mickey count by the factor *before* the mickey-to-pixel ratio is applied, the absolute maximum obtainable speed is 1 mickey to 8 pixels, multiplied by a factor of 3.5 (sensitivity rate 100), for a total of (8×3.5) or 28 pixels per one mickey count. Additionally, if the double-speed threshold kicked in, the mouse could move at 56 pixels per mickey count.

That about does it for cursor speed—on to the next chapter and a discussion of changing the shape of and managing the graphics mouse cursor.

Chapter 14

Changing and Managing the Graphics Mouse Cursor

The ability to change the shape of the mouse's graphics cursor is one of the most useful functions provided by the mouse driver. It gives the programmer a mechanism to convey information to the user *visually*. For instance, when long operations occur that require no user interaction, changing the mouse cursor's shape to an hourglass is very helpful in letting users know the computer is currently processing, and to wait. Perhaps you (or your end users) prefer to use a hand as the mouse cursor shape instead of the standard arrow. For so many tasks, changing the shape of the mouse cursor to meet specific operational needs polishes off any mouse application with an extra touch of elegance.

In this chapter, you learn about the mechanics of the graphics mouse cursor, and how to redefine its shape. After you have read the necessary discussions, an example is presented to demonstrate changing the mouse cursor's shape to a hand and an hourglass. If you are really adventurous, an additional example defines every standard cursor shape found in Windows and builds a window cursor management routine that automatically changes the mouse cursor shape as the mouse cursor moves in and out of a window or rectangular border. This is similar to the way Windows manages the cursor shape around window borders. First, though, you need some mouse cursor basics.

Graphics Mouse Cursor Mechanics

The graphics mouse cursor that moves around on the display occupies 16 pixels across, and 16 pixels down. Therefore, the mouse cursor is a square image occupying 256 pixels. How this image is generated, and how it operates against the background it is moving over is a bit difficult to conceptualize. I'll try to make it as painless as possible.

The Screen and Cursor Masks

The graphics mouse cursor image is defined by a 16-bit integer array, containing 32 elements. The first 16 elements are known as the *screen mask*, and the last 16 elements are known as the *cursor mask*.

Each 16-bit integer contained within the array should not be thought of as one value, but as 16 individual bits, where each bit represents a specific pixel location. Therefore, the first 16 elements, or screen mask, and the last 16 elements, or cursor mask, can be thought of as two individual 16 × 16-bit arrays, or masks.

Figure 14-1 is an illustration of the 32-element array and how the 16-bit integers are used in the masks, according to their individual bit values. The figure represents the default graphics mouse cursor.

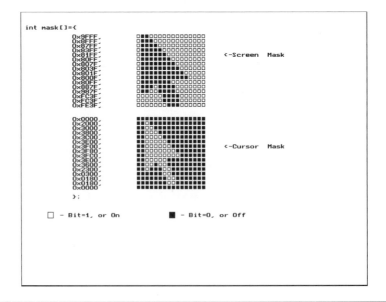

Figure 14-1.   *32-element array containing the screen and cursor masks*

The screen mask and the cursor mask work together to form the actual mouse cursor shape and background. Here's how:

1. The screen mask is logically ANDed into the corresponding location of the video buffer. The location is relative to the mouse cursor position, which is relative to the mouse cursor's hot spot.

2. The cursor mask is then logically XORed over the screen mask.

The mouse cursor hot spot is explained in the section, "The Hot Spot."

The following table is a guide to how individual bit values in each mask affect the final outcome of the mouse cursor image, and underlying background:

Bit Value (1 or 0)

Screen Mask	1	1	0	0	1	1	0	0
Cursor Mask	1	0	1	0	1	0	1	0
Pixel Value	1	1	1	1	0	0	0	0
Resulting	0	1	1	0	1	0	1	0
Bit on Display	REV	UNC	ON	OFF	ON	OFF	ON	OFF

where

Value	Meaning
REV	The underlying pixel value is reversed.
UNC	The underlying pixel value is unchanged.
ON	The underlying pixel value is that of the cursor's color.
OFF	The underlying pixel value is that of the background color.

With this in mind, when the display and cursor masks illustrated in Figure 14-1 are used, the outcome is the actual graphics mouse cursor shown in Figure 14-2. The border is black (or the current background color), inside the border is the solid cursor color, and the pixels outside the border do not modify the background they are writing over.

Bit Expansion

In some graphics modes, the bit masks are expanded or compressed internally by the mouse driver. The effect on you, the programmer, is minimal. With the exception of two modes (modes 4 and 5 hex), you only need concern yourself with setting the

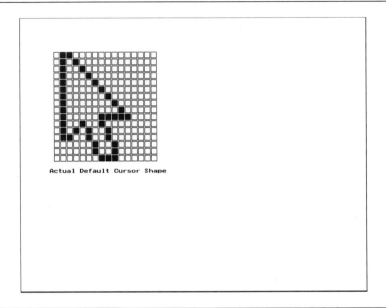

Actual Default Cursor Shape

Figure 14-2.   *The actual graphics mouse cursor*

two 16 × 16 bit masks. Here is the expansion (or compression) data for the various graphics modes. All graphics modes not listed use the 16 × 16 bit masks with no expansion.

Graphics Modes 4 and 5

In modes 4 and 5, the bit masks are actually compressed. In these modes, the graphics mouse cursor is represented by an 8 × 16 pixel region. You should take this into consideration when defining the masks in these modes, because every two bit pairs act as one pixel. All other modes use one-to-one mapping when defining the masks.

Graphics Mode D Hex

In mode D hex, every bit expands to four bits to produce a 16-color range. This means every 1 expands to 1111, and every 0 expands to 0000.

Graphics Mode 13 Hex

In mode 13 hex, every bit expands to eight bits to produce a 256-color range. This means every 1 expands to 11111111, and every 0 expands to 00000000.

The Hot Spot

The *hot spot* defines the pixel distance the mouse driver positions the upper-left element of the 16 × 16 mouse cursor image (mask location 0,0), away from the location used to set the mouse cursor's position. For instance, Figure 14-3 illustrates both the default hot spot of (0,–1) and a modified hot spot of (7,7). If the mouse cursor's position is set to location (100,100), then the checked box (pixel) is where the mouse driver considers location (100,100), in respect to the mouse cursor.

The hot spot's distance range is from –128 to 127 pixels, in any direction, from the upper-left corner of the 16 × 16 pixel mouse cursor image.

Setting the Mouse Cursor Shape

The graphics mouse cursor shape and hot spot can be modified with mouse function 9, set graphics cursor block. Mouse function 9 is located in the optional library function set_graphics_cursor(). The address of the screen and cursor mask array is sent to the mouse driver, along with the x and y hot spot coordinates. Examine the function set_graphics_cursor(), found in OPTIONAL.INC, for exact implementation and address management.

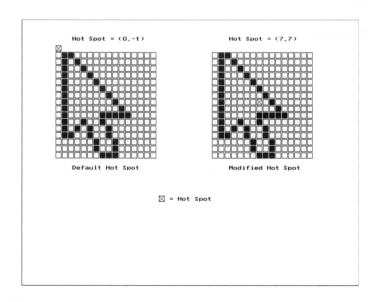

Figure 14-3.   *Default and modified mouse cursor hot spot*

The following example provides a simple demonstration by defining a hand and hourglass mouse cursor. The example uses the hand at startup. Press the left mouse button to change to the hourglass mouse cursor, and press the right mouse button to return to the hand mouse cursor. Both cursors are suitable for use in real-time applications.

Here is the project file, MOUSE21.PRJ:

```
EVENT.OBJ
MOUSE21.C
```

 Run this example in graphics modes only!

Here is MOUSE21.C:

```
/*--------------------------------------------------------------*/
/*                      MOUSE21.C                          */
/*                                                         */
/* Demonstration of changing the cursor shape. Hand and    */
/* hourglass cursors are demonstrated.                     */
/* RUN THIS ONLY IN GRAPHICS MODE !!!                      */
/*--------------------------------------------------------------*/

#include "header3.h"          /* New header with optional funcs*/

                             /* Screen and cursor mask defines*/

int hand[]=                  /* Hand cursor                 */
        {
        0xE1FF,   /* 1110000111111111 */
        0xE1FF,   /* 1110000111111111 */
        0xE1FF,   /* 1110000111111111 */
        0xE03F,   /* 1110000000111111 */
        0xE007,   /* 1110000000000111 */
        0xE000,   /* 1110000000000000 */
        0xE000,   /* 1110000000000000 */
        0xE000,   /* 1110000000000000 */
        0x0000,   /* 0000000000000000 */
        0x0000,   /* 0000000000000000 */
        0x0000,   /* 0000000000000000 */
        0x0000,   /* 0000000000000000 */
        0x0000,   /* 0000000000000000 */
        0x0000,   /* 0000000000000000 */
        0x0000,   /* 0000000000000000 */
        0x0000,   /* 0000000000000000 */
```

```
    0x1E00,   /* 0001111000000000 */
    0x1200,   /* 0001001000000000 */
    0x1200,   /* 0001001000000000 */
    0x13C0,   /* 0001001111000000 */
    0x1278,   /* 0001001001111000 */
    0x124F,   /* 0001001001001111 */
    0x1249,   /* 0001001001001001 */
    0x1249,   /* 0001001001001001 */
    0xF249,   /* 1111001001001001 */
    0x9001,   /* 1001000000000000 */
    0x9001,   /* 1001000000000000 */
    0x9001,   /* 1001000000000000 */
    0x8001,   /* 1000000000000000 */
    0x8001,   /* 1000000000000000 */
    0x8001,   /* 1000000000000000 */
    0xFFFF    /* 1111111111111111 */
    };

int hourglass[]=                  /* Hourglass cursor          */
    {
    0x8001,   /* 1000000000000001 */
    0xC003,   /* 1100000000000011 */
    0xC003,   /* 1100000000000011 */
    0xC003,   /* 1100000000000011 */
    0xC003,   /* 1100000000000011 */
    0xE007,   /* 1110000000000111 */
    0xF00F,   /* 1111000000001111 */
    0xF81F,   /* 1111100000011111 */
    0xF81F,   /* 1111100000011111 */
    0xF00F,   /* 1111000000001111 */
    0xE007,   /* 1110000000000111 */
    0xC003,   /* 1100000000000011 */
    0xC003,   /* 1100000000000011 */
    0xC003,   /* 1100000000000011 */
    0xC003,   /* 1100000000000011 */
    0x8001,   /* 1000000000000001 */

    0x7FFE,   /* 0111111111111110 */
    0x2004,   /* 0010000000000100 */
    0x2004,   /* 0010000000000100 */
    0x2004,   /* 0010000000000100 */
    0x2664,   /* 0010011001100100 */
    0x13C8,   /* 0001001111001000 */
    0x0990,   /* 0000100110010000 */
```

```
    0x0420,   /* 0000010000100000 */
    0x0420,   /* 0000010000100000 */
    0x0990,   /* 0000100110010000 */
    0x13C8,   /* 0001001111001000 */
    0x27E4,   /* 0010011111100100 */
    0x2FF4,   /* 0010111111110100 */
    0x2FF4,   /* 0010111111110100 */
    0x2004,   /* 0010000000000100 */
    0x7FFE    /* 0111111111111110 */
    };

void main()
   {
   install_video(GMODE);      /* Install video system     */
   header();                  /* Draw header              */
   reset_mouse();             /* Reset mouse              */

   if (MOUSE_THERE)
      {
                             /* Set horiz & vert limits   */
      set_mouse_hlimits(1,VID_MAXX-MOUSE_SIZE+1);
      set_mouse_vlimits(1,VID_MAXY-MOUSE_SIZE);

                             /* Install the event handler */
      install_event_handler();

      out_text_xy(10,4,"Changing the graphics cursor shape.");
      out_text_xy(10,6,"Press LEFT mouse button to set
                       'Hourglass' cursor.");
      out_text_xy(10,7,"Press RIGHT mouse button to set 'Hand'
                       cursor.");

                             /* Set initial cursor shape to */
      change_color(15);       /* hand. Hot spot = (1,1)     */
      set_graphics_cursor(hand,1,1);
      show_mouse_cursor();

      while (!kbhit())
         {
         if (LBUTTON_DOWN)    /* Left button, change to     */
            {                 /* hourglass cursor.          */
            LBUTTON_DOWN=0;
            hide_mouse_cursor();
            set_graphics_cursor(hourglass,1,1);
            show_mouse_cursor();
```

```
                }

        if (RBUTTON_DOWN)     /* Right button, change to hand  */
                {                    /* cursor.                       */
                RBUTTON_DOWN=0;
                hide_mouse_cursor();
                set_graphics_cursor(hand,1,1);
                show_mouse_cursor();
                }

            }
        reset_mouse();
        }
    else mouse_error(10,4);

    getch();
    shut_down_video();
    }
```

After the program starts, if you press the left mouse button, the mouse cursor is changed to the hourglass cursor illustrated in Figure 14-4.

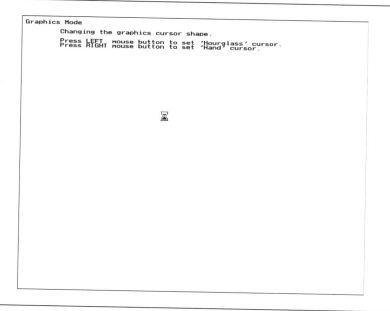

Figure 14-4.   *The hourglass mouse cursor shape*

Windows-Style Cursor Management in DOS

For all you budding GUI programmers who really want to impress users with DOS-based graphics applications, the following section should be of special interest. Not only is every standard cursor shape found in Windows defined, but a window/cursor border-management function utilizing the shapes is presented as well. The new mouse cursor shapes and their accompanying names are shown in Figure 14-5.

Sizing Arrows on Borders

Anybody familiar with Windows is familiar with window-sizing operations. When the mouse cursor moves to a window's border or one of its corners, the mouse cursor is changed to the appropriate sizing arrow. This is to inform the user that it's OK to resize the window from that location in the direction indicated. When the mouse cursor moves away from the window's borders, its shape automatically changes back to the default mouse cursor, which can also be one of a any number of shapes, including the sizing arrows.

The GUI presented in this book (the video function library), is not nearly complex enough to handle actual window resizing. Therefore, the example presented simply

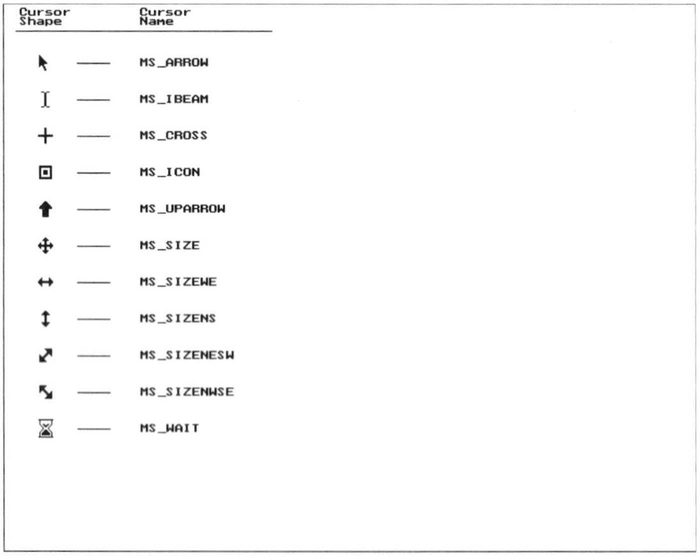

Cursor Shape	Cursor Name
▸	MS_ARROW
I	MS_IBEAM
+	MS_CROSS
▣	MS_ICON
↑	MS_UPARROW
✛	MS_SIZE
↔	MS_SIZEWE
↕	MS_SIZENS
↗	MS_SIZENESW
↖	MS_SIZENWSE
⧖	MS_WAIT

Figure 14-5. *The Windows-style cursor shapes*

demonstrates how the mouse cursor shape is managed when moving in and out of a window's border. To represent window borders, a rectangle is drawn in the center of the display. The rectangle coordinates are considered window coordinates.

The cursor management routine in the following example changes the shape of the mouse cursor to the appropriate sizing arrow whenever the mouse cursor is eight pixels (MOUSE_SIZE/2) or closer from the rectangle borders, in any direction. It changes the mouse cursor shape back to the default mouse cursor when it is eight pixels away from the rectangle borders. All that is required from you is sending the rectangle (or window) coordinates to the following function:

```
void manage_window_cursor(int x,int y,
                          int x1,int y1,int x2,int y2)
```

You send the coordinates every time the mouse cursor moves, where x and y are the current mouse cursor coordinates, and x1, y1, x2, and y2 are the rectangle, or window, borders. Since the function operates on coordinates, and not a predefined window, it should be portable to most other GUI's with little or no modification.

The Default Mouse Cursor Shape

In addition to automatically managing the sizing arrows, the following example allows you to change the default mouse cursor to any of the defined cursor shapes. You do this by pressing either the left or right mouse buttons. The new cursor shape is used as the default mouse cursor until it is changed again.

Go ahead and run the example. Move the mouse cursor around the rectangular borders to observe the mouse cursor shape changes. Study the code carefully to determine when shape changes are occurring and how a change is determined.

Here is the project file, MOUSE22.PRJ:

```
EVENT.OBJ
MOUSE22.C
```

Run this example in graphics modes only!

Here is MOUSE22.C:

```
/*------------------------------------------------------------*/
/*                        MOUSE22.C                           */
/*                                                            */
/* This example demonstrates Windows type of cursor           */
/* management.The standard default Windows cursors are defined*/
/* and the function manage_window_cursor()  will change the   */
/* shape of the cursor automatically on window borders or a   */
/* defined rectangular region. The user can also manually     */
/* change the default shape by pressing left and right buttons*/
/*------------------------------------------------------------*/

#include "header3.h"          /* New header with optional funcs*/

#define MS_ARROW    1          /* Constants for cursor names    */
#define MS_IBEAM    2          /* Names are the same as in      */
#define MS_CROSS    3          /* Windows, except in Windows    */
#define MS_ICON     4          /* they are preceded by IDC_,    */
#define MS_UPARROW  5          /* not MS_.                      */
#define MS_SIZE     6
#define MS_SIZEWE   7
#define MS_SIZENS   8
#define MS_SIZENESW 9
#define MS_SIZENWSE 10
#define MS_WAIT     11

int DEFAULT_CURSOR=1;          /* The default cursor when sizing*/
                               /* arrows are not being used.    */

int CURRENT_CURSOR=1;          /* Whatever cursor is currently  */
                               /* being used.                   */


/*                        THE SHAPES                          */
/*------------------------------------------------------------*/
/* The actual screen and cursor masks to define all the       */
/* standard cursor shaped used by Windows. These are not EXACT*/
/* replications, and the author has designed the shapes to be */
/* as similar as possible. Also, the color of the shapes will */
/* always be white with a black border.                       */
/* NOTE : Notice the names are the same as the defined         */
/*        constants, only preceded by an underscore( _ ).     */
/*------------------------------------------------------------*/
```

```
int _MS_ARROW[]=
       {
       0x9FFF,   /* 1001111111111111 */
       0x8FFF,   /* 1000111111111111 */
       0x87FF,   /* 1000011111111111 */
       0x83FF,   /* 1000001111111111 */
       0x81FF,   /* 1000000111111111 */
       0x80FF,   /* 1000000011111111 */
       0x807F,   /* 1000000001111111 */
       0x803F,   /* 1000000000111111 */
       0x801F,   /* 1000000000011111 */
       0x800F,   /* 1000000000001111 */
       0x80FF,   /* 1000000011111111 */
       0x887F,   /* 1000100001111111 */
       0x987F,   /* 1001100001111111 */
       0xFC3F,   /* 1111110000111111 */
       0xFC3F,   /* 1111110000111111 */
       0xFE3F,   /* 1111111000111111 */

       0x0000,   /* 0000000000000000 */
       0x2000,   /* 0010000000000000 */
       0x3000,   /* 0011000000000000 */
       0x3800,   /* 0011100000000000 */
       0x3C00,   /* 0011110000000000 */
       0x3E00,   /* 0011111000000000 */
       0x3F00,   /* 0011111100000000 */
       0x3F80,   /* 0011111110000000 */
       0x3FC0,   /* 0011111111000000 */
       0x3E00,   /* 0011111000000000 */
       0x3600,   /* 0011011000000000 */
       0x2300,   /* 0010001100000000 */
       0x0300,   /* 0000001100000000 */
       0x0180,   /* 0000000110000000 */
       0x0180,   /* 0000000110000000 */
       0x0000    /* 0000000000000000 */
       };

int _MS_IBEAM[]=
       {
       0xE187,   /* 1110000110000111 */
       0xE007,   /* 1110000000000111 */
       0xFC3F,   /* 1110000000000111 */
       0xFC3F,   /* 1111110000111111 */
       0xFC3F,   /* 1111110000111111 */
       0xFC3F,   /* 1111110000111111 */
```

```
        0xFC3F,   /* 1111110000111111 */
        0xFC3F,   /* 1111110000111111 */
        0xFC3F,   /* 1111110000111111 */
        0xFC3F,   /* 1111110000111111 */
        0xFC3F,   /* 1111110000111111 */
        0xFC3F,   /* 1111110000111111 */
        0xFC3F,   /* 1111110000111111 */
        0xFC3F,   /* 1110000000000111 */
        0xE007,   /* 1110000000000111 */
        0xE187,   /* 1110000110000111 */

        0x0000,   /* 0000000000000000 */
        0x0E70,   /* 0000111001110000 */
        0x0180,   /* 0000000110000000 */
        0x0180,   /* 0000000110000000 */
        0x0180,   /* 0000000110000000 */
        0x0180,   /* 0000000110000000 */
        0x0180,   /* 0000000110000000 */
        0x0180,   /* 0000000110000000 */
        0x0180,   /* 0000000110000000 */
        0x0180,   /* 0000000110000000 */
        0x0180,   /* 0000000110000000 */
        0x0180,   /* 0000000110000000 */
        0x0180,   /* 0000000110000000 */
        0x0180,   /* 0000000110000000 */
        0x0E70,   /* 0000111001110000 */
        0x0000    /* 0000000000000000 */
        };

int _MS_CROSS[]=
        {
        0xFC3F,   /* 1111110000111111 */
        0xFC3F,   /* 1111110000111111 */
        0xFC3F,   /* 1111110000111111 */
        0xFC3F,   /* 1111110000111111 */
        0xFC3F,   /* 1111110000111111 */
        0xFC3F,   /* 1111110000111111 */
        0x0000,   /* 0000000000000000 */
        0x0000,   /* 0000000000000000 */
        0x0000,   /* 0000000000000000 */
        0x0000,   /* 0000000000000000 */
        0xFC3F,   /* 1111110000111111 */
        0xFC3F,   /* 1111110000111111 */
        0xFC3F,   /* 1111110000111111 */
        0xFC3F,   /* 1111110000111111 */
```

```
    0xFC3F,    /* 1111110000111111 */
    0xFC3F,    /* 1111110000111111 */

    0x0000,    /* 0000000000000000 */
    0x0180,    /* 0000000110000000 */
    0x0180,    /* 0000000110000000 */
    0x0180,    /* 0000000110000000 */
    0x0180,    /* 0000000110000000 */
    0x0180,    /* 0000000110000000 */
    0x0180,    /* 0000000110000000 */
    0x7FFE,    /* 0111111111111110 */
    0x7FFE,    /* 0111111111111110 */
    0x0180,    /* 0000000110000000 */
    0x0180,    /* 0000000110000000 */
    0x0180,    /* 0000000110000000 */
    0x0180,    /* 0000000110000000 */
    0x0180,    /* 0000000110000000 */
    0x0180,    /* 0000000110000000 */
    0x0000     /* 0000000000000000 */
    };

int _MS_ICON[]=
    {
    0xFFFF,    /* 1111111111111111 */
    0xFFFF,    /* 1111111111111111 */
    0xC003,    /* 1100000000000011 */
    0xC003,    /* 1100000000000011 */
    0xC003,    /* 1100000000000011 */
    0xC003,    /* 1100000000000011 */
    0xC003,    /* 1100000000000011 */
    0xC003,    /* 1100000000000011 */
    0xC003,    /* 1100000000000011 */
    0xC003,    /* 1100000000000011 */
    0xC003,    /* 1100000000000011 */
    0xC003,    /* 1100000000000011 */
    0xC003,    /* 1100000000000011 */
    0xC003,    /* 1100000000000011 */
    0xFFFF,    /* 1111111111111111 */
    0xFFFF,    /* 1111111111111111 */

    0x0000,    /* 0000000000000000 */
    0x0000,    /* 0000000000000000 */
    0x3FFC,    /* 0011111111111100 */
    0x3FFC,    /* 0011111111111100 */
    0x300C,    /* 0011000000001100 */
```

```
        0x300C,   /* 0011000000001100 */
        0x33CC,   /* 0011001111001100 */
        0x33CC,   /* 0011001111001100 */
        0x33CC,   /* 0011001111001100 */
        0x33CC,   /* 0011001111001100 */
        0x300C,   /* 0011000000001100 */
        0x300C,   /* 0011000000001100 */
        0x3FFC,   /* 0011111111111100 */
        0x3FFC,   /* 0011111111111100 */
        0x0000,   /* 0000000000000000 */
        0x0000    /* 0000000000000000 */
        };

int _MS_UPARROW[]=
        {
        0xFE7F,   /* 1111111001111111 */
        0xFC3F,   /* 1111110000111111 */
        0xF81F,   /* 1111100000011111 */
        0xF00F,   /* 1111000000001111 */
        0xE007,   /* 1110000000000111 */
        0xC003,   /* 1100000000000011 */
        0x8001,   /* 1000000000000001 */
        0x8001,   /* 1000000000000001 */
        0x8001,   /* 1000000000000001 */
        0xF00F,   /* 1111000000001111 */
        0xF00F,   /* 1111000000001111 */
        0xF00F,   /* 1111000000001111 */
        0xF00F,   /* 1111000000001111 */
        0xF00F,   /* 1111000000001111 */
        0xF00F,   /* 1111000000001111 */
        0xF00F,   /* 1111000000001111 */

        0x0000,   /* 0000000000000000 */
        0x0180,   /* 0000000110000000 */
        0x03C0,   /* 0000001111000000 */
        0x07E0,   /* 0000011111100000 */
        0x0FF0,   /* 0000111111110000 */
        0x1FF8,   /* 0001111111111000 */
        0x3FFC,   /* 0011111111111100 */
        0x3FFC,   /* 0011111111111100 */
        0x07E0,   /* 0000011111100000 */
        0x07E0,   /* 0000011111100000 */
        0x07E0,   /* 0000011111100000 */
        0x07E0,   /* 0000011111100000 */
        0x07E0,   /* 0000011111100000 */
```

```
        0x07E0,   /* 0000011111100000 */
        0x07E0,   /* 0000011111100000 */
        0x0000    /* 0000000000000000 */
        };

int _MS_SIZE[]=
        {
        0xFE7F,   /* 1111111001111111 */
        0xFC3F,   /* 1111110000111111 */
        0xF81F,   /* 1111100000011111 */
        0xF00F,   /* 1111000000001111 */
        0xE007,   /* 1110000000000111 */
        0xC423,   /* 1100010000100011 */
        0x8001,   /* 1000000000000001 */
        0x0000,   /* 0000000000000000 */
        0x0000,   /* 0000000000000000 */
        0x8001,   /* 1000000000000001 */
        0xC423,   /* 1100010000100011 */
        0xE007,   /* 1110000000000111 */
        0xF00F,   /* 1111000000001111 */
        0xF81F,   /* 1111100000011111 */
        0xFC3F,   /* 1111110000111111 */
        0xFE7F,   /* 1111111001111111 */

        0x0000,   /* 0000000000000000 */
        0x0180,   /* 0000000110000000 */
        0x03C0,   /* 0000001111000000 */
        0x07E0,   /* 0000011111100000 */
        0x0180,   /* 0000000110000000 */
        0x1188,   /* 0001000110001000 */
        0x318C,   /* 0011000110001100 */
        0x7FFE,   /* 0111111111111110 */
        0x7FFE,   /* 0111111111111110 */
        0x318C,   /* 0011000110001100 */
        0x1188,   /* 0001000110001000 */
        0x0180,   /* 0000000110000000 */
        0x07E0,   /* 0000011111100000 */
        0x03C0,   /* 0000001111000000 */
        0x0180,   /* 0000000110000000 */
        0x0000    /* 0000000000000000 */
        };

int _MS_SIZEWE[]=
        {
        0xFFFF,   /* 1111111111111111 */
```

```
        0xFFFF,    /* 1111111111111111 */
        0xFFFF,    /* 1111111111111111 */
        0xF3CF,    /* 1111001111001111 */
        0xE3C7,    /* 1110001111000111 */
        0xC3C3,    /* 1100001111000011 */
        0x8001,    /* 1000000000000001 */
        0x0000,    /* 0000000000000000 */
        0x0000,    /* 0000000000000000 */
        0x8001,    /* 1000000000000001 */
        0xC3C3,    /* 1100001111000011 */
        0xE3C7,    /* 1110001111000111 */
        0xF3CF,    /* 1111001111001111 */
        0xFFFF,    /* 1111111111111111 */
        0xFFFF,    /* 1111111111111111 */
        0xFFFF,    /* 1111111111111111 */

        0x0000,    /* 0000000000000000 */
        0x0000,    /* 0000000000000000 */
        0x0000,    /* 0000000000000000 */
        0x0000,    /* 0000000000000000 */
        0x0810,    /* 0000100000010000 */
        0x1818,    /* 0001100000011000 */
        0x381C,    /* 0011100000011100 */
        0x7FFE,    /* 0111111111111110 */
        0x7FFE,    /* 0111111111111110 */
        0x381C,    /* 0011100000011100 */
        0x1818,    /* 0001100000011000 */
        0x0810,    /* 0000100000010000 */
        0x0000,    /* 0000000000000000 */
        0x0000,    /* 0000000000000000 */
        0x0000,    /* 0000000000000000 */
        0x0000     /* 0000000000000000 */
        };

int _MS_SIZENS[]=
        {
        0xFE7F,    /* 1111111001111111 */
        0xFC3F,    /* 1111110000111111 */
        0xF81F,    /* 1111100000011111 */
        0xF00F,    /* 1111000000001111 */
        0xE007,    /* 1110000000000111 */
        0xE007,    /* 1110000000000111 */
        0xFC3F,    /* 1111110000111111 */
        0xFC3F,    /* 1111110000111111 */
        0xFC3F,    /* 1111110000111111 */
```

```
        0xFC3F,   /* 1111110000111111 */
        0xE007,   /* 1110000000000111 */
        0xE007,   /* 1110000000000111 */
        0xF00F,   /* 1111000000001111 */
        0xF81F,   /* 1111100000011111 */
        0xFC3F,   /* 1111110000111111 */
        0xFE7F,   /* 1111111001111111 */

        0x0000,   /* 0000000000000000 */
        0x0180,   /* 0000000110000000 */
        0x03C0,   /* 0000001111000000 */
        0x07E0,   /* 0000011111100000 */
        0x0FF0,   /* 0000111111110000 */
        0x0180,   /* 0000000110000000 */
        0x0180,   /* 0000000110000000 */
        0x0180,   /* 0000000110000000 */
        0x0180,   /* 0000000110000000 */
        0x0180,   /* 0000000110000000 */
        0x0180,   /* 0000000110000000 */
        0x0FF0,   /* 0000111111110000 */
        0x07E0,   /* 0000011111100000 */
        0x03C0,   /* 0000001111000000 */
        0x0180,   /* 0000000110000000 */
        0x0000    /* 0000000000000000 */
        };

int _MS_SIZENESW[]=
        {
        0xFFFF,   /* 1111111111111111 */
        0xF801,   /* 1111100000000001 */
        0xFC01,   /* 1111110000000001 */
        0xFE01,   /* 1111111000000001 */
        0xFF01,   /* 1111111100000001 */
        0xBF01,   /* 1011111100000001 */
        0x9E01,   /* 1001111000000001 */
        0x8C01,   /* 1000110000000001 */
        0x8031,   /* 1000000000110001 */
        0x8079,   /* 1000000001111001 */
        0x80FD,   /* 1000000011111101 */
        0x80FF,   /* 1000000011111111 */
        0x807F,   /* 1000000001111111 */
        0x803F,   /* 1000000000111111 */
        0x801F,   /* 1000000000011111 */
        0xFFFF,   /* 1111111111111111 */
```

```
        0x0000,  /* 0000000000000000 */
        0x0000,  /* 0000000000000000 */
        0x01FC,  /* 0000000111111100 */
        0x00FC,  /* 0000000011111100 */
        0x007C,  /* 0000000001111100 */
        0x007C,  /* 0000000001111100 */
        0x00FC,  /* 0000000011111100 */
        0x21CC,  /* 0010000111001100 */
        0x3384,  /* 0011001110000100 */
        0x3F00,  /* 0011111100000000 */
        0x3E00,  /* 0011111000000000 */
        0x3E00,  /* 0011111000000000 */
        0x3F00,  /* 0011111100000000 */
        0x3F80,  /* 0011111110000000 */
        0x0000,  /* 0000000000000000 */
        0x0000   /* 0000000000000000 */
    };

int  _MS_SIZENWSE[]=
        {
        0xFFFF,  /* 1111111111111111 */
        0x801F,  /* 1000000000011111 */
        0x803F,  /* 1000000000111111 */
        0x807F,  /* 1000000001111111 */
        0x80FF,  /* 1000000011111111 */
        0x80FD,  /* 1000000011111101 */
        0x8079,  /* 1000000001111001 */
        0x8031,  /* 1000000000110001 */
        0x8C01,  /* 1000110000000001 */
        0x9E01,  /* 1001111000000001 */
        0xBF01,  /* 1011111100000001 */
        0xFF01,  /* 1111111100000001 */
        0xFE01,  /* 1111111000000001 */
        0xFC01,  /* 1111110000000001 */
        0xF801,  /* 1111100000000001 */
        0xFFFF,  /* 1111111111111111 */

        0x0000,  /* 0000000000000000 */
        0x0000,  /* 0000000000000000 */
        0x3F80,  /* 0011111110000000 */
        0x3F00,  /* 0011111100000000 */
        0x3E00,  /* 0011111000000000 */
        0x3E00,  /* 0011111000000000 */
        0x3F00,  /* 0011111100000000 */
        0x3384,  /* 0011001110000100 */
```

```
    0x21CC,  /* 0010000111001100 */
    0x00FC,  /* 0000000011111100 */
    0x007C,  /* 0000000001111100 */
    0x007C,  /* 0000000001111100 */
    0x00FC,  /* 0000000011111100 */
    0x01FC,  /* 0000000111111100 */
    0x0000,  /* 0000000000000000 */
    0x0000   /* 0000000000000000 */
    };

int _MS_WAIT[]=
    {
    0x8001,  /* 1000000000000001 */
    0xC003,  /* 1100000000000011 */
    0xC003,  /* 1100000000000011 */
    0xC003,  /* 1100000000000011 */
    0xC003,  /* 1100000000000011 */
    0xE007,  /* 1110000000000111 */
    0xF00F,  /* 1111000000001111 */
    0xF81F,  /* 1111100000011111 */
    0xF81F,  /* 1111100000011111 */
    0xF00F,  /* 1111000000001111 */
    0xE007,  /* 1110000000000111 */
    0xC003,  /* 1100000000000011 */
    0xC003,  /* 1100000000000011 */
    0xC003,  /* 1100000000000011 */
    0xC003,  /* 1100000000000011 */
    0x8001,  /* 1000000000000001 */

    0x7FFE,  /* 0111111111111110 */
    0x2004,  /* 0010000000000100 */
    0x2004,  /* 0010000000000100 */
    0x2004,  /* 0010000000000100 */
    0x2664,  /* 0010011001100100 */
    0x13C8,  /* 0001001111001000 */
    0x0990,  /* 0000100110010000 */
    0x0420,  /* 0000010000100000 */
    0x0420,  /* 0000010000100000 */
    0x0990,  /* 0000100110010000 */
    0x13C8,  /* 0001001111001000 */
    0x27E4,  /* 0010011111100100 */
    0x2FF4,  /* 0010111111110100 */
    0x2FF4,  /* 0010111111110100 */
    0x2004,  /* 0010000000000100 */
```

```
        0x7FFE    /* 0111111111111110 */
        };


/* MODULE: WRITE CURSOR NAME                                    */
/*------------------------------------------------------------*/
/* Writes the cursor name base on the number or defined        */
/* constant passed in. Writes text at (42, y).                 */
/* Input parameters                                            */
/*    number - Cursor name to write                            */
/*         y - Vert coord to write name at                     */
/*                                                             */
void write_cursor_name(int number,int y)
    {
    switch(number)
        {
        case MS_ARROW:clear_line_from(y,42,15,0);
                      out_text_xy(42,y,"MS_ARROW");
                      break;
        case MS_IBEAM:clear_line_from(y,42,15,0);
                      out_text_xy(42,y,"MS_IBEAM");
                      break;
        case MS_CROSS:clear_line_from(y,42,15,0);
                      out_text_xy(42,y,"MS_CROSS");
                      break;
        case MS_ICON: clear_line_from(y,42,15,0);
                      out_text_xy(42,y,"MS_ICON");
                      break;
        case MS_UPARROW:clear_line_from(y,42,15,0);
                      out_text_xy(42,y,"MS_UPARROW");
                      break;
        case MS_SIZE: clear_line_from(y,42,15,0);
                      out_text_xy(42,y,"MS_SIZE");
                      break;
        case MS_SIZEWE:clear_line_from(y,42,15,0);
                      out_text_xy(42,y,"MS_SIZEWE");;
                      break;
        case MS_SIZENS:clear_line_from(y,42,15,0);
                      out_text_xy(42,y,"MS_SIZENS");;
                      break;
        case MS_SIZENESW:clear_line_from(y,42,15,0);
                      out_text_xy(42,y,"MS_SIZENESW");;
                      break;
        case MS_SIZENWSE:clear_line_from(y,42,15,0);
                      out_text_xy(42,y,"MS_SIZENWSE");;
                      break;
```

```
    case MS_WAIT: clear_line_from(y,42,15,0);
                  out_text_xy(42,y,"MS_WAIT");
                  break;
    }
  }


/* MODULE: CHANGE CURSOR                                           */
/*---------------------------------------------------------------*/
/* Function sets the cursor shape corresponding to the number,*/
/* or defined constant passed in. Cursor should be hidden      */
/* before calling this function.                               */
/* Input parameters                                            */
/*    number - Cursor shape to change to                       */
/*                                                             */
/* NOTE: Notice hot spots are changed on many of the shapes.   */
/*                                                             */
void change_cursor(int number)
  {

  switch(number)
    {
    case MS_ARROW:set_graphics_cursor(_MS_ARROW,0,-1);
                  write_cursor_name(MS_ARROW,6);
                  break;

    case MS_IBEAM:set_graphics_cursor(_MS_IBEAM,7,7);
                  write_cursor_name(MS_IBEAM,6);
                  break;

    case MS_CROSS:set_graphics_cursor(_MS_CROSS,7,7);
                  write_cursor_name(MS_CROSS,6);
                  break;

    case MS_ICON: set_graphics_cursor(_MS_ICON,7,7);
                  write_cursor_name(MS_ICON,6);
                  break;

    case MS_UPARROW:set_graphics_cursor(_MS_UPARROW,7,1);
                  write_cursor_name(MS_UPARROW,6);
                  break;

    case MS_SIZE: set_graphics_cursor(_MS_SIZE,7,7);
                  write_cursor_name(MS_SIZE,6);
                  break;
```

```
        case MS_SIZEWE:set_graphics_cursor(_MS_SIZEWE,7,7);
                  write_cursor_name(MS_SIZEWE,6);
                  break;

        case MS_SIZENS:set_graphics_cursor(_MS_SIZENS,7,7);
                  write_cursor_name(MS_SIZENS,6);
                  break;

        case MS_SIZENESW:set_graphics_cursor(_MS_SIZENESW,7,7);
                  write_cursor_name(MS_SIZENESW,6);
                  break;

        case MS_SIZENWSE:set_graphics_cursor(_MS_SIZENWSE,7,7);
                  write_cursor_name(MS_SIZENWSE,6);
                  break;

        case MS_WAIT: set_graphics_cursor(_MS_WAIT,1,1);
                  write_cursor_name(MS_WAIT,6);
                  break;
        }
    }


/* MODULE: MANAGE WINDOW CURSOR                                 */
/*------------------------------------------------------------*/
/* This function manages the cursor on a rectangle defined by */
/* the programmer. The cursor shape will change when the      */
/* cursor comes within 8 pixels of the border, from any       */
/* direction. Changes are made in the four corners, the       */
/* horizontal borders, the vertical borders, and when the     */
/* cursor moves away from the region, to the default cursor    */
/* shape.                                                      */
/* Input parameters                                           */
/*      x,y - Cursor's current location                       */
/*      x1,y2,x2,y2 - Rectangle border to change shape on     */
/*                                                            */
/* NOTE : Notice else statements are NOT nested in code       */
/*        layout, but are nested logically.                   */
/*                                                            */
void manage_window_cursor(int x,int y,
                          int x1,int y1,int x2,int y2)
    {
                              /* Cursor INSIDE borders?        */
    if (
       ((x>x1+MOUSE_SIZE/2)&&(y>y1+MOUSE_SIZE/2)&&
```

```
      (x<x2-MOUSE_SIZE/2)&&(y<y2-MOUSE_SIZE/2))
      &&(CURRENT_CURSOR!=DEFAULT_CURSOR)
      )
         {
         change_cursor(DEFAULT_CURSOR);
         CURRENT_CURSOR=DEFAULT_CURSOR;
         }
                            /* Cursor OUTSIDE borders?    */
else
if (
      (x<x1-MOUSE_SIZE/2)||(y<y1-MOUSE_SIZE/2)||
      (x>x2+MOUSE_SIZE/2)||(y>y2+MOUSE_SIZE/2)
      )
         {
         if (CURRENT_CURSOR!=DEFAULT_CURSOR)
            {
            CURRENT_CURSOR=DEFAULT_CURSOR;
            change_cursor(DEFAULT_CURSOR);
            }
         }
else                       /* Cursor on vertical line?   */
if (
      (
      ((x<=x1+MOUSE_SIZE/2)||(x>=x2-MOUSE_SIZE/2))&&
      ((y>y1+MOUSE_SIZE/2)&&(y<y2-MOUSE_SIZE/2))
      )&&(CURRENT_CURSOR!=MS_SIZEWE)
      )
         {
         change_cursor(MS_SIZEWE);
         CURRENT_CURSOR=MS_SIZEWE;
         }
else                       /* Cursor on horizontal line?  */
if (
      (
      ((y<=y1+MOUSE_SIZE/2)||(y>=y2-MOUSE_SIZE/2))&&
      ((x>x1+MOUSE_SIZE/2)&&(x<x2-MOUSE_SIZE/2))
      )&&(CURRENT_CURSOR!=MS_SIZENS)
      )
         {
         change_cursor(MS_SIZENS);
         CURRENT_CURSOR=MS_SIZENS;
         }
                            /* Cursor in UPPER-left corner  */
else                        /* or LOWER-right corner?       */
if (
```

```
        (
        ((x<=x1+MOUSE_SIZE/2)&&(y<=y1+MOUSE_SIZE/2))||
        ((x>=x2-MOUSE_SIZE/2)&&(y>=y2-MOUSE_SIZE/2))
        )&&(CURRENT_CURSOR!=MS_SIZENWSE)
        )
            {
            change_cursor(MS_SIZENWSE);
            CURRENT_CURSOR=MS_SIZENWSE;
            }
                            /* Cursor in UPPER-right corner */
    else                    /* or LOWER-left corner?        */
    if (
        (
        ((x>=x2-MOUSE_SIZE/2)&&(y<=y1+MOUSE_SIZE/2)) ||
        ((x<=x1+MOUSE_SIZE/2)&&(y>=y2-MOUSE_SIZE/2))
        )&&(CURRENT_CURSOR!=MS_SIZENESW)
        )
            {
            change_cursor(MS_SIZENESW);
            CURRENT_CURSOR=MS_SIZENESW;
            }
    }


/* MODULE: MENU                                                */
/*-----------------------------------------------------------*/
/* Initial display write specifically for this example.       */
/*                                                            */
void menu(int wx1,int wy1,int wx2,int wy2)
    {
    clear_line_from(2,2,20,0);

    change_color(4);
    draw_rectangle(wx1,wy1,wx2,wy2);

    change_color(11);
    out_text_xy(15,2,"Window's Style Cursor Managment In
                    DOS Applications");

    change_color(15);
    out_text_xy(25,5,"Default Cursor - ");
    out_text_xy(25,6,"Current Cursor - ");

    out_text_xy(26,(wy1+((wy2-wy1)/2))/VFONT_SIZE-2,
                " Cursor shape will change");
```

```
out_text_xy(26,(wy1+((wy2-wy1)/2))/VFONT_SIZE,
            "  AUTOMATICALLY as it moves");

out_text_xy(26,(wy1+((wy2-wy1)/2))/VFONT_SIZE+2,
            "in and out of window borders.");

out_text_xy(5,(VID_MAXY/VFONT_SIZE)-1,
            "Press the left or right mouse button
            to change the default cursor shape.");

change_color(14);
}

            /*----------------------*/
            /*          MAIN        */
            /*----------------------*/

void main()
   {
   int wx1,wx2,wy1,wy2;      /* Rectangular border coordinates*/

   install_video(GMODE);    /* Install video system         */
   header();                /* Draw header                  */
   reset_mouse();           /* Reset mouse                  */

   if (MOUSE_THERE)
      {
      wx1=VID_MAXX/4;       /* Figure middle rectangle or   */
      wx2=VID_MAXX/4*3;     /* "window" borders, based on   */
      wy1=VID_MAXY/4;       /* video mode.                  */
      wy2=VID_MAXY/4*3;

      menu(wx1,wy1,wx2,wy2); /* Do initial display write    */

                            /* Install event handler        */
      install_event_handler();

                            /* Set horiz & vert limits      */
      set_mouse_hlimits(1,VID_MAXX-MOUSE_SIZE+1);
      set_mouse_vlimits(1,VID_MAXY-MOUSE_SIZE);

                            /* Change to default cursor     */
                            /* Initially 1, or MS_ARROW     */
      change_cursor(DEFAULT_CURSOR);
      write_cursor_name(DEFAULT_CURSOR,5);
```

```
        show_mouse_cursor();

    while (!kbhit())         /* Do until user presses a key   */
        {

        if (LBUTTON_DOWN)    /* Left button pressed, increase */
            {                /* current cursor number and     */
            LBUTTON_DOWN=0;  /* set default cursor to new.    */

            ++CURRENT_CURSOR;
            if (CURRENT_CURSOR>11) CURRENT_CURSOR=1;
            DEFAULT_CURSOR=CURRENT_CURSOR;

                             /* Now change to new cursor shape*/
            hide_mouse_cursor();
            change_cursor(DEFAULT_CURSOR);
            write_cursor_name(DEFAULT_CURSOR,5);
            show_mouse_cursor();
            }

        if (RBUTTON_DOWN)    /* Right button pressed, decrease*/
            {                /* current cursor number and     */
            RBUTTON_DOWN=0;  /* set default cursor to new.    */

            -CURRENT_CURSOR;
            if (CURRENT_CURSOR<1) CURRENT_CURSOR=11;
            DEFAULT_CURSOR=CURRENT_CURSOR;

                             /* Now change to new cursor shape*/
            hide_mouse_cursor();
            change_cursor(DEFAULT_CURSOR);
            write_cursor_name(DEFAULT_CURSOR,5);
            show_mouse_cursor();
            }

        if (CURSOR_MOVED)    /* If cursor moved, see if it is */
            {                /* on a border.                  */
            CURSOR_MOVED=0;
            manage_window_cursor(CMX,CMY,wx1,wy1,wx2,wy2);
            }
        }
    reset_mouse();
    }

else mouse_error(5,4);
```

```
getch();

shut_down_video();
}
```

Figure 14-6 was generated by using the default arrow at startup and moving the mouse cursor into the upper-left corner of the rectangular border.

This should give you plenty to think about when you design your next GUI. With the tools presented here, you have everything needed to manage the cursor shape around a sizeable window in any DOS based application.

Be sure to hide the mouse cursor before changing the cursor shape and show it afterward. If the mouse cursor is over background text or graphics and the cursor shape is changed before being hidden, the background image is wholly or partially destroyed at the mouse cursor's location.

Figure 14-6.   *Windows-style cursor management in DOS applications*

Chapter *15*

The Mouse's Text Cursor

Like the mouse's graphics cursor, the text-mode mouse cursor can be modified to meet specific needs or provide special effects. However, in text modes, there are two distinct types of mouse cursors available.

The Two Types of Text Cursors

In text modes, you can choose between using the mouse driver's software text cursor or the system's hardware text cursor. The two types of text cursors are defined as follows:

- The *software cursor* is the default text cursor used by the mouse driver. It is a single character block whose operations on the underlying background are defined using two masks: the screen mask and the cursor mask.

- The *hardware cursor* is same text cursor used by the operating system. For example, the blinking cursor at the DOS command line is the hardware text cursor. This type of cursor can be modified by changing the starting and ending scan lines of the cursor.

The Software Text Cursor

To understand the mouse's software text cursor, you must first understand how a character is displayed in text modes.

A text character and its attributes are stored as a 16-bit integer value. This 16-bit integer value contains specific information regarding the character's color, background color, blinking attribute, intensity attribute, and the actual character value. The specific bits of the integer and their meanings are defined in Table 15-1.

When a character is written to the display in text modes, these values are used to determine the actual character, colors, and attributes.

The mouse's software text cursor, like the graphics cursor, uses two separate masks to define how the cursor operates against the background image. The first mask is called the *screen mask*, and the second is called the *cursor mask*. However, these masks are much simpler than the masks used by the graphics mouse cursor, as each is defined in one 16-bit integer, following the format illustrated in Table 15-1. Here's how the masks work:

1. The screen mask is logically ANDed with the character attributes on the display, corresponding to the mouse cursor's location.

2. The cursor mask is then logically XORed with the result of operation 1.

The outcome of these two operations is the software text cursor.

The default masks are defined as the following:

Mask	16-Bit Binary Value	Hexadecimal Value
Screen mask	0111111111111111	7FFF
Cursor mask	0111011100000000	7700

When these mask values are used for the software text cursor, the result is a cursor with a reversed background and inverted character color.

The Hardware Text Cursor

The hardware text mouse cursor is the system cursor used in text processing. It is modified by changing the starting scan line and the ending scan line of the cursor.

The number of scan lines for the cursor is dependent on the type of video system being used. CGA and EGA systems with color monitors use eight scan lines, numbered from 0 to 7. VGA and monochrome systems use 14 scan lines, numbered from 0 to 13.

If the system is using a cursor with 14 scan lines, then setting the starting scan line to 0 and the ending scan line to 13 will produce a solid block. If the starting scan is set to 13, and the ending scan line is set to 13, the cursor will resemble an underscore, with only the last line of the cursor block being visible.

Bit(s)	Meaning	Range or Value
0-7	ASCII character value	0-255
8-10	Foreground color	0-7
11	Intensity attribute	1=high, 0=normal
12-14	Background color	0-7
15	Blink attribute	1=blink, 0=no blink

Table 15-1.   Bits of a 16-Bit Integer That Describes a Text Character

Using the set_text_cursor() Function

To modify either the software or hardware text cursor, use the mouse library function set_text_cursor(), which calls mouse function 10, set text cursor. Three values are sent to the function set_text_cursor(), in the following order:

1. ctype, sent first, specifies the type of cursor to use. A value of 0 specifies the software text cursor, and a value of 1 specifies the hardware text cursor.

2. sm_or_sl is sent next. If ctype is 0, then sm_or_sl is the value for the screen mask used by the software text cursor. If ctype is 1, then sm_or_sl is the starting scan line number for the hardware text cursor.

3. cm_or_el is sent last. If ctype is 0, then cm_or_el if the value for the cursor mask used by the software text cursor. If ctype is 1, then cm_or_el is the ending scan line number for the hardware text cursor.

Modifying the Software Text Cursor

The following example modifies the mouse's software text cursor to three distinct, usable cursors, including the default software text cursor.

Here is the project file, MOUSE23.C:

```
EVENT.OBJ
MOUSE23.C
```

Here is MOUSE23.C:

```
/*-------------------------------------------------------------*/
/*                        MOUSE23.C                            */
/*                                                             */
```

```
/* Demonstration of setting the text SOFTWARE cursor.        */
/* Software cursor is set by setting the text screen and     */
/* cursor masks.                                             */
/* RUN THIS ONLY IN TEXT MODE !!!                            */
/*----------------------------------------------------------*/

#include "header3.h"        /* New header with optional funcs*/

void main()
    {
    int cloop=1,loop1,loop2;   /* Misc. loops              */
    int mask_count;            /* What masks are being used?  */

    install_video(TMODE);      /* Install video system        */
    header();                  /* Draw header                 */
    reset_mouse();             /* Reset mouse                 */

    if (MOUSE_THERE)
        {
                               /* Install event handler       */
        install_event_handler();

                               /* Set horiz & vert limits     */
        set_mouse_hlimits(1,VID_MAXX-MOUSE_SIZE+1);
        set_mouse_vlimits(1,VID_MAXY-MOUSE_SIZE);

        out_text_xy(10,4,"Demonstration of setting the text
                    SOFTWARE cursor.");
        out_text_xy(10,6,"Press LEFT  mouse button for next
                    mask setting.");
        out_text_xy(10,7,"Press RIGHT mouse button for previous
                    mask setting.");

        out_text_xy(10, 9,"Mask Number  : ");
        out_text_xy(10,10,"Mask Type    : ");
        out_int_xy(27,9,1);
        out_text_xy(27,10,"Defualt");

                               /* Write some text on display   */
        for (loop1=15;loop1<=20;loop1++)
           for (loop2=5;loop2<=68;loop2+=12)
              {
              change_color(cloop);
              out_text_xy(loop2,loop1,"SAMPLETEXT");
              ++cloop;
```

```
        if (cloop==16) cloop=1;
        }

change_color(15);
mask_count=1;              /* Set the mask count to 1       */

show_mouse_cursor();

while (!kbhit())
    {                          /* Either button pressed        */
    if ((LBUTTON_DOWN)||(RBUTTON_DOWN))
        {

        if (LBUTTON_DOWN)
            {                  /* Left button, inc mask count  */
            LBUTTON_DOWN=0;
            ++mask_count;
            if (mask_count>3) mask_count=1;
            }

        if (RBUTTON_DOWN)
            {                  /* Right button, dec mask count */
            RBUTTON_DOWN=0;
            —mask_count;
            if (mask_count<1) mask_count=4;
            }

        hide_mouse_cursor();
        clear_line_from(9,27,2,0);
        clear_line_from(10,27,40,0);
        out_int_xy(27,9,mask_count);

                        /* Change to new masks,write info*/
        switch(mask_count)
            {
            case 1:set_text_cursor(0,0x7FFF,0x7700);
                    out_text_xy(27,10,"Default");
                    break;
            case 2:set_text_cursor(0,0xFFFF,0xFF00);
                    out_text_xy(27,10,
                            "Character blinking/reversed");
                    break;
            case 3:set_text_cursor(0,0xFFFF,0xF000);
                    out_text_xy(27,10,"Character blinking");
```

```
                  break;
              }

          show_mouse_cursor();
              }
          }
      reset_mouse();
      }
  else mouse_error(10,4);

  getch();
  shut_down_video();
  }
```

Modifying the Hardware Text Cursor

To demonstrate modifying the mouse's hardware text cursor, the following example sets the starting and ending scan lines for the hardware text cursor to four different settings. The example assumes you are using a 14-scan-line system. If you use a system with eight scan lines (CGA or EGA), you can still run the program, but the hardware text cursor will become invisible when the third and fourth settings are used. This is because both the starting and ending scan lines are beyond the maximum scan line allowed for those modes. If the ending scan line is past the maximum but the starting scan line is valid, the cursor is drawn from the starting scan line to the maximum scan line, so the first two settings will work fine.

You could easily determine the available scan lines by first determining the video card and monitor type. To keep matters simple, the following example does not make this determination.

Here is the project file, MOUSE24.PRJ:

```
EVENT.OBJ
MOUSE24.C
```

Here is MOUSE24.C:

```
/*-----------------------------------------------------------*/
/*                       MOUSE24.C                         */
/*                                                         */
/* Demonstration of setting the text HARDWARE cursor.      */
/* Hardware cursor is set w/ start and ending scan line number*/
/* RUN THIS ONLY IN TEXT MODE !!!                          */
/*-----------------------------------------------------------*/
```

```
#include "header3.h"            /* New header with optional funcs*/

void main()
   {
   int cloop=1,loop1,loop2;   /* Misc. loops, coords        */
   int scan_count;            /* What scan line setting?     */

   install_video(TMODE);      /* Install video system        */
   header();                  /* Draw header                 */
   reset_mouse();             /* Reset mouse                 */

   if (MOUSE_THERE)
      {
                              /* Install event handler       */
      install_event_handler();

                              /* Set horiz & vert limits     */
      set_mouse_hlimits(1,VID_MAXX-MOUSE_SIZE+1);
      set_mouse_vlimits(1,VID_MAXY-MOUSE_SIZE);

      out_text_xy(10,4,"Demonstration of setting the text
                     HARDWARE cursor.");
      out_text_xy(10,6,"Press LEFT  mouse button for next
                     scan line setting.");
      out_text_xy(10,7,"Press RIGHT mouse button for previous
                     scan line setting.");

      out_text_xy(10, 9,"Mask Number   : ");
      out_text_xy(10,10,"Start Line    : ");
      out_text_xy(10,11,"End Scan Line: ");

      out_int_xy(27,9,1);
      out_int_xy(27,10,1);
      out_int_xy(27,11,14);

                              /* Write some text on display    */
      for (loop1=15;loop1<=20;loop1++)
         for (loop2=5;loop2<=68;loop2+=12)
            {
            change_color(cloop);
            out_text_xy(loop2,loop1,"SAMPLETEXT");
            ++cloop;
            if (cloop==16) cloop=1;
            }
```

```
change_color(15);
scan_count=1;              /* Set the scan count to 1      */
                          /* Set text cursor to default   */
set_text_cursor(1,1,14);
show_mouse_cursor();

while (!kbhit())
    {                      /* Either button pressed        */
    if ((LBUTTON_DOWN)||(RBUTTON_DOWN))
        {
        if (LBUTTON_DOWN)
            {              /* Left button, inc scan count  */
            LBUTTON_DOWN=0;
            ++scan_count;
            if (scan_count>4) scan_count=1;
            }

        if (RBUTTON_DOWN)
            {              /* Right button, dec scan count */
            RBUTTON_DOWN=0;
            —scan_count;
            if (scan_count<1) scan_count=4;
            }

        hide_mouse_cursor();
        clear_line_from(9,27,2,0);
        clear_line_from(10,27,40,0);
        clear_line_from(11,27,40,0);
        out_int_xy(27,9,scan_count);

                          /* Change to new scan lines      */
        switch(scan_count)
            {
            case 1:set_text_cursor(1,0,13);
                    out_int_xy(27,10,0);
                    out_int_xy(27,11,13);
                    break;
            case 2:set_text_cursor(1,7,13);
                    out_int_xy(27,10,7);
                    out_int_xy(27,11,13);
                    break;
            case 3:set_text_cursor(1,11,13);
                    out_int_xy(27,10,11);
                    out_int_xy(27,11,13);
                    break;
```

```
         case 4:set_text_cursor(1,13,13);
                out_int_xy(27,10,13);
                out_int_xy(27,11,13);
                break;
         }

       show_mouse_cursor();
         }
      }
   reset_mouse();
   }

else mouse_error(10,4);

getch();
shut_down_video();
}
```

There you have it. By studying the previous two examples, you should be able to determine how to modify the mouse's text cursor(s) to suit any text-based DOS application.

Chapter **16**

Combining the Functions into One Library

With the 16 mouse library functions you created in Chapter 3 and Chapter 12, the event handler and processor you created in Chapter 7, and the techniques you have learned in all the previous chapters, you should be able to utilize the mouse in any DOS-based application with total confidence. However, there is one final process you must complete to make the mouse functions, event handler, and event processor truly flexible, manageable, and reusable. That process is combining everything into one complete library file.

The mouse functions not covered in the previous chapters are documented in detail in Appendix A, and sample code fragments are provided for each function.

A Real Mouse Function Library

Throughout the previous chapters, the mouse library functions and event processor resided in separate source code files that got recompiled in every example. When you use the functions in your own application, there is no reason for you to continually recompile these source files, and doing so wastes valuable processing and development time. A better method is to precompile every source file, including the assembly language event handler, and combine them into one complete library file.

Library Files

A *library file* is a module composed of precompiled object (.OBJ) files. If you are building a resource (like a function library) composed of one or more object files, combining them into a library file is very advantageous. To illustrate why, consider the steps you have taken to compile most of the programming examples in the previous chapters:

- Up to this point, you've had to build a separate project file that contains the event handler (EVENT.OBJ) and the C program file. This is because EVENT.ASM is coded in assembly language, and does not compile with the C compiler. Therefore, EVENT.ASM must be compiled with an assembler and integrated in the program at link time as an object file.

- The ten necessary mouse functions, the six optional mouse functions, and the C event processor have all been developed in separate files, and you've had to code many #include statements to incorporate them into the programming examples. Additionally, these files have been recompiled in every programming example.

If all the mouse functions were combined and compiled into one object file, say MOUSELIB.OBJ, they too could simply be used in a project file and not be recompiled with each and every application. However, the project file would need to contain EVENT.OBJ, MOUSELIB.OBJ, and the application source file. If the librarian is used, both EVENT.OBJ and MOUSELIB.OBJ can be combined into one file, called MOUSELIB.LIB. The project file for an application would then need only MOUSELIB.LIB, and the application source file.

Alternatively, Microsoft C 6.0 and C/C++ 7.0 compiler users can add MOUSELIB.LIB to the Additional Libraries options. If you do this, there is no need for a project file, unless your application uses other .OBJ or source files.

Creating the Library File

Combining the C mouse library functions, the C event processor, and the assembly language event handler into one library file is exactly what you do in this chapter. The steps you must take to complete this process are as follows:

1. Combine the C mouse library functions and C event processor into one source file. The source file is called MOUSELIB.C.

2. Compile MOUSELIB.C to MOUSELIB.OBJ.

3. Compile EVENT.ASM to EVENT.OBJ.

4. Combine MOUSELIB.OBJ and EVENT.OBJ into MOUSELIB.LIB using the librarian.

5. Create a header file for applications that use MOUSELIB.LIB.

Memory Models

There is one restriction the object files in the library, and applications you create must adhere to. They *must* all be compiled in the same memory model. If you usually compile all your applications in the same memory model, this should not be a problem, but if you write many applications using different memory models, you need to compile MOUSELIB.C and EVENT.ASM to .OBJ files using the same memory model as the specific application before combining them into the library file.

Alternatively, you could take care of all memory models in one shot, by building a library file for each model, and using the appropriate library file as needed. For instance, the naming convention you could use might be MOUSELBH.LIB, MOUSELBL.LIB, MOUSELBC.LIB, MOUSELBM.LIB, and MOUSELBS.LIB, where the last letter in the filename represents the memory model in which the library file was compiled.

There are even more sophisticated methods to work around different memory models in library files. If you are interested, refer to your compiler's manuals for more detailed information.

Step 1

The first step in creating MOUSELIB.LIB is to combine all the C mouse library functions and the C event processor into one file, MOUSELIB.C, and compile that to MOUSELIB.OBJ. Here is MOUSELIB.C:

```
/*-----------------------------------------------------------*/
/*                    MOUSELIB.C                          */
/*                                                        */
/*  The complete mouse function library. All mouse functions */
/*  and event processing files are combined here. This file */
/*  MUST be compiled to MOUSELIB.OBJ. Next MOUSLELIB.OBJ and */
/*  EVENT.OBJ are combined to MOUSELIB.LIB with the         */
/*  librarian (Borland = TLIB.EXE, Microsoft = LIB.EXE).    */
/*  MOUSELIB.LIB is then ready for use with all external    */
/*  applications with no need for recompiling. The external */
/*  application will also need to include the header        */
/*  "MOUSELIB.H" within the application.                    */
/*-----------------------------------------------------------*/
```

```
#include "compiler.h",     /* Include compiler macros      */

#include "mouse.h"         /* Include the mouse vars       */
#include "mouse.inc"       /* Include 10 nec. mouse functs */
#include "optional.inc"    /* Include optional mouse functs */
#include "mevent.inc"      /* C Event processor            */
```

Compile MOUSELIB.C to MOUSELIB.OBJ.

Microsoft users must turn stack checking off when compiling MOUSELIB.C.

Step 2

The next step is to compile EVENT.ASM to EVENT.OBJ. Make sure you change the statement .MODEL *xxx* to match the memory model MOUSELIB.OBJ was compiled in, where *xxx* is HUGE, LARGE, COMPACT, MEDIUM, or SMALL. Also be sure to use the /mx compiler option with the assembler.

If you do not have an assembler, EVENT.ASM has been compiled for each individual memory model, and the .OBJ files are included with the companion disk supplied with this book. The file naming convention for the various memory models are as follows:

Filename	Memory Model
EVENTH.OBJ	Huge memory model
EVENTL.OBJ	Large memory model
EVENTC.OBJ	Compact memory model
EVENTM.OBJ	Medium memory model
EVENTS.OBJ	Small memory model

Compiling EVENT.ASM is detailed in Chapter 7. If you have not yet compiled EVENT.ASM or do not know how to use your assembler, refer to Chapter 7.

Step 3

The next step is to combine the files MOUSELIB.OBJ and EVENT.OBJ into MOUSELIB.LIB. The librarian TLIB.EXE (LIB.EXE for Microsoft compilers) must be either in the same directory as MOUSELIB.OBJ and EVENT.OBJ or in the environment path. Proceed as follows:

- If you are using a Borland librarian enter the command

    TLIB MOUSELIB +EVENT +MOUSELIB

- If you are using a Microsoft librarian, first enter the command

    LIB MOUSELIB +EVENT +MOUSELIB

    then press ENTER when the librarian asks for the list filename.

What these commands do is tell the librarian to add EVENT.OBJ (+EVENT) and MOUSELIB.OBJ (+MOUSELIB) to the library file MOUSELIB.LIB. If MOUSELIB.LIB does not exist, it is created. If it does exist, you need to erase it before the new library file can be created. Otherwise, the linker disregards the attempt to add the new object files into the library.

With Borland compilers, Microsoft C 6.0, and Microsoft C/C++ 7.0, the order of +EVENT and +MOUSELIB is irrelevant. However, with Microsoft QuickC, the order must be +EVENT +MOUSELIB; otherwise, when an application using MOUSELIB.LIB is compiled, the link fails due to _TEXT segment fixup errors.

Step 4

Finally, a header file must be created to inform any application using MOUSELIB.LIB of the functions and global variables existing therein. The header file is named MOUSELIB.H. Here it is:

```
/*-------------------------------------------------------------*/
/*                      MOUSELIB.H                          */
/*                                                         */
/* Header file for application using MOUSELIB.LIB.          */
/*-------------------------------------------------------------*/

#define MV_LBUTTON 1        /* For event driver button    */
#define MV_RBUTTON 2        /* status when CURSOR_MOVED    */
#define MV_BBUTTON 3        /* message is trapped.         */

    /*--------------------------------------------*/
    /* External Variables Declared in MOUSELIB.LIB */
    /*--------------------------------------------*/

extern int NUMBER_BUTTONS;   /* Number of mouse buttons     */

extern int HCELL_SIZE,       /* Cursor cell sizes - text mode */
           VCELL_SIZE;
```

```
extern int MOUSE_SIZE;          /* Mouse cursor size. Use 16 in  */
                                /* graphics mode, 1 in text.     */

extern unsigned char IN_GMODE;/* 1 in graphics mode, 0 in text*/

extern unsigned char MOUSE_THERE;   /* 1 if present, 0 if not */
extern unsigned char MOUSE_VISIBLE; /* Is mouse visible?      */

extern unsigned char LBUTTON_DOWN, /* Boolean vars or messags */
                     RBUTTON_DOWN, /* set by event processor. */
                     BBUTTON_DOWN,
                     LBUTTON_UP,
                     RBUTTON_UP,
                     BBUTTON_UP,
                     CURSOR_MOVED;

extern int CMX,CMY;             /* Mouse coords set by event   */
extern int BSTATE;              /* handler. Also button state. */

extern union  REGS  mregs;    /* DOS/mouse registers         */
extern struct SREGS msegregs;/* DOS/mouse segment register  */

extern unsigned char EGA_REG_READ;   /* EGA regs handled?   */
                                     /* Default YES         */

        /*---------------------------------------------*/
        /* Functions Found in MOUSELIB.LIB             */
        /*---------------------------------------------*/

/*---------------------*/
/* Standard Functions  */
/*---------------------*/
void reset_mouse(void);
void pascal show_mouse_cursor(void);
void pascal hide_mouse_cursor(void);
void pascal set_hide_bounds(int x1,int y1,int x2,int y2);
void pascal set_mouse_position(int x,int y);
void pascal set_mouse_hlimits(int x1,int x2);
void pascal set_mouse_vlimits(int y1,int y2);
void pascal get_mouse_button(unsigned char *button1,
                             unsigned char *button2,
                             int *x,int *y);
unsigned char pascal get_button_rls_info(int butt_no,
                                         int *count,
```

```
                                    int *x,int *y);
void pascal set_event_handler(int call_mask,
                              void (far *location)(void));



/*----------------------*/
/* Optional Functions   */
/*----------------------*/
void pascal get_mouse_type(int *maj_ver,int *min_ver,
                           int *mtype,int *irq_num);
int pascal get_crt_page(void);
void pascal get_mouse_sensitivity(int *h_speed,int *v_speed,
                                  int *threshold);
void pascal set_mouse_sensitivity(int h_speed,int v_speed,
                                  int threshold);
void pascal set_graphics_cursor(int far *cursor_mask,
                                int hotx,int hoty);
void pascal set_text_cursor(int ctype,int sm_or_sl,int cm_or_el);



/*------------------*/
/* Event Processor  */
/*------------------*/
void near event_processor(int event_status,int button_status,
                          int x,int y);
void install_event_handler(void);
void reset_event_status(void);
```

Using the Library

To demonstrate the use of MOUSELIB.LIB, the program MOUSE12.C from Chapter 8 is duplicated as MOUSE25.C. The only changes made are the initial #include <*filename*> statements.

If you use a Borland compiler or Microsoft QuickC and are compiling in the integrated environment, a project file is needed. Here is MOUSE25.PRJ:

```
MOUSELIB.LIB
MOUSE25.C
```

If you are using the Microsoft C 6.0 or C/C++ 7.0 compiler and are compiling in the Programmers Workbench, add MOUSELIB to the Additional Libraries Linker option.

If you are compiling from the command line with any Borland or Microsoft compiler, add MOUSELIB.LIB to the link libraries command-line option.

The remaining header and include files are discussed in the following section, "Using the Library with Your Own Applications."
Here is MOUSE25.C:

```c
/*-------------------------------------------------------------*/
/*                     MOUSE25.C                          */
/*                                                         */
/* This example is a copy of MOUSE12.C, with the exception */
/* that the library files MOUSELIB.LIB and MOUSELIB.H are  */
/* used instead of the individual mouse #include files.    */
/*                                                         */
/* Be sure to compile using the same memory model as       */
/* MOUSELIB.OBJ and EVENT.OBJ located in MOUSELIB.LIB!!!    */
/*-------------------------------------------------------------*/

#include "compiler.h"        /* Compiler directives        */
#include "mouselib.h"        /* Mouse library header file   */

#include graphics            /* Graphics and video files    */
#include videolib

void main()
   {
   install_video(GMODE);     /* Install video system        */
   header();                 /* Draw header                 */
   reset_mouse();            /* Reset mouse                 */

   if (MOUSE_THERE)
      {
      out_text_xy(25, 2,"Event Handler/Processor");
      out_text_xy(20, 5,"Press buttons and move the mouse
                 around.");
      out_text_xy(30, 10,"X -     , Y - ");

                              /* Set mouse horiz & vert limits */
      set_mouse_hlimits(1,VID_MAXX-MOUSE_SIZE+1);
      set_mouse_vlimits(1,VID_MAXY-MOUSE_SIZE);

                              /* Install event handler       */
      install_event_handler();
      show_mouse_cursor();

      while (!kbhit()) ,      /* Do until keypressed         */
         {
```

```
        show_mouse_cursor();
        if (CURSOR_MOVED)    /* If cursor moved              */
            {
            CURSOR_MOVED=0;
                            /* Clear last coords, write new */
            change_color(14);
            hide_mouse_cursor();
            clear_line_from(10,34,3,0);
            clear_line_from(10,43,3,0);
            out_int_xy(34,10,CMX);
            out_int_xy(43,10,CMY);
            show_mouse_cursor();
            }

        if (LBUTTON_DOWN)    /* Left button pressed          */
            {
            LBUTTON_DOWN=0;
            change_color(11);
            hide_mouse_cursor();
            clear_line_from(15,28,22,0);
            out_text_xy(28,15,"Left Button Pressed");
            show_mouse_cursor();
            }

        if (RBUTTON_DOWN)    /* Right button pressed         */
            {
            RBUTTON_DOWN=0;
            change_color(11);
            hide_mouse_cursor();
            clear_line_from(15,28,22,0);
            out_text_xy(28,15,"Right Button Pressed");
            show_mouse_cursor();
            }
        }
    }

else mouse_error(5,4);

getch();
                        /* Need to reset,no event handler*/
if (MOUSE_THERE) reset_mouse();

shut_down_video();
}
```

Using the Library with Your Own Applications

Perhaps you noticed that the previous example, MOUSE25.C, still contains COM-PILER.H, and the video functions library. That's because you're still using the programming examples and video function library presented in this book. When you integrate the library into your own applications, take the following steps.

These steps are not required and do not affect the libraries' performance. However, if you are an optimization fiend, continue on.

Borland Compilers

In the file MOUSELIB.C, Borland users can change the statement #include "compiler.h" to #include <dos.h>, recompile it to MOUSELIB.OBJ, and add it to MOUSELIB.LIB. The file COMPILER.H is not required for the Borland compiler.

The previous example, MOUSE25.C, can also be compiled without COM-PILER.H. Instead, the following headers and #include files can be used:

```
#include <dos.h>
#include "mouselib.h"
#include <stdio.h>
#include <graphics.h>
#include <conio.h>
#include "tcvidlib.inc"
```

Microsoft Compilers

Microsoft users need to modify the individual mouse library functions in order to compile without using COMPILER.H. If you do this, use COMPILER.H as a guideline to the necessary renaming conventions. Alternatively, you could strip COMPILER.H of the Borland macro definitions, and leave the Microsoft macro definitions intact.

Once MOUSELIB.C is compiled to an object file and added to MOUSELIB.LIB, MOUSE25.C can be compiled without COMPILER.H. Instead, the following headers and #include files can be used:

```
#include <dos.h>
#include "mouselib.h"
#include <stdio.h>
#include <graph.h>
#include <conio.h>
#include "msvidlib.inc"
```

QuickC users also need to modify MSVIDLIB.INC to match the OLDC compiler directives in COMPILER.H.

Both Compilers

Look at the following statements, which are used in MOUSE25.C when COM-PILER.H is not used:

```
#include <dos.h>
#include "mouselib.h"
#include <stdio.h>
#include <graphics.h>
#include <conio.h>
#include "tcvidlib.inc"
```

DOS.H   The file DOS.H was previously included in the file COMPILER.H. If you include DOS.H in your application, it must precede MOUSELIB.H. If you do not normally use DOS.H in your applications, you may choose to include it in MOUSELIB.H and not worry about it in your application's source code.

Other Files   The requirements for using STDIO.H, (GRAPHICS.H or GRAPH.H), and CONIO.H, will vary depending on your application's needs. Consult your compiler's reference manual for the individual function prototypes defined in these files.

The files TCVIDLIB.INC (Borland video function library) and MSVIDLIB.INC (Microsoft video function library) are only required for the examples presented in this book. As you will more than likely use your own video functions in your applications, they are irrelevant except within the context of this book.

That's it. You now have one complete library filled with mouse functions and tools, ready to be employed in your own applications. Enjoy 'em!

Part *II*

Building Your Own Mouse Cursor and the Elusive 800 × 600 16-Color Mode

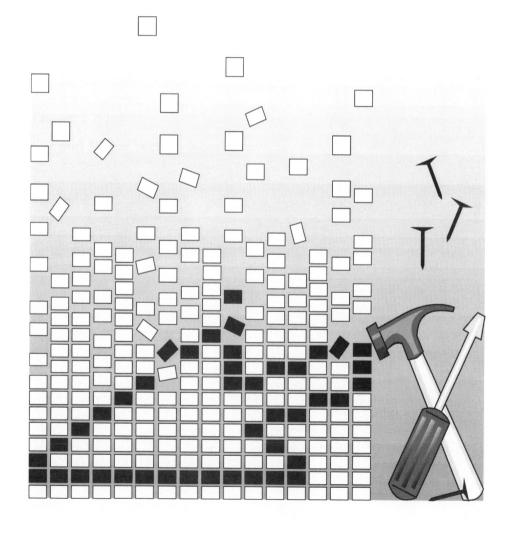

Chapter 17

Building Your Own Mouse Cursor

This chapter and the following four chapters are dedicated to one topic: building a graphics mouse cursor. After you complete these chapters, you will possess a new mouse function library capable of implementing either the default graphics mouse cursor or your own graphics mouse cursor, containing many new and exciting features. In addition, you will gain valuable insight regarding sprite and mouse cursor mechanics.

Although the task of building a graphics mouse cursor is not one for the timid, enthusiastic beginners should not be discouraged. It is not necessary to understand every (or any) concept and idea put forth. It helps, but the only requirement is entering the code, and using it as specified. It is is a good idea to read every chapter thoroughly and try to comprehend as much as possible, but again, it is not a requirement.

The Reason for Building Your Own Mouse Cursor

Originally, the graphics mouse cursor created in this book was developed to rectify a problem that has plagued mouse programmers for some time: the inability to display the mouse cursor using the Super VGA 800 × 600 16-color mode. Unless specific device-dependent mechanisms are in place, the default graphics mouse cursor never becomes visible in the 800 × 600 16-color mode. All other mouse operations function properly, but it's of little consequence if the mouse cursor is always invisible.

The mouse cursor you create in this book corrects this problem. However, the methods developed to manage the new mouse cursor presented such a wide array of new and exciting possibilities that the Super VGA 800 × 600 16-color mode has become a secondary topic. While this chapter explores the problems associated with this particular graphics mode, the new graphics mouse cursor operates in *all* of the following video modes:

- 640 × 200 16-color mode

- 640 × 350 16-color and monochrome modes

- 640 × 480 16-color and monochrome modes

- 800 × 600 16-color mode

Additionally, the new graphics mouse cursor and the accompanying sprite driver are built independently of any compiler or third-party graphics library and can be utilized in any graphics library you desire.

Some of new and exciting possibilities available with the new mouse cursor include the following:

- Mouse cursors of any color

- Multicolor mouse cursors

- Dual mouse cursors, or more if desired

- Easy-write mode-switching capability

- A device-independent graphics mouse cursor that operates in the 800 × 600 16-color mode.

The remainder of this chapter discusses the problems, and solutions, that originally inspired the building of a graphics mouse cursor.

The 800 × 600 16-Color Super VGA Mode

The 800 × 600 16-color mode is a simple extension of the standard EGA and VGA graphics modes. Almost every VGA and Super VGA card manufactured today has the ability to implement this mode, provided the appropriate monitor is used as well. However, unless you've ventured into low-level graphics programming, you might not even be aware that this mode exists. That's because most standard graphics libraries do not support it. It is a non-DOS supported graphics mode.

Setting the Mode

The blame for this mode not being widely supported falls on the shoulders of the graphics-card manufacturers. In DOS-supported graphics modes, such as the VGA 640 × 480 16-color mode, every graphics card implements setting the video mode in the same manner, conforming to the IBM/DOS standard. However, when moving into non-DOS (OEM) video modes, the manufacturers do not follow any standard whatsoever and implement the high-resolution modes however they see fit.

The nonstandard methods used to set the 800 × 600 16-color mode is by far the biggest reason the mode is not supported in most standard graphics packages or utilities, such as a compiler's graphics library or the mouse's graphics cursor. How can manufacturers of these products be expected to support a mode that is initially implemented differently on virtually every graphics card? They can't. If the graphics-card manufacturers could get together and decide on some standard, this problem could finally be put to rest.

Some technicians in the graphics-card business argue that even if a standard method for implementing the mode were used, the problem would still exist, because each manufacturer implements the high-resolution modes differently in many other aspects as well. That may be the true for most high-resolution Super VGA graphics modes, but for the 800 × 600 16-color mode, all other implementation is the same on so many VGA and Super VGA cards that it should be considered a standard.

Planar Memory

The 800 × 600 16-color mode is, with very few exceptions, implemented in exactly the same manner as the standard EGA 640 × 350 16-color mode and VGA 640 × 480 16-color mode. The reason is because these graphics modes all use *planar memory*. Planar memory is the method of storing graphics memory using four memory planes, one for red, one for green, one for blue, and one for intensity. Each memory plane has the capacity to store 64K of graphics memory. The EGA 640 × 350 16-color mode uses 28K per plane, the VGA 640 × 480 16-color mode uses 38.4K per plane, and the 800 × 600 16-color mode uses 60K per plane.

The important point is that since each plane can be maintained within the 64K limit, there is no change to the way planar memory is manipulated internally in any of the previously listed video modes.

The Horizontal Offset

One modification you must make to graphics routines using the 800 × 600 16-color mode is to the *horizontal offset*. The horizontal offset is used for vertical address calculation, and is calculated by dividing the maximum number of horizontal locations by 8 (one byte). For video modes with 640 horizontal locations, this works out to be $640/8 = 80$. For the 800×600 mode, it works out to be $800/8 = 100$.

Maximum Absolute Coordinates

Another item you need to change is the maximum absolute display coordinates. In the 800×600 16-color mode, the maximum horizontal coordinate is 799, and the maximum vertical coordinate is 599.

Graphics Code and Libraries

Since planar memory is handled in the same manner for the EGA 650×350 16-color mode, the VGA 640×480 16-color mode, and the VGA 800×600 16-color mode, if you have the ability to modify the horizontal offset and the maximum absolute coordinates, the remaining graphics code should operate properly in all of these modes, with no additional modification.

Most standard graphics libraries do not allow you to directly modify the horizontal offset, and that's a shame, because the 800×600 16-color mode could be implemented using the libraries if this were allowed, provided that the library also allowed you to directly set the video mode. As it is, you must either write the graphics code yourself (all of it), or rely on third-party graphics libraries.

Existing Solutions

In recent years, some graphics-card and mouse manufacturers have developed solutions for the mouse cursor visibility problem. The following are a few of these solutions.

Video Hardware Cursors

Some Super VGA cards, such as the Video 7 VRAM II Ergo card, implement the graphics mouse cursor directly in video hardware. These cards allow the graphics mouse cursor to operate in any graphics *or text* mode. The Microsoft mouse driver supports the 800×600 16-color mode using these cards, but it is a misnomer. What is actually supported is the graphics card, not the video mode. Any mouse driver supports the video mode, provided the particular graphics card is being used.

 Mouse function 40, set video mode, does allow you to directly set the mouse's video mode. However, it is mainly used to determine if a video mode is valid or to set the mouse's video mode independent of the active video mode.

Proprietary Software Cursors

Some Super VGA cards, such as the ATI Graphics Ultra Accelerator card, are bundled with an InPort mouse built directly into the graphics card. The mouse driver supplied with the ATI InPort mouse maintains the mouse cursor in the high-resolution modes, and you can take immediate advantage of it.

VESA VCI Overlay

Logitech now supports high-resolution graphics modes with the incorporation of a VESA (Video Electronics Standards Association) VCI (Video Cursor Interface) overlay. The VCI separates the video cursor functions from the mouse driver and places them in an overlay, which is loaded either from the disk at run time or linked through interrupt 10h as a ROM/TSR-based overlay. If the VCI is supplied with the video card, you can take immediate advantage of the high-resolution graphics modes; otherwise the VCI can be incorporated directly into the mouse driver.

In order to promote the acceptance of VESA, Logitech has subsequently stopped supporting all OEM video modes. Programmers interested should contact Logitech, and request the *Logitech Mouse Technical Reference & Programming Guide Addendum*, which contains a full description of Logitech's VCI overlay and how to incorporate it into the mouse driver.

Device Dependence

The problem with all of the solutions listed above is that they are device dependent. While VESA is making huge strides in standardizing the high-resolution graphics modes, only Logitech has made the decision to support a VCI directly in their mouse driver, and in that sense, the solution is device dependent to the Logitech mouse. The hardware graphics cursor and the InPort mouse driver supplied with the high-end video cards are specific to those cards, and most VGA cards provide neither.

A Universal Solution

The only universal solution to cure the problem and maintain compatibility with all VGA cards and mouse drivers is to build your own graphics mouse cursor and use it instead of the default graphics mouse cursor. In the following four chapters you learn how this feat is accomplished.

This solution is only universal in the 800×600 16-color mode. Other OEM Super VGA modes are implemented differently in many regards, depending on the video-card manufacturer.

Although the inspiration for building a graphics mouse cursor arose from the problems associated with the 800×600 16-color mode, only two programming examples presented in this book utilizes the mode. The reason is because neither the Borland nor Microsoft graphics libraries provide direct support for this mode, and some additional low-level code has to be written in order to demonstrate it. However, there are several examples using the new mouse cursor with the standard graphics libraries and video functions you have been using in the previous chapters. Therefore, even if you do not have a graphics card or monitor that supports the 800 × 600 16-color mode, there are many examples that should still be of considerable interest to you.

Microsoft does support the 800× 600 16-color mode in the Microsoft C/C++ 7.0 compiler, but the VESA TSR might be required.

It should be pointed out that the new mouse cursor does not represent any cursor implementation employed by Microsoft or any OEM mouse manufacturer. Although the methods presented in this book might follow similar fundamental sprite mechanics, the new mouse cursor is defined and written to the display much differently. While it lacks the feature of a definable border edge, it does contain many proprietary features not found in the standard mouse cursor.

One more point: do not assume you can use the 800 × 600 16-color mode simply because you have a graphics card (VGA) that supports it. The 800 × 600 16-color mode also requires a variable frequency display, such as the NEC MultiSynch or compatible monitor. Check both your graphics card and monitor documentation to determine if you can use the 800 × 600 16-color mode. You *must* also determine the correct mode number for your graphics card and how to set the mode using the graphics card, since it varies from manufacturer to manufacturer. Again, consult your video card's documentation.

Attempting to run the 800× 600 16-color mode on the wrong type of monitor can result in damage to the monitor! Be sure to first consult your video card and video monitor documentation to determine if you can use this mode.

Chapter *18*

Building the Sprite Driver

In this chapter, you build the functions necessary to generate a new graphics mouse cursor. You learn about the EGA/VGA's write mode 0, why write mode 0 is important to the mouse cursor, and basic sprite/cursor mechanics.

Before beginning, some terminology is required. The new graphics mouse cursor you create in this book is called a *sprite*. A sprite is a small, high-resolution object, of a known size, that does not disturb the background text or graphics it moves over (or under). Although the default graphics mouse cursor is also a sprite, to avoid confusion, the default graphics mouse cursor is called the *mouse cursor*, and the graphics mouse cursor you create in this book is called the *sprite cursor*. The functions used to generate the sprite cursor are collectively known as the *sprite driver*.

The following discussions, the algorithms presented, and the actual source code, are the author's own interpretation of how the mouse cursor's graphics routines are implemented. It is not the author's intent to assert that these are the exact methods used by Microsoft, or any OEM mouse manufacturer. As these operations are proprietary to the specific mouse manufacturer, no technical information has been made available regarding them. The mechanisms and similarities discussed here refer only to the concepts of background image saving, background image restoring, and cursor image management.

The Graphics Mouse Cursor

The graphics mouse cursor is a 16 × 16 square image that moves around the display without disturbing the background image it moves over. To accomplish this, the mouse driver is constantly saving and restoring the background image the mouse cursor is moving over.

It is the general assumption that the mouse driver saves and restores a 16 × 16 square background image for every pixel move the mouse cursor makes, and redraws the mouse cursor for every pixel move as well. Only two parts of this assumption are true: for every pixel move the background image is restored and the mouse cursor is redrawn. However, the underlying background image is only saved every *eight* pixel moves in any *one* direction. To understand how and why, you must first understand some basics about writing to the EGA/VGA video card.

EGA/VGA Read/Write Mode 0

Both the EGA and VGA video cards allow you to read and write graphics information to display memory using various methods, known as *read and write modes*. Each read and write mode manages graphics data in a different manner. Some modes are available only on the VGA, while others are available on the EGA and VGA. The mouse cursor, and the sprite cursor, use read and write mode 0, which are available on all EGA and VGA video cards. Write mode 0 has the ability to make logical comparisons with the data being written, and the background it is writing over. It is perfectly suited for use with a graphics mouse cursor. Read mode 0 operates the same as write mode 0, only graphics data is read from display memory and no logical operations occur.

Using write mode 0, graphics data is written to the display eight bits (one byte) at a time. Each byte can be thought of as eight pixels, where bit 7 corresponds to the starting pixel location of the display write, and bits 6-0 are the right neighboring pixels. Figure 18-1 illustrates writing eight bits, or pixels, at one time, starting at display location 0,0.

Even Byte Boundaries

The one limitation of write mode 0 is that the eighth bit (bit 7) must reside on an *even byte boundary*, or pixel location. An even byte boundary is a horizontal display location that can be evenly divided by 8, or one byte. The display write can start at horizontal location 0, 8, 16, 24, and so on, but not at location 4, 12, 20, 28, and so on. Byte (eight-pixel) display writes must begin on even byte boundaries. Figure 18-2 is an illustration of valid, even, byte boundaries and nonvalid boundary locations.

To write a single bit, or pixel, using write mode 0, the appropriate bit must be located in the byte (eight bits), and the remaining 7 bits masked out. If the display's horizontal coordinates range from 0 to 639, then writing a single pixel at horizontal

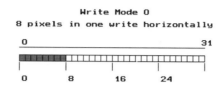

Figure 18-1.   *Write mode 0—eight pixels in one write horizontally*

location 2 requires writing a byte with bit 5 set to 1 and the remaining bits set to 0. Figure 18-3 illustrates masking out seven bits, or pixels, to write one bit, or pixel.

The byte value represented in Figure 18-3 is 0×20, or 32 decimal. The binary representation is 00100000. Bytes are written to the display beginning with the most significant bits. Using the previous illustration as an example, bit 7 corresponds to location 0, bit 6 to location 1, bit 5 to location 2, bit 4 to location 3, and so on.

Since the graphics mouse cursor is defined as a 16 × 16-bit image, one row of the mouse cursor's image represents two bytes (16 bits). These two bytes can be written to the display using two one-byte writes, masking out the cursor image from the bytes as they are written. The problem is that when a 16-bit row is shifted (moved) one pixel at a time, it only resides on even byte boundaries once every eight moves. This means the 16-bit (two-byte) row actually resides within three even byte boundaries, and must be loaded appropriately into a 24-bit row and written to the display as three

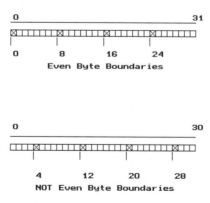

Figure 18-2.   *Byte boundaries*

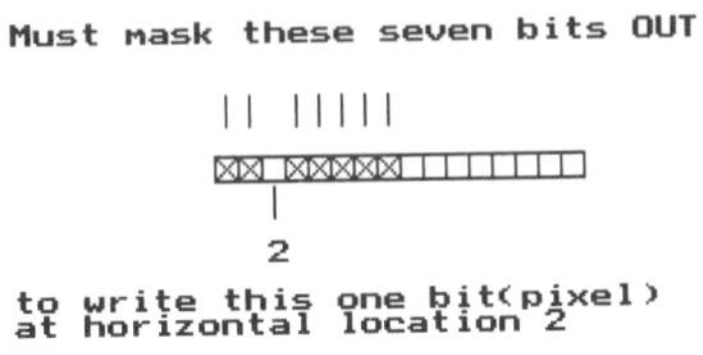

```
Must mask these seven bits OUT

      || |||||
    ▓▓ ▓▓▓▓▓ ┌┬┬┬┬┬┬┬┐
       |
       2
to write this one bit(pixel)
at horizontal location 2
```

Figure 18-3.   Masking seven bits to write one bit at horizontal location 2

bytes. This process occurs every seven consecutive *single* pixel moves, as the eighth move resides on an even byte boundary and can be written as two bytes. It is in this small bit of logic, which at first appears to be a hindrance, that the speed and performance of the mouse cursor is obtained.

Cursor/Sprite Mechanics

Internally, the mouse cursor's image is *actually* a 24 × 24-bit image, *not* 16 × 16. The 16 × 16-bit image used to define the mouse's cursor shape is imported, internally, into a 24 × 24-bit image. When the 16 × 16-bit image is initially imported into the 24 × 24-bit image, each 24-bit row has eight empty (padded) bits to the right (least significant), and the last eight rows of the image are completely empty (padded). This is illustrated in Figure 18-4.

When the mouse cursor is initially written to the display, the background image behind the 24 × 24-bit image is saved. As the mouse cursor moves pixel by pixel, the original background is restored, the 16 × 16-bit image is *shifted* appropriately inside the 24 × 24-bit image, and the 24 × 24-bit image is redrawn, at the same location, on three even byte boundaries. When the 16 × 16-bit image reaches a border *inside* the 24 × 24-bit image (bit 0 or bit 23), either horizontally or vertically, it is *only* then that the 24 × 24-bit image is relocated, by one byte (eight pixels), and a new background image saved. The 16 × 16-bit image is then shifted to a new corner of the 24 × 24-bit image, appropriate to the direction of the move, and the 24 × 24-bit image is redrawn at the new location. This means that the mouse driver only saves the mouse cursor's underlying background image when the mouse cursor travels a distance of eight pixels from the last even byte boundary, horizontally or vertically!

To hold the 24 × 24-bit image, a 24-element array of long integers (32 bits) is used. There are eight unused bits in each long integer (which you could use to define a 32 × 32-bit image if you are really adventurous).

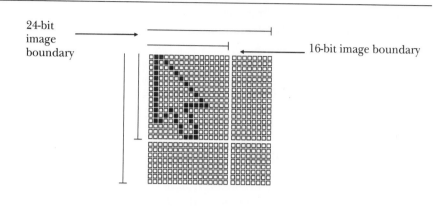

Figure 18-4.   *16 × 16-bit image imported into 24 × 24-bit image*

COPYPUT/XOR Mode

The sprite cursor you create in this book operates in either COPYPUT (replace) mode or XOR (eXclusive OR) mode. If the sprite cursor is operating in the COPYPUT mode, the previously discussed background image saving and restoring is performed. However, if the sprite cursor is operating in XOR mode, the sprite driver performs *zero* image saving and *zero* image restoring, as the sprite cursor is simply XORed against the display background to become visible and XORed again at the same location to become invisible, leaving the background image intact.

The Sprite Driver

The sprite driver functions presented in this chapter use the exact techniques described in the previous sections. The graphics functions that handle image saving, restoring, and drawing the cursor shape are written at the lowest level possible, directly to the video card itself. This allows complete independence of any existing graphics library, and provides the speed required for sprite animation. It also requires some fairly complex code.

However, beginners needn't be discouraged. Although the sprite driver's graphics functions are written in assembly language, it is all coded using *inline assembly*. Inline assembly allows you to write assembly code directly in a C source file. As such, function calls and the arguments passed in to the function can all be managed as regular C code. Probably the biggest hurdle for programmers learning assembly language to get over is handling the arguments passed into assembly functions. Since the graphics functions are coded using inline assembly, beginners can concentrate on the actual graphics code and what the code does. Experienced programmers wishing to optimize further can modify the source code to pure assembly.

There is no requirement for you to completely understand the source code, only that you use it properly.

Low-Level Graphics Functions

The following low-level graphics functions have been adapted from the book *The Programmer's Guide to EGA and VGA Card,* by Richard F. Ferraro, Addison Wesley, 1990. The functions operate in the EGA 640 × 200 16-color mode, EGA 640 × 350 16-color and monochrome modes, VGA 640 × 480 16-color and monochrome modes, and the 800 × 600 16-color mode. If you wish to utilize the sprite driver in graphics modes beyond the 800 × 600 16-color mode, such as the 1024 × 768 256-color mode, the information you seek is provided in Mr. Ferraro's book. Since modes higher than the 800 × 600 16-color mode (Super VGA modes) follow no standard of implementation, it is beyond the scope of this book to utilize them.

To give you a general feeling for what the low-level graphics functions do internally, the following provides a brief description of each function. It should be pointed out that several of these functions, especially those used to modify the EGA/VGA registers, have many uses, and the descriptions provided specify how the functions are used relative to the code found in this book.

The source code for the graphics functions is heavily commented, and provides additional information regarding the functions, and how they are implemented.

LL_modereg(unsigned char *mode*)   This function modifies the mode register. It is used to specify the EGA/VGA write mode.

LL_mapmask(unsigned char *plane*)   This function modifies the map mask register. It is used to specify which memory plane data is written to.

LL_setres(unsigned char *value*)   This function modifies the set reset resister. It is used to modify the color of a sprite row.

LL_esetres(unsigned char *mask*)   This function modifies the enable set reset register. It is used to specify which display planes are used with the LL_setres() function, set reset register.

LL_readmap(unsigned char *mapcode*)   This function modifies the read map select register. It is used to specify which bit plane is accessed in read mode 0.

LL_bitmask(unsigned char *val*)   This function modifies the bit mask register. It is used to allow all bits in a sprite cursor row to modify display memory.

LL_setfunction(int *mode*)   This function modifies the data rotate register. It is used to modify the logical mode a sprite uses (XOR or COPYPUT).

LL_rdgwin(int *segment*,int *offst*,
        unsigned char far **buf*,
        int *nbyte*,int *nrow*,int *bpvrow*)   This function reads data from one bit plane.

LL_wrgwin(int *segment*,int *offst*,
        unsigned char far **buf*,
        int *nbyte*,int *nrow*,int *bpvrow*)   This function writes data to one bit plane.

LL_planerd(int *segment*,int *address*,
        unsigned char far **buf*,
        int *numbyte*,int *nrow*,int *offset*)   This function reads data from all four bit planes, one plane at a time.

LL_planewr(int *segment*,int *address*,
        unsigned char far **buf*,
        int *numbyte*,int *nrow*,int *offset*)   This function writes data to all four bit planes, one plane at a time.

LL_readwin(int *page*,int *x1*,int *y1*,
        unsigned char far **buf*,
        int *mode*)   This function reads and saves the contents of display memory defined by rectangular region, or window.

LL_writewin(int *page*,int *x1*,int *y1*,
        unsigned char far **buf*,
        int *mode*)   This function writes data for a rectangular region, or window, to display memory.

LL_write3byte(int *address*,char *mask1*,
        char *mask2*,char *mask3*)   This function writes 24 bits (three bytes) of data to display memory, one byte at a time.

Sprite Functions

The following are the actual sprite driver functions. They are used to create, destroy, write, move, hide, and show sprites.

The sprite driver functions can be implemented in any graphics mode (such as the 1024 × 768 256-color mode), providing the underlying low- level graphics code is available for that mode. See the introduction to the previous section, "Low-Level Graphics Functions."

sprite_imagesize(int *BIT_SIZE*)   This function returns the amount of memory needed to save a sprite image whose size is equal to BIT_SIZE × BIT_SIZE.

sprite_type *new_sprite(void)   This function allocates memory for a sprite and returns a pointer to that memory.

load_sprite(char *mask*[16][17],
              int *hotx*,int *hoty*,
              sprite_type **sprite*,int *mode*)   This function loads and initializes a sprite.

destroy_sprite_(sprite_type **sprite*)   This function destroys a sprite.

do_sprite(sprite_type **sprite*)   This function writes a sprite to the display. This function is used internally by other sprite function, and you should not use it directly.

draw_sprite(int *x*,int *y*,sprite_type **sprite*)   This function sets the display location of a sprite. If the location is different from the current location, the sprite is moved. This function is the heart of the sprite driver. All internal shifting logic, background saving logic, and background restoring logic, is contained within this function.

change_sprite_line_color(sprite_type **sprite*,int *linenum*,
                           int *newcolor*)   This function changes the color of an individual row in a sprite.

change_sprite_color(sprite_type **sprite*,int *newcolor*)   This function changes the color of an entire sprite.

set_sprite_mode(sprite_type **sprite*,int *mode*)   This function changes the current logical write mode of a sprite to COPYPUT or XOR modes.

hide_sprite(sprite_type **sprite*)   This function makes a sprite invisible if it is currently visible.

show_sprite(sprite_type **sprite*)   This function makes a sprite visible if it is currently invisible.

The Sprite Driver Source Code

The file containing all of the previous functions is called SPRITELL.C. Compiling instructions are provided following the source code listing.

Here is SPRITELL.C:

```
/*------------------------------------------------------------*/
/*                      SPRITELL.C                        */
/*                                                        */
/* Sprite drivers, low-level window save/restore, and 3-byte */
/* line drawing. All the necessary components to build a  */
/* driver independent of any graphics library. The sprite is */
/* used in this book for the mouse cursor, but can be used */
/* on its own as well for other needs.                    */
/*------------------------------------------------------------*/

#include "compiler.h"
#include allocate

#define XOR_MODE 24             /* Write mode identifiers      */
#define COPYPUT_MODE 0

int BITMAP_SIZE=16;             /* Size of bitmap image        */



/* The Sprite Structure Type */
/*----------------------------*/
typedef struct
   {
   unsigned long bigmask[24];  /* Actual sprite mask          */
   unsigned char *image_buffer;/* Image buffer for sprite     */
   unsigned char color[16];    /* Color of each line in mask  */
   int left_shift;             /* Blank bits - left side mask */
   int right_shift;            /* Blank bits - right side mask*/
   int up_shift;               /* Blank bits - upper side mask*/
   int down_shift;             /* Blank bits - lower side mask*/
   int tx,ty;                  /* Text coords-3byte wide mask */
   int gx,gy;                  /* Graf coords-3byte wide mask */
   int hotx,hoty;              /* Hot spot                    */
   int sprite_mode;            /* COPY/PUT or XOR sprite?      */
   unsigned char SPRITE_ON;    /* Sprite on or off k          */
   }sprite_type;

                               /* Mode number for 800x600 16-  */
                               /* color mode. You can hard-code */
                               /* this or take it out. If you   */
                               /* take it out, the case stmnts  */
                               /* will consider DEFAULT to be   */
```

```c
                              /* the 800X600 16-color mode.    */
                              /* 0x62 is for Video-7 card.     */
#define MODE_800X600X16 0x62

int HORIZ_OFFSET=80;          /* Horizontal offset for vertical*/
                              /* pixel addressing.             */
                              /* Assign value in main() !!!    */

int MODE_NUMBER;              /* Video mode number; set in     */
                              /* LL_setmode() or by programmer.*/

int PAGE=0;                   /* Current video page number.    */
                              /* Assign value in main() !!!    */


void evp_type draw_sprite(int x,int y,sprite_type *sprite);


              /*---------------------------*/
              /* EGA/VGA REGISTER FUNCTIONS */
              /*---------------------------*/

/* Load the "mode" register with the byte "mode"              */
/*----------------------------------------------------------*/
void far pascal LL_modereg(unsigned char mode)
    {outp(0x3CE,5);outp(0x3CF,mode);}

/* Load the map mask register with the byte "plane"           */
/*----------------------------------------------------------*/
void far pascal LL_mapmask(unsigned char plane)
    {outp(0x3C4,2);outp(0x3C5,plane);}

/* Load the "set reset" register with byte "value"            */
/*----------------------------------------------------------*/
void far pascal LL_setres(unsigned char value)
    {outp(0x3CE,0);outp(0x3CF,value);}

/* Load the enable set reset register with "mask"             */
/*----------------------------------------------------------*/
void far pascal LL_esetres(unsigned char mask)
    {outp(0x3CE,1);outp(0x3CF,mask);}
```

```
/* Load the "read map select" register                      */
/*------------------------------------------------------------*/
void far pascal LL_readmap(unsigned char mapcode)
   {outp(0x3CE,4);outp(0x3CF,mapcode);}


/* Load the "bit mask" register to the byte "val"            */
/*------------------------------------------------------------*/
void far pascal LL_bitmask(unsigned char val)
   {outp(0x3CE,8);outp(0x3CF,val);}


/* Load the "write mode" register bit 4 & 5 to COPY=0,XOR=24, */
/* AND=8,OR=16                                               */
/*------------------------------------------------------------*/
void far pascal LL_setfunction(int mode)
   {outp(0x3CE,3);outp(0x3CF,mode);}



            /*----------------------------*/
            /* LOW-LEVEL GRAPHICS FUNCTIONS*/
            /*----------------------------*/



/* MODULE : LL RDGWIN                                        */
/*------------------------------------------------------------*/
/* Read a plane of data from the display memory.             */
/* Input parameters                                          */
/*      segment    - Segment address of starting coordinates */
/*      offset     - Address of starting coordinates         */
/*      buffer     - Host "c" buffer containing the data      */
/*      nbyte      - Number of bytes per row                 */
/*      nrow       - Number of rows                           */
/*      bpvrow     - Bytes per virtual row                   */
/*                                                          */
void evp_type pascal LL_rdgwin(int segment,int offst,
                               unsigned char far *buf,
                               int nbyte,int nrow,int bpvrow)
   {
   unsigned char nnbyte;     /* Dummy for Microsoft C        */
   asm push ds;              /* Save for code; all others     */
   asm push si;              /* are saved automatically.      */
   asm push di;
```

```
/* Load segment:offset address to display memory in DS:SI  */
/*-----------------------------------------------------------*/
asm mov ax,segment;        /* Get segment to display buffer */
asm mov ds,ax;             /* Load into DS                  */
asm mov si,offst;          /* Get offset to display memory  */

/* Load segment:offset address of the "c" buffer in ES:DI   */
/*-----------------------------------------------------------*/
asm les di,buf;            /* Get segment - offset of buffer*/

/* Set up constants for the data moving                     */
/*-----------------------------------------------------------*/
asm mov dx,nrow;           /* Get number of rows per window */
asm mov bx,bpvrow;         /* Get window bytes per row      */
asm sub bx,nbyte;          /* (Virtual window) bytes per row*/
nnbyte=nbyte;              /* MC won't compile unless subbed*/
asm mov ah,nnbyte;         /* Get bytes per window          */
asm xor ch,ch;             /* Clear the CH                  */

/* Move one row per loop                                    */
/*-----------------------------------------------------------*/
RUNLOOP:
asm mov cl,ah;             /* Number of bytes per row       */
asm rep movsb;             /* Move the data                 */
asm add si,bx;             /* Add byte increment            */
asm dec dx;                /* Decrement the row counter     */
asm jg  RUNLOOP;           /* Repeat for all rows           */

asm pop di;                /* Restore for code              */
asm pop si;
asm pop ds;
}


/* MODULE : LL WRGWIN                                        */
/*-----------------------------------------------------------*/
/* Write a plane of data from the display memory.           */
/* Input parameters                                         */
/*    segment    - Segment address of starting coordinates  */
/*    offset     - Address of starting coordinates          */
/*    buffer     - Host "c" buffer containing the data       */
/*    nbyte      - Number of bytes per row                  */
/*    nrow       - Number of rows                           */
```

```
/*     bpvrow      - Bytes per virtual row                     */
/*                                                             */
void evp_type pascal LL_wrgwin(int segment,int offst,
                              unsigned char far *buf,
                              int nbyte,int nrow,int bpvrow)
    {
    unsigned char nnbyte;       /* Dummy for Microsoft C       */
    asm push si;                /* Save for code, all others are */
    asm push di;                /* saved automatically.        */
    asm push es;

    /* Load segment:offset address to display memory in ES:DI  */
    /*-----------------------------------------------------------*/
    asm mov ax,segment;         /* Get segment to display memory */
    asm mov es,ax;              /* Load into es                */
    asm mov di,offst;           /* Get offset to display memory  */

    /* Load segment:offset address of the "c" buffer in DS:SI  */
    /*-----------------------------------------------------------*/
    asm lds si,buf;             /* Segment and offset of buffer  */

    /* Set up constants fo the data moving                     */
    /*-----------------------------------------------------------*/
    asm mov dx,nrow;            /* Get number of rows per window */
    asm mov bx,bpvrow;          /* Get window bytes per row    */
    asm sub bx,nbyte;           /* (Virtual window) bytes per row*/
    nnbyte=nbyte;               /* MC Won't compile unless subbed*/
    asm mov ah,nnbyte;          /* Get bytes per window        */
    asm xor ch,ch;              /* Clear the CH                */

    /* Move one row per loop                                   */
    /*-----------------------------------------------------------*/
RUNLOOP:
    asm mov cl,ah;              /* Number of bytes per row     */
    asm rep movsb;              /* Move the data               */
    asm add di,bx;              /* Add offset for display address*/
    asm dec dx;                 /* Decrement the row counter   */
    asm jg RUNLOOP;             /* Repeat for all rows         */

    asm pop es;                 /* Restore for code            */
    asm pop di;
    asm pop si;
    }
```

```
/* MODULE : LL PLANERD                                         */
/*------------------------------------------------------------*/
/* Read the data from all four bit planes.                     */
/* Input parameters                                            */
/*     segment     - Segment portion the display address       */
/*     address     - Offset portion of display memory address  */
/*     buf         - Buffer which will contain the data        */
/*     numbyte     - Number of bytes per row                   */
/*     nrow        - Number of rows in the window              */
/*     offset      - Number of bytes per horizontal offset     */
/*                                                             */
void evp_type pascal LL_planerd(int segment,int address,
                                unsigned char far *buf,
                                int numbyte,int nrow,int offset)

    {
    unsigned char far *pntbuf;
    int byteperwin;

    byteperwin=numbyte*nrow;   /* Calc bytes per window/plane   */

    pntbuf=buf;                /* Pointer pntbuf points to buf  */
    byteperwin=(unsigned long) (numbyte*nrow);
    LL_readmap(0);
    LL_rdgwin(segment,address,pntbuf,numbyte,nrow,offset);

    pntbuf+=byteperwin;        /* Plane 1 after plane 0 in buf  */
    LL_readmap(1);
    LL_rdgwin(segment,address,pntbuf,numbyte,nrow,offset);

    pntbuf+=byteperwin;        /* Plane 2 after plane 1 in buf  */
    LL_readmap(2);
    LL_rdgwin(segment,address,pntbuf,numbyte,nrow,offset);

    pntbuf+=byteperwin;        /* Plane 3 after plane 2 in buf  */
    LL_readmap(3);
    LL_rdgwin(segment,address,pntbuf,numbyte,nrow,offset);
    }


/* MODULE : LL PLANEWR                                          */
/*------------------------------------------------------------*/
/* Write the data to all four bit planes.                      */
/* Input parameters                                            */
/*     segment     - Segment portion of the display address    */
```

```
/*      address       - Offset portion of display memory address  */
/*      buf           - Buffer which will contain the data         */
/*      numbyte       - Number of bytes per row                    */
/*      nrow          - Number of rows in the window               */
/*      offset        - Number of bytes per horizontal offset      */
/*                                                                 */
void evp_type pascal LL_planewr(int segment,int address,
                                unsigned char far *buf,
                                int numbyte,int nrow,int offset)
    {
    unsigned char far *pntbuf;
    int byteperwin;

    byteperwin=numbyte*nrow;   /* Calc bytes per window/plane     */

    pntbuf=buf;                /* Pointer pntbuf points to buf    */
    byteperwin=(unsigned long) (numbyte*nrow);
    LL_mapmask(1);
    LL_wrgwin(segment,address,pntbuf,numbyte,nrow,offset);

    pntbuf+=byteperwin;        /* Plane 1 after plane 0 in buf    */
    LL_mapmask(2);
    LL_wrgwin(segment,address,pntbuf,numbyte,nrow,offset);

    pntbuf+=byteperwin;        /* Plane 2 after plane 1 in buf    */
    LL_mapmask(4);
    LL_wrgwin(segment,address,pntbuf,numbyte,nrow,offset);

    pntbuf+=byteperwin;        /* Plane 3 after plane 2 in buf    */
    LL_mapmask(8);
    LL_wrgwin(segment,address,pntbuf,numbyte,nrow,offset);

    LL_mapmask(0xff);          /* Enable all planes               */
    }


/* MODULE : LL READWIN                                            */
/*--------------------------------------------------------------*/
/* Read a rectangular region (bound on even bytes, text sizes)*/
/* to the display memory. These routines are coded to save.     */
/* BITMAP region sizes only.                                    */
/* Input parameters                                             */
/*      page    - Page number to read from                      */
/*      x1,y1   - Upper-left coordinates of region to be saved  */
/*      buf     - Address to image data; must be allocated      */
/*                first!!!                                       */
```

```c
/*      mode    -  Current video mode we are in            */
/*                                                          */
void evp_type pascal LL_readwin(int page,int x1,int y1,
                               unsigned char far *buf,
                               int mode)
    {
    int address,nrow,numbyte;

    x1*=8;y1*=8;                /* Make 'em into graphics coords */
    nrow=BITMAP_SIZE+8;         /* 1 byte more than the bitmap   */
    numbyte=nrow>>3;            /* Even bytes = (nrow / 8)        */

    switch(mode)
       {
       case 0x0E:/* Mode 0x0E , 640 x 200 16-COLOR */
                 address=(page&3)*0x4000 + (y1*80) + (x1>>3);
                 LL_planerd(0xA000,address,buf,numbyte,nrow,80);
                 break;

       case 0x0F:/* Mode 0x0F , 640 x 350 MONO     */
                 address=(page&1)*0x8000 + (y1*80) + (x1>>3);
                 LL_rdgwin(0xA000,address,buf,numbyte,nrow,80);
                 break;

       case 0x10:/* Mode 0x10 , 640 x 350 16-COLOR */
                 address=(page&1)*0x8000 + (y1*80) + (x1>>3);
                 LL_planerd(0xA000,address,buf,numbyte,nrow,80);
                 break;

       case 0x11:/* Mode 0x11 , 640 x 480 MONO     */
                 address=(y1*80) + (x1>>3);
                 LL_rdgwin(0xA000,address,buf,numbyte,nrow,80);
                 break;

       case 0x12:/* Mode 0x12 , 640 x 480 16-COLOR */
                 address=(y1*80) + (x1>>3);
                 LL_planerd(0xA000,address,buf,numbyte,nrow,80);
                 break;

       /* Since the mode # on SVGA cards for 800 x 600 16-color*/
       /* is different for all cards, this makes the 800 x 600 */
       /* 16-color mode either:  1) the default, in which case */
       /* if it's not EGA/VGA mode, it will assume 800 x 600 or*/
       /* 2) by the mode number defined at the top of the code.*/
       /* Remember, you CANNOT use variables in switch         */
```

```
        /* statements; it must be used with constant values.    */

        case MODE_800X600X16:
        default:
                /* 800 x 600 16-Color */
                address=(y1*100) + (x1>>3);
                LL_planerd(0xA000,address,buf,numbyte,nrow,100);
                break;
        }
    }



/* MODULE : LL WRITEWIN                                            */
/*-------------------------------------------------------------*/
/* Write a rectangular region (bound on even bytes,text sizes)*/
/* to the display memory. These routines are coded to write    */
/* BITMAP region sizes only.                                   */
/* Input parameters                                            */
/*     page   -  Page number to write to                       */
/*     x1,y1  -  Upper-left coordinates of region to write to  */
/*     buf    -  Address to image data                         */
/*     mode   -  Current video mode                            */
/*                                                             */
void evp_type pascal LL_writewin(int page,int x1,int y1,
                                 unsigned char far *buf,
                                 int mode)
    {
    int address,nrow,numbyte;

    x1*=8;y1*=8;              /* Make 'em into graphics coords */
    nrow=BITMAP_SIZE+8;       /* 1 byte more than the bitmap    */
    numbyte=nrow>>3;          /* Even bytes = (nrow / 8)        */

    switch(mode)
        {
        case 0x0E:/* Mode 0x0E , 640 x 200 16-COLOR */
                address=((page&3)*0x4000) + (y1*80) + (x1>>3);
                LL_planewr(0xA000,address,buf,numbyte,nrow,80);
                break;

        case 0x0F:/* Mode 0x0F , 640 x 350 MONO       */
                address=((page&1)*0x8000) + (y1*80) + (x1>>3);
                LL_wrgwin(0xA000,address,buf,numbyte,nrow,80);
                break;
```

```
case 0x10:/* Mode 0x10 , 640 x 350 16-COLOR */
         address=((page&1)*0x8000) + (y1*80) + (x1>>3);
         LL_planewr(0xA000,address,buf,numbyte,nrow,80);
         break;

case 0x11:/* Mode 0x11 , 640 x 480 MONO     */
         address=(y1*80) + (x1>>3);
         LL_wrgwin(0xA000,address,buf,numbyte,nrow,80);
         break;

case 0x12:/* Mode 0x12 , 640 x 480 16-COLOR */
         address=(y1*80) + (x1>>3);
         LL_planewr(0xA000,address,buf,numbyte,nrow,80);
         break;

/* Since the mode # on SVGA cards for 800 x 600 16-color*/
/* is different for all cards, this makes the 800 x 600 */
/* 16-color mode either: 1) the default, in which case  */
/* if it's not EGA/VGA mode, it will assume 800 x 600 or*/
/* 2) by the mode number defined at the top of the code.*/
/* Remember, you CANNOT use variables in switch          */
/* statements, it must be used with constant values.     */

case MODE_800X600X16:
default:
         /* 800 x 600 16-Color */
         address=(y1*100) + (x1>>3);
         LL_planewr(0xA000,address,buf,numbyte,nrow,100);
         break;


   }
}


/* MODULE : LL WRITE3BYTE                                 */
/*------------------------------------------------------*/
/* Output a horizontal contained within three bytes.     */
/* Input assumptions                                     */
/*    Enable set/reset register set to desired planes.   */
/*    Set/reset register set to color.                   */
/* Input parameters                                      */
/*    address = Display memory offset address            */
/*    mask1   = First (left) mask for line               */
/*    mask2   = Second (middle) mask for line            */
/*    mask3   = Third (right) mask for line               */
```

```
/*                                                    */
void evp_type pascal LL_write3byte(int address,char mask1,
                                    char mask2,char mask3)
   {
   asm push ds;                    /* Save for code, the rest are  */
   asm push si;                    /* saved automatically.         */

   asm mov ax,0A000h;              /* Point to display address     */
   asm mov ds,ax;
   asm mov si,address;             /* Get address                  */

   /* Load the bit mask regstr*/
   /*------------------------*/
   asm mov ax,3CEh;                /* Point to mask address        */
   asm mov dx,ax;
   asm mov al,8;                   /* 8 for mask                   */
   asm out dx,al;
   asm inc dx;                     /* Point to mask register       */

   /* Output first byte      */
   /*------------------------*/
   asm mov al,mask1;               /* Get mask                     */
   asm out dx,al;                  /* Load mask                    */

   asm mov al,ds:[si];             /* Dummy read before write      */
   asm mov ds:[si],al;             /* Output color                 */

   /* Output second byte     */
   /*------------------------*/
   asm mov al,mask2;               /* Get mask                     */
   asm out dx,al;                  /* Load mask                    */

   asm inc si;                     /* Increment address            */

   asm mov al,ds:[si];             /* Dummy read before write      */
   asm mov ds:[si],al;             /* Output color                 */

   /* Output third byte      */
   /*------------------------*/
   asm mov al,mask3;               /* Get mask                     */
   asm out dx,al;                  /* Load mask                    */

   asm inc si;                     /* Increment address            */

   asm mov al,ds:[si];             /* Dummy read before write      */
```

```
asm mov ds:[si],al;        /* Output color              */

asm pop si;                /* Restore for code          */
asm pop ds;
   }


        /*--------------------------*/
        /* SPRITE DRIVER FUNCTIONS  */
        /*--------------------------*/


/* MODULE : SRITE_IMAGESIZE                                */
/*-------------------------------------------------------*/
/* Determine image size of sprite.                         */
/* Input parameters                                        */
/*     BIT_SIZE - size of bitmap image (NOT region)        */
/* Output parameters                                       */
/*     Size of region                                      */
/*                                                         */
int pascal sprite_imagesize(int BIT_SIZE)
   {
   int nrow,numbytes;         /* Number columns, rows, bytes  */
   int byteperwin;            /* Bytes per window/plane        */
   nrow=BIT_SIZE+8;           /* Number rows=bitmap size+1 byte*/
   numbytes=nrow/2;           /* Number of bytes = rows / 2    */
                              /* Bytes per = window/ 4 planes  */
   byteperwin=numbytes*nrow*4;
   return(byteperwin);        /* Return size                   */
   }


/* MODULE : NEW SPRITE                                     */
/*-------------------------------------------------------*/
/* Allocates memory and returns pointer to the new sprite. */
/* Output parameters                                       */
/*     memory pointer to sprite                            */
/*                                                         */
sprite_type *new_sprite(void)
   {
   return((sprite_type *)malloc(sizeof(sprite_type)));
   }
```

```
/* MODULE : LOAD SPRITE                                          */
/*-------------------------------------------------------------*/
/* Load the sprite mask.                                         */
/* Input parameters                                              */
/*    mask      - Mask with values to load                       */
/*  hotx,hoty - Sprite's hot spot                                */
/*    sprite    - Address of sprite structure to load up         */
/*    mode      - Mode for sprite to initialize as, COPY/PUT or  */
/*                XOR                                             */
/* Output parameters                                             */
/*    sprite    - Memory is loaded up with values                */
/*                                                               */
void evp_type load_sprite(char mask[16][17],
                          int hotx,int hoty,
                          sprite_type *sprite,int mode)
   {
   int loop1,loop2;          /* Row/column loops                 */
   unsigned long binary_counter; /* Bit counter                  */

                             /* Vertical mask loop               */
   for (loop1=0;loop1<=15;loop1++)
      {
                             /* First set it to zero             */
      sprite->bigmask[loop1]=0L;
                             /* Counter = 31st bit               */
      binary_counter=0x80000000;
                             /* Horizontal loop                  */
      for (loop2=0;loop2<=15;loop2++)

         {                   /* If mask byte NOT 0, turn the     */
                             /* bigmask bit on.                  */

         if (mask[loop1][loop2]!=0)
            sprite->bigmask[loop1]+=binary_counter;

         binary_counter/=2;  /* Binary count=next bit down       */
         }
                             /* Set color for bit row            */
      sprite->color[loop1]=mask[loop1][BITMAP_SIZE];
      }
                             /* Set last 8 bytes to zero         */
   for (loop1=BITMAP_SIZE;loop1<=BITMAP_SIZE+8-1;loop1++)
```

```
        sprite->bigmask[loop1]=0L;

                                /* Set hot spot                 */
    sprite->hotx=hotx;sprite->hoty=hoty;

                                /*Alloc image, initialize shifts */
    sprite->image_buffer=malloc(sprite_imagesize(BITMAP_SIZE));
    sprite->left_shift=0;sprite->right_shift=8;
    sprite->up_shift=0;sprite->down_shift=8;
                                /* Mouse cursor defaults to      */
                                /* center of display.            */


    sprite->SPRITE_ON=0;        /* Sprite not on yet             */
    sprite->sprite_mode=mode;   /* Sprite drawing mode           */

                                /* Default mouse cursor starts in*/
                                /* center of display. Set start  */
                                /* values appropriately, and YES,*/
                                /* they are set using values as  */
                                /* if disp. coords were 1-640,   */
                                /* not 0-639.                    */
    switch(MODE_NUMBER)
      {
      case 0x0E:/* Mode 0x0E , 640 x 200 16-COLOR */
              sprite->tx=0;sprite->ty=0;
              sprite->gx=640/2;sprite->gy=200/2;
              break;

      case 0x0F:/* Mode 0x0F , 640 x 350 MONO     */
      case 0x10:/* Mode 0x10 , 640 x 350 16-COLOR */
              sprite->tx=0;sprite->ty=0;
              sprite->gx=640/2;sprite->gy=350/2;
              break;

      case 0x11:/* Mode 0x11 , 640 x 480 MONO     */
      case 0x12:/* Mode 0x12 , 640 x 480 16-COLOR */
              sprite->tx=0;sprite->ty=0;
              sprite->gx=640/2;sprite->gy=480/2;
              break;

      case MODE_800X600X16:
      default:  /* 800 x 600 16-COLOR             */
              sprite->tx=0;sprite->ty=0;
              sprite->gx=800/2;sprite->gy=600/2;
```

```
                break;
        }
                                /* Note this call to draw_sprite!*/
                                /* Since sprite is not on yet, no*/
                                /* image saving, restoring, or   */
                                /* drawing is performed. It is    */
                                /* only used to adjust the        */
                                /* default mask shift amounts so */
                                /* the cursor will be in the      */
                                /* center.                        */
        draw_sprite(sprite->gx,sprite->gy,sprite);
        }


/* MODULE : DESTROY SPRITE                                    */
/*----------------------------------------------------------*/
/* Destroy the sprite image buffer.                          */
/* Input parameters                                          */
/*     sprite - Address to sprite                            */
/*                                                           */
void destroy_sprite(sprite_type *sprite)
    {free(sprite->image_buffer);
     free(sprite);}


/* MODULE : DO SPRITE (INTERNAL)                             */
/*----------------------------------------------------------*/
/* The actual routine to draw the sprite. This routine is    */
/* INTERNAL and should be called only by draw_sprite().      */
/* Input parameters                                          */
/*     sprite - Address to sprite                            */
/*                                                           */
void evp_type do_sprite(sprite_type *sprite)
    {
    int address,loop,ender;    /* Start address, loopers     */
    char mask1,mask2,mask3;    /* Actual mask bytes to draw   */
    int x,y;

    LL_esetres(15);            /* Enable set/reset registers  */
                               /* Set draw mode to COPY/PUT-XOR */
    LL_setfunction(sprite->sprite_mode);

    x=sprite->tx*8;            /* Now make coords graf coords  */
    y=sprite->ty*8;
```

```
    ender=BITMAP_SIZE+8-1;     /* Determ size of bigmask        */

                               /* Loop down thru mask           */
    for (loop=0;loop<=ender;loop++)
       {                       /* Get current address           */
                               /* Incrmt y for next write       */
       address=(y*HORIZ_OFFSET)+(x >> 3);
       ++y;
                               /* Upper 8 bits                  */
       mask1=(sprite->bigmask[loop] & 0xFF000000) >> 24;

                               /* Mid-left 8 bits               */
       mask2=(sprite->bigmask[loop] & 0x00FF0000) >> 16;

                               /* Mid-right 8 bits              */
       mask3=(sprite->bigmask[loop] & 0x0000FF00) >> 8;

                               /* Set the color for line        */
       if ((loop>=sprite->up_shift)&&
           (loop<sprite->up_shift+BITMAP_SIZE))
           LL_setres(sprite->color[loop-sprite->up_shift]);

                               /* Write the 3 bytes             */
       LL_write3byte(address,mask1,mask2,mask3);
       }
                               /* Reset the registers           */
    LL_bitmask(255);LL_esetres(0);
    LL_mapmask(15);LL_setfunction(0);
    }


/* MODULE : DRAW SPRITE                                         */
/*------------------------------------------------------------*/
/*                                                              */
/* HEART OF SPRITE DRIVER                                       */
/*                                                              */
/* Main routine used to draw sprite.                            */
/* Input parameters                                             */
/*    x,y     - Graphics cursor location to draw sprite at      */
/*    sprite  - Address to sprite                               */
/*                                                              */
void evp_type draw_sprite(int x,int y,sprite_type *sprite)
    {
    int loop;               /* Loop counter                     */
    int tx,ty;              /* x,y coordinates-TEXT locations*/
```

```
int gx,gy;                  /* x,y coordinates-GRAF locations*/
int gyu,gxl;                /* Graf Y-upper shft,X-Left shft */
int nys,nxs;                /* Y shft(if any), X shft(if any)*/


                            /* MUST DO IF CALLED FROM EVENT  */
                            /* PROCESSOR!!!                   */
                            /* Fill bitmask, write mode 0     */
LL_bitmask(255);LL_modereg(0);


x-=sprite->hotx;            /* Adjust position according to  */
y-=sprite->hoty;            /* hot spot.                     */

if (sprite->SPRITE_ON)     /* If sprite is ON               */
   {
                            /* If in COPYPUT mode,           */
                            /* lay down background.          */
   if (sprite->sprite_mode==COPYPUT_MODE)
      LL_writewin(PAGE,sprite->tx,sprite->ty,
                  sprite->image_buffer,
                  MODE_NUMBER);
   else
      do_sprite(sprite); /* If XOR mode erase by redrawing */
   }


tx=x>>3;                    /* Figure text coords(x/8,y/8)    */
ty=y>>3;
                            /* If text boundries changed -    */
if ((tx!=sprite->tx)||(ty!=sprite->ty))
   {
   sprite->tx=tx;           /* Update curr TEXT x,y locations */
   sprite->ty=ty;
   if ((sprite->SPRITE_ON)&&
       (sprite->sprite_mode==COPYPUT_MODE))
      LL_readwin(PAGE,sprite->tx,sprite->ty,
                 sprite->image_buffer,MODE_NUMBER);
   }

gx=tx<<3;                   /* Define curr GRAF x,y locations*/
gy=ty<<3;                   /* as even byte boundry.(x*8,y*8)*/
sprite->gx=x;sprite->gy=y;/* Update curr GRAF x,y locations*/
gxl=x-gx;                   /* Amount of X shift difference  */
gyu=y-gy;                   /* Amount of Y shift difference  */

                            /* If curr X shift!=last X shift */
if (gxl!=sprite->left_shift)
```

```
      {
                                  /* Need to shift it right?      */
      if (gxl>sprite->left_shift)
         {
                                  /* Figure how much to shift right*/
         nxs=gxl-sprite->left_shift;

                                  /* Now loop thru entire mask     */
         for (loop=0;loop<=23;loop++)
            sprite->bigmask[loop]=sprite->bigmask[loop] >> nxs;
         }
      else                        /* Else needs to be shifted left */
         {
                                  /* Figure how much to shift left */
         nxs=sprite->left_shift-gxl;

                                  /* Now loop thru entire mask     */
         for (loop=0;loop<=23;loop++)
            sprite->bigmask[loop]=sprite->bigmask[loop] << nxs;
         }
                                  /* Set current shift amounts to  */
                                  /* new shift amounts.            */
      sprite->left_shift=gxl;
      sprite->right_shift=8-gxl;
      }
                                  /* If curr Y shift!=last Y shift */
   if (gyu!=sprite->up_shift)
      {
                                  /* Need to shift it down?        */
      if (gyu>sprite->up_shift)
         {
                                  /* Figure how much to shift down */
         nys=gyu-sprite->up_shift;

                                  /* Now loop thru mask and shift  */
         for (loop=23;loop>=nys;loop--)
            sprite->bigmask[loop]=sprite->bigmask[loop-nys];

                                  /* Set other bits to 0           */
         for (loop=nys-1;loop>=0;loop--)
            sprite->bigmask[loop]=0;
         }
      else                        /* Else we need to shift it up   */
         {
                                  /* Figure how much to shift up   */
```

```
        nys=sprite->up_shift-gyu;


                                /* Now loop thru mask and shift  */
        for (loop=0;loop<=23-nys;loop++)
           sprite->bigmask[loop]=sprite->bigmask[loop+nys];


                                /* Set other bits to 0            */
        for (loop=23-nys;loop<=23;loop++)
           sprite->bigmask[loop]=0;
        }


     sprite->up_shift=gyu;   /* Set current shift amounts     */
     sprite->down_shift=8-gyu;
     }
                                /* Redraw the sprite             */
   if (sprite->SPRITE_ON) do_sprite(sprite);
   }




/* MODULE : CHANGE SPRITE LINE COLOR                            */
/*------------------------------------------------------------*/
/* Changes the color of one row in the sprite mask.            */
/* Input parameters                                            */
/*      sprite   - Address to sprite                           */
/*      linenum  - Row number of mask to change color on       */
/*      newcolor - Color to change the mask line               */
/*                                                             */
void change_sprite_line_color(sprite_type *sprite,int linenum,
                               int newcolor)
   {
   -linenum;                    /* Array starts at 0, not 1     */
   sprite->color[linenum+sprite->up_shift]=newcolor;
   }




/* MODULE : CHANGE SPRITE COLOR                                 */
/*------------------------------------------------------------*/
/* Change the color of the entire sprite to one solid color.   */
/* Input parameters                                            */
/*      sprite   - Address to sprite                           */
/*      newcolor - Color to change the mask line               */
/*                                                             */
void change_sprite_color(sprite_type *sprite,int newcolor)
   {
```

```
    int loop;
    for (loop=0;loop<=BITMAP_SIZE-1;loop++)
       sprite->color[loop]=newcolor;
    }


/* MODULE : SET SPRITE MODE                                      */
/*-------------------------------------------------------------*/
/* Set the sprite mode to either COPY/PUT (0) or XOR (24) mode*/
/* Input parameters                                             */
/*      *sprite  - Address to sprite                            */
/*       mode     - Mode to set sprite to                       */
/*                                                              */
void set_sprite_mode(sprite_type *sprite,int mode)
    {
                                    /* If new mode is different     */
    if (mode!=sprite->sprite_mode)
       sprite->sprite_mode=mode;
    }


/* MODULE : HIDE SPRITE                                          */
/*-------------------------------------------------------------*/
/* Hides the current sprite so that you can write to the        */
/* screen where the sprite is. Like the standard mouse cursor,  */
/* you should hide it whenever you do screen writes, because    */
/* you really don't know where it is at any given time. This    */
/* sprite driver also does not keep shadow maps of the EGA      */
/* registers.                                                   */
/* Input parameters                                             */
/*      sprite  - Address to sprite                             */
/*                                                              */
void evp_type hide_sprite(sprite_type *sprite)
    {
                                    /* MUST DO IF CALLED FROM EVENT */
                                    /* PROCESSOR!!!                 */
                                    /* Fill Bitmask, write mode 0   */
    LL_bitmask(255);LL_modereg(0);

    if (sprite->SPRITE_ON)     /* If sprite is on hide it      */
       {
       if (sprite->sprite_mode==COPYPUT_MODE)
          LL_writewin(PAGE,sprite->tx,sprite->ty,
                     sprite->image_buffer,MODE_NUMBER);
       else do_sprite(sprite);
       sprite->SPRITE_ON=0;
```

```
        }
    }



/* MODULE : SHOW SPRITE                                          */
/*-------------------------------------------------------------*/
/* Shows a previously hidden sprite back on the screen.          */
/* Input parameters                                              */
/*     sprite  - Address to sprite                               */
/*                                                               */
void evp_type show_sprite(sprite_type *sprite)
    {
                                /* MUST DO IF CALLED FROM EVENT  */
                                /* PROCESSOR!!!                  */
                                /* Fill Bitmask, write mode 0    */
    LL_bitmask(255);LL_modereg(0);

                                /* If a sprite is there          */
    if ((!sprite->SPRITE_ON)&&(sprite->image_buffer!=NULL))
        {
                                /* and off, save sprite image    */
                                /* and redraw it.                */
    if (sprite->sprite_mode==COPYPUT_MODE)
        LL_readwin(PAGE,sprite->tx,sprite->ty,
                    sprite->image_buffer,MODE_NUMBER);

    do_sprite(sprite);
    sprite->SPRITE_ON=1;
        }
    }
```

The DATA Segment

Before compiling SPRITELL.C, take a look at the following #define statements found in COMPILER.H:

```
#ifdef BORLAND
    #define evp_type huge
#ifdef MICROSOFT
    #define evp_type far
```

With the exception of the EGA/VGA register functions, every sprite driver function called either directly or indirectly from the C event processor (which is presented in the following chapter) must save the previous data segment, load the current data segment, and restore the previous data segment upon termination. This *must* occur or the sprite driver functions will only operate in the SMALL memory model. To force the Borland compiler to do this, the functions in question must be declared as huge functions. Microsoft C compilers do not allow functions to be of type huge, therefore they are declared as far functions. Microsoft users *must* compile SPRITELL.C with the /Au compiler switch to force the compiler to maintain the data segment.

 This applies only when the sprite driver is used in interrupt-driven graphics routines, such as those used to implement a sprite cursor. If you use the sprite driver in other situations that are not interrupt driven (called by an event handler or processor), it is not required to maintain the data segment within the sprite driver functions.

Compiling SPRITELL.C

Use the following instructions to compile SPRITELL.C with either the integrated environment or command-line compilers.

Integrated Environment Compiling

If compiling with Borland Turbo C 2.0, you must compile SPRITELL.C using the command-line compiler because the integrated environment compiler will not compile inline assembly code. If you are compiling with Borland Turbo C++ 1.0 or later, you can compile SPRITELL.C within the integrated environment.

If you are compiling with a Microsoft compiler, you *must* use the /Au compiler switch. If you use Microsoft C 6.0 or C/C++ 7.0, enter /**Au** in the Additional Global Options or Additional Release Options. If you use QuickC, enter /**Au** in the Compiler Custom Flags Global options. You *must* also turn stack checking off and set the Build flags to Release, not Debug.

No matter which compiler you use, you must set the memory model to the model you will compile programs using the sprite driver in.

Compile SPRITELL.C to SPRITELL.OBJ. The file must be an object file so it can be included in the new mouse function library presented in the following chapter.

Command-Line Compiling

If you prefer compiling with command-line compilers, use the following instructions:

Borland Compilers   Compile SPRITELL.C to SPRITELL.OBJ by entering the following at the DOS command line:

```
TCC –B –c -mh –IC:\TC\INCLUDE –LC:\TC\LIB
    –nC:\TC\EXAMPLE SPRITELL.C
```

where:

- *TCC* is the Borland Turbo C command-line compiler. Use BCC if you are compiling with a Borland C++ compiler (non-Turbo).

- *–B* means compile via assembly and invoke TASM.EXE.

- *–c* means compile only (object file).

- *–mh* means model huge. Change this to match the memory model you are compiling in. ms=SMALL, mm=MEDIUM, mc=COMPACT, ml=LARGE, mh=HUGE.

- *–IC:\TC\INCLUDE* is the directory location for your #include files.

- *–LC:\TC\LIB* is the directory location for your library files.

- *–nC:\TC\EXAMPLE* is the directory location you are compiling in.

- *SPRITELL.C* is the name of the source code file.

Make sure TASM.EXE is in the current directory or path. Additionally, the compiler switches are case sensitive and should be entered in exactly as shown.

If you use Turbo C 2.0, and do not have TASM.EXE, SPRITELL.C has been compiled for each individual memory model, and the .OBJ files are included with the companion disk supplied with this book. The file-naming conventions for the various memory models are as follows:

Filename	Memory Model Compiled In
SPRITLLH.OBJ	HUGE memory model
SPRITLLL.OBJ	LARGE memory model
SPRITLLC.OBJ	COMPACT memory model
SPRITLLM.OBJ	MEDIUM memory model
SPRITLLS.OBJ	SMALL memory model

Microsoft Compilers   Compile SPRITELL.C to SPRITELL.OBJ by entering the following at the DOS command line:

CL /c /AH /Au /Gs SPRITELL.C

where:

- *CL* is the Microsoft command-line compiler. Use QCL if compiling with QuickC.

- */c* means compile only (object file).

- */AH* means model HUGE. Change this to match the memory model you are compiling in. AS=SMALL, AM=MEDIUM, AC=COMPACT, AL=LARGE, AH=HUGE.

- */Au* means Assume SS!=DS. DS is reloaded on function entry.

- */Gs* means remove stack check calls.

- *SPRITELL.C* is the name of the source code file.

 The compiler switches are case sensitive and should be entered in exactly as shown.

On to the New Mouse Function Library

There is still much work to be done before the sprite driver functions can be utilized. In the following chapter you create new mouse function library to interface with the sprite driver, so you can actually implement a sprite cursor.

Chapter 19

The New Mouse Function Library and Sprite Cursor

In this chapter, you actually generate and use a sprite cursor. First though, you need to modify the mouse function library (which you created in Chapters 3, 7, 12, and 16) in order for it to interface properly with the sprite driver.

Modifying the Mouse Function Library

Substituting the sprite cursor for the default mouse cursor is really very easy. It is accomplished by never allowing the default mouse cursor to become visible, and tying the sprite cursor to the mouse driver via the event handler and event processor, which in turn move the sprite cursor whenever the mouse is moved.

However, in order for you to properly maintain the sprite cursor and have the ability to utilize either the sprite cursor or the default mouse cursor, the following modifications must be made to the mouse library functions.

Show and Hide Functions

The mouse library functions show_mouse_cursor() and hide_mouse_cursor() must examine the variable USING_SPRITE, defined in MOUSEDRV.C to determine which cursor is being used. If USING_SPRITE is 0, the default mouse cursor is being used and operations occur as normal. If USING_SPRITE is 1, the sprite cursor is being used and the sprite driver functions show_sprite() and hide_sprite() must be called instead of mouse function 1, show cursor, and mouse function 2, hide cursor.

Additionally, if the event handler moves the sprite cursor while the functions show_sprite() and hide_sprite() are processing, phantom cursors or misplaced backgrounds can occur. To ensure that this does not happen, the event handler must be partially deactivated immediately before the call to show_sprite() or hide_sprite(), and fully reactivated immediately after. All other events (button presses and releases) must call the event handler as normal, to ensure that button presses and releases are not missed. The event handler can be partially deactivated by setting the call mask's movement bit (bit 0) to 0 (see Chapter 7 regarding the call mask) and can be reactivated with the mouse library function install_event_handler().

Setting an Exclusion Area

The sprite driver does not maintain shadow maps of the EGA/VGA registers (see Chapter 4) and therefore cannot implement an exclusion area. The mouse library function set_hide_bounds() must be modified to accommodate this limitation. When the sprite cursor is in use, the function set_hide_bounds() must call the mouse library function hide_mouse_cursor() instead of setting an exclusion area with mouse function 16. If the default mouse cursor is in use and the EGA/VGA registers can be read (see Chapter 4), the exclusion area can be set as normal.

Event Processor

The C event processor function, event_processor(), must be modified so that whenever a user moves the mouse, the event processor in turn moves the sprite cursor.

Additionally, event_processor() must be modified to accommodate turning movement events off in the functions show_mouse_cursor() and hide_mouse_cursor(). To satisfy this accommodation, the variable event_status must be examined in conjunction with the current display coordinates to determine if the mouse has moved. This makes it possible to turn off movement events without needing to fully deactivate the event handler.

Cursor Position

As with the functions show_mouse_cursor() and hide_mouse_cursor(), the mouse library function set_mouse_position() must be modified to determine which cursor is being used. If the sprite cursor is in use, the function draw_sprite(x,y,sprite_cursor) must be called. The mouse driver won't move the sprite cursor, so it must be done manually.

The New Mouse Function Library

Only a few changes to the original mouse function library are necessary to implement the previously described modifications. However, they are *mandatory*. When these changes are complete, you can use either the default mouse cursor or the sprite cursor, with only a few addition lines of initialization code in your application. After that, everything is handled internally, and you don't need to think twice about it.

Here is the modified mouse function library, MOUSEDRV.C:

```
/*------------------------------------------------------------*/
/*                    MOUSEDRV.C                          */
/*                                                        */
/*  The new mouse function library.                       */
/*  With these functions either the regular graphics mouse */
/*  cursor or a sprite being used as a mouse cursor will be */
/*  handled appropriately.                                */
/*                                                        */
/*  Compile this to MOUSEDRV.OBJ, use the librarian to link */
/*  EVENT.OBJ, MOUSEDRV.OBJ, and SPRITELL.OBJ to make      */
/*  MOUSEDRV.LIB.                                          */
/*------------------------------------------------------------*/

#include "compiler.h"         /* Compiler directives         */

#define MV_LBUTTON 1          /* For event driver button     */
#define MV_RBUTTON 2          /* status when CURSOR_MOVED     */
#define MV_BBUTTON 3          /* message is trapped.          */

int NUMBER_BUTTONS=2;         /* Number of mouse buttons      */

int HCELL_SIZE=8,            /* Cursor cell sizes - text mode */
    VCELL_SIZE=8;

int MOUSE_SIZE=16;            /* Mouse cursor size. Use 16 in */
                              /* graphics mode, 1 in text.    */

unsigned char IN_GMODE;       /* 1 in graphics mode, 0 in text */

unsigned char MOUSE_THERE;    /* 1 if mouse present, 0 if not */
unsigned char MOUSE_VISIBLE;  /* Internal for HIDE_CURSOR and */
                              /* SHOW_CURSOR functions; 1 if  */
                              /* mouse currently visible, 0 if */
                              /* not.                         */
```

```
unsigned char LBUTTON_DOWN,  /* Boolean vars or 'messages'  */
         RBUTTON_DOWN,       /* set by event processor.     */
         BBUTTON_DOWN,
         LBUTTON_UP,
         RBUTTON_UP,
         BBUTTON_UP,
         CURSOR_MOVED;

int CMX=0,CMY=0;             /* Mouse coords set by event   */
int BSTATE=0;                /* handler; also button state. */

union  REGS  mregs;          /* DOS/mouse registers         */
struct SREGS msegregs;       /* DOS/mouse segment register  */

unsigned char EGA_REG_READ=1;/* EGA regs handled properly?  */

                             /* New sprite mouse cursor=1   */
                             /* Normal mouse cursor=0       */
unsigned char USING_SPRITE=0;

/* The Sprite Structure Type */
/*--------------------------*/
typedef struct
   {
   unsigned long bigmask[24];  /* Actual sprite mask        */
   unsigned char *image_buffer;/* Image buffer for sprite   */
   unsigned char color[16];    /* Color of each line in mask */
   int left_shift;             /* Blank bits - left side mask */
   int right_shift;            /* Blank bits - right side mask*/
   int up_shift;               /* Blank bits - upper side mask*/
   int down_shift;             /* Blank bits - lower side mask*/
   int tx,ty;                  /* Text coords-3byte wide mask */
   int gx,gy;                  /* Graf coords-3byte wide mask */
   int hotx,hoty;              /* Hot spot                  */
   int sprite_mode;            /* COPY/PUT or XOR sprite?    */
   unsigned char SPRITE_ON;    /* Sprite on or off?         */
   }sprite_type;

sprite_type *sprite_cursor;   /* Hard assigment pointer->   */
                              /* for event processor.       */

                              /* External prototypes for    */
                              /* SPRITELL.C                 */
void evp_type draw_sprite(int x,int y,sprite_type *sprite);
```

```
void evp_type hide_sprite(sprite_type *sprite);
void evp_type show_sprite(sprite_type *sprite);


                               /* Prototypes for mouse funcs  */
void far event_handler(void);
void pascal set_event_handler(int call_mask,
                      void (far *location)(void));
void install_event_handler(void);

/* MODULE : RESET MOUSE                                      */
/*----------------------------------------------------------*/
/* Reset mouse and get status.                              */
/* Output parameters                                        */
/*     None. Global variables set inside function.          */
/*                                                          */
void reset_mouse(void)
   {

   MOUSE_THERE=0;                       /* Default NOT there   */
   MOUSE_SIZE=16;                       /* Default graphic size*/
   HCELL_SIZE=8;VCELL_SIZE=8;           /* Default text cell sz*/
   MOUSE_VISIBLE=0;                     /* Default not visible */

   if (getvect(0x33)!=0L)               /* If Int 33 installed-*/
      {
      mregs.x.ax=0;                     /* Mouse function  0   */
      int86(0x33,&mregs,&mregs);        /* Reset mouse         */

      if (mregs.x.ax!=0)                /* If AX=0, no mouse   */
         {                              /* If mouse is present-*/
         MOUSE_THERE=1;                 /* Set global variable */

         NUMBER_BUTTONS=mregs.x.bx;     /* Number buttons in BX*/

         if (!IN_GMODE)                 /* If in text mode -   */
            {
            mregs.h.ah=0x0F;            /* NONmouse function   */
            int86(0x10,&mregs,&mregs);  /* Int 10h, func 0Fh,  */
            switch(mregs.h.al)          /* get video mode.     */
               {
               case 0:                  /* If 40 char mode-    */
               case 1:                  /* Adjust cell size    */
                     HCELL_SIZE=16;break;
               }
```

```
                MOUSE_SIZE=1;                    /* Text cursor=one char*/
                  }

             LBUTTON_DOWN=0;                     /* Reset status vars   */
             RBUTTON_DOWN=0;                     /* used in event prcess*/
             BBUTTON_DOWN=0;
                  }
            }
       }


/* MODULE : SHOW MOUSE CURSOR                                          */
/*------------------------------------------------------------------*/
/* Make mouse cursor visible.                                         */
/*                                                                    */
void pascal show_mouse_cursor(void)
     {
     if (MOUSE_THERE)
        {
        MOUSE_VISIBLE=1;          /* Set flag to 1 - on              */

        if (!USING_SPRITE)        /* If normal mouse cursor then     */
           {
           mregs.x.ax=1;          /* Mouse function  1, show cursor*/
           int86(0x33,&mregs,&mregs);
           }
        else                      /* Else show the sprite cursor     */
           {
                                  /* Event handler move events       */
                                  /* turned off to avoid phantom     */
                                  /* cursors (bit 0 in call mask=0)*/
           if (NUMBER_BUTTONS==3)
              set_event_handler(126,event_handler);
           else
              set_event_handler(30,event_handler);

                                  /* Show the sprite cursor          */
           show_sprite(sprite_cursor);

                                  /* Reactivate full event handler */
           install_event_handler();
           }
        }
     }
```

```
/* MODULE : HIDE MOUSE CURSOR                                      */
/*----------------------------------------------------------------*/
/* Hide the mouse cursor.                                          */
/*                                                                 */
void pascal hide_mouse_cursor(void)
   {                              /* Is mouse already hidden?      */
   if ((MOUSE_VISIBLE)&&(MOUSE_THERE))
     {
     MOUSE_VISIBLE=0;           /* Set first so if int subroutine*/
                                /* is called before exit out.    */
     if (!USING_SPRITE)         /* If normal mouse cursor then - */
        {
        mregs.x.ax=2;           /* Mouse function 2, hide cursor */
        int86(0x33,&mregs,&mregs);
        }
     else                       /* Else hide the sprite          */
        {
                                /* Event handler move events     */
                                /* turned off to avoid misplaced */
                                /* bckgrnd (bit 0 in call mask=0)*/
        if (NUMBER_BUTTONS==3)
           set_event_handler(126,event_handler);
        else
           set_event_handler(30,event_handler);

                                /* Hide the sprite cursor        */
        hide_sprite(sprite_cursor);

                                /* Reactivate full event handler */
        install_event_handler();
        }
     }
   }


/* MODULE : SET HIDE BOUNDS                                        */
/*----------------------------------------------------------------*/
/* Set a rectangular region of the display that the mouse         */
/* cursor is to be hidden in.                                      */
/* Input parameters                                               */
/*     x1 - Left horizontal bound of region                       */
/*     y1 - Upper vertical bound of region                        */
/*     x2 - Right horizontal bound of region                      */
/*     y2 - Bottom vertical bound of region                       */
/*                                                                 */
```

```c
void pascal set_hide_bounds(int x1,int y1,int x2,int y2)
    {
                                    /* If EGA regs in tact and not */
                                    /* using sprite as cursor -    */
    if ((EGA_REG_READ)&&(!USING_SPRITE)&&(MOUSE_THERE))
        {
        if (!IN_GMODE)                      /* If in text mode-    */
            {
            x1=(x1*HCELL_SIZE)-HCELL_SIZE;/* x1 to graf coord      */
            x2=(x2*HCELL_SIZE)-HCELL_SIZE;/* x2 to graf coord      */
            y1=(y1*VCELL_SIZE)-VCELL_SIZE;/* y1 to graf coord      */
            y2=(y2*VCELL_SIZE)-VCELL_SIZE;/* y2 to graf coord      */
            }
        mregs.x.ax=16;                      /* Mouse function 16,  */
        mregs.x.cx=x1;                      /* set exclusion area. */
        mregs.x.dx=y1;
        mregs.x.si=x2;
        mregs.x.di=y2;
        int86(0x33,&mregs,&mregs);
        }
                                    /* EGA registers not   */
    else hide_mouse_cursor();       /* intact or using     */
    }                               /* sprite as cursor.   */

/* MODULE : SET MOUSE POSITION                                     */
/*---------------------------------------------------------------*/
/* Set the current mouse cursor position.                         */
/* Input parameters                                               */
/*     x,y - coordinates of where to place mouse cursor           */
/*                                                                */
void pascal set_mouse_position(int x,int y)
    {
    if (MOUSE_THERE)
        {
        if (!IN_GMODE)                      /* If in text mode-    */
            {
            x=(x*HCELL_SIZE)-HCELL_SIZE;  /* x to graf coord       */
            y=(y*VCELL_SIZE)-VCELL_SIZE;  /* y to graf coord       */
            }

        mregs.x.ax=4;                       /* Mouse function 4    */
        mregs.x.cx=x;                       /* Load reg cx with x  */
        mregs.x.dx=y;                       /* Load reg dx with y  */
        int86(0x33,&mregs,&mregs);          /* Change cursor pos   */
```

```
                                         /* If using sprite and */
     if ((USING_SPRITE)&&(IN_GMODE))  /* in graphics mode -  */
        draw_sprite(x,y,sprite_cursor);
     CMX=x;CMY=y;


     }

   }


/* MODULE : SET MOUSE HLIMITS                                 */
/*----------------------------------------------------------*/
/* Set the maximum horizontal mouse cursor display region.   */
/* Input parameters                                          */
/*     x1,x2 - Horizontal mouse cursor display boundary      */
/*                                                           */
void pascal set_mouse_hlimits(int x1,int x2)
   {
   if (MOUSE_THERE)
      {
      if (!IN_GMODE)                     /* If in text mode-    */
         {
         x1=(x1*HCELL_SIZE)-HCELL_SIZE;/* x1 to graf coord    */
         x2=(x2*HCELL_SIZE)-HCELL_SIZE;/* x2 to graf coord    */
         }

      mregs.x.ax=7;                      /* Mouse function 7   */
      mregs.x.cx=x1;                     /* Reg cx = start x   */
      mregs.x.dx=x2;                     /* Reg dx = end x     */
      int86(0x33,&mregs,&mregs);         /* Set horiz limits   */
      }
   }


/* MODULE : SET MOUSE VLIMITS                                 */
/*----------------------------------------------------------*/
/* Set the maximum vertical mouse cursor display region.     */
/* Input parameters                                          */
/*     y1,y2 - Vertical mouse cursor display boundary        */
/*                                                           */
void pascal set_mouse_vlimits(int y1,int y2)
   {
   if (MOUSE_THERE)
      {
      if (!IN_GMODE)                     /* If in text mode-    */
         {
         y1=(y1*VCELL_SIZE)-VCELL_SIZE;/* y1 to graf coord    */
```

```
            y2=(y2*VCELL_SIZE)-VCELL_SIZE;/* y2 to graf coord    */
            }

        mregs.x.ax=8;                       /* Mouse function 8    */
        mregs.x.cx=y1;                      /* Reg cx = start y    */
        mregs.x.dx=y2;                      /* Reg dx = end y      */
        int86(0x33,&mregs,&mregs);          /* Set vertical limits */
        }
    }


/* MODULE : GET MOUSE BUTTON                                       */
/*---------------------------------------------------------------*/
/* Get the status of the mouse buttons and the current            */
/* location of the mouse cursor.                                  */
/* Input parameters                                               */
/*      *button1 - Address to button1 status var                  */
/*      *button2 - Address to button2 status var                  */
/*      *x       - Address to x coordinate var                    */
/*      *y       - Address to y coordinate var                    */
/* Output parameters                                              */
/*      button status vars = 1 if button pressed, 0 if not        */
/*      x,y variables contain current mouse cursor location       */
/*                                                                */
void pascal get_mouse_button(unsigned char *button1,
                             unsigned char *button2,
                             int *x,int *y)
    {
    if (MOUSE_THERE)
        {
        mregs.x.ax=3;                       /* Mouse function 3    */
        int86(0x33,&mregs,&mregs);          /* Button & coord stats*/

        *button1 =(mregs.x.bx == 1) ? 1 : 0; /* Button1 pressed?*/
        *button2 =(mregs.x.bx == 2) ? 1 : 0; /* Button2 pressed?*/

        if (mregs.x.bx==3)                  /* Both buttons pressd?*/
            {*button1=1;*button2=1;}

        if (IN_GMODE)                       /* If in graphics mode-*/
            {
            *x=mregs.x.cx;                  /* Reg cx = x coord    */
            *y=mregs.x.dx;                  /* Reg dx = y coord    */
            }
        else                                /* If in text mode-    */
```

```
          {                              /* Convert to text crds*/
     *x=(mregs.x.cx+HCELL_SIZE)/HCELL_SIZE;
     *y=(mregs.x.dx+VCELL_SIZE)/VCELL_SIZE;
          }
     }
  }



/* MODULE : GET BUTTON RLS INFO                               */
/*-----------------------------------------------------------*/
/* Get information about button releases since last call to   */
/* function.                                                  */
/* Input parameters                                          */
/*      butt_no - which button? 0=left, 1=right               */
/*      *count  - Address to var-how many times butt released */
/*      *x,*y   - Address to new coordinate variables         */
/* Output parameters                                         */
/*      If butt_no =0 and left button released, returns 1     */
/*      If butt_no =0 and left button not released, returns 0 */
/*      If butt_no =1 and right button released, returns 1    */
/*      If butt_no =1 and right button not released, returns 0*/
/*                                                           */
/*                                                           */
unsigned char pascal get_button_rls_info(int butt_no,
                                    int *count,
                                    int *x,int *y)
   {
   if (MOUSE_THERE)
      {
      mregs.x.ax=6;                      /* Mouse function 6    */
      mregs.x.bx=butt_no;                /* Which button,       */
                                         /* 0=left, 1=right     */
      int86(0x33,&mregs,&mregs);         /* Retrieve information*/

      *count=mregs.x.bx;                 /* bx = number releases*/
      *x=mregs.x.cx;                     /* cx = horiz coord     */
      *y=mregs.x.dx;                     /* dx = vert coord      */

                                         /* Bit 1 in ax contains*/
                                         /* left button status. */
                                         /* Released or not?     */
      if (butt_no==0) return(!(mregs.x.ax & 1));

                                         /* Bit 2 in ax contains*/
                                         /* right button status.*/
```

```
          else return(!((mregs.x.ax & 2) >> 1));
          }
      return(0);
      }


/* MODULE : SET EVENT HANDLER                                 */
/*------------------------------------------------------------*/
/* Function sets the EVENT handler subroutine to be called by */
/* the mouse driver.                                          */
/* Input parameters                                           */
/*    call_mask - Action that causes event handler to be calld*/
/*    location  - Pass in actual function name                */
/*                                                            */
void pascal set_event_handler(int call_mask,
                                  void (far *location)(void))
    {
    if (MOUSE_THERE)
        {
        mregs.x.ax=12;                      /* Mouse function 12   */
        mregs.x.cx=call_mask;               /* Call mask-action    */
        mregs.x.dx=FP_OFF(location);     /* Offset of e-handler */
        msegregs.es=FP_SEG(location);    /* Segment of e-handler*/
        int86x(0x33,&mregs,&mregs,&msegregs);
        }
    }


              /*------------------------------*/
              /* NOTE : The optional functions */
              /*          have not changed!     */
              /*------------------------------*/


#include "optional.inc"


/* MODULE : EVENT PROCESSOR                                   */
/*------------------------------------------------------------*/
/* This routine is FULLY internal and is ONLY called by the   */
/* assembly function Event_Handler.                           */
/* Event_Handler automatically calls this routine, at which   */
/* time it can take control based on the activity.            */
/*                                                            */
/*                                                            */
void near event_processor(int event_status,int button_status,
                          int x,int y)
    {
                                 /* Cursor moved?              */
```

```
if ((event_status & 1)&&((CMX!=x)||(CMY!=y)))
   {
   if (!IN_GMODE)           /* If in text mode          */
      {                     /* Convert coordinates      */
      x=(x+HCELL_SIZE)/HCELL_SIZE;
      y=(y+VCELL_SIZE)/VCELL_SIZE;
      }
   CURSOR_MOVED=1;          /* Set cursor moved to 1    */
   CMX=x;CMY=y;             /* Assign global vars       */

                           /* If mouse is visible, and vid */
                           /* is in graf mode, and using   */
                           /* the sprite then write the sprt*/
   if ((MOUSE_VISIBLE)&&(IN_GMODE)&&(USING_SPRITE))
      draw_sprite(CMX,CMY,sprite_cursor);
   }

BSTATE=button_status;      /* Set BSTATE every call    */

if (event_status & 2)      /* Left button down         */
   LBUTTON_DOWN=1;

if (event_status & 8)      /* Right button down        */
   RBUTTON_DOWN=1;

                           /* Both buttons down        */
if (((event_status & 2)||(event_status & 8))
   &&(button_status==3))
   BBUTTON_DOWN=1;

                           /* If 3-button, check for down */
if ((NUMBER_BUTTONS==3)&&(event_status & 32))
   BBUTTON_DOWN=1;

if (event_status & 4)      /* Left button up           */
   LBUTTON_UP=1;

if (event_status & 16)     /* Right button up          */
   RBUTTON_UP=1;

                           /* Both buttons up          */
if ((LBUTTON_UP)&&(RBUTTON_UP))
   BBUTTON_UP=1;

                           /* If 3-button, check for up */
if ((NUMBER_BUTTONS==3)&&(event_status & 64))
   BBUTTON_UP=1;
}
```

```
/* MODULE : INSTALL EVENT HANDLER                                 */
/*---------------------------------------------------------------*/
/* Installs the global mouse event handler. Sets the mask so     */
/* all first five bits are on with two-button mice, and first    */
/* seven bits are on with three-button mice.                     */
/*                                                               */
void install_event_handler(void)
    {
    if (NUMBER_BUTTONS==3)                    /* Set for 3-button*/
        set_event_handler(127,event_handler);
    else                                      /* Set for 2-button*/
        set_event_handler(31,event_handler);
    }


/* MODULE : RESET EVENT STATUS                                    */
/*---------------------------------------------------------------*/
/* Resets all event status variables to 0.                       */
/*                                                               */
void reset_event_status(void)
    {
    CURSOR_MOVED=0;
    LBUTTON_DOWN=0;LBUTTON_UP=0;
    RBUTTON_DOWN=0;RBUTTON_UP=0;
    BBUTTON_DOWN=0;BBUTTON_UP=0;
    }
```

Compiling MOUSEDRV.C

Use the following instructions to compile MOUSEDRV.C with either the integrated environment or command-line compilers.

Integrated Environment Compiling

If you are compiling with a Microsoft compiler, you *must* turn stack checking off. See you compiler's reference manual regarding turning stack checking off within the integrated environment.

No matter what compiler you use, be sure to set the memory model to the model you will compile programs using the sprite driver and mouse function library in. The memory model must also be the same as the model you compiled SPRITELL.C with in the previous chapter.

Compile MOUSEDRV.C to MOUSEDRV.OBJ.

Command-Line Compiling

If you prefer compiling with command line compilers, use the following instructions.

Borland Compilers   Compile MOUSEDRV.C to MOUSEDRV.OBJ by entering the following at the DOS command line:

```
TCC -c -mh -IC:\TC\INCLUDE -LC:\TC\LIB
     -nC:\TC\EXAMPLE MOUSEDRV.C
```

where:

- *TCC* is the Borland Turbo C command-line compiler. Use BCC if compiling with a Borland C++ compiler (non-Turbo).

- *–c* means compile only (object file).

- *–mh* means model HUGE. Change this to match the memory model you are compiling in. ms=SMALL, mm=MEDIUM, mc=COMPACT, ml=LARGE, mh=HUGE.

- *–IC:\TC\INCLUDE* is the directory location for your #include files.

- *–LC:\TC\LIB* is the directory location for your library files.

- *–nC:\TC\EXAMPLE* is the directory location you are compiling in.

- *MOUSEDRV.C* is the name of the source code file.

The compiler switches are case sensitive and should be entered in exactly as shown.

Microsoft Compilers   Compile MOUSEDRV.C to MOUSEDRV.OBJ by entering the following at the DOS command line:

```
CL /c /AH /Gs MOUSEDRV.C
```

where:

- *CL* is the Microsoft command-line compiler. Use QCL if you are compiling with QuickC.

- */c* means compile only (object file).

- */AH* means model HUGE. Change this to match the memory model you are compiling in. AS=SMALL, AM=MEDIUM, AC=COMPACT, AL=LARGE, AH=HUGE.

- */Gs* means remove stack-check calls.

- *MOUSEDRV.C* is the name of the source code file.

The compiler switches are case sensitive and should be entered in exactly as shown.

Combining the Event Handler, Mouse Function Library, and Sprite Driver

In order to provide a single, self-contained, mouse function/sprite driver library, the event handler, the new mouse function library, and the sprite driver must be combined. The new library file is called MOUSEDRV.LIB. Use the following instructions to build MOUSEDRV.LIB:

1. Compile EVENT.ASM, SPRITELL.C, and MOUSEDRV.C into individual object (.OBJ) files. Use the same memory model for every file. For details about compiling EVENT.ASM, refer to Chapter 7. For details about compiling SPRITELL.C, refer to Chapter 18. Use the previous instructions to compile MOUSEDRV.C.

2. Combine the separate object files in one library file.
   For Borland users, enter the following at the DOS command line:

   TLIB MOUSEDRV +EVENT +MOUSEDRV +SPRITELL

   For Microsoft users, enter the following at the DOS command line:

   LIB MOUSEDRV +EVENT +MOUSEDRV +SPRITELL

With Borland compilers and Microsoft C 6.0 and 7.0 compilers, the order of +EVENT, +MOUSEDRV, and +SPRITELL is not relevant. However, with Microsoft QuickC, the order must be +EVENT +MOUSEDRV +SPRITELL. Otherwise, when an application utilizing MOUSEDRV.LIB is compiled, the link fails due to _TEXT segment fixup errors.

The New Library Header File

To inform applications of the functions and global variables contained within MOUSEDRV.LIB, a header file is required. The header file for the modified mouse function library is called MOUSEDRV.H and is shown here:

```
/*------------------------------------------------------------*/
/*                    MOUSEDRV.H                          */
/*                                                        */
/* Header file for MOUSEDRV.LIB.                          */
/*                                                        */
/*------------------------------------------------------------*/

#define XOR_MODE 24           /* Sprite write mode constants   */
#define COPYPUT_MODE 0


#define MV_LBUTTON 1          /* For event driver button       */
#define MV_RBUTTON 2          /* status when CURSOR_MOVED       */
#define MV_BBUTTON 3          /* message is trapped.            */

      /*---------------------------------------------*/
      /* External Variables Declared in MOUSEDRV.LIB */
      /*---------------------------------------------*/

extern int NUMBER_BUTTONS;    /* Number of mouse buttons        */

extern int HCELL_SIZE,        /* Cursor cell sizes - text mode */
           VCELL_SIZE;

extern int MOUSE_SIZE;        /* Mouse cursor size. Use 16 in   */
                              /* graphics mode, 1 in text.      */

extern unsigned char IN_GMODE;/* 1 in graphics mode, 0 in text*/

extern unsigned char MOUSE_THERE;    /* 1 if present, 0 if not */
extern unsigned char MOUSE_VISIBLE;  /* Is mouse visible?      */

extern unsigned char LBUTTON_DOWN,    /* Boolean vars or messags*/
                     RBUTTON_DOWN,    /* set by event processor.*/
                     BBUTTON_DOWN,
                     LBUTTON_UP,
                     RBUTTON_UP,
                     BBUTTON_UP,
                     CURSOR_MOVED;
```

```
extern int CMX,CMY;              /* Mouse coords set by event    */
extern int BSTATE;               /* handler; also button state.  */

extern union  REGS  mregs;    /* DOS/mouse registers            */
extern struct SREGS msegregs;/* DOS/mouse segment register      */

extern unsigned char EGA_REG_READ;     /* EGA regs handled?    */
                                       /* Default YES          */

                                 /* New sprite mouse cursor=1   */
                                 /* Normal mouse cursor=0       */
extern unsigned char USING_SPRITE;

/* The Sprite Structure Type */
/*---------------------------*/
typedef struct
    {
    unsigned long bigmask[24];  /* Actual sprite mask        */
    unsigned char *image_buffer;/* Image buffer for sprite    */
    unsigned char color[16];    /* Color of each line in mask */
    int left_shift;             /* Blank bits - left side mask */
    int right_shift;            /* Blank bits - right side mask*/
    int up_shift;               /* Blank bits - upper side mask*/
    int down_shift;             /* Blank bits - lower side mask*/
    int tx,ty;                  /* Text coords-3byte wide mask */
    int gx,gy;                  /* Graf coords-3byte wide mask */
    int hotx,hoty;              /* Hot spot                   */
    int sprite_mode;            /* COPY/PUT or XOR sprite?    */
    unsigned char SPRITE_ON;    /* Sprite on or off k         */
    }sprite_type;

                                /* Hard assigment pointer->    */
                                /* for event processor.        */
extern sprite_type *sprite_cursor;

extern int BITMAP_SIZE;         /* Size of bitmap image        */

extern int HORIZ_OFFSET;        /* Horiz offset for vertical   */
                                /* pixel addressing.           */
                                /* Assign value in main() !!!  */

extern int MODE_NUMBER;         /* Video mode number; set in   */
                                /* LL_setmode() or by programmr*/
```

```
extern int PAGE;                    /* Current video page number   */
                                    /* Assign value in main() !!!  */



/*---------------------*/
/* Standard Functions   */
/*---------------------*/
void reset_mouse(void);
void pascal show_mouse_cursor(void);
void pascal hide_mouse_cursor(void);
void pascal set_hide_bounds(int x1,int y1,int x2,int y2);
void pascal set_mouse_position(int x,int y);
void pascal set_mouse_hlimits(int x1,int x2);
void pascal set_mouse_vlimits(int y1,int y2);
void pascal get_mouse_button(unsigned char *button1,
                             unsigned char *button2,
                             int *x,int *y);
unsigned char pascal get_button_rls_info(int butt_no,
                                         int *count,
                                         int *x,int *y);
void pascal set_event_handler(int call_mask,
                              void (far *location)(void));


/*---------------------*/
/* Optional Functions   */
/*---------------------*/
void pascal get_mouse_type(int *maj_ver,int *min_ver,
                           int *mtype,int *irq_num);
int pascal get_crt_page(void);
void pascal get_mouse_sensitivity(int *h_speed,int *v_speed,
                                  int *threshold);
void pascal set_mouse_sensitivity(int h_speed,int v_speed,
                                  int threshold);
void pascal set_graphics_cursor(int far *cursor_mask,
                                int hotx,int hoty);
void pascal set_text_cursor(int ctype,int sm_or_sl,int cm_or_el);



/*-----------------*/
/* Event Processor  */
/*-----------------*/
void far event_handler(void);
void near event_processor(int event_status,int button_status,
                          int x,int y);
```

```
void install_event_handler(void);
void reset_event_status(void);


/*----------------------*/
/* Sprite Functions     */
/*----------------------*/
sprite_type *new_sprite(void);
void evp_type load_sprite(char mask[16][17],
                          int hotx,int hoty,
                          sprite_type *sprite,int mode)
void destroy_sprite(sprite_type *sprite);
void evp_type draw_sprite(int x,int y,sprite_type *sprite);
void change_sprite_line_color(sprite_type *sprite,
                              int linenum,int newcolor);
void change_sprite_color(sprite_type *sprite,int newcolor);
void set_sprite_mode(sprite_type *sprite,int mode);
void evp_type hide_sprite(sprite_type *sprite);
void evp_type show_sprite(sprite_type *sprite);
```

Using the Sprite Cursor

The following example demonstrates using the sprite cursor as the graphics mouse cursor. Go ahead and enter, compile, and run the program. Some of the finer details are discussed after the example.

If you are compiling within the integrated environment and are using a Borland compiler or the Microsoft QuickC compiler, a project file is required to contain the mouse function library and the C source file. The project file is called MOUSE26.PRJ. Here it is:

```
MOUSEDRV.LIB
MOUSE26.C
```

If you use Microsoft C 6.0 or C/C++ 7.0, you do not need a project file. Just add MOUSEDRV.LIB to the Additional Libraries Linker option.

If you are compiling from the command line with any Borland or Microsoft compiler, add MOUSELIB.LIB to the link library's command-line option.

Here is MOUSE26.C:

```
/*---------------------------------------------------------------*/
/*                      MOUSE26.C                      */
/*                                                     */
/* First demonstration of using a sprite as the mouse cursor. */
/* Example compiles with the file MOUSEDRV.LIB and the header */
/* file MOUSEDRV.H.                                     */
/*---------------------------------------------------------------*/

#include "compiler.h"      /* Compiler directives        */
#include "mousedrv.h"      /* Header file for mouse/sprite */
#include graphics
#include videolib

                           /* 1st 16 bytes in row   = MASK  */
char hand[16][17]=         /* 17th Byte in each row = COLOR */
    {
    0,0,0,1,1,0,0,0,0,0,0,0,0,0,0,0, 12,
    0,0,0,1,1,0,0,0,0,0,0,0,0,0,0,0, 12,
    0,0,0,1,1,0,0,0,0,0,0,0,0,0,0,0, 12,
    0,0,0,1,1,0,1,1,0,1,1,0,1,1,0,0, 12,
    0,0,0,1,1,0,1,1,0,1,1,0,1,1,0,0, 12,
    0,0,0,1,1,1,1,1,1,1,1,1,1,1,0,0, 15,
    1,1,0,1,1,1,1,1,1,1,1,1,1,1,0,0, 15,
    1,1,0,1,1,1,1,1,1,1,1,1,1,1,0,0, 15,
    1,1,1,1,1,1,1,1,1,1,1,1,1,0,0,0, 15,
    1,1,1,1,1,1,1,1,1,1,1,1,0,0,0,0, 15,
    1,1,1,1,1,1,1,1,1,1,1,0,0,0,0,0, 15,
    1,1,1,1,1,1,1,1,1,1,1,0,0,0,0,0,  9,
    0,1,1,1,1,1,1,1,1,1,0,0,0,0,0,0,  9,
    0,0,1,1,1,1,1,1,1,0,0,0,0,0,0,0,  9,
    0,0,0,1,1,1,1,1,1,0,0,0,0,0,0,0,  9,
    0,0,0,1,1,1,1,1,1,0,0,0,0,0,0,0,  9
    };



/* MODULE : INIT SPRITE                                */
/*---------------------------------------------------------------*/
/* Initialize sprite, event handler, and all relevant vars.  */
```

```
/*                                                    */
void init_sprite(void)
   {
   switch(VID_MAXY)             /* EGA or VGA graphics adapter?  */
      {
      case 199:MODE_NUMBER=0x0E;break;
      case 349:MODE_NUMBER=0x10;break; /* Mono switch to 0x0F */
      case 479:MODE_NUMBER=0x12;break; /* Mono switch to 0x11 */
      }

   PAGE=0;                      /* Video page to write on        */

   HORIZ_OFFSET=80;             /* Horizontal offset for vertical*/
                                /* address calulation.           */
                                /* 80 is for all modes where 640 */
                                /* is the max horizontal coord.  */
                                /* If you choose the 800 x 600 16*/
                                /* color mode be SURE to change   */
                                /* this to 100  !!!!!!!          */


   USING_SPRITE=1;             /* Set USING_SPRITE to 1 for      */
                                /* sprite cursor, 0 for default   */
                                /* cursor.                        */

   if (USING_SPRITE)
      {                         /* Grab memory for sprite         */
      sprite_cursor=new_sprite();

                                /* Load the sprite with mask      */
                                /* Initialize in COPYPUT mode     */
      load_sprite(hand,0,-1,sprite_cursor,COPYPUT_MODE);
      }

   install_event_handler();  /* Install the event handler        */
   }



void main()
   {
   install_video(GMODE);     /* Install video system          */
   header();                 /* Draw header                   */
   reset_mouse();            /* Reset mouse                   */
```

```
if (MOUSE_THERE)
   {
   init_sprite();              /* Initialize the sprite as the  */
                              /* mouse cursor.                 */

                              /* Set horiz and vertical limits */
   set_mouse_hlimits(1,VID_MAXX-MOUSE_SIZE);
   set_mouse_vlimits(1,VID_MAXY-MOUSE_SIZE);

   out_text_xy(15,4,"Using the sprite cursor instead of
                     the default mouse cursor.");
   out_text_xy(15,5,"Sprite cursor should now be a
                     RED/WHITE/BLUE hand.");
   out_text_xy(15,6,"Move it around with the mouse.");
   out_text_xy(15,8,"Press any key to exit.");

   show_mouse_cursor();
   }
else
   mouse_error(5,4);

getch();                      /* Wait for keypress             */
                              /* Reset mouse due to event hndlr*/
if (MOUSE_THERE) reset_mouse();

                              /* LOOK !!!!!                    */
                              /* If using sprite,destroy it!   */
if (USING_SPRITE) destroy_sprite(sprite_cursor);

shut_down_video();
}
```

When the program is run, the sprite cursor is a red, white, and blue hand, illustrated in Figure 19-1.

Initializing the Sprite Cursor

The following discussions relate to how the sprite cursor is defined and initialized in the previous example. Many of the subjects discussed will be expanded on in the following two chapters.

Figure 19-1.   *The sprite cursor*

Cursor Mask

The sprite cursor's shape is defined in a different fashion than the default mouse cursor. Notice from the previous example the cursor mask hand[] is actually loaded with char values of 1 or 0, not bit values contained within an integer (as with the default mouse cursor). The mask is defined this way for two reasons:

- You can enter the mask visually, without the need to convert binary values (mask rows) into decimal or hexadecimal equivalents. This is much easier because visual patterns are always more readable than numeric values. The sprite driver function load_sprite() makes the necessary conversions to long integers.

- Notice that the mask is actually a 16 × 17 char array. The seventeenth value of each mask row is used to specify the color of the particular row, and each row in the cursor mask can be a separate color. Again, the appropriate conversions are handled inside the sprite driver function *load_sprite()*.

The init_sprite() Function

Take a look at the function init_sprite() in MOUSE26.C. This is where the sprite cursor is initialized. The reason the initialization code is not a mouse library function is because your sprite needs may vary from application to application, and you may want to modify the initialization code without having to recompile the mouse function library. Therefore, the initialization code is left outside of the mouse function library.

The following is a breakdown of the statements within the function init_sprite():

switch(VID_MAXY)   The current video mode is determined by examining the variable VID_MAXY. Within the switch statements, the variable MODE_NUMBER is set accordingly.

Since MOUSE26.C uses either the standard Borland or Microsoft graphics library and the sprite driver uses its own low-level graphics functions, the sprite driver must be informed of the current video mode.

No matter which graphics library you use in your own applications or which method you use to set or determine the video mode, you *must* inform the sprite driver of the current mode by setting the variable MODE_NUMBER appropriately.

The sprite driver uses more modes than those utilized in the previous example, and those are covered in the following two chapters.

PAGE=0;   This statement specifies which video page the sprite cursor is displayed on. 0 specifies page 1, and 1 specifies page 2. If you use only the default page in your applications (page 1), you can remove this statement, since PAGE defaults to 0.

HORIZ_OFFSET=80;   This statement specifies the horizontal offset used in vertical address calculations (see Chapter 17). For the 640 × 200, 640 × 350, and 640 × 480 modes, you must set HORIZ_OFFSET to 80. For the 800 × 600 mode, you must set HORIZ_OFFSET to 100. If you do not use graphics modes higher than 640 × 480 in your applications, you can remove this statement, as HORIZ_OFFSET defaults to 80.

USING_SPRITE=1;   This statement specifies which cursor the mouse function library is to use. If you want to use the sprite cursor, set USING_SPRITE to 1. If you want to use the default mouse cursor, set USING_SPRITE to 0.

sprite_cursor=new_sprite();   This statement allocates memory for the sprite cursor and points sprite_cursor to the memory location. The pointer sprite_cursor is a global pointer declared in MOUSEDRV.C. Although you may implement more than one sprite at a time (dual sprite cursors are demonstrated in Chapter 21), the sprite cursor pointer used internally by the mouse function library is always sprite_cursor.

load_sprite(hand,0,–1,sprite_cursor,
        COPYPUT_MODE);   This statement loads the sprite cursor with the mask values in hand[] and specifies a hot spot of 0,–1 (for specific information regarding the hot spot, see Chapter 14). The sprite cursor is initialized in the

COPYPUT_MODE mode. The available modes are COPYPUT_MODE and XOR_MODE.

install_event_handler();   The event handler is activated, and the sprite cursor is ready to use.

Destroying the Sprite Cursor

If you use the sprite cursor (or any other sprite), you must destroy it upon program termination. Otherwise, the memory allocated to the sprite cursor is unavailable to the system after program termination.

When MOUSE26.C is terminated, the sprite is destroyed with following statement:

```
if (USING_SPRITE) destroy_sprite(sprite_cursor);
```

The Default Mouse Cursor

To verify that the default mouse cursor still functions as normal, change the statement USING_SPRITE=1 to USING_SPRITE=0 in MOUSE26.C, recompile and run. Notice that the default mouse cursor still functions normally.

Additionally, the new mouse function library still operates in text modes. Just change the statement install_video(GMODE) to install_video(TMODE), set USING_SPRITE to 0, recompile the program, and run it.

The next chapter demonstrates using the sprite cursor in the 800×600 16-color mode.

Chapter *20*

The Sprite Cursor in the 800 × 600 16-Color Mode

Since the 800 × 600 16-color graphics mode was the initial inspiration for building a sprite cursor, it seems only fitting to demonstrate the sprite cursor using that mode.

The VGA 800× 600 16-color mode requires a variable frequency display such as the NEC MultiSynch or compatible monitor. Attempting to run the 800 × 600 16-color mode on the wrong type of monitor may result in damage to the monitor! Be sure to first read the documentation supplied with your video card and video monitor to determine if you can use this mode.

New Video Functions

Since the Borland and Microsoft standard graphics libraries do not support the 800 × 600 16-color mode (without VESA being loaded), some new video functions are needed in order to utilize the mode.

In this chapter, you create six new video functions to interface with the video card. The functions use DOS interrupt 0x10 exclusively. The source code is kept to a bare minimum, just enough to verify that the sprite cursor does indeed operate in the 800 × 600 16-color mode. If you are currently programming applications that use this mode, you have either written your own graphics functions or are using a third-party graphics library. If you have never used the 800×600 16-color graphics mode, the new video functions you create in this chapter effectively demonstrate how to access and use the mode.

The following list of the six new video functions includes the function name, parameters, and a short description of what each function does.

LL_setmode(int *mode***)**   This function is used to set the video mode on most VGA cards.

LL_setvideo7mode(int *mode***)**   This function is used to set the high-resolution video modes on the Video 7 Super VGA card.

LL_clrscr(int *x1***,int** *y1***,int** *x2***,int** *y2***,int** *color***)**   This function clears a display area defined by the specified rectangular borders.

LL_gotoxy(int *x***,int** *y***,int** *PAGE***)**   This function locates the video cursor (not the mouse cursor) to the specified display location.

LL_outch(int *value***,int** *color***,int** *PAGE***)**   This function outputs a character to the display.

out_text_xy(int *x***,int** *y***,char** **str***,int** *color***)**   This function outputs a string of text to the display. The function is similar to the function out_text_xy() in the previous video function library, except the function is also sent the color.

The new video functions are used only in this chapter so the 800×600 16-color mode can be demonstrated.

Here are the six new video functions. The file they are located in is called **SMALLVID.INC**.

```
/*------------------------------------------------------------*/
/*                      SMALLVID.INC                       */
/*                                                          */
/* Small video functions for extended graphics modes.       */
/*------------------------------------------------------------*/

int VID_MAXX,VID_MAXY;

#include <string.h>

/* MODULE : LL SETMODE                                      */
/*------------------------------------------------------------*/
/* Sets the video mode. No modification needed for any DOS   */
/* supported mode, ATI SVGA card, and most other SVGA cards. */
```

```
/* Use setvideo7mode() to set the Video 7 card to 800 x 600.  */
/* Note that if a mode not supported is passed in, the         */
/* function assumes the 800 x 600 16-color mode!               */
/*                                                             */
/* Input parameters                                            */
/*      mode - Mode number                                     */
/*                                                             */
void pascal LL_setmode(int mode)
   {
   union REGS gregs;
   gregs.h.ah=0;              /* Function 00H, set mode        */
   gregs.h.al=mode;           /* Set mode number               */
   int86(0x10,&gregs,&gregs);/* Call int 10h                   */

   MODE_NUMBER=mode;          /* Set global variable           */

   switch(MODE_NUMBER)        /* Set maximum coordinates       */
      {
      case 0x0E:/* 640 x 200 16-COLOR */
               VID_MAXX=639;VID_MAXY=199;
               break;

      case 0x0F:/* 640 x 350 MONO     */
      case 0x10:/* 640 x 350 16-COLOR */
               VID_MAXX=639;VID_MAXY=349;
               break;

      case 0x11:/* 640 x 480 MONO     */
      case 0x12:/* 640 x 480 16-COLOR */
               VID_MAXX=639;VID_MAXY=479;
               break;

      default:/* NOTE !!! Any modes other than     */
               /* listed above sets to 800 x 600!!!*/
               VID_MAXX=799;VID_MAXY=599;
               break;
      }
   }

/* MODULE : LL SETVIDEO7MODE                             */
/*-----------------------------------------------------------*/
/* Sets the 800 x 600 16-color mode on a Video 7 card.   */
/* Use the function setmode() to set standard DOS supported  */
/* video modes.                                          */
```

```
/* Input parameters                                          */
/*      mode - Mode number                                   */
/*                                                           */
void pascal LL_setvideo7mode(int mode)
    {
    union REGS gregs;
    gregs.h.ah=0x06F;          /* Set up for Video 7 call    */
    gregs.h.al=0x05;
    gregs.h.bl=mode;           /* Set mode number            */
    int86(0x10,&gregs,&gregs);/* Call int 10h                */
    MODE_NUMBER=mode;          /* Set global variable         */

    VID_MAXX=799;VID_MAXY=599;
    }


/* MODULE : LL CLRSCR                                         */
/*----------------------------------------------------------*/
/* Clears the window at TEXT ABSOLUTE x1,y1,x2,y2, with the   */
/* value color. Even in graphics mode the values are TEXT     */
/* coordinates.                                               */
/* Input parameters                                          */
/*    x1,y1,x2,y2 - Region to clear in TEXT coordinates       */
/*          color - Color to clear as                         */
/*                                                           */
void pascal LL_clrscr(int x1,int y1,int x2,int y2,int color)
    {
    union REGS gregs;
    gregs.h.ah=0x06;           /* Function 6, init window     */
    gregs.h.al=00;             /* If al=0 screen is blanked   */
    gregs.h.bh=color;          /* Set the color               */
    gregs.h.ch=y1;             /* Set all the coordinates     */
    gregs.h.cl=x1;
    gregs.h.dh=y2;
    gregs.h.dl=x2;
    int86(0x10,&gregs,&gregs);/* Call int 10h                */
    }


/* MODULE : LL GOTOXY                                         */
/*----------------------------------------------------------*/
/* Goto X,Y TEXT coordinates, values are ABSOLUTE.            */
/* Input parameters                                          */
/*    x,y - X,Y TEXT coordinates                              */
/*    page- Page to move text cursor on                       */
/*                                                           */
```

```c
void pascal LL_gotoxy(int x,int y,int PAGE)
   {
   union REGS gregs;
   gregs.h.ah=0x02;            /* Function 2, set cursor pos  */
   gregs.h.bh=PAGE;            /* Set page number             */
   gregs.h.dh=y;               /* Set x,y coordinates         */
   gregs.h.dl=x;
   int86(0x10,&gregs,&gregs);/* Call int 10h                  */
   }


/* MODULE : LL OUTCH                                           */
/*-----------------------------------------------------------*/
/* Outputs a character and updates the TEXT cursor position,  */
/* even in graphics mode.                                     */
/* Input parameters                                           */
/*     value - ASCII value of character                       */
/*     color - Color to write as                              */
/*      page - Page to write it to                            */
/*                                                            */
void pascal LL_outch(int value,int color,int PAGE)
   {
   union REGS gregs;
   gregs.h.ah=0x0E;            /* Function E, teletype mode    */
   gregs.h.al=value;           /* ASCII value for character    */
   gregs.h.bh=PAGE;            /* Page to write it to          */
   gregs.h.bl=color;           /* Color                        */
   int86(0x10,&gregs,&gregs);/* Call int 10h                   */
   }


/* MODULE : OUT TEXT XY                                        */
/*-----------------------------------------------------------*/
/* Output a string of characters.                             */
/* Input parameters                                           */
/*     x,y   - Text locations                                 */
/*     str   - Address to string                              */
/*     color - Color to draw it in                            */
/*                                                            */
void out_text_xy(int x,int y,char *str,int color)
   {
   int loop;
   LL_gotoxy(x,y,PAGE);
   for (loop=0;loop<strlen(str);loop++)
      LL_outch(str[loop],color,PAGE);
   }
```

Running in Any 16-Color Mode

The following example utilizes the new video functions and the sprite cursor. It is set to run in the EGA/VGA 640 × 350 16-color mode. Instructions on how to change to the 800 × 600 16-color mode or the VGA 640 × 480 16-color mode are found in the function init_graphics() and are explained in detail following the source code listing.

Here is the project file, MOUSE27.PRJ:

```
MOUSEDRV.LIB
MOUSE27.C
```

   Run this example in graphics modes only!

Here is MOUSE27.C:

```
/*-------------------------------------------------------------*/
/*                      MOUSE27.C                              */
/*                                                             */
/*                                                             */
/* Demonstration of using the sprite cursor in EGA, VGA, or    */
/* 800 x 600 16-color mode.                                    */
/*                                                             */
/* Example is set to run in the 640 x 350 EGA mode.            */
/* YOU MUST MAKE THE CHANGES TO RUN IT IN 800 X 600 16-COLOR!  */
/*                                                             */
/* If running the 800 x 600 16-color mode, you MUST have a     */
/* capable graphics card and monitor!                          */
/*                                                             */
/* Read the comments carefully to determine how to integrate   */
/* and implement the 800 x 600 16-color mode.                  */
/*                                                             */
/* Example is set to run in the 640 x 350 EGA mode.            */
/* YOU MUST MAKE THE CHANGES TO RUN IT IN 800 X 600 16-COLOR.  */
/*-------------------------------------------------------------*/

#include "compiler.h"        /* Compiler directives           */
#include "mousedrv.h"        /* Mouse/sprite driver header     */
#include "smallvid.inc"      /* New graphics functions         */

                             /* 1st 16 bytes in row  = MASK   */
char hand[16][17]=           /* 17th byte in each row = COLOR  */
```

```
{
0,0,0,1,1,0,0,0,0,0,0,0,0,0,0,0,  12,
0,0,0,1,1,0,0,0,0,0,0,0,0,0,0,0,  12,
0,0,0,1,1,0,0,0,0,0,0,0,0,0,0,0,  12,
0,0,0,1,1,0,1,1,0,1,1,0,1,1,0,0,  12,
0,0,0,1,1,0,1,1,0,1,1,0,1,1,0,0,  12,
0,0,0,1,1,1,1,1,1,1,1,1,1,1,0,0,  15,
1,1,0,1,1,1,1,1,1,1,1,1,1,1,0,0,  15,
1,1,0,1,1,1,1,1,1,1,1,1,1,1,0,0,  15,
1,1,1,1,1,1,1,1,1,1,1,1,1,0,0,0,  15,
1,1,1,1,1,1,1,1,1,1,1,1,0,0,0,0,  15,
1,1,1,1,1,1,1,1,1,1,1,0,0,0,0,0,  15,
1,1,1,1,1,1,1,1,1,1,0,0,0,0,0,0,   9,
0,1,1,1,1,1,1,1,1,0,0,0,0,0,0,0,   9,
0,0,1,1,1,1,1,1,1,0,0,0,0,0,0,0,   9,
0,0,0,1,1,1,1,1,1,0,0,0,0,0,0,0,   9,
0,0,0,1,1,1,1,1,1,0,0,0,0,0,0,0,   9
};


/* MODULE : INIT GRAPHICS                                        */
/*--------------------------------------------------------------*/
/* Sets up the video system for EGA, VGA or 800 x 600 16-color*/
/* Be sure to READ the comments and make the appropriate       */
/* changes for each mode. NO MATTER WHAT GRAPHICS LIBRARY YOU */
/* USE, ALL variables in this function must be set. It's up   */
/* to you to integrate within your own graphics library.      */
/*                                                            */
void init_graphics(void)
   {
   LL_setmode(0x10);            /* Set video mode               */
                               /* 0x0E - EGA 640 x 200 16-color */
                               /* 0x0F - EGA 640 x 350 MONO    */
                               /* 0x10 - EGA 640 x 350 16-color */
                               /* 0x11 - VGA 640 x 480 MONO    */
                               /* 0x12 - VGA 640 x 480 16-color */
                               /* Check you SVGA card manual for*/
                               /* correct 800 x 600 16-color   */
                               /* mode. Video - 7 users use the */
                               /* function LL_setvideo7mode().  */

   HORIZ_OFFSET=80;            /* Horizontal offset for vertical*/
                               /* address calculation. 80 is for*/
                               /* all modes where 640 is the max*/
                               /* horizontal coordinate. If you */
```

```
                              /* choose the 800 x 600 16-color */
                              /* mode, be SURE to change this  */
                              /* to 100 !!!!!!!                */

    IN_GMODE=1;               /* Yes, in graphics mode         */

    PAGE=0;                   /* Video page to draw on         */
    }


/* MODULE : INIT SPRITE                                         */
/*----------------------------------------------------------*/
/* Initialize sprite, event handler, and all relevant vars.   */
/*                                                            */
void init_sprite(void)
    {
    USING_SPRITE=1;           /* Using sprite cursor           */

    if (USING_SPRITE)
        {                     /* Grab memory and address for   */
                              /* sprite.                       */
        sprite_cursor=new_sprite();

                              /* Load the sprite with values   */
                              /* from 'hand' and initialize in */
                              /* COPY/PUT mode.                */
        load_sprite(hand,0,-1,sprite_cursor,COPYPUT_MODE);
        }

    install_event_handler();  /* Install event handler         */
    }



void main(void)
    {
    char xstr[6],ystr[6];     /* Strings for coordinates       */

    init_graphics();          /* Initialize graphics system    */

    reset_mouse();

    if (MOUSE_THERE)
        {
```

```
      init_sprite();              /* Initialize sprite cursor   */


                                 /* Set horiz/vert limits      */
      set_mouse_hlimits(1,VID_MAXX-MOUSE_SIZE);
      set_mouse_vlimits(1,VID_MAXY-MOUSE_SIZE);


                                 /* If using 800 x 600 16-color,  */
                                 /* mouse's virtual screen may be */
                                 /* 799 x 199, so force it to     */
                                 /* default in the center of scr. */
      set_mouse_position(VID_MAXX/2,VID_MAXY/2);

      out_text_xy(5,2,"Demostrate using the sprite cursor in EGA,
                     VGA, and 800 x 600 16 color",15);
      out_text_xy(5,3,"Sprite cursor should be a
                     RED/WHITE/BLUE hand.",15);
      out_text_xy(5,4,"Move it around with the mouse all
                     you want.",15);
      out_text_xy(5,5,"Press Any Key When Finished.",15);


                                 /* Convert maximum coordinates   */
      sprintf(xstr,"%d",VID_MAXX);
      sprintf(ystr,"%d",VID_MAXY);

      out_text_xy(25,10,"Video Maximum X -",15);
      out_text_xy(43,10,xstr,11);
      out_text_xy(25,11,"Video Maximum Y -",15);
      out_text_xy(43,11,ystr,11);

      show_mouse_cursor();

      }
   else
      {
      out_text_xy(5,5,"No Mouse Is Installed!",10);
      out_text_xy(5,6,"Please Install The Mouse Driver
                     Before Continuing...",10);
      printf("%c",7);
      }

   getch();                          /* Wait for keypress          */

   if (MOUSE_THERE) reset_mouse();
```

```
                              /* LOOK !!!!!                */
                              /* If using sprite cursor,   */
                              /* destroy it!               */
        if (USING_SPRITE) destroy_sprite(sprite_cursor);

        LL_clrscr(0,0,79,24,0);
        LL_setmode(3);                /* Reset video to 80 x 25 text*/
        }
```

Setting the 800 × 600 16-Color Mode

Because the mode number for the 800 × 600 16-color mode varies from card to card, the previous example is set to run in the EGA 640 × 350 16-color mode. To change the video mode to the 800 × 600 16-color mode, follow these instructions:

1. In the function init_graphics(), the statement LL_setmode(0x10) sets the video mode to the EGA/VGA 640 × 350 16-color mode. To change to the VGA 800 × 600 16-color mode, change 0x10 to the correct mode number for your video card. Determine this from your video card documentation.

    If you use a Video-7 VGA card, use the function LL_setvideo7mode() instead of LL_setmode().

2. Change the statement HORIZ_OFFSET=80 to HORIZ_OFFSET=100.

Assuming you have a VGA video card and monitor capable of utilizing the 800 × 600 16-color mode and know the correct mode number for your video card, these changes allow you to run the previous example in the 800 × 600 16-color mode.

Verifying Proper Behavior

The following example writes text to the display in a continuous fashion (similar to the MOUSETORAT examples in Chapter 4), and the sprite cursor is hidden and shown between display writes. This is to verify that the sprite cursor does not cause graphics disruption during display writing. Move the sprite cursor around in the text as it is being written, to verify proper behavior.

Here is the project file, MOUSE28.PRJ:

```
MOUSEDRV.LIB
MOUSE28.C
```

Run this example in graphics modes only!

Here is MOUSE28.C:

```
/*------------------------------------------------------------*/
/*                      MOUSE28.C                          */
/*                                                        */
/*                                                        */
/* Demonstration of using the sprite cursor while writing  */
/* text to the display to verify no graphics disruption.   */
/*                                                        */
/* Example is set to run in the 640 x 350 EGA mode.        */
/* YOU MUST MAKE THE CHANGES TO RUN IT IN 800 X 600 16-COLOR! */
/*                                                        */
/* If running the 800 x 600 16-color mode, you MUST have a  */
/* capable graphics card and monitor!                      */
/*                                                        */
/* Read the comments carefully to determine how to integrate */
/* and implement the 800 x 600 16-color mode.              */
/*                                                        */
/* Example is set to run in the 640 x 350 EGA mode.        */
/* YOU MUST MAKE THE CHANGES TO RUN IT IN 800 X 600 16-COLOR. */
/*------------------------------------------------------------*/

#include "compiler.h"       /* Compiler directives          */
#include "mousedrv.h",       /* Mouse/sprite driver header    */
#include "smallvid.inc"      /* New graphics functions        */

                            /* Microsoft compilers!          */
#ifdef MICROSOFT            /* Since the delay function was   */
   #include <time.h>         /* located in the old video func */
   #include "delay.inc"      /* library, need it here as well.*/
#endif

                            /* 1st 16 bytes in row   = MASK  */
char hand[16][17]=           /* 17th byte in each row = COLOR */
    {
    0,0,0,1,1,0,0,0,0,0,0,0,0,0,0,0, 12,
    0,0,0,1,1,0,0,0,0,0,0,0,0,0,0,0, 12,
    0,0,0,1,1,0,0,0,0,0,0,0,0,0,0,0, 12,
    0,0,0,1,1,0,1,1,0,1,1,0,1,1,0,0, 12,
    0,0,0,1,1,0,1,1,0,1,1,0,1,1,0,0, 12,
    0,0,0,1,1,1,1,1,1,1,1,1,1,1,0,0, 15,
    1,1,0,1,1,1,1,1,1,1,1,1,1,1,0,0, 15,
    1,1,0,1,1,1,1,1,1,1,1,1,1,1,0,0, 15,
    1,1,1,1,1,1,1,1,1,1,1,1,1,0,0,0, 15,
```

```
1,1,1,1,1,1,1,1,1,1,1,1,1,0,0,0,0,  15,
1,1,1,1,1,1,1,1,1,1,1,1,0,0,0,0,0,  15,
1,1,1,1,1,1,1,1,1,1,0,0,0,0,0,0,   9,
0,1,1,1,1,1,1,1,1,0,0,0,0,0,0,0,   9,
0,0,1,1,1,1,1,1,1,0,0,0,0,0,0,0,   9,
0,0,0,1,1,1,1,1,1,0,0,0,0,0,0,0,   9,
0,0,0,1,1,1,1,1,1,0,0,0,0,0,0,0,   9
};


/* MODULE : INIT GRAPHICS                                   */
/*----------------------------------------------------------*/
/* Sets up the video system for EGA, VGA or 800 x 600 16-color*/
/* Be sure to READ the comments and make the appropriate    */
/* changes for each mode. NO MATTER WHAT GRAPHICS LIBRARY YOU */
/* USE, ALL variables in this function must be set. It's up  */
/* to you to integrate within your own graphics library.    */
/*                                                          */
void init_graphics(void)
    {
    LL_setmode(0x10);          /* Set video mode              */
                               /* 0x0E - EGA 640 x 200 16-color */
                               /* 0x0F - EGA 640 x 350 MONO     */
                               /* 0x10 - EGA 640 x 350 16-color */
                               /* 0x11 - VGA 640 x 480 MONO     */
                               /* 0x12 - VGA 640 x 480 16-color */
                               /* Check you SVGA card manual for*/
                               /* correct 800 x 600 16-color    */
                               /* mode. Video-7 users use the   */
                               /* function LL_setvideo7mode().  */

    HORIZ_OFFSET=80;           /* Horizontal offset for vertical*/
                               /* address calculation. 80 is for*/
                               /* all modes where 640 is the max*/
                               /* horizontal coordinate. If you */
                               /* choose the 800 x 600 16-color */
                               /* mode, be SURE to change this  */
                               /* to 100 !!!!!!!                */

    IN_GMODE=1;                /* Yes, in graphics mode         */

    PAGE=0;                    /* Video page to draw on         */
    }
```

```
/* MODULE : INIT SPRITE                                           */
/*--------------------------------------------------------------*/
/* Initialize sprite, event handler, and all relevant vars.     */
/*                                                               */
void init_sprite(void)
    {                             /* Grab memory and address for  */
                                  /* sprite.                      */

    sprite_cursor=new_sprite();

                                  /* Load the sprite with values  */
                                  /* from 'hand' and initialize in */
                                  /* COPY/PUT mode.               */
    load_sprite(hand,0,-1,sprite_cursor,COPYPUT_MODE);

    install_event_handler();  /* Install event handler            */
    USING_SPRITE=1;           /* Using sprite cursor              */
    }




void main(void)
    {
    int loop1,loop2,cloop,max;
    char xstr[6],ystr[6];     /* Strings for coordinates          */

    init_graphics();          /* Initialize graphics system       */

    reset_mouse();

    if (MOUSE_THERE)
        {
        init_sprite();        /* Initialize sprite cursor         */

                              /* Set horiz/vert limits            */
        set_mouse_hlimits(1,VID_MAXX-MOUSE_SIZE);
        set_mouse_vlimits(1,VID_MAXY-MOUSE_SIZE);

                              /* If using 800 x 600 16-color,     */
                              /* mouse's virtual screen may be    */
                              /* 799 x 199, so force it to        */
                              /* default in the center of scr.    */
        set_mouse_position(VID_MAXX/2,VID_MAXY/2);
```

```
out_text_xy(5,2,"Demonstrate using the sprite cursor in EGA,
                 VGA, and 800 x 600 16 color",15);
out_text_xy(5,3,"Sprite cursor should be a
                 RED/WHITE/BLUE hand.",15);
out_text_xy(5,4,"Move it around with the mouse all
                 you want.",15);
out_text_xy(5,5,"Press Any Key When Finished.",15);

                         /* Convert maximum coordinates  */
sprintf(xstr,"%d",VID_MAXX);
sprintf(ystr,"%d",VID_MAXY);

out_text_xy(5,10,"Video Maximum X -",15);
out_text_xy(23,10,xstr,11);
out_text_xy(5,11,"Video Maximum Y -",15);
out_text_xy(23,11,ystr,11);

show_mouse_cursor();

cloop=1;                 /* Start MOUSETORAT color       */
max=20;                  /* cycle for test.              */
while (!kbhit())
   {
   loop1=10;
   while ((loop1<=max)&&(!kbhit()))
      {
      loop2=40 ;         /* Start write halfway over      */
      while ((loop2<=66)&&(!kbhit()))
         {
                         /* Hide, write text, show        */
         hide_mouse_cursor();
         out_text_xy(loop2,loop1,"MOUSETORAT",cloop);
         show_mouse_cursor();

                         /* Update loops                  */
         ++cloop;loop2+=12;
         if (cloop==16) cloop=1;

         delay(100);    /* Delay 200 mllsecs              */
         }
      loop1+=2;
      }
   }
}
```

```
else
   {
   out_text_xy(5,5,"No Mouse Is Installed!",10);
   out_text_xy(5,6,"Please Install The Mouse Driver
                    Before Continuing...",10);
   printf("%c",7);
   }

getch();                          /* Wait for keypress        */

if (MOUSE_THERE) reset_mouse();

                                  /* LOOK !!!!!               */
                                  /* If using sprite cursor,  */
                                  /* destroy it!              */
if (USING_SPRITE) destroy_sprite(sprite_cursor);

LL_clrscr(0,0,79,24,0);
LL_setmode(3);                    /* Reset video to 80 x 25 text*/
   }
```

When the program runs, there should be no disruption of the text whatsoever.
   You should now be satisfied that the sprite cursor does indeed operate in the
800 × 600 16-color mode. The next chapter exploits the features and capabilities of
the sprite driver and sprite cursor, and you revert back to using the video function
library presented in Chapter 2.

Chapter **21**

Sprite Usage Rules and Features

When you use the sprite cursor, there are a few rules you must follow to ensure that it behaves properly within your applications. However, along with these additional rules come some additional features, such as color changing, write-mode switching, and multiple sprite capability. This chapter teaches you the sprite cursor usage rules, and provides examples demonstrating the additional features.

Sprite Cursor Usage Rules

The following rules must be observed to ensure that the sprite driver is initialized properly, no graphics disruption occurs during sprite cursor operations, and the event handler remains active.

Global Variables

Before you use the sprite cursor, you must appropriately set the global variables IN_GMODE, USING_SPRITE, HORIZ_OFFSET, and MODE_NUMBER, no matter what graphics library you are using. For details regarding these variables, and their possible values, see Chapter 19.

Valid Ranges

The sprite driver functions do not check for valid ranges of the hot spot, color values in the sprite cursor mask, or valid display coordinates. It's up to you, the programmer, to ensure that valid ranges are used.

Display Boundaries

If you draw the sprite cursor beyond the maximum horizontal display coordinate, it does not disappear like the default mouse cursor, but instead wraps around to the right side of the display, one line down. If you draw the sprite cursor beyond the maximum vertical display coordinate, it does disappear like the default mouse cursor.

To ensure that the cursor never goes past the maximum horizontal and vertical display boundaries, always use the following statements when your application initializes the sprite cursor, and before you make the sprite cursor visible:

```
set_mouse_hlimits(1,VID_MAXX-MOUSE_SIZE);
set_mouse_vlimits(1,VID_MAXY-MOUSE_SIZE);
```

This limits the sprite cursor's range to inside the valid display region.

Additionally, if you locate the sprite cursor's hot spot a considerable distance away from the actual sprite cursor (see Chapter 14), you should set the display range boundaries relative to the hot spot, as the following code fragment illustrates:

```
set_mouse_hlimits(1+sprite->hotx,
                  VID_MAXX-MOUSE_SIZE+sprite->hotx);
set_mouse_vlimits(1+sprite->hoty,
                  VID_MAXY-MOUSE_SIZE+sprite->hoty);
```

Use extreme caution when limiting the sprite cursor's range relative to the hot spot. If you switch to the default mouse cursor during program execution, do not limit the default mouse cursor's display range with the sprite cursor's hot spot, unless the hot spot values are the same as those used by the default mouse cursor. Otherwise, you will limit the default mouse cursor's range using incorrect coordinates.

Hiding the Sprite Cursor

You must hide the sprite cursor before any display updating occurs and show it immediately after. Although you cannot implement an exclusion area when you use the sprite cursor (see Chapter 19), you can still make calls to the mouse library function set_hide_bounds() as if you are setting an exclusion area. This is because in Chapter 19, you modified set_hide_bounds() to hide the sprite cursor instead of setting an exclusion area and set an exclusion area only if the default mouse cursor is in use. This allows you to use the function set_hide_bounds() no matter which cursor is being used.

Switching Cursors

You may switch back and forth between the sprite cursor and the default mouse cursor, provided you are in a video mode the default mouse cursor supports. To switch between cursors, use the following instructions, in the precise order listed.

When switching from the default mouse cursor to the sprite cursor you must

1. Hide the default mouse cursor.

2. Create and load the sprite cursor (if it is not previously loaded).

3. Set the variable USING_SPRITE to 1.

4. Show the sprite cursor.

When switching from the sprite cursor to the default cursor you must

1. Hide the sprite cursor.

2. Set the variable USING_SPRITE to 0.

3. Show the default mouse cursor.

Furthermore, if the sprite cursor is being used and you call mouse function 9, set graphics cursor block, or the mouse library function set_graphics_cursor(), there is no effect on the sprite cursor's shape or hot spot. However, the default mouse cursor is modified and remains invisible.

Keeping the Event Handler Active

When you use the sprite cursor, extreme caution must be exercised if you use mouse function 12, mouse function 20, or the mouse library function set_event_handler() in your application. After installing the sprite cursor, any call made to these functions disables the active event handler, leaving a dead sprite cursor on the display (end users do not appreciate a dead mouse).

Additionally, any new event handler you install by using mouse function 12, mouse function 20, or set_event_handler() is disabled when you make a call to the mouse library function show_mouse_cursor() or hide_mouse_cursor(). Look at the following code fragment from the function show_mouse_cursor():

```
if (!USING_SPRITE)
    {
    mregs.x.ax=1;
    int86(0x33,&mregs,&mregs);
    }
else
    {
    if (NUMBER_BUTTONS==3)
        set_event_handler(126,event_handler);
    else
        set_event_handler(30,event_handler);

    show_sprite(sprite_cursor);

    install_event_handler();
    }
```

Notice that if the sprite cursor is being used, the event handler is partially deactivated immediately before the call to show_sprite() and fully reactivated immediately after with a call to install_event_handler(). At that point, any existing event handler is deactivated.

If you use mouse function 12, mouse function 20, or the mouse library function set_event_handler() to temporarily perform some other event-driven operation and you are using the sprite cursor, be sure to reactivate the sprite cursor's event handler when your event routine terminates by calling install_event_handler() or show_mouse_cursor().

Destroying the Sprite Cursor

The sprite cursor must be destroyed when the application terminates. Otherwise, memory allocated to the sprite cursor is not freed and is unavailable to other applications. To destroy the sprite cursor, use the sprite driver function destroy_sprite().

Sprite Features

The sprite driver functions and the sprite cursor provide you with many unique and interesting features. For instance, you can change any line of the sprite cursor, or the entire sprite cursor, to 1 of 16 colors. Additionally, you can change the write mode used to draw the sprite cursor to either COPYPUT (replacement) mode or XOR (eXclusive OR) mode.

The sprite driver functions you have access to in your applications are defined in the header file, MOUSEDRV.H. The following provides a look at three of these functions:

change_sprite_line_color(sprite_type *sprite,
                          **int *linenum*,int *newcolor*)   Use this function to change the color of any line in the sprite cursor. The range of line numbers is 0 to 15, and the range of color is 0 to 15.

**change_sprite_color(sprite_type *sprite*,int *newcolor*)   Use this function to change the color of the entire sprite cursor to one solid color. The range of color is 0 to 15.

**set_sprite_mode(sprite_type *sprite*,int *mode*)   Use this function to set the drawing mode of the sprite. Use the constant COPYPUT_MODE or 0 for the COPYPUT mode and XOR_MODE or 24 for XOR drawing mode. In COPYPUT mode, the sprite cursor appears solid on the display, replacing the underlying background image. In XOR mode, the underlying background is inverted, and shows through the sprite cursor.

Modifying the Sprite Color and Write Mode

In the following example, the sprite cursor is shown as a red, white, and blue hand. The program then pauses and waits for a keypress. After you press a key, the sprite's cursor image is changed to a striped, multicolored cursor with the sprite driver function change_sprite_line_color(). The program then waits for another keypress, and after you press a key, the sprite cursor color is changed to solid green with the sprite driver function change_sprite_color(). The program then enters a keypress loop. While in the loop, you can change the sprite cursor's color by pressing the left mouse button, and you can cycle through all 16 available colors. You can change the sprite cursor's drawing mode to XOR by pressing the right mouse button, and pressing it again changes the drawing mode back to the COPYPUT mode.
Here is the project file, MOUSE29.PRJ:

```
MOUSEDRV.LIB
MOUSE29.C
```

Here is MOUSE29.C:

```
/*-----------------------------------------------------------*/
/*                                                           */
/*                        MOUSE29.C                          */
/*                                                           */
/*                                                           */
/* Demonstrate how to change color and drawing mode of sprite */
/* cursor, using the sprite driver functions.                */
/*-----------------------------------------------------------*/
```

```c
#include "compiler.h"        /* Compiler directives        */
#include "mousedrv.h"        /* Header file for mouse/sprite */
#include graphics
#include videolib
                            /* 1st 16 bytes in row  = MASK  */
char hand[16][17]=           /* 17th byte in each row = COLOR */
    {
    0,0,0,1,1,0,0,0,0,0,0,0,0,0,0,0, 12,
    0,0,0,1,1,0,0,0,0,0,0,0,0,0,0,0, 12,
    0,0,0,1,1,0,0,0,0,0,0,0,0,0,0,0, 12,
    0,0,0,1,1,0,1,1,0,1,1,0,1,1,0,0, 12,
    0,0,0,1,1,0,1,1,0,1,1,0,1,1,0,0, 12,
    0,0,0,1,1,1,1,1,1,1,1,1,1,1,0,0, 15,
    1,1,0,1,1,1,1,1,1,1,1,1,1,1,0,0, 15,
    1,1,0,1,1,1,1,1,1,1,1,1,1,1,0,0, 15,
    1,1,1,1,1,1,1,1,1,1,1,1,1,0,0,0, 15,
    1,1,1,1,1,1,1,1,1,1,1,1,0,0,0,0, 15,
    1,1,1,1,1,1,1,1,1,1,1,1,0,0,0,0, 15,
    1,1,1,1,1,1,1,1,1,1,1,0,0,0,0,0,  9,
    0,1,1,1,1,1,1,1,1,1,0,0,0,0,0,0,  9,
    0,0,1,1,1,1,1,1,1,0,0,0,0,0,0,0,  9,
    0,0,0,1,1,1,1,1,1,0,0,0,0,0,0,0,  9,
    0,0,0,1,1,1,1,1,1,0,0,0,0,0,0,0,  9
    };

/* MODULE : INIT SPRITE                                          */
/*-------------------------------------------------------------*/
/* Initialize sprite, event handler, and all relevant vars.    */
/*                                                             */
void init_sprite(void)
    {
    switch(VID_MAXY)              /* EGA or VGA graphics adapter? */
        {
        case 199:MODE_NUMBER=0x0E;break;
        case 349:MODE_NUMBER=0x10;break; /* Mono switch to 0x0F */
        case 479:MODE_NUMBER=0x12;break; /* Mono switch to 0x11 */
        }

    PAGE=0;                       /* Video page to write on        */

    HORIZ_OFFSET=80;              /* Horizontal offset for vertical*/
                                  /* address calculation.          */
                                  /* 80 is for all modes where 640 */
```

```
                              /* is the max horizontal coord.  */
                              /* If you choose the 800 x 600    */
                              /* 16-color mode be SURE to       */
                              /* change this to 100 !!!!!!!     */

    USING_SPRITE=1;           /* Set USING_SPRITE to 1 for      */
                              /* sprite cursor, 0 for default   */
                              /* cursor.                        */

    if (USING_SPRITE)
        {                     /* Grab memory for sprite         */
        sprite_cursor=new_sprite();

                              /* Load the sprite with mask      */
                              /* Initialize in COPYPUT mode     */
        load_sprite(hand,0,-1,sprite_cursor,COPYPUT_MODE);
        }

    install_event_handler();  /* Install the event handler      */
    }

void main()
    {
    int color,linenum;
    int loop1,loop2;

    install_video(GMODE);     /* Install video system           */
    header();                 /* Draw header                    */
    reset_mouse();            /* Reset mouse                    */

    if (MOUSE_THERE)
        {
        init_sprite();        /* Initialize the sprite as the   */
                              /* mouse cursor.                  */

                              /* Set horiz and vertical limits */
        set_mouse_hlimits(1,VID_MAXX-MOUSE_SIZE);
        set_mouse_vlimits(1,VID_MAXY-MOUSE_SIZE);

                              /* Set the mouse to center of     */
                              /* display.                       */
        set_mouse_position(VID_MAXX/2,VID_MAXY/2);

        clear_line_from(2,2,20,0);
```

```
out_text_xy(15,2,"Sprite cursor should be a
                  RED/WHITE/BLUE hand.");
out_text_xy(15,5,"Press any key to change to
                  MULTI-COLORED hand...");

show_mouse_cursor();    /* Show RED/WHITE/BLUE HAND   */
getch();                /* Wait for a key to be pressed */
hide_mouse_cursor();    /* Hide mouse cursor          */

                        /* Change sprite to multicolored */
color=11;               /* Start with hi cyan          */
                        /* Loop through all lines in mask*/
for (linenum=0;linenum<=15;linenum++)
   {
                        /* Change a single line in sprite*/
   change_sprite_line_color(sprite_cursor,linenum,color);

   color+=2;            /* Increase color by 2, check max*/
   if (color>15) color=9;
   }
clear_line_from(2,15,55,0);
clear_line_from(5,15,55,0);
out_text_xy(15,2,"Sprite Cursor should now be a
                  MULTI-COLORED hand.");
out_text_xy(15,4,"Try moving it around with the mouse.");
out_text_xy(15,6,"Press any key to continue...");

show_mouse_cursor();    /* Show new multicolored sprite  */
getch();                /* Wait for a key to be pressed  */

hide_mouse_cursor();    /* Hide the mouse cursor          */
clear_line_from(2,15,50,0);
clear_line_from(4,15,40,0);
clear_line_from(6,15,40,0);

out_text_xy(15,4,"Press the LEFT  button to change
                  sprite colors.");
out_text_xy(15,5,"Press the RIGHT button to change
                  sprite drawing modes.");
out_text_xy(15,7,"Press any key to exit....");

color=1;                /* Write some text to display     */
change_color(color);
for (loop1=10;loop1<=18;loop1+=2)
   {
```

```
    for (loop2=5;loop2<=68;loop2+=12)
       {
       out_text_xy(loop2,loop1,"SAMPLETEXT");
       color+=1;
       if (color>=16) color=1;
       change_color(color);
       }
    }

change_color(15);        /* Write initial values        */
out_text_xy(25,21,"Current Color# - ");
out_text_xy(25,22,"Current Mode   - ");

                         /* Write initial mode          */
out_int_xy(45,21,color);
if (sprite_cursor->sprite_mode==COPYPUT_MODE)
   out_text_xy(45,22,"COPYPUT Mode");
else out_text_xy(45,22,"XOR Mode");

color=10;                /* Make sprite cursor solid green*/
change_sprite_color(sprite_cursor,color);
show_mouse_cursor();

while (!kbhit())
   {

   if (LBUTTON_DOWN)
      {                  /* Change color of sprite cursor */
      LBUTTON_DOWN=0;
      ++color;
      if (color>15) color=1;

      hide_mouse_cursor();
      change_sprite_color(sprite_cursor,color);

                         /* Write new color to display    */
      clear_line_from(21,45,5,0);
      out_int_xy(45,21,color);
      show_mouse_cursor();
      }

   if (RBUTTON_DOWN)
      {                  /* Change mode of sprite cursor  */
      RBUTTON_DOWN=0;
      hide_mouse_cursor();
```

```
        if (sprite_cursor->sprite_mode==COPYPUT_MODE)
            set_sprite_mode(sprite_cursor,XOR_MODE);
        else
            set_sprite_mode(sprite_cursor,COPYPUT_MODE);

                            /* Write new mode to display    */
        clear_line_from(22,45,15,0);
        if (sprite_cursor->sprite_mode==COPYPUT_MODE)
            out_text_xy(45,22,"COPYPUT Mode");
        else out_text_xy(45,22,"XOR Mode");
        show_mouse_cursor();
        }


    }

    }
    else mouse_error(5,4);

    getch();

    if (MOUSE_THERE) reset_mouse();

                        /* LOOK !!!!!                     */
                        /* If using sprite, destroy it!   */
    if (USING_SPRITE) destroy_sprite(sprite_cursor);

    shut_down_video();
    }
```

When the program starts, press a key. The striped, multicolored sprite cursor appears as illustrated in Figure 21-1.

When you run the previous example, if you change the sprite cursor's drawing mode to XOR and place the sprite on top of a letter in the underlying background, the color of the letter is reversed, and shows through the sprite cursor as illustrated in Figure 21-2.

Changing the Sprite Cursor Mask

Changing the sprite cursor's image mask is a bit different than changing the default mouse cursor's image mask (see Chapter 14). To change the sprite cursor's image mask, use the following instructions in the precise order listed:

1. Hide the sprite cursor.

2. Deactivate the event handler.

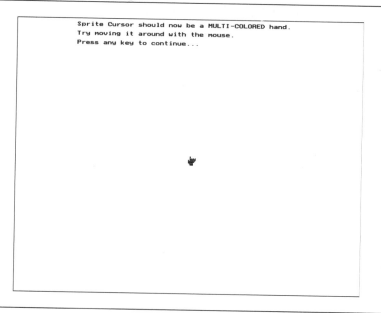

Figure 21-1.   *A multicolored sprite cursor*

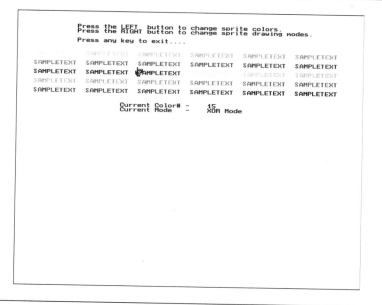

Figure 21-2.   *The sprite cursor in XOR mode*

3. Destroy the sprite cursor and then reallocate it.

4. Load the sprite cursor with the new mask.

5. Set the sprite cursor's position to the display location it resided in prior to the event handler being deactivated. This aligns the sprite cursor mask's internal shift positions with the last display location.

6. Show the sprite cursor.

The following example demonstrates changing the sprite cursor's image mask on the fly. When the program starts, the sprite cursor is a solid blue hand. Pressing the left mouse button changes the sprite cursor image to a solid yellow arrow. Pressing the right mouse button changes the sprite cursor image back to the solid blue hand.
    Here is the project file, MOUSE30.PRJ:

```
MOUSEDRV.LIB
MOUSE30.C
```

Here is MOUSE30.C:

```
/*------------------------------------------------------------*/
/*                       MOUSE30.C                        */
/*                                                        */
/* Demonstrate how to change sprite masks on the fly.     */
/*------------------------------------------------------------*/

#include "compiler.h"      /* Compiler directives              */
#include "mousedrv.h"      /* Header file for mouse/sprite     */
#include graphics
#include videolib

char hand[16][17]=
    {
    0,0,0,1,1,0,0,0,0,0,0,0,0,0,0,0, 11,
    0,0,0,1,1,0,0,0,0,0,0,0,0,0,0,0, 11,
    0,0,0,1,1,0,0,0,0,0,0,0,0,0,0,0, 11,
    0,0,0,1,1,0,1,1,0,1,1,0,1,1,0,0, 11,
    0,0,0,1,1,0,1,1,0,1,1,0,1,1,0,0, 11,
    0,0,0,1,1,1,1,1,1,1,1,1,1,1,0,0, 11,
    1,1,0,1,1,1,1,1,1,1,1,1,1,1,0,0, 11,
    1,1,0,1,1,1,1,1,1,1,1,1,1,1,0,0, 11,
    1,1,1,1,1,1,1,1,1,1,1,1,1,0,0,0, 11,
    1,1,1,1,1,1,1,1,1,1,1,1,0,0,0,0, 11,
    1,1,1,1,1,1,1,1,1,1,1,1,0,0,0,0, 11,
```

```
   1,1,1,1,1,1,1,1,1,1,0,0,0,0,0,0, 11,
   0,1,1,1,1,1,1,1,1,0,0,0,0,0,0,0, 11,
   0,0,1,1,1,1,1,1,1,0,0,0,0,0,0,0, 11,
   0,0,0,1,1,1,1,1,1,0,0,0,0,0,0,0, 11,
   0,0,0,1,1,1,1,1,1,0,0,0,0,0,0,0, 11
   };

char right_arrow[16][17]=
   {
   0,1,1,0,0,0,0,0,0,0,0,0,0,0,0,0, 14,
   0,1,1,1,0,0,0,0,0,0,0,0,0,0,0,0, 14,
   0,1,1,1,1,0,0,0,0,0,0,0,0,0,0,0, 14,
   0,1,1,1,1,1,0,0,0,0,0,0,0,0,0,0, 14,
   0,1,1,1,1,1,1,0,0,0,0,0,0,0,0,0, 14,
   0,1,1,1,1,1,1,1,0,0,0,0,0,0,0,0, 14,
   0,1,1,1,1,1,1,1,1,0,0,0,0,0,0,0, 14,
   0,1,1,1,1,1,1,1,1,1,0,0,0,0,0,0, 14,
   0,1,1,1,1,1,1,1,1,1,1,0,0,0,0,0, 14,
   0,1,1,1,1,1,1,1,1,1,1,1,0,0,0,0, 14,
   0,1,1,1,1,1,1,1,0,0,0,0,0,0,0,0, 14,
   0,1,1,1,0,1,1,1,1,0,0,0,0,0,0,0, 14,
   0,1,1,0,0,1,1,1,1,0,0,0,0,0,0,0, 14,
   0,0,0,0,0,0,1,1,1,1,0,0,0,0,0,0, 14,
   0,0,0,0,0,0,1,1,1,1,0,0,0,0,0,0, 14,
   0,0,0,0,0,0,0,1,1,1,0,0,0,0,0,0, 14
   };

/* MODULE : INIT SPRITE                                  */
/*------------------------------------------------------------*/
/* Initialize sprite, event handler, and all relevant vars.  */
/*                                                        */
void init_sprite(void)
   {
   switch(VID_MAXY)              /* EGA or VGA graphics adapter?  */
      {
      case 199:MODE_NUMBER=0x0E;break;
      case 349:MODE_NUMBER=0x10;break; /* Mono switch to 0x0F */
      case 479:MODE_NUMBER=0x12;break; /* Mono switch to 0x11 */
      }

   PAGE=0;                       /* Video page to write on       */

   HORIZ_OFFSET=80;              /* Horizontal offset for vertical*/
                                 /* address calculation.        */
                                 /* 80 is for all modes where 640 */
```

```
                               /* is the max horizontal coord.  */
                               /* If you choose the 800 x 600   */
                               /* 16-color mode be SURE to       */
                               /* change this to 100 !!!!!!!     */

    USING_SPRITE=1;            /* Set USING_SPRITE to 1 for     */
                               /* sprite cursor, 0 for default  */
                               /* cursor.                       */

    if (USING_SPRITE)
        {                      /* Grab memory for sprite        */
        sprite_cursor=new_sprite();

                               /* Load the sprite with mask     */
                               /* Initialize in COPYPUT mode    */
        load_sprite(hand,0,-1,sprite_cursor,COPYPUT_MODE);
        }

    install_event_handler();  /* Install the event handler     */
    }

void main()
    {

    install_video(GMODE);     /* Install video system          */
    header();                 /* Draw header                   */
    reset_mouse();            /* Reset mouse                   */

    if (MOUSE_THERE)
        {
        init_sprite();        /* Initialize the sprite as the  */
                              /* mouse cursor.                 */

                              /* Set horiz and vertical limits */
        set_mouse_hlimits(1,VID_MAXX-MOUSE_SIZE);
        set_mouse_vlimits(1,VID_MAXY-MOUSE_SIZE);

        out_text_xy(15,4,"Sprite cursor is a solid cyan hand");
        out_text_xy(15,6,"Press LEFT  mouse button to change to
                        a yellow arrow.");
        out_text_xy(15,7,"Press RIGHT mouse button to change back
                        to cyan hand");
        out_text_xy(15,9,"Press any key to exit..");
```

```
    show_mouse_cursor();

while (!kbhit())
    {
    if (LBUTTON_DOWN)
        {                    /* Change to red arrow         */
        LBUTTON_DOWN=0;
                             /* Hide sprite cursor          */
        hide_mouse_cursor();

                             /* Deactivate e-handler, destroy */
                             /* sprite cursor.              */
        set_event_handler(0,0);
        destroy_sprite(sprite_cursor);

                             /* Reallocate sprite, load new */
                             /* mask.                       */
        sprite_cursor=new_sprite();
        load_sprite(right_arrow,0,-1,
                 sprite_cursor,COPYPUT_MODE);

                             /* Redraw sprite at previous   */
                             /* location.                   */
        draw_sprite(CMX,CMY,sprite_cursor);

                             /* Show sprite, which reactivates*/
                             /* event handler as well.      */
        show_mouse_cursor();
        }

    if (RBUTTON_DOWN)
        {                    /* Change to blue hand         */
        RBUTTON_DOWN=0;
        hide_mouse_cursor();
        set_event_handler(0,0);
        destroy_sprite(sprite_cursor);
        sprite_cursor=new_sprite();
        load_sprite(hand,0,-1,sprite_cursor,COPYPUT_MODE);
        draw_sprite(CMX,CMY,sprite_cursor);
        show_mouse_cursor();
        }
    }
}
else mouse_error(5,4);
```

```
    getch();

    if (MOUSE_THERE) reset_mouse();

    if (USING_SPRITE) destroy_sprite(sprite_cursor);

    shut_down_video();
    }
```

Using Other Sprites

Although the sprite driver was designed to implement a sprite cursor, it can be used for many other types of sprite animation, and the number of sprites the system can use at one time is limited only to available memory.

If you create a sprite that is not used as a sprite cursor, or is used as a replicate sprite cursor, the following functions are available to move, hide, and show it:

draw_sprite(int *x*,int *y*,sprite_type **sprite*) Use this function to move a sprite to a new display location. The function handles all image saving and restoring internally. If the sprite is invisible when you use this function, the position is changed, and the sprite remains invisible.

hide_sprite(sprite_type **sprite*) Use this function to hide a sprite. If the sprite is interrupt driven (like the sprite cursor), you must hide it before any display updating takes place.

show_sprite(sprite_type **sprite*) Use this function to make a sprite visible.

Dual Sprite Cursors

One of the nicest features of the sprite driver is the ability to create and use multiple sprites. Consider the following possibility of using two sprite cursors simultaneously.

Mirror Image CAD Functions

If you have ever used any type of CAD application, you are probably familiar with *mirroring* functions. A *mirror image* is an exact duplicate of some graphics object, except reversed, or "flipped over". Mirror functions are very useful when complex, symmetrical images are being created. You concentrate on drawing one half of an image and then use a mirror function to replicate and reverse the image. When you place the mirrored image side by side, or top to bottom with the original image, one perfectly symmetrical image is produced.

The image reversing is managed internally, usually by swapping bits from the original graphics image. Using horizontal mirror images, left becomes right, and right becomes left. Using vertical mirror images, top become bottom, and bottom becomes top. For the purpose of the following discussion, assume the mirror is defined horizontally.

New Mirror Techniques with Dual Cursors

With the ability to use two sprite cursors simultaneously, a new concept of implementing mirroring techniques comes to life. Here's how the new method works.

The display screen is divided into two horizontal regions, left and right, and a line is drawn down the center. In the right-hand display region, the sprite cursor is defined as an arrow pointing left. In the left-hand display region, a replicate sprite cursor is defined as an arrow pointing right. You can choose either side of the display as the drawing reference. Assuming you choose the right-hand display region as the drawing reference, then when you stretch a graphics object in that region, the replicate cursor in the left-hand display region mirrors the operation, producing an exact mirror image of the graphics object when the operation is complete.

The following section describes the steps required to implement this technique.

Initializing Two Sprite Cursors

Initializing two sprites is easy. Instead of defining one sprite mask, you define two, and instead of loading one sprite, you load two. In the following example, the mirroring CAD technique is presented, and the masks used to define the two cursors are called left_arrow, and right_arrow. Since the sprite cursor moved by the event handler is always the global pointer sprite_cursor, the second sprite pointer is called mirror_cursor.

Initializing both sprites in the COPYPUT drawing mode requires the following code:

```
sprite_cursor=new_sprite();
mirror_cursor=new_sprite();
load_sprite(left_arrow,0,-1,sprite_cursor,COPYPUT_MODE);
load_sprite(right_arrow,0,-1,mirror_cursor,COPYPUT_MODE);
```

Moving Both Mouse Cursors

Actually moving both cursors at once is a bit tricky. Since the sprite cursor is moved automatically by the event handler, the technique is to trap CURSOR_MOVED events and manually move the mirror cursor inside the trap. This effectively provides two event-driven cursors.

If the sprite cursor is using the right side of the display and the mirror cursor is using the left, then the following code is required to move mirror_cursor when the event processor moves sprite_cursor:

```
if (CURSOR_MOVED)
   {
   CURSOR_MOVED=0;
   mirror_x=(VID_MAXX/2)-(CMX-VID_MAXX/2);
   draw_sprite(mirror_x-MOUSE_SIZE+1,CMY,mirror_cursor);
   }
```

When the CURSOR_MOVED status variable is trapped, mirror_x is determined by figuring the distance sprite_cursor is from the display's halfway point (VID_MAXX/2), to its current location (CMX–VID_MAXX/2). The result is subtracted from the halfway point ((VID_MAXX/2)–(CMX–VID_MAXX/2)). Since the mirror cursor is using reverse reference points, the cursor position must be adjusted to reflect the correct reverence, so mirror_cursor is drawn at mirror_x–MOUSE_SIZE+1.

The Event Handler

When using two sprite cursors simultaneously, both of which are event driven, the event handler must be partially deactivated before hiding and showing either cursor and while drawing the mirror sprite cursor.

The event handler is automatically deactivated and reactivated for the sprite cursor inside the mouse library functions hide_mouse_cursor() and show_mouse_cursor() (see Chapter 19). However, you must manually perform these operations when hiding, showing, and drawing the mirror cursor. In the following example, a new function is presented called turn_off_move_event(). This function partially deactivates the event handler by resetting the call mask move bit (bit 0) to 0. The event handler is fully reactivated by calling either install_event_handler() or show_mouse_cursor().

The Dual Cursor CAD Mirror Program

The following example demonstrates the concept of a mirrored-cursor CAD-type application. The example allows you to draw lines on either side of the display. Use the right cursor as the reference cursor. A discussion on how to switch reference cursors follows the source code listing.

Here is the project file, MOUSE31.PRJ:

```
MOUSEDRV.LIB
MOUSE31.C
```

Here is MOUSE31.C:

```
/*------------------------------------------------------------*/
/*                        MOUSE31.C                        */
/*                                                         */
/* Demonstrate how to implement and use two sprite cursors at */
/* once. The example also demonstrates a new concept for      */
/* mirror functions in CAD type programs.                     */
/*------------------------------------------------------------*/

#include "compiler.h"      /* Compiler directives          */
#include "mousedrv.h"      /* Header file for mouse/sprite  */
#include graphics
#include videolib

sprite_type *mirror_cursor;

char right_arrow[16][17]=
    {
    0,1,1,0,0,0,0,0,0,0,0,0,0,0,0,0, 15,
    0,1,1,1,0,0,0,0,0,0,0,0,0,0,0,0, 15,
    0,1,1,1,1,0,0,0,0,0,0,0,0,0,0,0, 15,
    0,1,1,1,1,1,0,0,0,0,0,0,0,0,0,0, 15,
    0,1,1,1,1,1,1,0,0,0,0,0,0,0,0,0, 15,
    0,1,1,1,1,1,1,1,0,0,0,0,0,0,0,0, 15,
    0,1,1,1,1,1,1,1,1,0,0,0,0,0,0,0, 15,
    0,1,1,1,1,1,1,1,1,1,0,0,0,0,0,0, 15,
    0,1,1,1,1,1,1,1,1,1,1,0,0,0,0,0, 15,
    0,1,1,1,1,1,1,1,1,1,1,1,0,0,0,0, 15,
    0,1,1,1,1,1,1,1,0,0,0,0,0,0,0,0, 15,
    0,1,1,1,0,1,1,1,1,0,0,0,0,0,0,0, 15,
    0,1,1,0,0,1,1,1,1,0,0,0,0,0,0,0, 15,
    0,0,0,0,0,0,1,1,1,1,0,0,0,0,0,0, 15,
    0,0,0,0,0,0,1,1,1,1,0,0,0,0,0,0, 15,
    0,0,0,0,0,0,0,1,1,1,0,0,0,0,0,0, 15
    };

char left_arrow[16][17]=
    {
    0,0,0,0,0,0,0,0,0,0,0,0,0,1,1,0, 15,
    0,0,0,0,0,0,0,0,0,0,0,0,1,1,1,0, 15,
```

```
         0,0,0,0,0,0,0,0,0,0,0,1,1,1,1,0,  15,
         0,0,0,0,0,0,0,0,0,0,1,1,1,1,1,0,  15,
         0,0,0,0,0,0,0,0,0,1,1,1,1,1,1,0,  15,
         0,0,0,0,0,0,0,0,1,1,1,1,1,1,1,0,  15,
         0,0,0,0,0,0,0,1,1,1,1,1,1,1,1,0,  15,
         0,0,0,0,0,0,1,1,1,1,1,1,1,1,1,0,  15,
         0,0,0,0,0,1,1,1,1,1,1,1,1,1,1,0,  15,
         0,0,0,0,1,1,1,1,1,1,1,1,1,1,1,0,  15,
         0,0,0,0,0,0,0,0,1,1,1,1,1,1,1,0,  15,
         0,0,0,0,0,0,0,1,1,1,1,0,1,1,1,0,  15,
         0,0,0,0,0,0,0,1,1,1,1,0,0,1,1,0,  15,
         0,0,0,0,0,0,1,1,1,1,0,0,0,0,0,0,  15,
         0,0,0,0,0,0,1,1,1,1,0,0,0,0,0,0,  15,
         0,0,0,0,0,0,1,1,1,0,0,0,0,0,0,0,  15
      };


/* MODULE : INIT SPRITE                                         */
/*-------------------------------------------------------------*/
/* Initialize sprite, event handler, and all relevant vars.    */
/*                                                              */
void init_sprite(void)
   {
   switch(VID_MAXY)              /* EGA or VGA graphics adapter?  */
      {
      case 199:MODE_NUMBER=0x0E;break;
      case 349:MODE_NUMBER=0x10;break;  /* Mono switch to 0x0F */
      case 479:MODE_NUMBER=0x12;break;  /* Mono switch to 0x11 */
      }

   PAGE=0;                       /* Video page to write on        */

   HORIZ_OFFSET=80;              /* Horizontal offset for vertical*/
                                 /* address calculation.          */
                                 /* 80 is for all modes where 640 */
                                 /* is the max horizontal coord.  */
                                 /* If you choose the 800 x 600   */
                                 /* 16-color mode be SURE to       */
                                 /* change this to 100 !!!!!!!    */

   USING_SPRITE=1;               /* Set USING_SPRITE to 1 for     */
                                 /* sprite cursor, 0 for default  */
                                 /* cursor.                       */
```

```
    if (USING_SPRITE)
       {                              /* Grab memory for sprite      */
       sprite_cursor=new_sprite();
       mirror_cursor=new_sprite();

                                      /* Load the sprite with mask   */
                                      /* Initialize in COPYPUT mode   */
       load_sprite(right_arrow,0,-1,sprite_cursor,COPYPUT_MODE);
       load_sprite(left_arrow,0,-1,mirror_cursor,COPYPUT_MODE);
       }

    install_event_handler();  /* Install the event handler    */
    }




/* MODULE: TURN OFF MOVE EVENT                                    */
/*--------------------------------------------------------------*/
/* Resets the event handler so that cursor movement does not     */
/* initiate an event, but left, right, and middle(if any)        */
/* button messages will still be recorded properly.              */
/*                                                               */
void turn_off_move_event(void)
   {
   if (NUMBER_BUTTONS==3)
      set_event_handler(126,event_handler);
   else
      set_event_handler(30,event_handler);
   }

/* MODULE : MENU                                                 */
/*--------------------------------------------------------------*/
/* Write initial text on display.                                */
/*                                                               */
void menu(void)
   {
   change_color(11);
   clear_line_from(2,2,15,0);
   out_text_xy(25,2,"Cursor Mirror CAD Line Drawing");
   change_color(14);
   out_text_xy(10,3,"Press and hold left mouse button to drag
                     lines on the display.");
```

```
      out_text_xy(10,4,"     Release left button for lines to
                    become stationary.");
      out_text_xy(10,5,"      Press right mouse button to 'undo'
                    last lines drawn.");
      change_color(11);
      out_text_xy(29,6,"Press any key to exit...");
      }

void main()
   {
   int mirror_x;              /* Horiz coord for mirror cursor */
   int newx=0,newy=0;         /* Cursor position              */
   int anchorx=0,anchory=0;   /* Anchor's, coords for last line*/
   int lastx1=0,lasty1=0,lastx2=0,lasty2=0;

   int lnewx=0;               /* Mirror cursor position       */
   int lanchorx=0;            /* Mirror cursor anchor and     */
   int lastlx1=0,lastlx2=0;   /* coords for last line.        */

   unsigned char draw_on=0;   /* Currently drawing line?      */

   install_video(GMODE);      /* Install video system         */
   header();                  /* Draw header                  */
   reset_mouse();             /* Reset mouse                  */

   if (MOUSE_THERE)           /* If the mouse is there -       */
      {
      init_sprite();          /* Initialize sprite cursor     */

                              /* Set horiz and vert limits    */
                              /* Limit to right half, lower   */
                              /* 3/4 display.                 */
      set_mouse_hlimits(VID_MAXX/2+1,VID_MAXX-MOUSE_SIZE);
      set_mouse_vlimits(VID_MAXY/4+1,VID_MAXY-MOUSE_SIZE);

                              /* Draw line thru halfway mark  */
      change_color(4);
      line(VID_MAXX/2,VID_MAXY/4,VID_MAXX/2,VID_MAXY);
      line(1,VID_MAXY/4,VID_MAXX,VID_MAXY/4);

      menu();

                              /* Set sprite cursor to right   */
                              /* side.                        */
```

```
set_mouse_position(VID_MAXX/2+1,VID_MAXY/2);

                        /* Set mirror cursor on left     */
                        /* side.                         */
draw_sprite(VID_MAXX/2-MOUSE_SIZE,VID_MAXY/2,
            mirror_cursor);

show_mouse_cursor();    /* Make 'em both visible         */
show_sprite(mirror_cursor);

while (!kbhit())
    {
    if (CURSOR_MOVED)   /* Trap cursor movement          */
        {
        CURSOR_MOVED=0;
                        /* Figure mirror cursor pos and  */
                        /* draw it at new location.      */
        mirror_x=(VID_MAXX/2)-(CMX-VID_MAXX/2);

                        /* Turn off move events, draw    */
                        /* mirror cursor, reactivate     */
                        /* move events.                  */
        turn_off_move_event();
        draw_sprite(mirror_x-MOUSE_SIZE+1,CMY,mirror_cursor);
        install_event_handler();

        if (draw_on)    /* If line being dragged         */
            {
                        /* Hide both cursors             */
            hide_mouse_cursor();

                        /* Turn off move events          */
                        /* show_cursor() reactivates it. */
            turn_off_move_event();
            hide_sprite(mirror_cursor);

                        /* Erase last line, old coords   */
            line(anchorx,anchory,newx,newy);
            line(lanchorx,anchory,lnewx,newy);

                        /* Figure new line coords        */
            newx=CMX;newy=CMY;

                        /* Figure mirror line coords     */
            lnewx=(VID_MAXX/2)-(newx-VID_MAXX/2);
```

```
                            /* Draw both lines at new local  */
            line(anchorx,anchory,newx,newy);
            line(lanchorx,anchory,lnewx,newy);

                            /* Show both cursors              */
            show_sprite(mirror_cursor);
            show_mouse_cursor();
            }

        }
    else if (!draw_on)   /* If not in drawing mode-           */
        {

        if (LBUTTON_DOWN)
            {
            LBUTTON_DOWN=0;
            draw_on=1;      /* Start drawing, set to 1         */

            newx=CMX;       /* Figure starting line coords     */
            lnewx=(VID_MAXX/2)-(newx-VID_MAXX/2);

            newy=CMY;       /* Set the anchors                 */
            anchorx=newx;
            lanchorx=lnewx;
            anchory=newy;
                            /* Hide both cursors               */
            hide_mouse_cursor();

                            /* Turn off move events            */
                            /* show_cursor() reactivates it    */
            turn_off_move_event();
            hide_sprite(mirror_cursor);

                            /* MODE TO XOR! Draw init lines     */
            setwritemode(XOR_PUT);
            change_color(10);
            line(anchorx,anchory,newx,newy);
            line(lanchorx,anchory,lnewx,newy);

                            /* Show both cursors               */
            show_sprite(mirror_cursor);
            show_mouse_cursor();
            }
                            /* Erase last lines, Undo          */
```

```
    if (RBUTTON_DOWN)
       {
       RBUTTON_DOWN=0;
                      /* Make sure there are lines to  */
                      /* erase; IF SO-                  */
       if (lastx1!=0)
          {
                      /* Hide both cursors              */
          hide_mouse_cursor();

                      /* Turn off move events           */
                      /* show_cursor() reactivates it   */
          turn_off_move_event();
          hide_sprite(mirror_cursor);

                      /* MODE TO XOR! Erase last lines  */
          setwritemode(XOR_PUT);
          line(lastx1,lasty1,lastx2,lasty2);
          line(lastlx1,lasty1,lastlx2,lasty2);

                      /* Set mode back to COPY_PUT      */
          setwritemode(COPY_PUT);
          lastx1=0;
                      /* Show both cursors              */
          show_sprite(mirror_cursor);
          show_mouse_cursor();
          }
       }
    }
                      /* Left button rlsd, in draw mode*/
if ((LBUTTON_UP)&&(draw_on))
   {
   LBUTTON_UP=0;

   draw_on=0;        /* Stop drawing, set to 0         */

   lastx1=anchorx;   /* Set coords for last lines      */
   lasty1=anchory;   /* drawn so it can be erased       */
   lastx2=newx;      /* with the Undo feature.          */
   lasty2=newy;
                      /* Set last mirror coords         */
   lastlx1=lanchorx;
   lastlx2=lnewx;
                      /* Set mode back to COPY_PUT      */
   setwritemode(COPY_PUT);
```

```
              }
          }
       }
    else
       mouse_error(5,4);

    getch();

    if (MOUSE_THERE) reset_mouse();
    if (USING_SPRITE) destroy_sprite(sprite_cursor);

    shut_down_video();
    }
```

Figure 21-3 was generated using the mirrored sprite and line drawing routines.

Changing Reference Cursors

In the previous example, the sprite cursor in the right-hand region of the display moved in the direction you moved the mouse, but the mirror cursor in the left-hand region moved in the opposite direction. Therefore, you used the sprite cursor in the right hand region as the *reference cursor.*

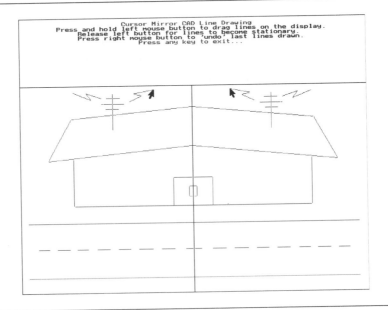

Figure 21-3.   Using dual sprite cursors in CAD applications

To change the reference cursor to the left-hand region of the display, you must reverse the mirror formula to the following:

```
if (CURSOR_MOVED)
   {
   CURSOR_MOVED=0;
   mirror_x=(VID_MAXX/2)+(VID_MAXX/2-CMX);
   draw_sprite(mirror_x-MOUSE_SIZE+1,CMY,mirror_cursor);
   }
```

When the CURSOR_MOVED status variable is trapped, mirror_x is determined by figuring the distance sprite_cursor is from the display's halfway point (VID_MAXX/2), to its current location (VID_MAXX/2–CMX). The result is added to the halfway point ((VID_MAXX/2)+(VID_MAXX/2–CMX)), and mirror_cursor is drawn at mirror_x–MOUSE_SIZE+1.

The other necessary modifications include switching the display regions for each cursor and drawing the lines appropriately. If you are curious about reversing the reference cursor, replace the contents of main() from the previous example with the following source code, which is also included on the companion disk supplied with this book and is called REV_REF.INC.

```
void main()
   {
   int mirror_x;              /* Horiz coord for mirror cursor */
   int newx=0,newy=0;         /* Cursor position               */
   int anchorx=0,anchory=0;   /* Anchors, coords for last line */
   int lastx1=0,lasty1=0,lastx2=0,lasty2=0;

   int lnewx=0;               /* Mirror cursor position        */
   int lanchorx=0;            /* Mirror cursor anchor and      */
   int lastlx1=0,lastlx2=0;   /* coords for last line.         */

   unsigned char draw_on=0;   /* Currently drawing line?       */

   install_video(GMODE);      /* Install video system          */
   header();                  /* Draw header                   */
   reset_mouse();             /* Reset mouse                   */

   if (MOUSE_THERE)           /* If the mouse is there -        */
      {
      init_sprite();          /* Initialize sprite cursor       */
```

```
                                /* Set horiz and vert limits    */
                                /* Limit to left half, lower     */
                                /* 3/4 display.                  */
set_mouse_hlimits(2,VID_MAXX/2-MOUSE_SIZE-1);
set_mouse_vlimits(VID_MAXY/4+1,VID_MAXY-MOUSE_SIZE);

                                /* Draw line thru halfway mark   */
change_color(4);
line(VID_MAXX/2,VID_MAXY/4,VID_MAXX/2,VID_MAXY);
line(1,VID_MAXY/4,VID_MAXX,VID_MAXY/4);

menu();

                                /* Set sprite cursor to left     */
                                /* side.                         */
set_mouse_position(VID_MAXX/2-MOUSE_SIZE,VID_MAXY/2);

                                /* Set mirror cursor on right    */
                                /* side.                         */
draw_sprite(VID_MAXX/2+1,VID_MAXY/2,
            mirror_cursor);

show_mouse_cursor();    /* Make 'em both visible         */
show_sprite(mirror_cursor);

while (!kbhit())
    {
    if (CURSOR_MOVED)     /* Trap cursor movement          */
        {
        CURSOR_MOVED=0;
                                /* Figure mirror cursor pos and  */
                                /* draw it at new location.      */
        mirror_x=(VID_MAXX/2)+(VID_MAXX/2-CMX);

                                /* Turn off move events, draw    */
                                /* mirror cursor, reactivate     */
                                /* move events.                  */
        turn_off_move_event();
        draw_sprite(mirror_x-MOUSE_SIZE+1,CMY,mirror_cursor);
        install_event_handler();

        if (draw_on)      /* If line being dragged         */
            {
```

```
                /* Hide both cursors          */
      hide_mouse_cursor();

                  /* Turn off move events         */
                  /* show_cursor() reactivates it  */
      turn_off_move_event();
      hide_sprite(mirror_cursor);

                  /* Erase last line, old coords   */
      line(anchorx,anchory,newx,newy);
      line(lanchorx,anchory,lnewx,newy);

                  /* Figure new line coords       */
      newx=CMX;newy=CMY;

                  /* Figure mirror line coords    */
      lnewx=(VID_MAXX/2)+(VID_MAXX/2-newx);

                  /* Draw both lines at new local  */
      line(anchorx,anchory,newx,newy);
      line(lanchorx,anchory,lnewx,newy);

                  /* Show both cursors            */
      show_sprite(mirror_cursor);
      show_mouse_cursor();
      }

    }
else if (!draw_on)  /* If not in drawing mode-     */
    {

    if (LBUTTON_DOWN)
      {
      LBUTTON_DOWN=0;
      draw_on=1;     /* Start drawing, set to 1      */

      newx=CMX;      /* Figure starting line coords  */
      lnewx=(VID_MAXX/2)-(newx-VID_MAXX/2);

      newy=CMY;      /* Set the anchors              */
      anchorx=newx;
      lanchorx=lnewx;
      anchory=newy;
                  /* Hide both cursors            */
      hide_mouse_cursor();
```

```
                    /* Turn off move events      */
                    /* show_cursor() reactivates it  */
      turn_off_move_event();
      hide_sprite(mirror_cursor);

                    /* MODE TO XOR! Draw init lines  */
      setwritemode(XOR_PUT);
      change_color(10);
      line(anchorx,anchory,newx,newy);
      line(lanchorx,anchory,lnewx,newy);

                    /* Show both cursors          */
      show_sprite(mirror_cursor);
      show_mouse_cursor();
      }
                    /* Erase last lines, Undo      */
  if (RBUTTON_DOWN)
      {
      RBUTTON_DOWN=0;
                    /* Make sure there are lines to  */
                    /* erase; IF SO-               */
      if (lastx1!=0)
        {
                    /* Hide both cursors          */
        hide_mouse_cursor();

                    /* Turn off move events      */
                    /* show_cursor() reactivates it  */
        turn_off_move_event();
        hide_sprite(mirror_cursor);

                    /* MODE TO XOR! Erase last lines */
        setwritemode(XOR_PUT);
        line(lastx1,lasty1,lastx2,lasty2);
        line(lastlx1,lasty1,lastlx2,lasty2);

                    /* Set mode back to COPY_PUT    */
        setwritemode(COPY_PUT);
        lastx1=0;
                    /* Show both cursors          */
        show_sprite(mirror_cursor);
        show_mouse_cursor();
        }
      }
    }
```

```
                                    /* Left button rlsd, in draw mode*/
        if ((LBUTTON_UP)&&(draw_on))
           {
           LBUTTON_UP=0;

           draw_on=0;        /* Stop drawing, set to 0        */

           lastx1=anchorx;   /* Set coords for last lines     */
           lasty1=anchory;   /* drawn so it can be erased      */
           lastx2=newx;      /* with the Undo feature.         */
           lasty2=newy;
                             /* Set last mirror coords         */
           lastlx1=lanchorx;
           lastlx2=lnewx;
                             /* Set mode back to COPY_PUT      */
           setwritemode(COPY_PUT);
           }
        }
     }
else
   mouse_error(5,4);

getch();

if (MOUSE_THERE) reset_mouse();
if (USING_SPRITE) destroy_sprite(sprite_cursor);

shut_down_video();
}
```

Other Ideas

The previous example, MOUSE31.C, is only one possible use of dual, simultaneous cursors. Other ideas might include split menus, graphics tracing, and quad cursors for games. How about utilizing a three-button mouse and implementing dual (or more) cursors, with only one cursor being active at any given time? To switch active cursors, a user presses the middle button. The possibilities are as limitless as the human imagination.

When using dual sprite cursors, do not initialize them to the same location at startup. If you do, the sprite cursor written last contains the other's image in its background and a phantom cursor is the result.

Part III

Interfacing with the Mouse in Windows

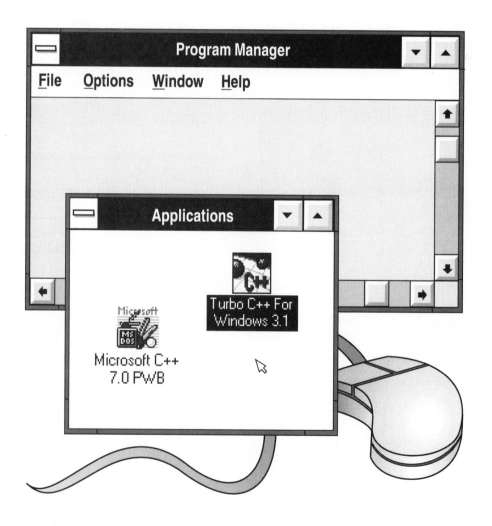

Chapter 22

The Generic Windows Program

With the advent of Microsoft Windows, application users now enjoy what was once the domain of operating systems other than MS-DOS: a standard, multi-tasking, graphical user interface (GUI). The popularity of Windows is easy to understand. Once a user learns one Windows application, learning another is only a matter of understanding the application, not the interface. As the programmer, Windows offers you many new opportunities, and many new challenges as well. This chapter and the following three chapters concentrate on one particular challenge: interfacing with the mouse in Windows.

This book assumes that you are at least familiar with using Windows and Windows applications. If you have never used Windows, or a Windows application, you should do so now. At the very least, read the small manual, *Getting Started with Microsoft Windows*, that is bundled with the Windows package.

Additionally, you should be familiar with your C compiler. Both the Borland and Microsoft compilers are bundled with excellent reference material, guides for beginners, and a bounty of helpful programming examples and compiling tips to get you started.

In this chapter, you create a generic Windows application that performs "all the right stuff." For those of you already familiar with Windows programming, a quick skim over the generic application should suffice. For those of you having little or no experience programming in Windows, the generic Windows program serves very well as an entry point into Windows programming. However, following this chapter, no attempt is made to explain Windows programming except when relating to the mouse, or when necessary.

 Windows 3.1 programmers wishing to learn more about Windows programming should see Windows 3.1 Programming, *by Murray and Pappas, Osborne McGraw-Hill, 1992.*

Windows, the Big Event Processor

The most fundamental difference between Windows applications and traditional DOS-based applications is that Windows applications are event driven, and DOS applications are generally sequentially driven. Conceptually understanding the difference between these two methodologies is the biggest hurdle you must overcome to write successful Windows applications.

In *sequentially structured* applications, you, as the programmer, have complete control over system resources. The order of operations in an application occur exactly as you specify, and the user must follow the order to properly run the application. In *event-driven applications*, the user has control over system resources, and the order of operations occur in the order the user chooses.

In Windows, your application, in most cases, does not have direct access to the operations or events that have occurred in the system, except through messages sent by Windows. Windows is continuously dispatching messages to applications about what events have occurred in the system. You trap these messages and take action based upon their meaning. In this sense, Windows is a big event processor.

If you have read Parts I and II of this book, you are one step closer to understanding event processing. The event handler and C event processor you created in Chapter 7 operate very similarly to the way Windows processes and dispatches messages, except that the C event processor is dispatching the messages (events), not Windows. Additionally, *everything* in Windows is event driven, not just mouse events.

Communicating with the Mouse in Windows

Communicating with the mouse in Windows is a snap. Unlike DOS applications, you do not make function calls to the mouse driver using DOS interrupt 0x33. Windows uses its own mouse driver, and DOS interrupt 0x33 is meaningless. Instead, Windows sends messages to your application regarding specific mouse activity.

Windows handles all mouse cursor initialization, hiding, showing, border management (if desired), and other maintenance-related items. You are free from the problems associated with DOS-based mouse programming, and can concentrate more on the application itself.

The Fundamental Windows Program

The first order of business is to create a fundamental Windows program. The program should provide all the essential Windows features such as sizing, moving, scrolling, and so on.

The following C source code is the fundamental Windows application. It is called GENERIC.C, and serves as the basis for all remaining Windows programming examples in this book.

```c
/*------------------------------------------------------------*/
/*                      GENERIC.C                         */
/*                                                        */
/* Basic fundamental Windows 3.1 program.                 */
/* Mouse cursor initialized as the default arrow.         */
/*------------------------------------------------------------*/

#define STRICT              /* Strict 3.1 compliance     */
#include <windows.h>        /* Standard Windows header    */

HINSTANCE gInstance;        /* Global instance handle     */

                            /* Function prototype for     */
                            /* MainWndProc().             */
LRESULT FAR PASCAL MainWndProc(HWND hWnd,UINT iMessage,
                        WPARAM wParam,LPARAM lParam);

/* Module : WinMain                                       */
/* ---------------------------------------------------------*/
/* Initializes window and processes message loop.         */
/*                                                        */
int PASCAL WinMain(HINSTANCE hInstance,
                   HINSTANCE hPrevInstance,
                   LPSTR lpszcmdparam,int nCmdShow)
   {
   HWND hWnd;
   MSG Message;
   WNDCLASS WndClass;

   gInstance=hInstance;     /* Assign global instance     */

   if (!hPrevInstance)
      {
      WndClass.cbClsExtra =0;
      WndClass.cbWndExtra =0;
```

```
       WndClass.hbrBackground=GetStockObject(WHITE_BRUSH);

                               /* Load Windows default arrow   */
       WndClass.hCursor=LoadCursor(NULL,IDC_ARROW);

       WndClass.hIcon=LoadIcon(NULL,"END");
       WndClass.hInstance=hInstance;
       WndClass.lpfnWndProc=MainWndProc;
       WndClass.lpszClassName="GENERIC";
       WndClass.lpszMenuName=NULL;
       WndClass.style=CS_HREDRAW | CS_VREDRAW;

       RegisterClass(&WndClass);
       }

   hWnd= CreateWindow("GENERIC",           /* Class name      */
                                           /* Caption         */
                   "GENERIC.C - Generic Windows 3.1 Program",

                   WS_OVERLAPPEDWINDOw      /* Style           */
                   CW_USEDEFAULT,           /* Horiz position */
                   0,                       /* Vert position   */
                   CW_USEDEFAULT,           /* Width           */
                   0,                       /* Height          */
                   NULL,                    /* Parent Window   */
                   NULL,                    /* Menu            */
                   hInstance,               /* Program instanc*/
                   NULL);                   /* Parameters      */

                           /* If no create, exit              */
   if (hWnd==NULL) return FALSE;

   ShowWindow(hWnd,nCmdShow);/* Make window visible            */
   UpdateWindow(hWnd);       /* Send paint mssg                */

                           /* Message loop                    */
   while(GetMessage(&Message,0,0,0))
      {
      TranslateMessage(&Message);
      DispatchMessage(&Message);
      }
   return Message.wParam;
   }
```

```
/* Module : MainWndProc                                          */
/*--------------------------------------------------------------*/
/* Message processor.                                            */
/*                                                              */
LRESULT FAR PASCAL MainWndProc(HWND hWnd,UINT iMessage,
                                WPARAM wParam,LPARAM lParam)
    {
    switch(iMessage)
        {
        case WM_DESTROY:
                        PostQuitMessage(0);
                        return 0;

        default:return(DefWindowProc(hWnd,iMessage,wParam,lParam));
        }
    }
```

The Module Definition File

Along with the C source code, every Windows application has a *module definition file*. Module definition files provide information to the linker regarding the contents and requirements of the Windows application.

Borland C++ and Turbo C++ linkers have other means of determining the information provided in the module definition file, and supply default values for the definition fields if the file is not present. Therefore, the definition file is not actually required for the Borland compilers. However, if you use a Borland compiler, you should at least be aware of module definition files, and how to use them.

The following is the module definition file for the fundamental Windows application. It is called GENERIC.DEF:

```
NAME         GENRIC
DESCRIPTION  'Generic Windows 3.1 Program'
EXETYPE      WINDOWS
STUB         "WINSTUB.EXE"
CODE         PRELOAD MOVEABLE
DATA         PRELOAD MOVEABLE MULTIPLE
HEAPSIZE     1024
STACKSIZE    5120
EXPORTS      MainWndProc @1
```

Compiling GENERIC.C

To compile GENERIC.C, use the following instructions. All other Windows programming examples presented in this book are compiled in the same manner.

You must have a compiler capable of compiling Windows 3.1 source code.

Integrated Environment Compiling

If you are compiling within the Borland integrated environment or the Microsoft Programmers Workbench, you need a project file for all remaining Windows programming examples.

The Project File   A project file is used to manage individual files that an application is composed of. These files can be source files, module definition files, precompiled object and library files, or Windows resource files.

The project files you create in this book always include a module definition file and the C source code file. One example presented in Chapter 24 also contains a cursor resource file.

The project file for GENERIC.C is as follows:

```
GENERIC.DEF
GENERIC.C
```

Compiling Steps   To compile GENERIC.C to GENERIC.EXE, use the following instructions:

1. Create the project file.

2. Set the application type to a Windows .EXE application.

3. Compile the program.

See your compiler's reference manual for further details about integrated environment compiling.

Command-Line Compiling

If you prefer compiling with command-line compilers, use the following instructions:

Turbo C++ for Windows 3.1, Borland C++ 3.1, and Later   Compile GENERIC.C to GENERIC.EXE by entering the following at the DOS command line:

```
TCC –W GENERIC.C
```

where

- *TCC* is the Turbo C++ command-line compiler. Use BCC if compiling with the Borland C++ command-line compiler.

- *–W* means compile a Windows executable program. See your compiler's reference manual for more detailed Windows compiling options.

- *GENERIC.C* is the name of the source code file.

The compiler switches are case sensitive and must be entered as shown.

Microsoft C/C++ 7.0 and Later   Compile GENERIC.C to GENERIC.EXE by entering the following at the DOS command line:

1. Enter

    CL /c /Gw /Zp GENERIC.C

    where

    - *CL* is the Microsoft command-line compiler.

    - */c* means compile only (object file).

    - */Gw* means generate entry/exit code for real-mode Windows functions.

    - */Zp* means pack structure variables.

    - *GENERIC.C* is the name of the source code file.

2. Enter

    link /nod generic,,,slibcew libw,GENERIC.DEF

    where

    - *link* is the Microsoft linker.

    - */nod* means do not search default libraries named in object file.

    - *generic* is GENERIC.OBJ, compiled in step 1.

    - *slibcew* is the Windows version of the C run-time library.

    - *libw* is the Windows library.

    - *GENERIC.DEF* is the module definition file.

The compiler switches are case sensitive and must be entered as shown.

Running GENERIC.EXE

To run GENERIC.EXE from within Turbo C++ 3.1 (or later) for Windows, open the Run menu, and choose Run (ALT-R, R). Microsoft C/C++ 7.0 does not allow you to run a Windows program from within the Programmer's Workbench, and it must be run from the Windows environment.

To run GENERIC.EXE from the Windows environment, open the File menu in Windows and choose Run (ALT-F, R). Enter the directory and filename. If GENERIC.EXE if located on drive C in a directory called \WINCODE, enter **C:\WINCODE\GENERIC.EXE**.

When you run the program, the window shown in Figure 22-1 is generated.

If you are an experienced Windows programmer, you are probably familiar with the layout of the basic window and its capabilities. If this is your first Windows program, you may be amazed at how much functionality this tiny little program has.

Notice in Figure 22-1 that the window has minimize, maximize, and system menu buttons built right in. For a complete demonstration of the built-in capabilities, take the following steps while running GENERIC.EXE:

1. Move the mouse cursor over the minimize button and click the left mouse button. The window becomes an inactive icon, as illustrated in Figure 22-2.

2. Move the mouse cursor over the icon and click the left mouse button. The system menu (also called the control menu) appears, as illustrated in Figure 22-3.

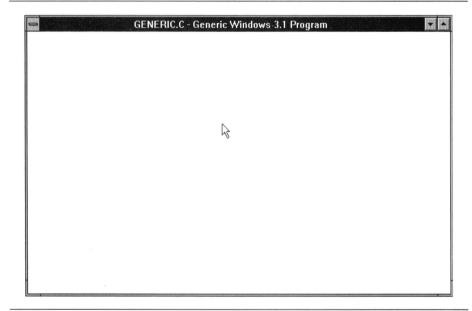

Figure 22-1.   *The GENERIC Windows program*

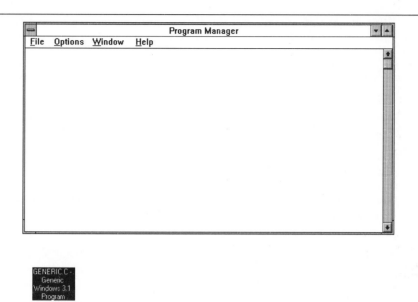

Figure 22-2.   *GENERIC.EXE as an icon*

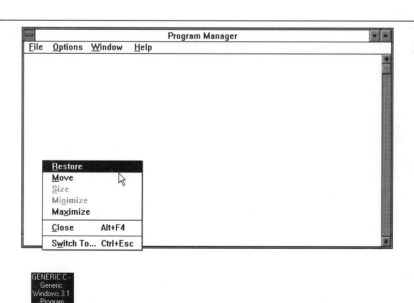

Figure 22-3.   *The system menu (also called the control menu)*

3. Move the mouse cursor over the Restore option and click the left mouse button. The window is restored to its previous size and becomes active.

4. Move the mouse over one of the window borders. A sizing arrow appears. Press the left mouse button, stretch the window to a new size, and release the mouse button.

5. Move the cursor over the maximize button and click the left mouse button. The window is maximized to the entire display region.

6. Move the mouse cursor over the system menu button and click the left mouse button. The system menu appears as illustrated in Figure 22-4.

7. Move the mouse cursor over the Close option and click the left mouse button. The window is closed and the program terminates.

Wow—all that from such a small amount of code! If you are a beginning Windows programmer, understanding and getting past the GENERIC.C program will put you on the fast track to Windows mania. The following sections describe the fundamental aspects of the generic Windows application.

Understanding GENERIC.C

The following sections cover the details of GENERIC.C. If you're new to Windows programming, don't be worried about understanding everything right away. After

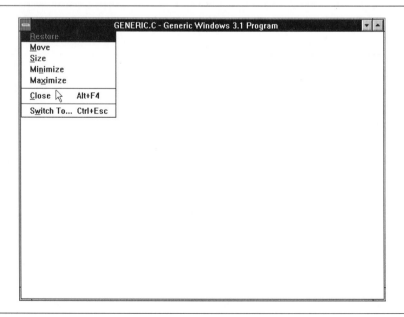

Figure 22-4.   Fully maximized window and the system menu

studying and running a few of the programming examples to follow, it will start to sink in and make sense.

In GENERIC.C, the functions called within WinMain() and MainWndProc() are Windows API (Application Programming Interface) functions—that is, they are part of Windows.

STRICT Compliance, WINDOWS.H, and gInstance

In GENERIC.C and every programming example to follow, the first four statements are always these:

```
#define STRICT
#include <windows.h>
HINSTANCE gInstance;
LRESULT FAR PASCAL MainWndProc(HWND hWnd,UINT iMessage,
                               WPARAM wParam,LPARAM lParam);
```

The keyword STRICT forces WINDOWS.H to follow strict Windows 3.1 type definitions, and must precede the WINDOWS.H header file. WINDOWS.H is where the Windows API function prototypes, structures, and messages are defined, and you must include it in any Windows application. The variable gInstance is used as a global instance reference outside of the function WinMain(). The last statement is the prototype for the function MainWndProc().

WinMain()

The next portion of code is the function WinMain(). WinMain() is the entry and exit point for all Windows applications, and has four basic parts to it: procedure declaration, program initialization, message loop processing, and program termination.

Procedure Declaration   The WinMain() function is declared as follows:

```
int PASCAL WinMain(HINSTANCE hInstance,
                   HINSTANCE hPrevInstance,
                   LPSTR lpszcmdparam,int nCmdShow)
```

where the parameters used are as follows:

Function Parameter	Meaning
hInstance	Handles identifying the program.
hPrevInstance	If another instance of the program is running, hPreviousInstance contains the handle of that instance, otherwise it is NULL.
lpszcmdparam	Specifies command-line arguments for the program.
nCmdShow	Specifies the state of the main window, icon, or on screen, when first opened.

Program Initialization   Program initialization represents the bulk of WinMain(). The first task is declaring the local variables and assigning the global instance handle:

```
{
HWND hWnd;
MSG Message;
WNDCLASS WndClass;

gInstance=hInstance;       /* Assign global instance        */
```

where the local variables mean the following:

Local Variable	Meaning
hWnd	Handle of window
Message	Message
WndClass	Class attributes of window

Notice that the global instance reference is assigned with the statement gInstance=hInstance.

Next, it is determined whether the application is the only instance of itself running. If it is, the window is registered:

```
if (!hPrevInstance)
    {
    WndClass.cbClsExtra =0;
    WndClass.cbWndExtra =0;
    WndClass.hbrBackground=GetStockObject(WHITE_BRUSH);
    WndClass.hCursor=LoadCursor(NULL,IDC_ARROW);
    WndClass.hIcon=LoadIcon(NULL,"END");
    WndClass.hInstance=hInstance;
    WndClass.lpfnWndProc=MainWndProc;
    WndClass.lpszClassName="GENERIC";
```

```
WndClass.lpszMenuName=NULL;
WndClass.style=CS_HREDRAW | CS_VREDRAW;
RegisterClass(&WndClass);
 }
```

Next the window is created:

```
hWnd= CreateWindow("GENERIC",          /* Class name    */
                                       /* Caption       */
               "GENERIC.C - Generic Windows 3.1 Program",

               WS_OVERLAPPEDWINDOW, /* Style           */
               CW_USEDEFAULT,       /* Horiz position */
               0,                   /* Vert position  */
               CW_USEDEFAULT,       /* Width          */
               0,                   /* Height         */
               NULL,                /* Parent Window  */
               NULL,                /* Menu           */
               hInstance,           /* Program Instanc*/
               NULL);               /* Parameters     */
```

After creating the window, the next line of code determines whether the window was created properly. If not, the application is terminated:

```
if (hWnd==NULL) return FALSE;
```

If the window was created properly, the window is made visible with ShowWindow(), and a **WM_PAINT** message is sent to the application with UpdateWindow():

```
ShowWindow(hWnd,nCmdShow);
UpdateWindow(hWnd);
```

Message Processing   At this point, the message processing loop takes over. Messages are retrieved via the GetMessage() function loop, and are processed and dispatched to Windows, which sends the message to the correct window:

```
while(GetMessage(&Message,0,0,0))
   {
   TranslateMessage(&Message);
   DispatchMessage(&Message);
   }
```

Program Termination   When GetMessage() receives a WM_QUIT message from MainWndProc() sent with PostQuitMessage(), the program instance is terminated and returns the message sent from PostQuitMessage():

```
return Message.wParam;
```

MainWndProc()

The function MainWndProc() is where GENERIC.C takes action based on messages sent from Windows. It is declared as follows:

```
LRESULT FAR PASCAL MainWndProc(HWND hWnd,UINT iMessage,
                        WPARAM wParam,LPARAM lParam)
```

where the parameters mean the following:

Variable	Meaning
hWnd	Handle of window
iMessage	Message type
wParam	Additional information regarding iMessage
lParam	Additional information regarding iMessage

Inside MainWndProc(), messages are trapped or processed back to Windows:

```
{

switch(iMessage)
    {
    case WM_DESTROY:
                  PostQuitMessage(0);
                  return 0;

    default:return(DefWindowProc(hWnd,iMessage,wParam,lParam));
    }
}
```

Understanding GENERIC.DEF

If this is your first attempt at programming in Windows, the module definition file probably seems very foreign. Every Windows application must have a module definition file to specify the application's name, type, code and data segments, memory requirements, and exported functions (although the Borland compilers will supply the default values if you do not provide a module definition file). The following describes what each statement in the module definition file means.

NAME GENERIC

NAME specifies that the application GENERIC is an executable program. Dynamically linked libraries use the LIBRARY keyword instead.

DESCRIPTION 'Generic Windows 3.1 Program'

This is usually used as a program's copyright notice or version identification.

EXETYPE WINDOWS

EXETYPE specifies that the program is an executable Windows application, and is required for any Windows executable application.

STUB "WINSTUB.EXE"

This attaches WINSTUB.EXE to the beginning of the application. If the application is run outside of Windows, WINSTUB.EXE generates the familiar message: "This program must be run under Microsoft Windows." You can create and use your own stub if desired.

CODE PRELOAD MOVEABLE

This specifies that the code segment is MOVABLE and can be relocated.

DATA PRELOAD MOVEABLE MULTIPLE

This specifies that the data segment is MOVEABLE and can be relocated. The MULTIPLE keyword is standard for Windows applications, and specifies that more than one copy of the program is allowed to run at the same time.

HEAPSIZE 1024

This sets the initial size of the application's local heap. The local heap is private to the program. The heap can grow beyond its initial size but not more than a value of 64K.

STACKSIZE 5120

The stack is used for storing local variables, function arguments, and saving return addresses to allow anonymous calling. Windows uses 3K of the stack, and your program uses whatever is left. 5K is considered the minimum stack size for a Windows application.

EXPORTS MainWndProc @1

All functions that are called by other Windows functions must be exported. The one exception is the function WinMain(). Each exported function gets an ordinal value assigned to it, which can be any integer value, but is usually assigned sequentially.

 See your compiler's reference manuals regarding other possible settings in the module definition file.

That concludes the explanation of the fundamental Windows application. The programming examples presented in the following three chapters are all based on this generic application.

Chapter 23

Windows Mouse
Button Messages

As with DOS applications, the mouse wouldn't be of much use in Windows if users couldn't press buttons to make choices and take action based on those choices. In a Windows application, no polling for button presses or releases is ever necessary, as messages regarding specific mouse events are sent automatically by Windows. As the programmer, you only need to set the trap, and the mouse comes walking in.

Button Press and Release Messages

When a user presses a mouse button in Windows, Windows sends a message specific to that button. For instance, the message WM_LBUTTONDOWN signifies that the user pressed the left mouse button, and the message WM_RBUTTONUP signifies that the user released the right mouse button. The messages are also specific to either the client area or the nonclient area. In the client area, messages are always preceded by a WM_, and in the nonclient area, messages are always preceded by WM_NC. This means that when a user presses the right mouse button in the client area, the message WM_RBUTTONDOWN is sent. When a user presses the right button in the nonclient area, the message WM_NCRBUTTONDOWN is sent.

Special care must be taken if you trap the WM_NCLBUTTONDOWN message. This message signifies that a user pressed the left mouse button in the nonclient area. If it is trapped, the system menu and all window sizing functions are lost. If you wish to capture the WM_NCLBUTTONDOWN message, you must control the system menu and window sizing functions when they are selected with the mouse. It is possible to trap the WM_NCLBUTTONDOWN message and process it back out to

Windows with the function DefWindowProc(), but you lose the button release message WM_NCLBUTTONUP. It's up to you how this is handled. In most applications, letting Windows control everything is just fine. In certain circumstances, you want to control everything.

The following example traps all Windows button press and release messages, in both the client and nonclient areas, and writes a string of text informing you of the message sent by Windows. Double-click messages are trapped as well.

In the following example, the message WM_NCLBUTTONDOWN is trapped, and the system menu and sizing functions are not available to the mouse. To exit the program, press ALT-SPACEBAR, *and choose Close.*

The project file is called WMOUSE1.PRJ. Here it is:

```
WMOUSE1.DEF
WMOUSE1.C
```

The module definition file is called WMOUSE1.DEF:

```
NAME          WMOUSE1
DESCRIPTION   'Mouse Button Messages'
EXETYPE       WINDOWS
STUB          "WINSTUB.EXE"
CODE          PRELOAD MOVEABLE
DATA          PRELOAD MOVEABLE MULTIPLE
HEAPSIZE      1024
STACKSIZE     5120
EXPORTS       MainWndProc @1
```

Here is WMOUSE1.C:

```
/*------------------------------------------------------------*/
/*                    WMOUSE1.C                          */
/*                                                      */
/* Capturing mouse button messages in Windows.          */
/*------------------------------------------------------------*/

#define STRICT              /* Strict 3.1 compliance      */
#include <windows.h>        /* Standard Windows header    */
#include <string.h>         /* Need for strlen prototype  */

HINSTANCE gInstance;        /* Global instance handle     */
```

```
                              /* Function prototype for        */
                              /* MainWndProc().                */
LRESULT FAR PASCAL MainWndProc(HWND hWnd,UINT iMessage,
                    WPARAM wParam,LPARAM lParam);


/* Module : WinMain                                            */
/* -----------------------------------------------------------*/
/* Initializes window and processes message loop.             */
/*                                                            */
int PASCAL WinMain(HINSTANCE hInstance,
                    HINSTANCE hPrevInstance,
                    LPSTR lpszcmdparam,int nCmdShow)
    {
    HWND hWnd;
    MSG Message;
    WNDCLASS WndClass;

    gInstance=hInstance;        /* Assign global instance       */

    if (!hPrevInstance)
        {
        WndClass.cbClsExtra =0;
        WndClass.cbWndExtra =0;
        WndClass.hbrBackground=GetStockObject(WHITE_BRUSH);

                              /* Load Windows default arrow     */
        WndClass.hCursor=LoadCursor(NULL,IDC_ARROW);

        WndClass.hIcon=LoadIcon(NULL,"END");
        WndClass.hInstance=hInstance;
        WndClass.lpfnWndProc=MainWndProc;
        WndClass.lpszClassName="WMOUSE1";
        WndClass.lpszMenuName=NULL;


                              /* Note CS_DBLCLKS                */
        WndClass.style=CS_HREDRAW | CS_VREDRAW | CS_DBLCLKS;
        RegisterClass(&WndClass);
        }

    hWnd= CreateWindow("WMOUSE1",          /* Class name     */
                                            /* Caption        */
                    "WMOUSE1.C - Mouse Button Messages",
                    WS_OVERLAPPEDWINDOW,  /* Style          */
                    CW_USEDEFAULT,        /* Horiz position */
                    0,                    /* Vert position  */
```

```
                            CW_USEDEFAULT,          /* Width          */
                            0,                      /* Height         */
                            NULL,                   /* Parent window  */
                            NULL,                   /* Menu           */
                            hInstance,              /* Program instanc*/
                            NULL);                  /* Parameters     */

                                /* If no create, exit            */
    if (hWnd==NULL) return FALSE;

    ShowWindow(hWnd,nCmdShow);/* Make window visible              */
    UpdateWindow(hWnd);
                                /* Message loop                  */
    while(GetMessage(&Message,0,0,0))
        {
        TranslateMessage(&Message);
        DispatchMessage(&Message);
        }
    return Message.wParam;
    }


/* Module : out text                                             */
/*-------------------------------------------------------------*/
/* Outputs a string of text at TEXT coordinates. This is a      */
/* much more natural way to output text. Coords 1,1 represent    */
/* the upper-left coordinate of the client area.                */
/*                                                              */
void PASCAL out_text(int x,int y,char *text,HWND hWnd)
    {
    int x_scale,y_scale;    /* Scaling vars                     */
    HDC TheDC;              /* Device handle                    */
    TEXTMETRIC text_metrics; /* Text settings                   */

    TheDC=GetDC(hWnd);          /* Get device and text metrics   */
    GetTextMetrics(TheDC,&text_metrics);

                                /* Figure Y an X coordinates     */
    y_scale=(y-1)*(text_metrics.tmHeight);
    x_scale=(x-1)*(text_metrics.tmAveCharWidth);

                                /* Output string, release device */
    TextOut(TheDC,x_scale,y_scale,text,strlen(text));
    ReleaseDC(hWnd,TheDC);
    }
```

```
/* Module : MainWndProc                                       */
/*-----------------------------------------------------------*/
/* Message processor.                                         */
/*                                                            */
LRESULT FAR PASCAL MainWndProc(HWND hWnd,UINT iMessage,
                                WPARAM wParam,LPARAM lParam)
    {
    PAINTSTRUCT ps;              /* Paint structure - init mssg   */
    switch(iMessage)
        {
      case WM_PAINT:
            BeginPaint(hWnd,&ps);
            out_text(1,1,"Press mouse buttons to see messages.",
                    hWnd);
            out_text(1,2,"Since program traps left button in
                        non-client area,",hWnd);
            out_text(1,3,"the Systsem Menu and Window Sizing
                        Functions are not",hWnd);
            out_text(1,4,"available. To exit program, press
                        ALT-Spacebar, Close.",hWnd);

            out_text(1,6,"Button Messages In Client Area",hWnd);
            out_text(1,7,"----------------------------",hWnd);
            out_text(1,11,"Button Messages In Non Client Area",
                    hWnd);
            out_text(1,12,"---------------------------------",
                    hWnd);

            EndPaint(hWnd,&ps);
            return 0;

            /* Client Area Button Messages */
            /* -------------------------- */

      case WM_LBUTTONDOWN:
            out_text(1,8,"Left Button Pressed            ",hWnd);
            return 0;

      case WM_LBUTTONUP:
            out_text(1,9,"Left Button Released           ",hWnd);
            return 0;

      case WM_LBUTTONDBLCLK:
            out_text(1,8,"Left Button Double Clicked     ",hWnd);
            out_text(1,9,"                               ",hWnd);
            return 0;
```

```
    case WM_RBUTTONDOWN:
         out_text(1,8,"Right Button Pressed          ",hWnd);
         return 0;

    case WM_RBUTTONUP:
         out_text(1,9,"Right Button Released         ",hWnd);
         return 0;

    case WM_RBUTTONDBLCLK:
         out_text(1,8,"Right Button Double Clicked   ",hWnd);
         out_text(1,9,"                              ",hWnd);
         return 0;

    case WM_MBUTTONDOWN:
         out_text(1,8,"Middle Button Pressed         ",hWnd);
         return 0;

    case WM_MBUTTONUP:
         out_text(1,9,"Middle Button Released        ",hWnd);
         return 0;

    case WM_MBUTTONDBLCLK:
         out_text(1,8,"Middle Button Double Clicked  ",hWnd);
         out_text(1,9,"                              ",hWnd);
         return 0;

         /* Nonclient Area Button Messages  */
         /* ------------------------------- */

/* System menu and sizing functions are not available   */
/* when WM_NCLBUTTONDOWN is trapped, unless it is         */
/* processed back out with DefWindowProc(), and then      */
/* left releases are lost. So, to demonstrate trapping    */
/* buttons the system menu and sizing functions = unavail*/

    case WM_NCLBUTTONDOWN:
         out_text(1,13,"Left Button Pressed          ",hWnd);
         return 0;

    case WM_NCLBUTTONUP:
         out_text(1,14,"Left Button Released         ",hWnd);
         return 0;
```

```
    case WM_NCLBUTTONDBLCLK:
        out_text(1,13,"Left Button Double Clicked    ",hWnd);
        out_text(1,14,"                              ",hWnd);
        return 0;

    case WM_NCRBUTTONDOWN:
        out_text(1,13,"Right Button Pressed          ",hWnd);
        return 0;

    case WM_NCRBUTTONUP:
        out_text(1,14,"Right Button Released         ",hWnd);
        return 0;

    case WM_NCRBUTTONDBLCLK:
        out_text(1,13,"Right Button Double Clicked   ",hWnd);
        out_text(1,14,"                              ",hWnd);
        return 0;

    case WM_NCMBUTTONDOWN:
        out_text(1,13,"Middle Button Pressed         ",hWnd);
        return 0;

    case WM_NCMBUTTONUP:
        out_text(1,14,"Middle Button Released        ",hWnd);
        return 0;

    case WM_NCMBUTTONDBLCLK:
        out_text(1,13,"Middle Button Double Clicked  ",hWnd);
        out_text(1,14,"                              ",hWnd);
        return 0;

    case WM_DESTROY:
        PostQuitMessage(0);
        return 0;

    default:
        return(DefWindowProc(hWnd,iMessage,wParam,lParam));
    }
}
```

When you run the program, press and release the left mouse button; then press the right mouse button. Figure 23-1 is the result.

Notice the following items from the previous example:

- When the window is initialized, double-clicks are enabled by adding the CS_DBLCLKS constant to the window. Look at the actual assignment:

```
WndClass.style=CS_HREDRAW | CS_VREDRAW | CS_DBLCLKS;
```

  If you remove CS_DBLCLKS from the window style, double-click messages are not sent to the application. You can verify this by removing CS_DBLCLKS, recompiling the program, and running it.

- Double-clicking a mouse button actually generates four messages. If you double-click the left button, the messages WM_LBUTTONDOWN, WM_LBUTTONUP, WM_LBUTTONDBLCLK, and another WM_LBUTTONUP are sent.

Additional Information from Button Messages

The button messages Windows send actually include much more information than the previous example. When a button press or release message is sent, three additional values are sent along with it. These values are located in the wParam and

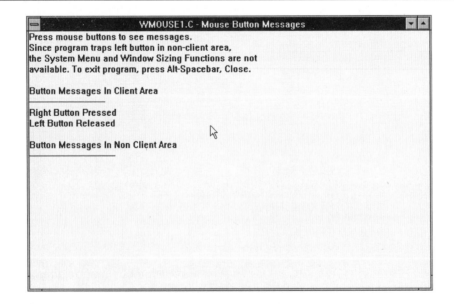

Figure 23-1.   Trapping button press and release messages

lParam parameters sent to MainWndProc(). The following details what these values mean, and how they are used.

Detailed Information in the Client Area

In the client area, the following values are sent along with a button message:

wParam   wParam indicates whether various virtual keys or buttons are down when a mouse button is pressed. This can be any combination of the following:

Value	Meaning
MK_CONTROL	Set if CTRL key is down
MK_SHIFT	Set if SHIFT key is down
MK_LBUTTON	Set if left button is down
MK_MBUTTON	Set if middle button is down
MK_RBUTTON	Set if right button is down

LOWORD (lParam)   LOWORD (lParam) specifies the horizontal position of the cursor in client coordinates.

HIWORD (lParam)   HIWORD (lParam) specifies the vertical position of the cursor in client coordinates.

With this in mind, the following example extracts the additional values and writes them to the display. Only messages in the client area are trapped.

The project file is called WMOUSE2.PRJ:

```
WMOUSE2.DEF
WMOUSE2.C
```

The module definition file is called WMOUSE2.DEF:

```
NAME          WMOUSE2
DESCRIPTION   'Detailed Button Messages'
EXETYPE       WINDOWS
STUB          "WINSTUB.EXE"
CODE          PRELOAD MOVEABLE#
DATA          PRELOAD MOVEABLE MULTIPLE
HEAPSIZE      1024
STACKSIZE     5120
EXPORTS       MainWndProc @1
```

Here is WMOUSE2.C:

```
/*------------------------------------------------------------*/
/*                      WMOUSE2.C                           */
/*                                                          */
/*  Capturing mouse button messages and detailed info inside */
/*  the client area.                                        */
/*------------------------------------------------------------*/

#define STRICT               /* Strict 3.1 compliance       */
#include <windows.h>         /* Standard Windows header      */
#include <stdio.h>           /* Need for sprintf prototype   */
#include <string.h>          /* Need for strlen prototype    */


HINSTANCE gInstance;         /* Global instance handle       */

                             /* Function prototype for       */
                             /* MainWndProc().               */
LRESULT FAR PASCAL MainWndProc(HWND hWnd,UINT iMessage,
                      WPARAM wParam,LPARAM lParam);


/* Module : WinMain                                          */
/* ---------------------------------------------------------*/
/* Initializes window and processes message loop.           */
/*                                                          */
int PASCAL WinMain(HINSTANCE hInstance,
                   HINSTANCE hPrevInstance,
                   LPSTR lpszcmdparam,int nCmdShow)

   {
   HWND hWnd;
   MSG Message;
   WNDCLASS WndClass;

   gInstance=hInstance;      /* Assign global instance       */

   if (!hPrevInstance)
      {
      WndClass.cbClsExtra =0;
      WndClass.cbWndExtra =0;
      WndClass.hbrBackground=GetStockObject(WHITE_BRUSH);

                            /* Load Windows default arrow    */
      WndClass.hCursor=LoadCursor(NULL,IDC_ARROW);

      WndClass.hIcon=LoadIcon(NULL,"END");
```

```
    WndClass.hInstance=hInstance;
    WndClass.lpfnWndProc=MainWndProc;
    WndClass.lpszClassName="WMOUSE2";
    WndClass.lpszMenuName=NULL;
    WndClass.style=CS_HREDRAW | CS_VREDRAW;
    RegisterClass(&WndClass);
    }

  hWnd= CreateWindow("WMOUSE2",                /* Class name    */
                                              /* Caption       */
                   "WMOUSE2.C - Detailed Button Messages",
                   WS_OVERLAPPEDWINDOW,  /* Style         */
                   CW_USEDEFAULT,        /* Horiz position */
                   0,                    /* Vert position  */
                   CW_USEDEFAULT,        /* Width         */
                   0,                    /* Height        */
                   NULL,                 /* Parent window  */
                   NULL,                 /* Menu          */
                   hInstance,            /* Program instanc*/
                   NULL);                /* Parameters    */


                         /* If no create, exit          */
  if (hWnd==NULL) return FALSE;

  ShowWindow(hWnd,nCmdShow);/* Make window visible        */
  UpdateWindow(hWnd);
                         /* Message loop                */
  while(GetMessage(&Message,0,0,0))
     {
     TranslateMessage(&Message);
     DispatchMessage(&Message);
     }
  return Message.wParam;
  }


/* Module : out text                                     */
/*-----------------------------------------------------------*/
/* Outputs a string of text at TEXT coordinates. This is a   */
/* much more natural way to output text. Coords 1,1 represent */
/* the upper-left coordinate of the client area.         */
/*                                                       */
void PASCAL out_text(int x,int y,char *text,HWND hWnd)
  {
  int x_scale,y_scale;     /* Scaling vars              */
```

```
    HDC TheDC;                   /* Device handle              */
    TEXTMETRIC text_metrics;   /* Text settings              */


    TheDC=GetDC(hWnd);           /* Get device and text metrics  */
    GetTextMetrics(TheDC,&text_metrics);


                                 /* Figure Y and X coordinates   */
    y_scale=(y-1)*(text_metrics.tmHeight);
    x_scale=(x-1)*(text_metrics.tmAveCharWidth);


                                 /* Output string, release device */
    TextOut(TheDC,x_scale,y_scale,text,strlen(text));
    ReleaseDC(hWnd,TheDC);
    }


/* Module : write control key                              */
/*----------------------------------------------------------*/
/* Write what control key is down when mouse button presses.  */
/*                                                          */
void write_control_key(WPARAM keyParam,int y,HWND hWnd)
    {
    if (keyParam & MK_LBUTTON)
        out_text(50,y,"Left Button Is Down       ",hWnd);
    if (keyParam & MK_MBUTTON)
        out_text(50,y,"Middle Button Is Down     ",hWnd);
    if (keyParam & MK_RBUTTON)
        out_text(50,y,"Right Button Is Down      ",hWnd);
    if (keyParam & MK_CONTROL)
        out_text(50,y,"CTRL Key Is Down          ",hWnd);
    if (keyParam & MK_SHIFT)
        out_text(50,y,"SHIFT Key Is Down         ",hWnd);
    if (keyParam==0)
        out_text(50,y,
            "                                    ",hWnd);
    }


/* Module : MainWndProc                                    */
/*----------------------------------------------------------*/
/* Message processor.                                       */
/*                                                          */
LRESULT FAR PASCAL MainWndProc(HWND hWnd,UINT iMessage,
                        WPARAM wParam,LPARAM lParam)
    {
    char coord_string[80];   /* For coords-string conversn  */
    PAINTSTRUCT ps;          /* Paint structure - init mssg  */
```

```
coord_string[0]=NULL;
switch(iMessage)
   {
   case WM_PAINT:
       BeginPaint(hWnd,&ps);
       out_text(1,1,"Press mouse buttons to see messages
                     and coordinates.",hWnd);
       out_text(1,2,"Hold CTRL or Shift keys while
                      pressing buttons, or",hWnd);
       out_text(1,3,"hold one button while pressing and
                      releasing the other.",hWnd);
       EndPaint(hWnd,&ps);
       return 0;


   case WM_LBUTTONDOWN:
       out_text(1,5,"Left Button Pressed      ",hWnd);


                          /* Get coords button presses at */
       sprintf(coord_string,"At - (%d , %d)      ",
               LOWORD(lParam),HIWORD(lParam));


                          /* Write coords                  */
       out_text(32,5,coord_string,hWnd);


                          /* Write what control key is down*/
                          /* Notice!! Remove MK_LBUTTON    */
                          /* from value, button known down.*/
       write_control_key(wParam-MK_LBUTTON,5,hWnd);
       return 0;


   case WM_LBUTTONUP:
       out_text(1,6,"Left Button Released     ",hWnd);


                          /* Get coords button presses at */
       sprintf(coord_string,"At - (%d , %d)     ",
               LOWORD(lParam),HIWORD(lParam));


                          /* Write coords and key          */
       out_text(32,6,coord_string,hWnd);
       write_control_key(wParam,6,hWnd);
       return 0;


   case WM_RBUTTONDOWN:
       out_text(1,5,"Right Button Pressed     ",hWnd);
```

```
                               /* Get coords button presses at */
         sprintf(coord_string,"At - ( %d , %d )      ",
                 LOWORD(lParam),HIWORD(lParam));

                               /* Write coords              */
         out_text(32,5,coord_string,hWnd);

                               /* Write what control key is down*/
                               /* Notice!! Remove MK_RBUTTON    */
                               /* from value, button known down.*/
         write_control_key(wParam-MK_RBUTTON,5,hWnd);
         return 0;

    case WM_RBUTTONUP:
         out_text(1,6,"Right Button Released   ",hWnd);

                               /* Get coords button presses at */
         sprintf(coord_string,"At - (%d , %d)      ",
                 LOWORD(lParam),HIWORD(lParam));

                               /* Write coords and key        */
         out_text(32,6,coord_string,hWnd);
         write_control_key(wParam,6,hWnd);
         return 0;

    case WM_DESTROY:
         PostQuitMessage(0);
         return 0;

    default:
         return(DefWindowProc(hWnd,iMessage,wParam,lParam));
    }
  }
```

Notice that the mouse cursor coordinates are converted directly in the statement:

```
sprintf(coord_string,"At - (%d , %d)      ",
        LOWORD(lParam),HIWORD(lParam));
```

When you run the program, if you press the left mouse button, then press the CTRL key, and then release the left mouse button, Figure 23-2 is generated.

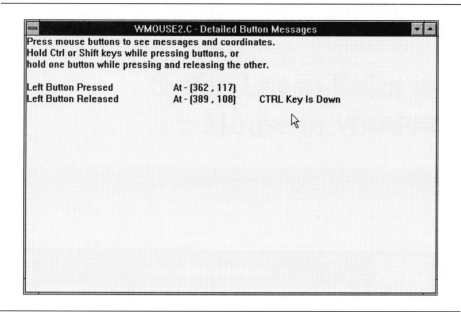

Figure 23-2. *Detailed information in the client area*

Extracting Proper Values

In the previous example, when a left button press is trapped, the value of MK_LBUTTON is subtracted from wParam when it is sent to the function write_control_key(), and when a right button press is trapped, the value of MK_RBUTTON is subtracted from wParam when it is sent to the function write_control_key(). To understand why, take a look at the following constant definitions for the various virtual keys and button-down parameters:

Constant	Value	Meaning
MK_CONTROL	0x0008	Set if CTRL key is down
MK_SHIFT	0x0004	Set if SHIFT key is down
MK_LBUTTON	0x0001	Set if left button is down
MK_RBUTTON	0x0002	Set if right button is down
MK_MBUTTON	0x0010	Set if middle button is down

Suppose your application receives a WM_LBUTTONDOWN message, and you scan for the CTRL key being down, which it is. Since the left button *is* down, Windows *adds* the value of MK_LBUTTON to the value of MK_CONTROL, totalling 0x0009. Next, suppose you use a direct comparisons to determine the additional keys or buttons, as in:

```
if (wParam==MK_CONTROL)
```

This comparison does not work because your application is scanning for a constant of 0x0008, and wParam is 0x0009. Additionally, bitwise comparisons such as the following may contain information you do not want:

```
if (wParam & MK_CONTROL)
```

While this determines the additional parameters correctly, duplicate messages are contained in the value. When the user presses the left button, there's no reason to extract MK_LBUTTON from wParam, because you already know the left button is down. However, MK_LBUTTON is contained in wParam along with MK_CONTROL.

The way to work around both potential pitfalls is to subtract the appropriate values from wParam. In the previous example, when WM_LBUTTONDOWN is trapped, since it is already known that the left button is down, MK_LBUTTON is subtracted from wParam. The same logic is applied when WM_RBUTTONDOWN is trapped, only MK_RBUTTON is subtracted from wParam. You do not need to do this for button releases, because MK_LBUTTON and MK_RBUTTON are only sent when a button is down.

One final note on this—suppose you trap a WM_LBUTTONDOWN message and use a direct comparison such as the following to determine if a virtual key is down:

```
if (wParam==MK_CONTROL)
```

If the user is also holding the right button down and has both the SHIFT and CTRL keys down, the value of wParam equals 0x0F, or the sum of (MK_LBUTTON+ MK_RBUTTON+MK_SHIFT+MK_CONTROL). It is always better to use bitwise logical comparisons to determine additional parameters.

Detailed Information in the Nonclient Area

In the nonclient area, the following values are sent along with a button message.

wParam   wParam specifies the nonclient area where the cursor is located. The possible locations can be any one of the following:

wParam	Nonclient Cursor Location
HTBOTTOM	Lower horizontal border
HTBOTTOMLEFT	Lower-left corner border
HTBOTTOMRIGHT	Lower-right corner border
HTCAPTION	Title bar area
HTERROR	Dividing line/background

wParam	Nonclient Cursor Location
HTGROWBOX	Size box
HTHSCROLL	Horizontal scroll box
HTLEFT	Left border
HTMENU	Menu area
HTREDUCE	Minimize button
HTRIGHT	Right border
HTSYSMENU	System menu
HTTOP	Upper horizontal border
HTTOPLEFT	Upper-left horizontal border
HTTOPRIGHT	Upper-right horizontal border
HTVSCROLL	Vertical scroll bar
HTZOOM	Maximize button

LOWORD (lParam)   LOWORD (lParam) specifies the horizontal position of the cursor in screen coordinates.

HIWORD (lParam)   HIWORD (lParam) specifies the vertical position of the cursor in screen coordinates.

The following example extracts the additional values and writes them to the display. When you run the program, move the cursor in all the nonclient regions. Press the right mouse button when you want the program to inform you of cursor location.

The project file is called WMOUSE3.PRJ. Here it is:

```
WMOUSE3.DEF
WMOUSE3.C
```

The module definition file is called WMOUSE3.DEF:

```
NAME          WMOUSE3
DESCRIPTION   'WMOUSE3.C - Detailed Nonclient Button Messages'
EXETYPE       WINDOWS
STUB          "WINSTUB.EXE"
CODE          PRELOAD MOVEABLE
DATA          PRELOAD MOVEABLE MULTIPLE
HEAPSIZE      1024
STACKSIZE     5120
EXPORTS       MainWndProc @1
```

Here is WMOUSE3.C:

```
/*------------------------------------------------------------*/
/*                        WMOUSE3.C                           */
/*                                                            */
/*   Capturing mouse button messages and detailed in the non-*/
/*   client area.                                             */
/*------------------------------------------------------------*/


#define STRICT               /* Strict 3.1 compliance         */
#include <windows.h>         /* Standard Windows header       */
#include <stdio.h>           /* Need for sprintf prototype    */
#include <string.h>          /* Need for strlen prototype     */


HINSTANCE gInstance;         /* Global instance handle        */

                             /* Function prototype for        */
                             /* MainWndProc().                */
LRESULT FAR PASCAL MainWndProc(HWND hWnd,UINT iMessage,
                        WPARAM wParam,LPARAM lParam);


/* Module : WinMain                                           */
/* ---------------------------------------------------------- */
/* Initializes window and processes message loop.             */
/*                                                            */
int PASCAL WinMain(HINSTANCE hInstance,
                   HINSTANCE hPrevInstance,
                   LPSTR lpszcmdparam,int nCmdShow)
   {
   HWND hWnd;
   MSG Message;
   WNDCLASS WndClass;

   gInstance=hInstance;       /* Assign global instance        */

   if (!hPrevInstance)
      {
      WndClass.cbClsExtra =0;
      WndClass.cbWndExtra =0;
      WndClass.hbrBackground=GetStockObject(WHITE_BRUSH);

                             /* Load Windows default arrow    */
      WndClass.hCursor=LoadCursor(NULL,IDC_ARROW);

      WndClass.hIcon=LoadIcon(NULL,"END");
```

```
    WndClass.hInstance=hInstance;
    WndClass.lpfnWndProc=MainWndProc;
    WndClass.lpszClassName="WMOUSE3";
    WndClass.lpszMenuName=NULL;
    WndClass.style=CS_HREDRAW | CS_VREDRAW | CS_DBLCLKS;
    RegisterClass(&WndClass);
    }


hWnd= CreateWindow("WMOUSE3",              /* Class name       */
                                          /* Caption          */
                "WMOUSE3.C -
                    Detailed Non-Client Button Messages",
                WS_OVERLAPPEDWINDOW, /* Style            */
                CW_USEDEFAULT,       /* Horiz position   */
                0,                   /* Vert position    */
                CW_USEDEFAULT,       /* Width            */
                0,                   /* Height           */
                NULL,                /* Parent window    */
                NULL,                /* Menu             */
                hInstance,           /* Program instanc  */
                NULL);               /* Parameters       */


                        /* If no create, exit           */
    if (hWnd==NULL) return FALSE;

    ShowWindow(hWnd,nCmdShow);/* Make window visible          */
    UpdateWindow(hWnd);

                        /* Message loop                 */
    while(GetMessage(&Message,0,0,0))
        {
        TranslateMessage(&Message);
        DispatchMessage(&Message);
        }
    return Message.wParam;
    }

/* Module : out text                                        */
/*--------------------------------------------------------------*/
/* Outputs a string of text at TEXT coordinates. This is a   */
/* much more natural way to output text. Coords 1,1 represent */
/* the upper-left coordinate of the client area.             */
/*                                                           */
void PASCAL out_text(int x,int y,char *text,HWND hWnd)
    {
```

```
    int x_scale,y_scale;        /* Scaling vars                 */
    HDC TheDC;                   /* Device handle                */
    TEXTMETRIC text_metrics;     /* Text settings                */

    TheDC=GetDC(hWnd);                  /* Get device and text metrics  */
    GetTextMetrics(TheDC,&text_metrics);

                                 /* Figure Y and X coordinates   */
    y_scale=(y-1)*(text_metrics.tmHeight);
    x_scale=(x-1)*(text_metrics.tmAveCharWidth);

                                 /* Output string, release device */
    TextOut(TheDC,x_scale,y_scale,text,strlen(text));
    ReleaseDC(hWnd,TheDC);
    }

/* Module : MainWndProc                                          */
/*-------------------------------------------------------------*/
/* Message processor.                                           */
/*                                                              */
LRESULT FAR PASCAL MainWndProc(HWND hWnd,UINT iMessage,
                                WPARAM wParam,LPARAM lParam)

    {
    char coord_string[80];      /* For coords-string conversn   */
    PAINTSTRUCT ps;             /* Paint structure - init mssg  */

    coord_string[0]=NULL;
    switch(iMessage)
        {
        case WM_PAINT:
            BeginPaint(hWnd,&ps);
            out_text(1,1,"Move mouse cursor to various regions
                        of the non client",hWnd);
            out_text(1,2,"area. Press the right mouse button
                        while in regions to",hWnd);
            out_text(1,3,"view message about location",hWnd);
            EndPaint(hWnd,&ps);
            return 0;

                                 /* Right button down           */
        case WM_NCRBUTTONDOWN:
            out_text(1,5,"Right Button Pressed      ",hWnd);

                                 /* Convert coords              */
            sprintf(coord_string,"At - (%d , %d)      ",
```

```
          LOWORD(lParam),HIWORD(lParam));
out_text(35,6,coord_string,hWnd);

switch(wParam)       /* Where is mouse?                      */
   {
   case HTBOTTOM:
        out_text(1,6,
           "In Lower Horiz Border            ",hWnd);
        break;
   case HTBOTTOMLEFT:
        out_text(1,6,
           "In Lower Left Corner Border      ",hWnd);
        break;
   case HTBOTTOMRIGHT:
        out_text(1,6,
           "In Lower Right Corner Border     ",hWnd);
        break;
   case HTCAPTION:
        out_text(1,6,
           "In Title Bar Area                ",hWnd);
        break;
   case HTERROR:
        out_text(1,6,
           "On Dividing Line/Background      ",hWnd);
        break;
   case HTGROWBOX:
        out_text(1,6,
           "In a Size Box                    ",hWnd);
        break;
   case HTHSCROLL:
        out_text(1,6,
           "In a Horiz Scroll Box            ",hWnd);
        break;
   case HTLEFT:
        out_text(1,6,
           "On Left Border                   ",hWnd);
        break;
   case HTMENU:
        out_text(1,6,
           "In a Menu Area                   ",hWnd);
        break;
   case HTREDUCE:
        out_text(1,6,
           "In a Minimize Button             ",hWnd);
        break;
```

```
              case HTRIGHT:
                   out_text(1,6,
                        "On Right Border                    ",hWnd);
                   break;
              case HTSYSMENU:
                   out_text(1,6,
                        "In a System Menu                   ",hWnd);
                   break;
              case HTTOP:
                   out_text(1,6,
                        "In Upper Horiz Border              ",hWnd);
                   break;
              case HTTOPLEFT:
                   out_text(1,6,
                        "In Upper Left Horiz Border         ",hWnd);
                   break;
              case HTTOPRIGHT:
                   out_text(1,6,
                        "In Upper Right Horiz Border        ",hWnd);
                   break;
              case HTVSCROLL:
                   out_text(1,6,
                        "In a Vertical Scroll Bar           ",hWnd);
                   break;
              case HTZOOM:
                   out_text(1,6,
                        "In a Maximize Button               ",hWnd);
                   break;

              default:
                   out_text(1,6,
                        "                                   ",hWnd);
                   break;
              }
          return 0;

     case WM_DESTROY:
          PostQuitMessage(0);
          return 0;

     default:
          return(DefWindowProc(hWnd,iMessage,wParam,lParam));
     }
}
```

When you run the program, move the cursor into the title area and press the right button. The program writes the message shown in Figure 23-3.

Double-Click Time

Double-click time is the maximum number of milliseconds that can occur between the first and second clicks of a mouse button double-click. If the double-click time is 500 milliseconds, a user must press a button twice within 500 milliseconds for a double-click to be registered by Windows.

In most instances, users set the mouse's double-click time to their own preference using the Windows Control Panel. However, there may be special circumstances where you want to set the time to a new value. You change the double-click time with the Windows function SetDoubleClickTime(), and retrieve the current time with the Windows function GetDoubleClickTime().

The following example creates a window and informs you of the current double-click time. Pressing the left mouse button doubles the time, until the value reaches 2000 milliseconds. At that point, the time is reset to 250 milliseconds. Use the right mouse button to see how the new time affects double-click activity.

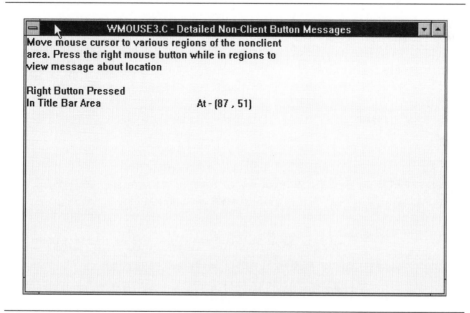

Figure 23-3.   Detailed information in the nonclient area

The project file is called WMOUSE4.PRJ:

```
WMOUSE4.DEF
WMOUSE4.C
```

The module definition file is called WMOUSE4.DEF:

```
NAME          WMOUSE4
DESCRIPTION   'Double-Click Time Functions'
EXETYPE       WINDOWS
STUB          "WINSTUB.EXE"
CODE          PRELOAD MOVEABLE
DATA          PRELOAD MOVEABLE MULTIPLE
HEAPSIZE      1024
STACKSIZE     5120
EXPORTS       MainWndProc @1
```

Here is WMOUSE4.C:

```c
/*----------------------------------------------------------*/
/*                    WMOUSE4.C                             */
/*                                                          */
/*  Double-click time functions.                           */
/*----------------------------------------------------------*/

#define STRICT              /* Strict 3.1 compliance       */
#include <windows.h>        /* Standard Windows header     */
#include <stdio.h>          /* Need for sprintf prototype  */
#include <string.h>         /* Need for strlen prototype   */

HINSTANCE gInstance;        /* Global instance handle      */

                            /* Function prototype for      */
                            /* MainWndProc().              */
LRESULT FAR PASCAL MainWndProc(HWND hWnd,UINT iMessage,
                        WPARAM wParam,LPARAM lParam);

/* Module : WinMain                                         */
/* -------------------------------------------------------- */
/* Initializes window and processes message loop.          */
/*                                                          */
int PASCAL WinMain(HINSTANCE hInstance,
                   HINSTANCE hPrevInstance,
                   LPSTR lpszcmdparam,int nCmdShow)
```

```
{
HWND hWnd;
MSG Message;
WNDCLASS WndClass;

gInstance=hInstance;        /* Assign global instance        */

if (!hPrevInstance)
    {
    WndClass.cbClsExtra =0;
    WndClass.cbWndExtra =0;
    WndClass.hbrBackground=GetStockObject(WHITE_BRUSH);

                            /* Load Windows default arrow     */
    WndClass.hCursor=LoadCursor(NULL,IDC_ARROW);

    WndClass.hIcon=LoadIcon(NULL,"END");
    WndClass.hInstance=hInstance;
    WndClass.lpfnWndProc=MainWndProc;
    WndClass.lpszClassName="WMOUSE4";
    WndClass.lpszMenuName=NULL;

                            /* Enable double-clicks           */
    WndClass.style=CS_HREDRAW | CS_VREDRAW | CS_DBLCLKS;
    RegisterClass(&WndClass);
    }

hWnd= CreateWindow("WMOUSE4",              /* Class name      */
                                           /* Caption         */
                "WMOUSE4.C - Double-Click Time Functions",
                WS_OVERLAPPEDWINDOW, /* Style                 */
                CW_USEDEFAULT,       /* Horiz position        */
                0,                   /* Vert position         */
                CW_USEDEFAULT,       /* Width                 */
                0,                   /* Height                */
                NULL,                /* Parent window         */
                NULL,                /* Menu                  */
                hInstance,           /* Program instanc       */
                NULL);               /* Parameters            */

                            /* If no create, exit             */
if (hWnd==NULL) return FALSE;

ShowWindow(hWnd,nCmdShow);/* Make window visible              */
UpdateWindow(hWnd);
```

```
                                    /* Message loop              */
    while(GetMessage(&Message,0,0,0))
        {
        TranslateMessage(&Message);
        DispatchMessage(&Message);
        }
    return Message.wParam;
    }


/* Module : out text                                         */
/*---------------------------------------------------------------*/
/* Outputs a string of text at TEXT coordinates. This is a    */
/* much more natural way to output text. Coords 1,1 represent */
/* the upper-left coordinate of the client area.              */
/*                                                            */
void PASCAL out_text(int x,int y,char *text,HWND hWnd)
    {
    int x_scale,y_scale;     /* Scaling vars               */
    HDC TheDC;               /* Device handle              */
    TEXTMETRIC text_metrics; /* Text settings              */

    TheDC=GetDC(hWnd);          /* Get device and text metrics   */
    GetTextMetrics(TheDC,&text_metrics);

                                /* Figure Y and X coordinates    */
    y_scale=(y-1)*(text_metrics.tmHeight);
    x_scale=(x-1)*(text_metrics.tmAveCharWidth);

                                /* Output string, release device */
    TextOut(TheDC,x_scale,y_scale,text,strlen(text));
    ReleaseDC(hWnd,TheDC);
    }

/* Module : MainWndProc                                      */
/*---------------------------------------------------------------*/
/* Message processor.                                        */
/*                                                           */
LRESULT FAR PASCAL MainWndProc(HWND hWnd,UINT iMessage,
                               WPARAM wParam,LPARAM lParam)
    {
    char coord_string[80];       /* For text string          */
    static int old_dblclk_time;  /* Orig DBLCLK time          */
    int new_dblclk_time;         /* New DBLCLK time           */
    PAINTSTRUCT ps;              /* Paint structure - init mssg  */
```

```
switch(iMessage)
    {
    case WM_CREATE:          /* Trap CREATE message        */
                             /* Get orig DBLCLK time       */
        old_dblclk_time=GetDoubleClickTime();
        return 0;

    case WM_PAINT:
        BeginPaint(hWnd,&ps);
        out_text(1,1,"Demonstration of setting the double
                    click speed.",hWnd);
        out_text(1,2,"Press the left mouse button to increase
                    delay time.",hWnd);
        out_text(1,3,"Double click with the right mouse
                    button. Notice the",hWnd);
        out_text(1,4,"amount of pause available between
                    clicks grows as the",hWnd);
        out_text(1,5,"time gets larger.",hWnd);
        EndPaint(hWnd,&ps);
        return 0;


    case WM_SIZE:            /* Trap for init write        */
                            /* Get DBLCLK Time             */
        new_dblclk_time=GetDoubleClickTime();


                            /* Convert coords to string    */
        sprintf(coord_string,
            "Orig Clk Time - %d, New Clk Time - %d    ",
            old_dblclk_time,new_dblclk_time);


                            /* Output coords               */
       out_text(1,7,coord_string,hWnd);
        return 0;

    case WM_LBUTTONDOWN:
                            /* Get double-click time       */
        new_dblclk_time=(GetDoubleClickTime() * 2);


                            /* Less than 2000?             */
        if (new_dblclk_time>2000) new_dblclk_time=250;


                            /* Set time                    */
        SetDoubleClickTime(new_dblclk_time);
```

```
                              /* Convert coords              */
              sprintf(coord_string,
                     "Orig Clk Time - %d, New Clk Time - %d    ",
                     old_dblclk_time,new_dblclk_time);

                               /* Output coords              */
              out_text(1,7,coord_string,hWnd);
              return 0;

     case WM_RBUTTONDBLCLK: /* Right button double-click     */
              out_text(1,9,
                     "Right Button Double Clicked         ",hWnd);
              return 0;

     case WM_RBUTTONDOWN:
              out_text(1,9,
                     "Right Button Pressed                ",hWnd);
              return 0;

     case WM_DESTROY:
                                /* Set time back to previous     */
              SetDoubleClickTime(old_dblclk_time);
              PostQuitMessage(0);
              return 0;

     default:
              return(DefWindowProc(hWnd,iMessage,wParam,lParam));
     }
  }
```

Figure 23-4 illustrates the double-click time set to 1000 milliseconds.

Notice when the window is destroyed, the double-click time is reset to its initial value. The double-click time is shared with all other Windows applications, and changing it inside your application changes it throughout the entire system. You should always reset the double-click time to its initial value upon program termination (unless it is your intent to set the speed globally).

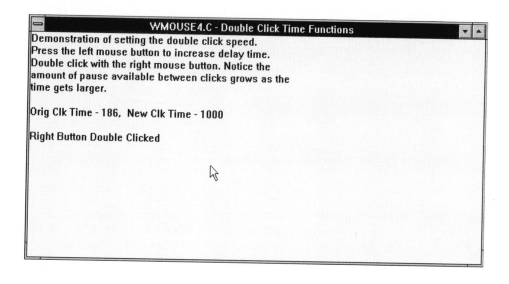

Figure 23-4.   *Setting the double-click time*

Chapter 24

Changing the Windows Cursor

Now for some real fun. As with DOS-based applications, the ability to change the shape of the cursor is one of the most useful functions available. It gives you a mechanism to convey information to users *visually*, such as using an hourglass cursor to inform users that the system is currently busy. Windows allows you to change the cursor using four possible methods:

- Using the standard Windows cursors, which are part of Windows

- Using resource cursors you create at development time, outside of the application

- Using device-dependent dynamic cursors created within the application

- Using device-independent dynamic cursors created within the application

In Windows, even though you can move cursors with the mouse, they are not called mouse cursors, but simply cursors. This is because most standard Windows cursors are system cursors (sizing arrows, hourglass, and so on), and Windows utilizes them whether a mouse is present or not.

The Standard Windows Cursors

When a Windows application is initialized, you inform Windows of the default cursor used in the application's client area. So far you have been loading the default cursor with the following statement:

```
                    /* Load default Windows arrow      */
WndClass.hCursor=LoadCursor(NULL,IDC_ARROW);
```

Setting the Default Registered Cursor

With Windows, you can set the cursor to be any one of the standard Windows cursors at startup by loading the desired cursor when the window is registered. This cursor is then used by Windows as the default client-area cursor, which means that when a user moves the cursor from the nonclient area to the client area, Windows loads the specified cursor. Usually, you'll want to use the standard arrow when the window is created and as the client-area cursor, but there may be circumstances when using a different cursor is appropriate.

To demonstrate loading other standard Windows cursors as the default registered cursor, make the following changes to GENERIC.C, which you created in Chapter 22, or any other previous Windows programming example.

Change

```
WndClass.hCursor=LoadCursor(NULL,IDC_ARROW)
```

to

```
WndClass.hCursor=LoadCursor(NULL,IDC_SIZE);
```

This loads the Windows north-south-east-west arrow cursor. Recompile the application and run it. You should see the cursor shape illustrated in Figure 24-1.

The possible Windows cursors you can load in this manner are illustrated in Figure 24-2. Go ahead and experiment a little—try out the cursor variety.

 You can also load a resource cursor as the default registered cursor.

Loading Windows Cursors on the Fly

Suppose you want to change the cursor to any standard Windows cursor on the fly, within the application. To do this you must inform Windows that you control the cursor inside the client area. It then becomes your responsibility to load the cursor(s) when needed.

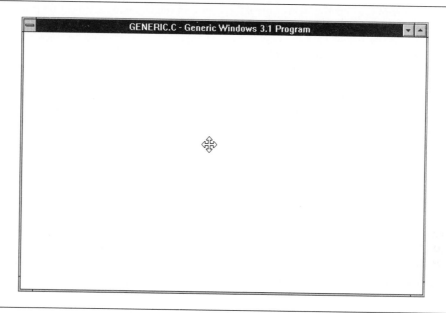

Figure 24-1. *The Windows north-south-east-west arrow cursor*

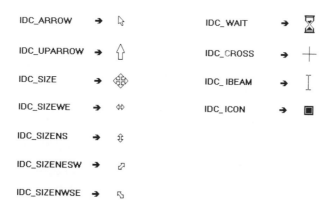

Figure 24-2. *The default Windows cursors*

To inform Windows that you control the cursor in the client area, simply do not load a default cursor. Instead, pass a NULL value to WndClass.hCursor, as in the following:

```
WndClass.hCursor=NULL;
```

After the application has been initialized and made active, simply load the standard Windows cursor you desire using the Windows functions LoadCursor() and SetCursor().

The following example allows you to cycle through all standard Windows cursors by pressing the left mouse button. When you run the program, notice that Windows still takes care of changing the cursors in the nonclient areas.

The project file is called WMOUSE5.PRJ. Here it is:

```
WMOUSE5.DEF
WMOUSE5.C
```

The module definition file, shown here, is called WMOUSE5.DEF:

```
NAME          WMOUSE5
DESCRIPTION   'Changing Default Cursor Shapes'
EXETYPE       WINDOWS
STUB          "WINSTUB.EXE"
CODE          PRELOAD MOVEABLE
DATA          PRELOAD MOVEABLE MULTIPLE
HEAPSIZE      1024
STACKSIZE     5120
EXPORTS       MainWndProc @1
```

Here is WMOUSE5.C:

```
/*-----------------------------------------------------------*/
/*                    WMOUSE5.C                              */
/*                                                          */
/* Loading and using default Windows cursors.               */
/*-----------------------------------------------------------*/

#define STRICT              /* Strict 3.1 compliance          */
#include <windows.h>        /* Standard Windows header        */

HINSTANCE gInstance;        /* Global instance handle         */

                            /* Function prototype for         */
                            /* MainWndProc().                 */
```

```
LRESULT FAR PASCAL MainWndProc(HWND hWnd,UINT iMessage,
                               WPARAM wParam,LPARAM lParam);


/* Module : WinMain                                         */
/* ---------------------------------------------------------*/
/* Initializes window and processes message loop.           */
/*                                                          */
int PASCAL WinMain(HINSTANCE hInstance,
                   HINSTANCE hPrevInstance,
                   LPSTR lpszcmdparam,int nCmdShow)
    {
    HWND hWnd;
    MSG Message;
    WNDCLASS WndClass;

    gInstance=hInstance;        /* Assign global instance        */

    if (!hPrevInstance)
        {
        WndClass.cbClsExtra =0;
        WndClass.cbWndExtra =0;
        WndClass.hbrBackground=GetStockObject(WHITE_BRUSH);

                            /* Notice the NULL statement!!!  */
                            /* Tells Windows you are in       */
                            /* control inside client area.    */
        WndClass.hCursor=NULL;

        WndClass.hIcon=LoadIcon(NULL,"END");
        WndClass.hInstance=hInstance;
        WndClass.lpfnWndProc=MainWndProc;
        WndClass.lpszClassName="WMOUSE5";
        WndClass.lpszMenuName=NULL;
        WndClass.style=CS_HREDRAW | CS_VREDRAW;
        RegisterClass(&WndClass);
        }

hWnd= CreateWindow("WMOUSE5",               /* Class name      */
                                            /* Caption         */
                    "WMOUSE5.C - Changing Default Cursor Shapes",
                    WS_OVERLAPPEDWINDOW,  /* Style          */
                    CW_USEDEFAULT,        /* Horiz position */
                    0,                    /* Vert position  */
                    CW_USEDEFAULT,        /* Width          */
                    0,                    /* Height         */
```

```
                    NULL,                   /* Parent window  */
                    NULL,                   /* Menu           */
                    hInstance,              /* Program instanc*/
                    NULL);                  /* Parameters     */

                            /* If no create, exit            */
    if (hWnd==NULL) return FALSE;

    ShowWindow(hWnd,nCmdShow);/* Make window visible          */
    UpdateWindow(hWnd);

                            /* Message loop                  */
    while(GetMessage(&Message,0,0,0))
        {
        TranslateMessage(&Message);
        DispatchMessage(&Message);
        }
    return Message.wParam;
    }

/* Module : get new cursor                                    */
/*----------------------------------------------------------*/
/* Get new cursor shape based on number.                      */
/*                                                            */
void PASCAL get_new_cursor(int number,HCURSOR *new_cursor)
    {
                            /* Change default cursor based    */
    switch(number)          /* on number.                     */
        {
        case  1:*new_cursor=LoadCursor(NULL,IDC_ARROW);    break;
        case  2:*new_cursor=LoadCursor(NULL,IDC_UPARROW);  break;
        case  3:*new_cursor=LoadCursor(NULL,IDC_CROSS);    break;
        case  4:*new_cursor=LoadCursor(NULL,IDC_IBEAM);    break;
        case  5:*new_cursor=LoadCursor(NULL,IDC_ICON);     break;
        case  6:*new_cursor=LoadCursor(NULL,IDC_SIZE);     break;
        case  7:*new_cursor=LoadCursor(NULL,IDC_SIZENESW);break;
        case  8:*new_cursor=LoadCursor(NULL,IDC_SIZENS);   break;
        case  9:*new_cursor=LoadCursor(NULL,IDC_SIZENWSE);break;
        case 10:*new_cursor=LoadCursor(NULL,IDC_SIZEWE);   break;
        case 11:*new_cursor=LoadCursor(NULL,IDC_WAIT);     break;
        }
    SetCursor(*new_cursor);
    }

/* Module : MainWndProc                                       */
/*----------------------------------------------------------*/
```

```
/* Message processor.                                          */
/*                                                             */
LRESULT FAR PASCAL MainWndProc(HWND hWnd,UINT iMessage,
                    WPARAM wParam,LPARAM lParam)
   {
   static HCURSOR new_cursor;/* New cursor in application      */
   static cursor_num=1;      /* Cursor count, start at 1       */
   PAINTSTRUCT ps;           /* Paint structure - init mssg    */
   HDC TheDC;                /* Device handle                  */

   switch(iMessage)
      {
      case WM_PAINT:
           BeginPaint(hWnd,&ps);
           TheDC=GetDC(hWnd);
           TextOut(TheDC,1,1,"Press Left Mouse Button To Change",
                   33);
           TextOut(TheDC,1,20,"Default Cursor Shape.",20);
           ReleaseDC(hWnd,TheDC);
           EndPaint(hWnd,&ps);
           return 0;

      case WM_MOUSEMOVE:     /* Trap MouseMove mssg            */
                             /* Grab current cursor            */
           get_new_cursor(cursor_num,&new_cursor);
           return 0;

      case WM_LBUTTONDOWN:   /* Trap left button down          */
           ++cursor_num;     /* Incr cursor numb, check max    */
           if (cursor_num>11) cursor_num=1;

                             /* Now get NEW cursor             */
           get_new_cursor(cursor_num,&new_cursor);
           return 0;

      case WM_DESTROY:
           PostQuitMessage(0);
           return 0;

      default:
           return(DefWindowProc(hWnd,iMessage,wParam,lParam));


      }

   }
```

In WMOUSE5.C, you might wonder why the current cursor is loaded every time a WM_MOUSEMOVE message is trapped. This is because of the way the cursor is managed in Windows.

WM_MOUSEMOVE

In Windows, the message WM_MOUSEMOVE is sent to an application whenever mouse movement is detected in the client area, and when the application becomes active.

When you use a cursor other than a default registered cursor, you must load it every time a WM_MOUSEMOVE message is sent by Windows. This is because when a user moves the cursor into the nonclient area, Windows automatically changes the cursor to a new cursor (sizing, arrow, and the like), depending on where the cursor is located. When the user moves the cursor back into the client area, Windows does not automatically change the cursor to the client-area cursor, because no cursor has been registered as the default cursor. Therefore, you must change it back to the client-area cursor manually. This does not cause any cursor flicker in the client area, because if the cursor you are setting is the same as the cursor currently in use, no internal action is taken by Windows.

So now you're wondering why you cannot register a default cursor upon program initialization. The reason is that if you do, Windows tries to load that cursor whenever the mouse is moved within the client area, *whether you load a different cursor later in the application or not.* The net effect is that Windows loads the default registered cursor, and your application loads the new cursor, *every time* the mouse is moved. This results in constant flicker and annoying "ghost" cursors. The only way to stop Windows from loading the default registered cursor is to not have a default registered cursor. You can verify this by changing the line the following line in WMOUSE5.C.

Change

```
WndClass.hCursor=NULL;
```

to

```
WndClass.hCursor=LoadCursor(NULL,IDC_ARROW);
```

Recompile it and run it. The effects are clearly visible.

WM_SETCURSOR

In situations where you want to manage the cursor in the nonclient area, instead of Windows, you trap the message WM_SETCURSOR instead of WM_MOUSEMOVE, and handle all cursor changes in the nonclient area. This requires checking the low word value of lParam and acting upon the value appropriately. Windows still manages the sizing functions and system menu, but does not manage the cursor changes.

When you trap the message WM_SETCURSOR, further cursor processing halts, and Windows does not try to load the default registered cursor in the client area automatically. Therefore, if you load a new Windows cursor later in the application, it is not necessary to load the cursor continuously when the mouse moves. Additionally, you can register a default cursor at program initialization.

The following example operates exactly as the previous example, but instead of trapping WM_MOUSEMOVE, the message WM_SETCURSOR is trapped instead, and the cursor is managed manually within the nonclient area.

The project file is called WMOUSE6.PRJ. Here it is:

```
WMOUSE6.DEF
WMOUSE6.C
```

The module definition file is called WMOUSE6.DEF:

```
NAME          WMOUSE6
DESCRIPTION   'Managing Default Windows Cursors'
EXETYPE       WINDOWS
STUB          "WINSTUB.EXE"
CODE          PRELOAD MOVEABLE
DATA          PRELOAD MOVEABLE MULTIPLE
HEAPSIZE      1024
STACKSIZE     5120
EXPORTS       MainWndProc @1
```

Here is WMOUSE6.C:

```
/*-------------------------------------------------------------*/
/*                    WMOUSE6.C                         */
/*                                                     */
/*  Managaing default Windows cursors in nonclient area.   */
/*-------------------------------------------------------------*/
#define STRICT            /* Strict 3.1 compliance        */
#include <windows.h>      /* Standard Windows header      */

HINSTANCE gInstance;      /* Global instance handle       */

                          /* Function prototype for       */
                          /* MainWndProc().               */
LRESULT FAR PASCAL MainWndProc(HWND hWnd,UINT iMessage,
                   WPARAM wParam,LPARAM lParam);
```

```
/* Module : WinMain                                         */
/* --------------------------------------------------------*/
/* Initializes window and processes message loop.           */
/*                                                          */
int PASCAL WinMain(HINSTANCE hInstance,
                   HINSTANCE hPrevInstance,
                   LPSTR lpszcmdparam,int nCmdShow)
    {
    HWND hWnd;
    MSG Message;
    WNDCLASS WndClass;

    gInstance=hInstance;        /* Assign global instance       */

    if (!hPrevInstance)
        {
        WndClass.cbClsExtra =0;
        WndClass.cbWndExtra =0;
        WndClass.hbrBackground=GetStockObject(WHITE_BRUSH);

                                /* Load Windows default arrow   */
        WndClass.hCursor=LoadCursor(NULL,IDC_ARROW);

        WndClass.hIcon=LoadIcon(NULL,"END");
        WndClass.hInstance=hInstance;
        WndClass.lpfnWndProc=MainWndProc;
        WndClass.lpszClassName="WMOUSE6";
        WndClass.lpszMenuName=NULL;
        WndClass.style=CS_HREDRAW | CS_VREDRAW;
        RegisterClass(&WndClass);
        }

    hWnd= CreateWindow("WMOUSE6",            /* Class name      */
                                             /* Caption         */
                    "WMOUSE6.C - Managing Windows Default
                     Cursors",
                    WS_OVERLAPPEDWINDOW,     /* Style           */
                    CW_USEDEFAULT,           /* Horiz position */
                    0,                       /* Vert position  */
                    CW_USEDEFAULT,           /* Width           */
                    0,                       /* Height          */
                    NULL,                    /* Parent window  */
                    NULL,                    /* Menu            */
                    hInstance,               /* Program instanc*/
```

```
                NULL);                      /* Parameters      */

                           /* If no create, exit           */
   if (hWnd==NULL) return FALSE;

   ShowWindow(hWnd,nCmdShow);/* Make window visible          */
   UpdateWindow(hWnd);

                           /* Message loop                 */
   while(GetMessage(&Message,0,0,0))
      {
      TranslateMessage(&Message);
      DispatchMessage(&Message);
      }
   return Message.wParam;
   }


/* Module : get new cursor                                  */
/*--------------------------------------------------------*/
/* Get new cursor shape based on number.                   */
/*                                                         */
void PASCAL get_new_cursor(int number,HCURSOR *new_cursor)
   {
                           /* Change default cursor based   */
   switch(number)          /* on number.                    */
      {
      case  1:*new_cursor=LoadCursor(NULL,IDC_ARROW);    break;
      case  2:*new_cursor=LoadCursor(NULL,IDC_UPARROW);  break;
      case  3:*new_cursor=LoadCursor(NULL,IDC_CROSS);    break;
      case  4:*new_cursor=LoadCursor(NULL,IDC_IBEAM);    break;
      case  5:*new_cursor=LoadCursor(NULL,IDC_ICON);     break;
      case  6:*new_cursor=LoadCursor(NULL,IDC_SIZE);     break;
      case  7:*new_cursor=LoadCursor(NULL,IDC_SIZENESW); break;
      case  8:*new_cursor=LoadCursor(NULL,IDC_SIZENS);   break;
      case  9:*new_cursor=LoadCursor(NULL,IDC_SIZENWSE); break;
      case 10:*new_cursor=LoadCursor(NULL,IDC_SIZEWE);   break;
      case 11:*new_cursor=LoadCursor(NULL,IDC_WAIT);     break;
      }
   SetCursor(*new_cursor);
   }
```

```
/* Module : MainWndProc                                    */
/*--------------------------------------------------------*/
/* Message processor.                                      */
/*                                                         */
LRESULT FAR PASCAL MainWndProc(HWND hWnd,UINT iMessage,
                   WPARAM wParam,LPARAM lParam)
   {
   static HCURSOR new_cursor;/* New cursor in application   */
   static cursor_num=1;      /* Cursor count, start at 1    */
   PAINTSTRUCT ps;           /* Paint structure - init mssg */
   HDC TheDC;                /* Device handle               */

   switch(iMessage)
      {
      case WM_PAINT:
            BeginPaint(hWnd,&ps);
            TheDC=GetDC(hWnd);
            TextOut(TheDC,1, 1,"Move mouse around in nonclient
                               areas.       ",45);
            TextOut(TheDC,1,15,"Nonclient cursor changed
                                within application. ",45);
            TextOut(TheDC,1,30,"Press left mouse button to
                                change default      ",45);
            TextOut(TheDC,1,45,"cursor shape in the client
                                area.            ",45);
            ReleaseDC(hWnd,TheDC);
            EndPaint(hWnd,&ps);
            return 0;
                            /* Trap SetCursor; you control  */
         case WM_SETCURSOR:  /* the cursor in nonclient area. */

                            /* Where is mouse?              */
            switch(LOWORD(lParam))
               {
                            /* Client area - user's choice  */
               case HTCLIENT:
                  get_new_cursor(cursor_num,&new_cursor);
                  break;
                            /* Bottom border   -IDC_SIZENS  */
               case HTBOTTOM:
                  get_new_cursor(8,&new_cursor);
                  break;
                            /* Bottom-left crnr- IDC_SIZENESW*/
```

```
case HTBOTTOMLEFT:
     get_new_cursor(7,&new_cursor);
     break;
               /* Bottom-right crnr-IDC_SIZENWSE*/
case HTBOTTOMRIGHT:
     get_new_cursor(9,&new_cursor);
     break;
               /* Title area      -IDC_ARROW    */
case HTCAPTION:
     get_new_cursor(1,&new_cursor);
     break;
               /* Horizontal scroll-IDC_ARROW   */
case HTHSCROLL:
     get_new_cursor(1,&new_cursor);
     break;
               /* Left border     -IDC_SIZEWE   */
case HTLEFT:
     get_new_cursor(10,&new_cursor);
     break;
               /* User menu       -IDC_ARROW    */
case HTMENU:
     get_new_cursor(1,&new_cursor);
     break;
               /* Minimize button -IDC_ARROW    */
case HTREDUCE:
     get_new_cursor(1,&new_cursor);
     break;
               /* Right border    -IDC_SIZEWE   */
case HTRIGHT:
     get_new_cursor(10,&new_cursor);
     break;
               /* System menu     -IDC_ARROW    */
case HTSYSMENU:
     get_new_cursor(1,&new_cursor);
     break;
               /* Top border      -IDC_SIZENS   */
case HTTOP:
     get_new_cursor(8,&new_cursor);
     break;
               /* Top-left border -IDC_SIZENWSE*/
case HTTOPLEFT:
     get_new_cursor(9,&new_cursor);
     break;
               /* Top-right border -IDC_SIZENESW*/
```

```
             case HTTOPRIGHT:
                  get_new_cursor(7,&new_cursor);
                  break;
                                /* Vertical scroll  -IDC_ARROW   */
             case HTVSCROLL:
                  get_new_cursor(1,&new_cursor);
                  break;
                                /* Maximize button  -IDC_ARROW   */
             case HTZOOM:
                  get_new_cursor(1,&new_cursor);
                  break;
             }
          return 0;

    case WM_LBUTTONDOWN:    /* Trap left button down        */
         ++cursor_num;      /* Incr cursor number, check max */
         if (cursor_num>11) cursor_num=1;

                                /* Now get NEW cursor          */
         get_new_cursor(cursor_num,&new_cursor);
         return 0;

    case WM_DESTROY:
         PostQuitMessage(0);
         return 0;

    default:
         return(DefWindowProc(hWnd,iMessage,wParam,lParam));
    }
}
```

Creating and Using Your Own Cursors

The previous examples demonstrated using the cursors supplied with Windows. However, you are not limited to using only these cursors—quite the contrary. In Windows, you can create your own cursors, and they can be any shape you desire. There are two methods available to create your own cursors in Windows:

- Create a cursor resource file.
- Create a dynamic cursor inside the application, very similar to setting the cursor shape in DOS-based applications.

If you are unfamiliar with resources and how to create them, please consult the manuals supplied with your compiler. Both the Borland and Microsoft compilers are bundled with resource management utilities. This book is not intended as a tutorial on resources, as that would constitute a book in itself.

Resource Cursors

The following example uses a cursor resource file created with the Resource Workshop (supplied with Borland compilers), and has two individual cursors defined. One cursor is called BIGARROW, and the other is called WAND1. Both cursors are in the resource file CURSORS.RES, which is included on the companion disk supplied with this book. CURSORS.RES must be in the same directory you are compiling in (unless you modify the project file).

The BIGARROW cursor shape looks like this:

The resource script file for BIGARROW is as follows:

```
BIGARROW CURSOR
BEGIN
    '00 00 02 00 01 00 20 20 02 00 00 00 00 00 30 01'
    '00 00 16 00 00 00 28 00 00 00 20 00 00 00 40 00'
    '00 00 01 00 01 00 00 00 00 00 00 02 00 00 00 00'
    '00 00 00 00 00 00 00 00 00 00 00 00 00 00 00 00'
    '00 00 FF FF FF 00 00 00 00 00 00 7F FF 00 00 40'
    '01 00 00 40 01 00 00 40 01 00 00 40 01 00 00 40'
    '01 00 00 40 01 00 00 40 01 00 00 40 01 00 00 40'
    '01 00 00 40 01 00 00 40 01 00 00 40 01 00 00 40'
    '01 00 00 40 01 00 1F C0 01 FC 08 00 00 08 04 00'
    '00 10 02 00 00 20 01 00 00 40 00 80 00 80 00 40'
    '01 00 00 20 02 00 00 10 04 00 00 08 08 00 00 04'
    '10 00 00 02 20 00 00 01 40 00 00 00 80 00 00 00'
    '00 00 00 00 00 00 FF 00 00 7F FF 00 00 7F FF 00'
    '00 7F FF 00 00 7F FF 00 00 7F FF 00 00 7F FF 00'
    '00 7F FF 00 00 7F FF 00 00 7F FF 00 00 7F FF 00'
    '00 7F FF 00 00 7F FF 00 00 7F FF 00 00 7F FF 00'
    '00 7F 00 00 00 00 80 00 00 00 C0 00 00 01 E0 00'
    '00 03 F0 00 00 07 F8 00 00 0F FC 00 00 1F FE 00'
    '00 3F FF 00 00 7F FF 80 00 FF FF C0 01 FF FF E0'
    '03 FF FF F0 07 FF FF F8 0F FF FF FC 1F FF FF FE'
    '3F FF FF FF 7F FF'
END
```

The WAND1 cursor looks like this:

The resource script file for WAND1 is as follows:

```
WAND1 CURSOR
BEGIN
    '00 00 02 00 01 00 20 20 02 00 00 00 00 00 30 01'
    '00 00 16 00 00 00 28 00 00 00 20 00 00 00 40 00'
    '00 00 01 00 01 00 00 00 00 00 00 02 00 00 00 00'
    '00 00 00 00 00 00 00 00 00 00 00 00 00 00 00 00'
    '00 00 FF FF FF 00 00 00 00 00 00 00 00 00 00 00'
    '00 00 00 00 00 00 00 00 00 00 00 00 80 00 00 00'
    '80 00 00 00 80 00 00 00 80 00 00 01 C0 00 00 01'
    'C0 00 00 01 C0 00 00 01 C0 00 00 03 E0 00 00 03'
    'E0 00 00 03 E0 00 00 00 00 00 00 00 00 00 00 3F'
    'FC 00 00 40 02 00 00 40 02 00 00 3F FC 00 00 00'
    '00 00 00 00 00 00 00 01 80 00 00 01 80 00 00 01'
    '80 00 00 01 80 00 00 00 00 00 00 00 00 00 00 00'
    '00 00 00 00 00 00 FF FF FF FF FF FF FF FF FF FF'
    '7F FF FF FF 7F FF FF FF 7F FF FF FE 3F FF FF FE'
    '3F FF FF FE 3F FF FF FE 3F FF FF FC 1F FF FF FC'
    '1F FF FF FC 1F FF FF FC 1F FF FF F8 0F FF FF F8'
    '0F FF FF F8 0F FF FF F0 0F FF FF 80 01 FF FF 00'
    '00 FF FF 00 00 FF FF 00 00 FF FF 00 00 FF FF 80'
    '01 FF FF F0 0F FF FF FC 3F FF FF FC 3F FF FF FC'
    '3F FF FF FC 3F FF FF FE 7F FF FF FF FF FF FF FF'
    'FF FF FF FF FF FF'
END
```

The project file for the Windows application must include the resource file along with the module definition and C source file.

The project file is called WMOUSE7.PRJ. Here it is:

```
CURSORS.RES
WMOUSE7.DEF
WMOUSE7.C
```

The module definition file is called **WMOUSE7.DEF**:

```
NAME        WMOUSE7
DESCRIPTION 'Loading Resource Cursors'
```

```
EXETYPE      WINDOWS
STUB         "WINSTUB.EXE"
CODE         PRELOAD MOVEABLE
DATA         PRELOAD MOVEABLE MULTIPLE
HEAPSIZE     1024
STACKSIZE    5120
EXPORTS      MainWndProc @1
```

Here is WMOUSE7.C:

```
/*-------------------------------------------------------------*/
/*                        WMOUSE7.C                            */
/*                                                             */
/*  Loading resource cursors.                                  */
/*  Note: Need the file "CURSORS.RES" in WMOUSE7.PRJ,          */
/*        project file.                                        */
/*-------------------------------------------------------------*/

#define STRICT              /* Strict 3.1 compliance           */
#include <windows.h>        /* Standard Windows header         */

HINSTANCE gInstance;        /* Global instance handle          */

static HCURSOR WAND1,BIGARROW;

                            /* Function protype for            */
                            /* MainWndProc().                  */
LRESULT FAR PASCAL MainWndProc(HWND hWnd,UINT iMessage,
                       WPARAM wParam,LPARAM lParam);

/* Module : WinMain                                            */
/* ----------------------------------------------------------- */
/* Initializes window and processes message loop.              */
/*                                                             */
int PASCAL WinMain(HINSTANCE hInstance,
               HINSTANCE hPrevInstance,
               LPSTR lpszcmdparam,int nCmdShow)
   {
   HWND hWnd;
   MSG Message;
   WNDCLASS WndClass;

   gInstance=hInstance;     /* Assign global instance          */
```

```c
if (!hPrevInstance)
   {
   WndClass.cbClsExtra =0;
   WndClass.cbWndExtra =0;
   WndClass.hbrBackground=GetStockObject(WHITE_BRUSH);

                           /* Notice the NULL statement!!!  */
                           /* Tells Windows you are in      */
                           /* control inside client area.   */
   WndClass.hCursor=NULL;
   WndClass.hIcon=LoadIcon(NULL,"END");
   WndClass.hInstance=hInstance;
   WndClass.lpfnWndProc=MainWndProc;
   WndClass.lpszClassName="WMOUSE7";
   WndClass.lpszMenuName=NULL;
   WndClass.style=CS_HREDRAW | CS_VREDRAW | CS_DBLCLKS;
   RegisterClass(&WndClass);
   }
                           /* Notice!!                      */
                           /* Load cursors now!             */
WAND1=LoadCursor(hInstance,"WAND1");
BIGARROW=LoadCursor(hInstance,"BIGARROW");

hWnd= CreateWindow("WMOUSE7",            /* Class name      */
                                         /* Caption         */
               "WMOUSE7.C - Loading Resource Cursors",
               WS_OVERLAPPEDWINDOW,  /* Style           */
               CW_USEDEFAULT,        /* Horiz position  */
               0,                    /* Vert position   */
               CW_USEDEFAULT,        /* Width           */
               0,                    /* Height          */
               NULL,                 /* Parent window   */
               NULL,                 /* Menu            */
               hInstance,            /* Program instanc */
               NULL);                /* Parameters      */

                           /* If no create, exit            */
if (hWnd==NULL) return FALSE;

ShowWindow(hWnd,nCmdShow);/* Make window visible           */
UpdateWindow(hWnd);

                           /* Message loop                  */
while(GetMessage(&Message,0,0,0))
   {
```

```
        TranslateMessage(&Message);
        DispatchMessage(&Message);
        }
    return Message.wParam;
    }


/* Module : get new cursor                                   */
/*-----------------------------------------------------------*/
/* Get new cursor shape based on number.                     */
/*                                                           */
void PASCAL get_new_cursor(int number,HCURSOR *new_cursor)
    {
    switch(number)              /* Change cursor based on number */
        {
        case  1:new_cursor=&WAND1;break;
        case  2:new_cursor=&BIGARROW;break;
        }
    SetCursor(*new_cursor);
    }


/* Module : MainWndProc                                      */
/*-----------------------------------------------------------*/
/* Message processor.                                        */
/*                                                           */
LRESULT FAR PASCAL MainWndProc(HWND hWnd,UINT iMessage,
                               WPARAM wParam,LPARAM lParam)
    {
    static HCURSOR *new_cursor;    /* Pointer to cursor        */
    static cursor_num=1;           /* Cursor count, start at 1 */
    PAINTSTRUCT ps;                /* Paint structure - init mssg */
    HDC TheDC;                     /* Device handle            */

    switch(iMessage)
        {
        case WM_PAINT:
            BeginPaint(hWnd,&ps);
            TheDC=GetDC(hWnd);
            TextOut(TheDC,1,1,"Press left mouse button to change",
                    33);
            TextOut(TheDC,1,15,"resource cursors.",16);
            ReleaseDC(hWnd,TheDC);
            EndPaint(hWnd,&ps);
            return 0;

        case WM_MOUSEMOVE:       /* Grab current cursor        */
```

```
        get_new_cursor(cursor_num,new_cursor);
        return 0;

case WM_LBUTTONDOWN:
        ++cursor_num;      /* Incr cursor number, check max */
        if (cursor_num>2) cursor_num=1;

                            /* Now get NEW cursor            */
        get_new_cursor(cursor_num,new_cursor);
        return 0;

case WM_DESTROY:           /* Must destroy cursors!         */
        DestroyCursor(WAND1);
        DestroyCursor(BIGARROW);
        PostQuitMessage(0);
        return 0;

default:
        return(DefWindowProc(hWnd,iMessage,wParam,lParam));
    }
}
```

When you run the program, press the left mouse button to cycle through the two resource cursors. When you do, the program generates the cursors in Figures 24-3 and 24-4.

When you use resource cursors, here are a few points to think about from the previous example:

- WAND1 and BIGARROW are defined globally. This ensures that they can be reached throughout the program.

- BIGARROW and WAND1 are loaded when the application is initialized in WinMain().

- A pointer to the resource cursor is passed into the function get_new_cursor(), and the function SetCursor() makes the resource cursor visible.

- When you use any cursor type other than the standard Windows cursors, you must destroy the cursor upon program termination. To do this, use the Windows function DestroyCursor(). If you do not, the cursor will still be floating around in memory, and that memory will be unavailable to other applications. When you use the standard Windows cursors, you do not need to destroy them when the application terminates.

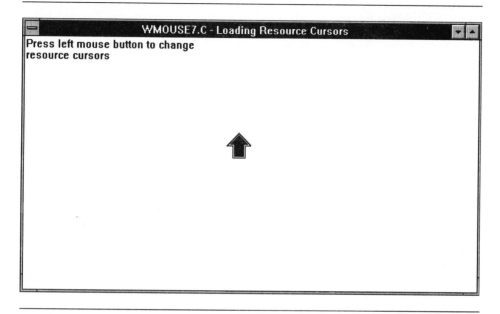

Figure 24-3. *Using the BIGARROW resource cursor*

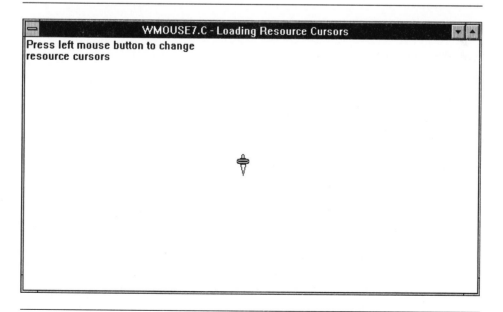

Figure 24-4. *Using the WAND1 resource cursor*

Dynamic Cursors

Both the standard Windows cursors and the resource cursors you have used so far are *static cursors*. Static cursors are created outside of the Windows application at development time. There may be instances when you want to create cursors *dynamically*, inside the application at execution time. Two types of cursors can be created dynamically; *device-dependent cursors*, and *device-independent cursors*.

Device-Dependent Cursors

In the following example, a dynamic cursor is created within the application using a bitmap mask as the cursor shape. The Windows function CreateCursor() is used to set the cursor shape, and the method is actually quite similar to those used in DOS applications (see Chapter 14). With CreateCursor(), the cursor shape is defined by setting the hot spot, size, and bitmap masks for the cursor shape.

The one limitation when using cursors created with bitmap masks is that they are device dependent, and the height and width you use to specify the cursor's size must be supported by the graphics card and monitor being used. Nevertheless, they do have their uses.

The project file is called WMOUSE8.PRJ. Here it is:

```
WMOUSE8.DEF
WMOUSE8.C
```

The module definition file is called WMOUSE8.DEF:

```
NAME          WMOUSE8
DESCRIPTION   'Device Dependent Dynamic Cursor'
EXETYPE       WINDOWS
STUB          "WINSTUB.EXE"
CODE          PRELOAD MOVEABLE
DATA          PRELOAD MOVEABLE MULTIPLE
HEAPSIZE      1024
STACKSIZE     5120
EXPORTS       MainWndProc @1
```

Here is WMOUSE8.C:

```
/*------------------------------------------------------------*/
/*                    WMOUSE8.C                               */
/*                                                            */
/*  Creating dynamic cursor within the program.              */
/*  Device dependent.                                        */
/*------------------------------------------------------------*/
```

```
#define STRICT                  /* Strict 3.1 compliance     */
#include <windows.h>            /* Standard Windows header    */

HINSTANCE gInstance;            /* Global instance handle     */

                               /* AND cursor mask, black outline*/
                               /* with checkerboard filling.  */
static unsigned char maskAND[]=
               {
               0x00, 0x00, 0x00, 0x00,   /* Scan Line 1    */
               0x7F, 0x00, 0xff, 0x00,   /* Scan line 2    */
               0x7F, 0x00, 0xFF, 0x00,   /* Scan Line 3    */
               0x7F, 0x00, 0xFF, 0x00,   /* Scan Line 4    */
               0x00, 0xFF, 0x00, 0xFE,   /* Scan Line 5    */
               0x00, 0xFF, 0x00, 0xFE,   /* Scan Line 6    */
               0x00, 0xFF, 0x00, 0xFE,   /* Scan Line 7    */
               0x00, 0xFF, 0x00, 0xFE,   /* Scan Line 8    */
               0x7F, 0x00, 0xFF, 0x00,   /* Scan Line 9    */
               0x7F, 0x00, 0xff, 0x00,   /* Scan line 10   */
               0x7F, 0x00, 0xFF, 0x00,   /* Scan Line 11   */
               0x7F, 0x00, 0xFF, 0x00,   /* Scan Line 12   */
               0x00, 0xFF, 0x00, 0xFE,   /* Scan Line 13   */
               0x00, 0xFF, 0x00, 0xFE,   /* Scan Line 14   */
               0x00, 0xFF, 0x00, 0xFE,   /* Scan Line 15   */
               0x00, 0xFF, 0x00, 0xFE,   /* Scan Line 16   */
               0x7F, 0x00, 0xFF, 0x00,   /* Scan Line 17   */
               0x7F, 0x00, 0xff, 0x00,   /* Scan line 18   */
               0x7F, 0x00, 0xFF, 0x00,   /* Scan Line 19   */
               0x7F, 0x00, 0xFF, 0x00,   /* Scan Line 20   */
               0x00, 0xFF, 0x00, 0xFE,   /* Scan Line 21   */
               0x00, 0xFF, 0x00, 0xFE,   /* Scan Line 22   */
               0x00, 0xFF, 0x00, 0xFE,   /* Scan Line 23   */
               0x00, 0xFF, 0x00, 0xFE,   /* Scan Line 24   */
               0x7F, 0x00, 0xFF, 0x00,   /* Scan Line 25   */
               0x7F, 0x00, 0xff, 0x00,   /* Scan line 26   */
               0x7F, 0x00, 0xFF, 0x00,   /* Scan Line 27   */
               0x7F, 0x00, 0xFF, 0x00,   /* Scan Line 28   */
               0x00, 0xFF, 0x00, 0xFE,   /* Scan Line 29   */
               0x00, 0xFF, 0x00, 0xFE,   /* Scan Line 30   */
               0x00, 0xFF, 0x00, 0xFE,   /* Scan Line 31   */
               0x00, 0x00, 0x00, 0x00    /* Scan Line 32   */
               };
```

```
                                 /* XOR Mask, set all to 0      */
static unsigned char maskXOR[]=
                          {0,0,0,0,0,0,0,0,
                           0,0,0,0,0,0,0,0,0,
                           0,0,0,0,0,0,0,0,0,
                           0,0,0,0,0,0,0,0,0,
                           0,0,0,0,0,0,0,0,0,
                           0,0,0,0,0,0,0,0,0,
                           0,0,0,0,0,0,0,0,0,
                           0,0,0,0,0,0,0,0,0,
                           0,0,0,0,0,0,0,0,0,
                           0,0,0,0,0,0,0,0,0,
                           0,0,0,0,0,0,0,0,0,
                           0,0,0,0,0,0,0,0,0,
                           0,0,0,0,0,0,0,0,0,
                           0,0,0,0,0,0,0,0,0,
                           0,0,0,0,0,0,0,0,
                           0,0,0,0,0,0,0,0};


                                 /* Function prototype for      */
                                 /* MainWndProc().              */
LRESULT FAR PASCAL MainWndProc(HWND hWnd,UINT iMessage,
                            WPARAM wParam,LPARAM lParam);


/* Module : WinMain                                            */
/* ----------------------------------------------------------*/
/* Initializes window and processes message loop.             */
/*                                                            */
int PASCAL WinMain(HINSTANCE hInstance,
                   HINSTANCE hPrevInstance,
                   LPSTR lpszcmdparam,int nCmdShow)
   {
   HWND hWnd;
   MSG Message;
   WNDCLASS WndClass;

   gInstance=hInstance;        /* Assign global instance       */

   if (!hPrevInstance)
      {
      WndClass.cbClsExtra =0;
      WndClass.cbWndExtra =0;
      WndClass.hbrBackground=GetStockObject(WHITE_BRUSH);
```

```
                            /* Notice the NULL statement!!!  */
                            /* Tells Windows you are in      */
                            /* control inside client area.   */
   WndClass.hCursor=NULL;
   WndClass.hIcon=LoadIcon(NULL,"END");
   WndClass.hInstance=hInstance;
   WndClass.lpfnWndProc=MainWndProc;
   WndClass.lpszClassName="WMOUSE8";
   WndClass.lpszMenuName=NULL;
   WndClass.style=CS_HREDRAW | CS_VREDRAW | CS_DBLCLKS;
   RegisterClass(&WndClass);
   }

hWnd= CreateWindow("WMOUSE8",          /* Class name     */
                                       /* Caption        */
                "WMOUSE8.C - Device Dependent Dynamic Cursor",
                WS_OVERLAPPEDWINDOW,   /* Style          */
                CW_USEDEFAULT,         /* Horiz position */
                0,                     /* Vert position  */
                CW_USEDEFAULT,         /* Width          */
                0,                     /* Height         */
                NULL,                  /* Parent window  */
                NULL,                  /* Menu           */
                hInstance,             /* Program instanc*/
                NULL);                 /* Parameters     */

                    /* If no create, exit             */
if (hWnd==NULL) return FALSE;

ShowWindow(hWnd,nCmdShow);/* Make window visible        */
UpdateWindow(hWnd);

                    /* Message loop                   */
while(GetMessage(&Message,0,0,0))
   {
   TranslateMessage(&Message);
   DispatchMessage(&Message);
   }
return Message.wParam;
}
```

```
/* Module : MainWndProc                                     */
/*---------------------------------------------------------*/
/* Message processor.                                       */
/*                                                          */
LRESULT FAR PASCAL MainWndProc(HWND hWnd,UINT iMessage,
                               WPARAM wParam,LPARAM lParam)
    {
    static HCURSOR new_cursor;/* New cursor                 */

    switch(iMessage)
       {
       case WM_MOUSEMOVE:
            SetCursor(NULL);   /* No cursor                 */
                               /* If already there, destroy */
            if (new_cursor) DestroyCursor(new_cursor);

                            /* Now create dynamic cursor     */
            new_cursor=CreateCursor(gInstance,   /* Instance */
                                          0,   /* X hotspot  */
                                          0,   /* Y hotspot  */
                                         32,   /* Width      */
                                         32,   /* Height     */
                                    maskAND,   /* AND BitMask*/
                                    maskXOR);  /* XOR Bitmask*/

                            /* Make cursor visible           */
            SetCursor(new_cursor);
            return 0;

       case WM_DESTROY:        /* Destroy cursor             */
            DestroyCursor(new_cursor);
            PostQuitMessage(0);
            return 0;

       default:
            return(DefWindowProc(hWnd,iMessage,wParam,lParam));
       }
    }
```

When you run the program, the cursor should be a checkerboard design outlined with a black border, as shown in Figure 24-5.

Cursors created in this manner flicker. This is because when you use a bitmap cursor, the area behind the bitmap must be restored every time the cursor position

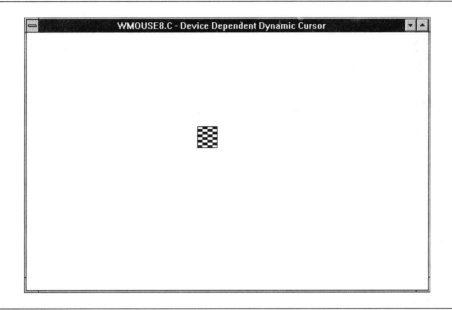

Figure 24-5.   *Device-dependent bitmap cursor*

changes. It would be very annoying in most Windows applications, but can be a useful technique under the appropriate circumstances.

Device-Independent Dynamic Cursors

The cursor created in the previous example is device dependent and must be supported by the graphics card and monitor being used. A better method is to use the Windows GDI (graphics device interface) functions to create the cursor shape, so the cursor is supported on all graphics cards and monitors.

The following example creates a cursor using the Windows GDI functions. The cursor is a very simple gray box. While the approach allows a lot of flexibility, it is also fairly involved.

The project file is called **WMOUSE9.PRJ**. Here it is:

```
WMOUSE9.DEF
WMOUSE9.C
```

The module definition file is called **WMOUSE9.DEF:**

```
NAME          WMOUSE9
DESCRIPTION   'Device Independent Dynamic Cursor'
EXETYPE       WINDOWS
STUB          "WINSTUB.EXE"
CODE          PRELOAD MOVEABLE
DATA          PRELOAD MOVEABLE MULTIPLE
HEAPSIZE      1024
STACKSIZE     5120
EXPORTS       MainWndProc @1
```

Here is WMOUSE9.C:

```c
/*------------------------------------------------------------*/
/*                      WMOUSE9.C                          */
/*                                                         */
/* Creating a dynamic cursor.                              */
/* Device independent.                                     */
/*------------------------------------------------------------*/


#define STRICT             /* Strict 3.1 compliance        */
#include <windows.h>       /* Standard Windows header       */
#include <string.h>        /* Use for _fmemset prototype    */

HINSTANCE gInstance;       /* Global instance handle        */

                           /* Function prototype for        */
                           /* MainWndProc().                */
LRESULT FAR PASCAL MainWndProc(HWND hWnd,UINT iMessage,
                        WPARAM wParam,LPARAM lParam);


/* Module : WinMain                                        */
/* ----------------------------------------------------------*/
/* Initializes window and processes message loop.          */
/*                                                         */
int PASCAL WinMain(HINSTANCE hInstance,
                HINSTANCE hPrevInstance,
                LPSTR lpszcmdparam,int nCmdShow)
    {
    HWND hWnd;
    MSG Message;
    WNDCLASS WndClass;

    gInstance=hInstance;       /* Assign global instance    */
```

```
if (!hPrevInstance)
   {
   WndClass.cbClsExtra =0;
   WndClass.cbWndExtra =0;
   WndClass.hbrBackground=GetStockObject(WHITE_BRUSH);
                           /* Notice the NULL statement!!!  */
                           /* Tells Windows you are in      */
                           /* control inside client area.   */
   WndClass.hCursor=NULL;
   WndClass.hIcon=LoadIcon(NULL,"END");
   WndClass.hInstance=hInstance;
   WndClass.lpfnWndProc=MainWndProc;
   WndClass.lpszClassName="WMOUSE9";
   WndClass.lpszMenuName=NULL;
   WndClass.style=CS_HREDRAW | CS_VREDRAW;
   RegisterClass(&WndClass);
   }

hWnd= CreateWindow("WMOUSE9",              /* Class name     */
                                           /* Caption        */
                  "WMOUSE9.C - Device Independent Dynamic
                               Cursor",
                  WS_OVERLAPPEDWINDOW,  /* Style          */
                  CW_USEDEFAULT,        /* Horiz position */
                  0,                    /* Vert position  */
                  CW_USEDEFAULT,        /* Width          */
                  0,                    /* Height         */
                  NULL,                 /* Parent window  */
                  NULL,                 /* Menu           */
                  hInstance,            /* Program instanc*/
                  NULL);                /* Parameters     */

                       /* If no create, exit        */
if (hWnd==NULL) return FALSE;

ShowWindow(hWnd,nCmdShow);/* Make window visible        */
UpdateWindow(hWnd);
                       /* Message loop               */
while(GetMessage(&Message,0,0,0))
   {
   TranslateMessage(&Message);
   DispatchMessage(&Message);
   }
return Message.wParam;
}
```

```
/* Module : MainWndProc                                         */
/*-------------------------------------------------------------*/
/* Message processor.                                           */
/*                                                              */
LRESULT FAR PASCAL MainWndProc(HWND hWnd,UINT iMessage,
                                WPARAM wParam,LPARAM lParam)
   {
   static HCURSOR new_cursor;            /* New cursor          */
   static int nCursX,nCursY,nByteArea;   /* Cursor size         */
   static HBITMAP hBM;                   /* Bitmap              */
   HDC hDC;                              /* DCHandle            */
   static HDC hDCBitmap;                 /* Bitmap DC           */
   static HANDLE hmemAND,hmemXOR;        /* Memory for cursor   */
   LPSTR lpAND,lpXOR;                    /* AND/XOR mask        */

   switch(iMessage)
      {
      case WM_CREATE:
                        /* Get cursor size                      */
            nCursX=GetSystemMetrics(SM_CXCURSOR);
            nCursY=GetSystemMetrics(SM_CYCURSOR);

                        /* Create bitmap                        */
            hBM=CreateBitmap(nCursX,nCursY,1,1,NULL);
            hDC=GetDC(hWnd);

                        /* Get bitmap DC                        */
            hDCBitmap=CreateCompatibleDC(hDC);
            ReleaseDC(hWnd,hDC);

                        /* Figure byte area                     */
            nByteArea=(nCursX/8)*nCursY;
            SelectObject(hDCBitmap,hBM);

                        /* Allocate memory                      */
            hmemAND=GlobalAlloc(GMEM_MOVEABLE,(DWORD)nByteArea);
            hmemXOR=GlobalAlloc(GMEM_MOVEABLE,(DWORD)nByteArea);

                        /* Lock memory                          */
            lpAND=GlobalLock(hmemAND);
            lpXOR=GlobalLock(hmemXOR);

                        /* Grey brush                           */
            SelectObject(hDCBitmap,GetStockObject(DKGRAY_BRUSH));
```

```
                                /* To bitmap                 */
        PatBlt(hDCBitmap,0,0,nCursX,nCursY,PATCOPY);

                                /* To AND mask                */
        GetBitmapBits(hBM,(DWORD)nByteArea,lpAND);

                                /* Set XOR mask to 0          */
        _fmemset(lpXOR,0,nByteArea);

                                /* Unlock memory              */
        GlobalUnlock(hmemAND);
        GlobalUnlock(hmemXOR);
        return 0;

case WM_MOUSEMOVE:
        SetCursor(NULL);   /* No cursor                       */
                                /* If already there, destroy  */
        if (new_cursor) DestroyCursor(new_cursor);

                                /* Lock memory                */
        lpAND=GlobalLock(hmemAND);
        lpXOR=GlobalLock(hmemXOR);

                                /* Create the cursor          */
        new_cursor=CreateCursor(gInstance,0,0,
                        nCursX,nCursY,lpAND,lpXOR);

                                /* Unlock memory              */
        GlobalUnlock(hmemAND);
        GlobalUnlock(hmemXOR);

                                /* Make cursor visible        */
        SetCursor(new_cursor);
        return 0;

case WM_DESTROY:
                                /* Destroy cursor             */
        DestroyCursor(new_cursor);

                                /* Delete objects             */
        DeleteObject(hBM);
        DeleteDC(hDCBitmap);

                                /* Free memory                */
```

```
            GlobalFree(hmemAND);
            GlobalFree(hmemXOR);
            PostQuitMessage(0);
            return 0;

    default:
            return(DefWindowProc(hWnd,iMessage,wParam,lParam));
    }
}
```

When you run the program, the gray cursor in Figure 24-6 appears.

And that's how you implement a device-independent dynamic cursor. You can elaborate all you want with the GDI routines and create some very nice, colorful cursors.

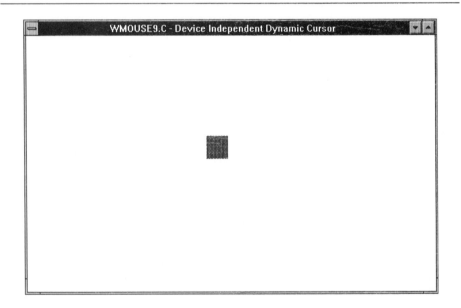

Figure 24-6.   *Device-independent bitmap cursor*

Chapter 25

Additional Windows Mouse-Related Topics

In Windows, button messages and cursor management are your biggest concern. Windows takes care of all cursor maintenance, and many DOS-related issues have simply disappeared. However, there are a few more Windows mouse issues to cover, including tracking the cursor's display location and managing the client area cursor when no mouse is present in the system.

Tracking Cursor Coordinates in Windows

It's a simple task to track the cursor's display coordinates in Windows. To retrieve the current cursor coordinates, you use the Windows function GetCursorPos(). To track the cursor coordinates as the mouse moves, you trap the messages WM_MOUSEMOVE and WM_NCMOUSEMOVE, which are sent by Windows whenever physical mouse movement is detected. WM_MOUSEMOVE is sent when the cursor is in the client area, and WM_NCMOUSEMOVE is sent when the cursor is in the nonclient area. You then determine the current cursor coordinates in the message traps.

The function GetCursorPos() returns the cursor coordinates in screen coordinates, which use the entire display as the mapping area. In Windows applications, it's common to use the cursor as a pointing tool inside the client area, and in these situations it's much better to know the cursor's location in client area coordinates. Converting screen coordinates to client coordinates is accomplished using the Windows function ScreenToClient().

The following example tracks cursor coordinates in the client and nonclient areas, converts screen coordinates to client coordinates, and writes all the coordinates to the display.

The project file is called WMOUSE10.PRJ. Here it is:

```
WMOUSE10.DEF
WMOUSE10.C
```

The module definition file is called **WMOUSE10.DEF**:

```
NAME          WMOUSE10
DESCRIPTION   'Tracking Mouse Coordinates'
EXETYPE       WINDOWS
STUB          "WINSTUB.EXE"
CODE          PRELOAD MOVEABLE
DATA          PRELOAD MOVEABLE MULTIPLE
HEAPSIZE      1024
STACKSIZE     5120
EXPORTS       MainWndProc @1
```

Here is **WMOUSE10.C**:

```c
/*-------------------------------------------------------------*/
/*                    WMOUSE10.C                            */
/*                                                         */
/*  Tracking mouse coordinates in both the client and non- */
/*  client areas, using both screen and client coordinates. */
/*-------------------------------------------------------------*/

#define STRICT              /* Strict 3.1 compliance       */
#include <windows.h>        /* Standard Windows header      */
#include <stdio.h>          /* Need for sprintf prototype   */
#include <string.h>         /* Need for strlen prototype    */

HINSTANCE gInstance;        /* Global instance handle       */

                            /* Function prototype for       */
                            /* MainWndProc().               */
LRESULT FAR PASCAL MainWndProc(HWND hWnd,UINT iMessage,
                      WPARAM wParam,LPARAM lParam);

/* Module : WinMain                                        */
/* -------------------------------------------------------------*/
```

```
/* Initializes Window and processes message loop.           */
/*                                                          */
int PASCAL WinMain(HINSTANCE hInstance,
                   HINSTANCE hPrevInstance,
                   LPSTR lpszcmdparam,int nCmdShow)
    {
    HWND hWnd;
    MSG Message;
    WNDCLASS WndClass;

    gInstance=hInstance;        /* Assign global instance    */

    if (!hPrevInstance)
        {
        WndClass.cbClsExtra =0;
        WndClass.cbWndExtra =0;
        WndClass.hbrBackground=GetStockObject(WHITE_BRUSH);

                                /* Load Windows default arrow    */
        WndClass.hCursor=LoadCursor(NULL,IDC_ARROW);

        WndClass.hIcon=LoadIcon(NULL,"END");
        WndClass.hInstance=hInstance;
        WndClass.lpfnWndProc=MainWndProc;
        WndClass.lpszClassName="WMOUSE10";
        WndClass.lpszMenuName=NULL;
        WndClass.style=CS_HREDRAW | CS_VREDRAW;

        RegisterClass(&WndClass);
        }

    hWnd= CreateWindow("WMOUSE10",            /* Class name    */
                                              /* Caption       */
                      "WMOUSE10.C - Tracking Mouse Coordinates",
                      WS_OVERLAPPEDWINDOW,  /* Style         */
                      CW_USEDEFAULT,        /* Horiz position */
                      0,                    /* Vert position  */
                      CW_USEDEFAULT,        /* Width          */
                      0,                    /* Height         */
                      NULL,                 /* Parent window  */
                      NULL,                 /* Menu           */
                      hInstance,            /* Program instanc*/
                      NULL);                /* Parameters     */

                        /* If no create, exit               */
```

```
    if (hWnd==NULL) return FALSE;

    ShowWindow(hWnd,nCmdShow);/* Make window visible       */
    UpdateWindow(hWnd);        /* Send paint mssg           */

                              /* Message loop               */
    while(GetMessage(&Message,0,0,0))
       {
       TranslateMessage(&Message);
       DispatchMessage(&Message);
       }
    return Message.wParam;


    }



/* Module : out text                                       */
/*-------------------------------------------------------*/
/* Outputs a string of text at TEXT coordinates. This is a */
/* much more natural way to output text. Coords 1,1 represent */
/* the upper-left coordinate of the client area.           */
/*                                                         */
void PASCAL out_text(int x,int y,char *text,HWND hWnd)
    {
    int x_scale,y_scale;       /* Scaling vars              */
    HDC TheDC;                 /* Device handle             */
    TEXTMETRIC text_metrics;   /* Text settings             */

    TheDC=GetDC(hWnd);         /* Get device and text metrics */
    GetTextMetrics(TheDC,&text_metrics);

                              /* Figure Y and X coordinates */
    y_scale=(y-1)*(text_metrics.tmHeight);
    x_scale=(x-1)*(text_metrics.tmAveCharWidth);

                              /* Output string, release device */
    TextOut(TheDC,x_scale,y_scale,text,strlen(text));
    ReleaseDC(hWnd,TheDC);
    }

/* Module : MainWndProc                                    */
/*-------------------------------------------------------*/
/* Message processor.                                      */
/*                                                         */
LRESULT FAR PASCAL MainWndProc(HWND hWnd,UINT iMessage,
```

```
                    WPARAM wParam,LPARAM lParam)
{
HDC text_DC;                /* Text output handle          */
POINT lpPoint;             /* Cursor tagPOINT structure    */
char coord_string[80];     /* For coords-string conversn   */
PAINTSTRUCT ps;            /* Paint structure - init mssg  */

switch(iMessage)
    {
    case WM_PAINT:
        BeginPaint(hWnd,&ps);
        out_text(1,1,"Move the mouse around to see the
                    display coordinates",hWnd);
        out_text(1,2,"in both the client and non-client
                    areas. Coordinates are",hWnd);
        out_text(1,3,"output using screen and client
                    coordinates.",hWnd);

        out_text(1,5,"Client Area Coordinates",hWnd);
        out_text(1,6,"--------------------------",hWnd);
        out_text(1,7,"Screen Coordinates : ",hWnd);
        out_text(1,8,"Client Coordinates : ",hWnd);

        out_text(1,10,"Non-Client Area Coordinates",hWnd);
        out_text(1,11,"--------------------------",hWnd);
        out_text(1,12,"Screen Coordinates : ",hWnd);
        out_text(1,13,"Client Coordinates : ",hWnd);
        EndPaint(hWnd,&ps);
        return 0;

    case WM_MOUSEMOVE:     /* Cursor moved in client area  */
                          /* Get cursor position          */
        GetCursorPos(&lpPoint);

                          /* Convert coordinates to string */
                          /* and output to display.        */
        sprintf(coord_string,"( %d , %d )     ",
                lpPoint.x,lpPoint.y);
        out_text(25,7,coord_string,hWnd);

                          /* Convert screen coordinates to */
                          /* client coordinates; then      */
                          /* output to display.            */
        ScreenToClient(hWnd,&lpPoint);
        sprintf(coord_string,"( %d , %d )     ",
```

```
                lpPoint.x,lpPoint.y);
            out_text(25,8,coord_string,hWnd);
            return 0;

    case WM_NCMOUSEMOVE:    /* Cursor moved—nonclient area  */
                            /* Get cursor position          */
            GetCursorPos(&lpPoint);

                            /* Convert coordinates to string */
                            /* and output to display.        */
            sprintf(coord_string,"( %d , %d )      ",
                    lpPoint.x,lpPoint.y);
            out_text(25,12,coord_string,hWnd);

                            /* Convert screen coordinates to */
                            /* client coordinates; then      */
                            /* output to display.            */
            ScreenToClient(hWnd,&lpPoint);
            sprintf(coord_string,"( %d , %d )      ",
                    lpPoint.x,lpPoint.y);
            out_text(25,13,coord_string,hWnd);
            return 0;

    case WM_DESTROY:
            PostQuitMessage(0);
            return 0;

    default:
            return(DefWindowProc(hWnd,iMessage,wParam,lParam));
    }
}
```

When you run the program, notice that if you move the cursor into the title bar, the nonclient area-client coordinates return negative values for the vertical coordinate, as Figure 25-1 illustrates.

Emulating Mouse Movement with the Keyboard

Although it is a common assumption that everybody using Windows uses a mouse, it is simply not true. Many users work though Windows using only the keyboard, and unless painting or CAD operations are involved, they may never have the desire to own a mouse (what a pity). When you write commercial Windows applications that require a cursor for a pointing tool, you can handle this situation in one of two ways:

- Provide the comment "Microsoft or 100% Compatible Mouse Required" on your software.

- Determine if a mouse is present, and if not, allow cursor movement to be emulated using the keyboard and manage the cursor manually inside your application.

Since it should be a goal of yours to please all end users, you should make the necessary arrangements to deal with a "no mouse" situation. Microsoft has given you three functions specifically for this task:

ShowCursor(BOOL *fShow*)   This function is used to make the cursor visible or invisible.

SetCursorPos(int *x*,int *y*)   This function moves the cursor to a new display location.

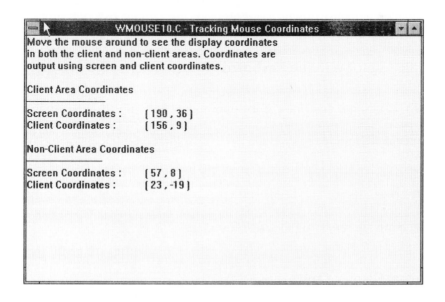

Figure 25-1.   *Tracking the cursor's display coordinates*

ClipCursor(const RECT FAR* *lprc*)   This function limits cursor movement to on and inside a predetermined rectangular region.

Although these three functions can be used if a mouse is present, they should not be. These functions can be very dangerous, and are a common cause of cursor mishap. There's no reason to use any of the functions if a mouse is present because, if one is, Windows takes care of everything for you.

Determining Mouse Presence

To determine if a mouse is present in the system, use the Windows function GetSystemMetrics(). Take a look at the following code fragment:

```
static BOOL MOUSE_THERE;

if (!GetSystemMetrics(SM_MOUSEPRESENT))
    MOUSE_THERE=FALSE;
else
    MOUSE_THERE=TRUE;
```

When the constant SM_MOUSEPRESENT is sent to GetSystsemMetrics(), the function returns 0 if no mouse is present and nonzero if a mouse is present. It's a good idea to save the value to a static global variable, such as MOUSE_THERE, so determination of mouse presence is easily made throughout an entire application.

Moving the Cursor with the Keyboard

To emulate cursor movement with the keyboard, you trap the Windows message **WM_KEYDOWN** and determine if the appropriate key (usually an arrow key) has been pressed. Next you determine the current cursor location, make the appropriate coordinate modifications, and set the new cursor location using SetCursorPos(), as in:

```
SetCursorPos(newpoint.x,newpoint.y);
```

This will move the cursor to the desired location.

The Internal Display Count

Whether or not the cursor is visible is determined by an internal display count kept by Windows. The display count is very similar to the DOS internal cursor flag (see Chapter 4). When the display count is 0 or greater, the cursor is visible. When the display count is –1 or less, the cursor is invisible. To increment the display count, you call ShowCursor(TRUE), and to decrement the display count, you call ShowCursor(FALSE). When a mouse is not present in the system, Windows makes no attempt to display the cursor, and the default display count is set to –1.

Like the DOS internal cursor flag, the internal display count can be decremented to values less than –1. However, unlike the DOS internal cursor flag, the internal display count can also be incremented to values greater than 0. This means that if you call ShowCursor(FALSE) five times consecutively, you must call ShowCursor(TRUE) five consecutive times before the cursor becomes visible again, and if you call ShowCursor(TRUE) five times consecutively, you must call ShowCursor(FALSE) five consecutive times for the cursor to become invisible.

Maintaining the Proper Display Count

In Windows, the cursor is a shared resource, and the display count is shared with all other Windows applications. If your application mishandles the display count, one of three things can happen:

- If no mouse is present and the display count is too high when the application terminates, the cursor will not become invisible, and an unusable phantom cursor appears on the display when the application terminates or goes iconic. This cursor remains on the display until Windows is terminated.

- If no mouse is present and the display count is too low when the application terminates, the cursor might not become visible in the next application desiring to use it, depending on the methods used in the next application.

- Whether a mouse is present or not, the next application to use the cursor might not be able to make it visible, hide it, or even use it all.

However, Windows gives you a feature not available in most DOS mouse drivers: access to the internal display count. When you call the function ShowCursor(), it returns the display count as an integer value. This means that no matter how badly other applications managed the internal display count, you will always be able to correct the situation (unless a phantom cursor is stuck on the display). Additionally, no matter how badly you handle the cursor count within the application, it's easy to get back to the correct value upon program termination or when focus is lost. The following code fragment illustrates how to make the cursor visible regardless of the display count:

```
dcount=ShowCursor(TRUE);
while (dcount<0)
   dcount=ShowCursor(TRUE);
```

The next code fragment illustrates how to make the cursor invisible, regardless of the display count:

```
dcount=ShowCursor(FALSE);
while (dcount>-1)
    dcount=ShowCursor(FALSE);
```

These operations should occur when Windows sends the message WM_ACTI-VATE. The proper determination must be made as to whether the window is becoming active or is being deactivated, and if the window was previously an icon.

 One final note on this. Always assume the previous application mishandled the display count, and take appropriate action. Never let the fate of your application rest in the hands of another.

Limiting Range of Movement

In Windows, you generally do not want to limit the display range in which the cursor can move. This would prohibit users from using the mouse to get to other applications or portions of your application. But when a mouse is not present in the system and your application uses the client area and a cursor for a pointing tool (maybe a CAD type application), limiting the cursor's display range to the client area is very desirable. There's no reason to let the cursor travel anywhere else; after all, there's no real mouse moving it, and no mouse messages are being sent by Windows.

To limit the display area the cursor can travel in, use the Windows function ClipCursor(). A RECT structure is used to inform ClipCursor() of the display range boundaries. To kill the display range boundaries, call ClipCursor(NULL).

Proper Coordinates

To retrieve a window's client coordinate region, use the Windows function GetClientRect(), which returns the region in client coordinates. However, when limiting the range of cursor movement, the function ClipCursor() uses screen coordinates, not client coordinates, and some nifty conversions are needed. The following code fragment demonstrates converting the client coordinates to screen coordinates for the upper-left corner of a window.

```
GetClientRect(hWnd,&clsize);
caPoint.x=clsize.left;caPoint.y=clsize.top;
ClientToScreen(hWnd,&caPoint);
clsize.left=caPoint.x;clsize.top=caPoint.y;
```

You must also convert the coordinates for the lower-left client coordinates, then set the range boundaries for the cursor.

Window Resizing

You must obtain the client coordinates every time a window is resized or moved, and reset the display boundaries to match the new client area. Use the messages WM_MOVE and WM_SIZE to determine when this is required. When WM_SIZE is trapped, you must also check the value in wParam to determine if the window is going iconic. If it is, you must kill the boundaries. Otherwise, when another application tries to use the cursor, the range is limited to your application's icon.

Termination and Lost Focus

Due to the multitude of various messages sent and the complexities of message ordering, it is best to kill the display boundaries whenever the messages WM_KILLFOCUS and WM_DESTROY are sent. When these are used in conjunction with the message WM_SIZE for iconic determination, proper behavior is assured.

Keyboard Mouse-Emulation Program

The following program demonstrates showing and hiding the cursor, moving it with the keyboard arrow keys, and limiting the range of cursor movement. If the mouse is present in your system, these operations will not occur, with the exception of moving the cursor with the arrow keys. To see how the routines operate when a mouse is not present, disconnect your mouse, restart Windows, and run the program.

The project file is called WMOUSE11.PRJ. Here it is:

```
WMOUSE11.DEF
WMOUSE11.C
```

The module definition file is called WMOUSE11.DEF:

```
    NAME          WMOUSE11
    DESCRIPTION   'Emulating the Mouse Cursor With No Mouse'
    EXETYPE       WINDOWS
    STUB          "WINSTUB.EXE"
    CODE          PRELOAD MOVEABLE
    DATA          PRELOAD MOVEABLE MULTIPLE
    HEAPSIZE      1024
    STACKSIZE     5120
    EXPORTS       MainWndProc @1
```

Here is WMOUSE11.C:

```
/*-------------------------------------------------------------*/
/*                     WMOUSE11.C                          */
/*                                                         */
/*  Emulating the mouse cursor with no mouse.              */
/*-------------------------------------------------------------*/

#define STRICT                /* Strict 3.1 compliance       */
#include <windows.h>          /* Standard Windows header     */
HINSTANCE gInstance;          /* Global instance handle      */

static BOOL MOUSE_THERE;      /* Global check for mouse presnce*/

                              /* Function prototype for      */
                              /* MainWndProc().              */
LRESULT FAR PASCAL MainWndProc(HWND hWnd,UINT iMessage,
                          WPARAM wParam,LPARAM lParam);


/* Module : WinMain                                        */
/* -------------------------------------------------------------*/
/* Initializes window and processes message loop.          */
/*                                                         */
int PASCAL WinMain(HINSTANCE hInstance,
                   HINSTANCE hPrevInstance,
                   LPSTR lpszcmdparam,int nCmdShow)
    {
    HWND hWnd;
    MSG Message;
    WNDCLASS WndClass;

    gInstance=hInstance;        /* Assign global instance      */

    if (!hPrevInstance)
       {
       WndClass.cbClsExtra =0;
       WndClass.cbWndExtra =0;
       WndClass.hbrBackground=GetStockObject(WHITE_BRUSH);

                              /* Load Windows default arrow   */
       WndClass.hCursor=LoadCursor(NULL,IDC_ARROW);

       WndClass.hIcon=LoadIcon(NULL,"END");
```

```
    WndClass.hInstance=hInstance;
    WndClass.lpfnWndProc=MainWndProc;
    WndClass.lpszClassName="WMOUSE11";
    WndClass.lpszMenuName=NULL;
    WndClass.style=CS_HREDRAW | CS_VREDRAW;

    RegisterClass(&WndClass);
    }

hWnd= CreateWindow("WMOUSE11",             /* Class name     */
                                           /* Caption        */
                "WMOUSE11.C - Emulating the
                              Mouse Cursor With No Mouse",
                WS_OVERLAPPEDWINDOW,  /* Style          */
                CW_USEDEFAULT,        /* Horiz position */
                0,                    /* Vert position  */
                CW_USEDEFAULT,        /* Width          */
                0,                    /* Height         */
                NULL,                 /* Parent window  */
                NULL,                 /* Menu           */
                hInstance,            /* Program instanc*/
                NULL);                /* Parameters     */

                        /* If no create, exit           */
if (hWnd==NULL) return FALSE;

ShowWindow(hWnd,nCmdShow);/* Make window visible         */
UpdateWindow(hWnd);       /* Send paint mssg             */

                        /* Message loop                 */
while(GetMessage(&Message,0,0,0))
    {
    TranslateMessage(&Message);
    DispatchMessage(&Message);
    }
return Message.wParam;
    }

/* Module : limit to client area                         */
/*-----------------------------------------------------*/
/* Limits the mouse cursor to the client area of a window. */
/* Use whenever window resized, moved, becomes active, or  */
/* gains focus.                                          */
/*                                                       */
void limit_to_client_area(HWND hWnd)
```

```
      {
      RECT clsize;                    /* Current client area       */
      POINT caPoint;                  /* Cursor tagPOINT structure  */
      if (!MOUSE_THERE)
         {
                                      /* Get client area boundaries */
         GetClientRect(hWnd,&clsize);
                                      /* Get top-left coordinates   */
         caPoint.x=clsize.left;caPoint.y=clsize.top;
                                      /* Convert to screen coordinates */
         ClientToScreen(hWnd,&caPoint);
                                      /* Reset top left             */
         clsize.left=caPoint.x;clsize.top=caPoint.y;
                                      /* Get bottom-right coordinates */
         caPoint.x=clsize.right;caPoint.y=clsize.bottom;
                                      /* Convert to screen coordinates */
         ClientToScreen(hWnd,&caPoint);
                                      /* Reset bottom right         */
         clsize.right=caPoint.x;clsize.bottom=caPoint.y;


                                      /* Limit cursor to client area */
         ClipCursor(&clsize);
                                      /* Set cursor to middle of disp */
         SetCursorPos(clsize.right/2,clsize.bottom/2);
         }
      }


/* Module : MainWndProc                                            */
/*---------------------------------------------------------------*/
/* Message processor.                                              */
/*                                                                 */
LRESULT FAR PASCAL MainWndProc(HWND hWnd,UINT iMessage,
                   WPARAM wParam,LPARAM lParam)
   {
   POINT cpPoint;                   /* Cursor tagPOINT structure   */
   PAINTSTRUCT ps;                  /* Paint structure - init mssg */
   HDC TheDC;                       /* Device handle               */
   static int dcount;
   int dloop;

   switch(iMessage)
      {                             /* When application created,   */
                                    /* check for mouse presence and */
                                    /* set global var MOUSE_THERE.  */
```

```
case WM_CREATE:
    if (!GetSystemMetrics(SM_MOUSEPRESENT))
        MOUSE_THERE=FALSE;
    else MOUSE_THERE=TRUE;
    return 0;

case WM_PAINT:
    BeginPaint(hWnd,&ps);
    TheDC=GetDC(hWnd);
    TextOut(TheDC,1, 1,"This program operates
                    differently when the mouse is",51);
    TextOut(TheDC,1,15,"not installed. Please refer to
                    chapter 24 for       ",51);
    TextOut(TheDC,1,30,"complete details.
                                         ",51);
    TextOut(TheDC,1,60,"Move the mouse cursor with the
                    keyboard arrow keys.",51);
    TextOut(TheDC,1,75,"If mouse not installed, cursor
                    limited to client   ",51);
    TextOut(TheDC,1,90,"area, otherwise range is not
                    limited.            ",51);
    ReleaseDC(hWnd,TheDC);
    EndPaint(hWnd,&ps);
    return 0;

                        /* If no mouse is present in    */
                        /* system, you must show it     */
                        /* manually, and MUST hide it   */
                        /* when the window is deactivated*/
case WM_ACTIVATE:
                        /* If NO mouse in system        */
    if (!MOUSE_THERE)
        {
                        /* If window becoming active    */
        if (wParam==WA_ACTIVE)
            {
                        /* From a min state, show it    */
            if (!HIWORD(lParam))
                {
                        /* Show cursor and get internal */
                        /* flag count. If less than 0,  */
                        /* keep showing until it equals 0*/
                dcount=ShowCursor(TRUE);
                while (dcount<0)
                    dcount=ShowCursor(TRUE);
                }
```

```
            }
        else
            {           /* Hide cursor and get internal  */
                        /* flag count.If greater than -1,*/
                        /* keep showing until it equals  */
                        /* -1.                           */
            dcount=ShowCursor(FALSE);
            while (dcount>-1)
                dcount=ShowCursor(FALSE);
            }
        }


                        /* Trap keydown to determine if  */
                        /* virtual arrow key pressed.    */
                        /* If so move cursor 5 pixels     */
                        /* over in direction of arrow.    */
    case WM_KEYDOWN:
        if ((wParam!=VK_LEFT)&&(wParam!=VK_RIGHT)&&
           (wParam!=VK_UP)&&(wParam!=VK_DOWN)) return 0;

                        /* Get current cursor position   */
        GetCursorPos(&cpPoint);

        switch(wParam)     /* Get virtual key and mdfy point*/
           {
           case VK_LEFT:
               cpPoint.x-=5;
               break;
           case VK_RIGHT:
               cpPoint.x+=5;
               break;
           case VK_UP:
               cpPoint.y-=5;
               break;
           case VK_DOWN:
               cpPoint.y+=5;
               break;
           default:
               return NULL;
           }
                        /* Set the new cursor position   */
        SetCursorPos(cpPoint.x,cpPoint.y);
        return 0;
```

```
    case WM_MOVE:               /* Get current window coords    */
        limit_to_client_area(hWnd);
        return 0;


                               /* Also need to limit or reset  */
    case WM_SIZE:              /* range when window is resized. */
        switch(wParam)
            {                  /* Going iconic                  */
                               /* Reset range to entire display */
            case SIZEICONIC:
            case SIZEZOOMHIDE:
                ClipCursor(NULL);
                break;
            default:           /* Normal resizing, limit range */
                               /* to new client area.          */
                limit_to_client_area(hWnd);
                break;
            }
        return 0;

    case WM_SETFOCUS:          /* Window gains focus            */
                               /* Limit range to client area    */
        limit_to_client_area(hWnd);
        return 0;

    case WM_KILLFOCUS:         /* Focus lost for some reason    */
        ClipCursor(NULL); /* Reset to entire display           */
        return 0;

    case WM_DESTROY:
        ClipCursor(NULL); /* And one final check when dtryd*/
        PostQuitMessage(0);
        return 0;

    default:
        return(DefWindowProc(hWnd,iMessage,wParam,lParam));
    }
}
```

Scope

There is a method to limiting the *scope* of the mouse messages to your application. What this means is that you can tell Windows to stop sending mouse messages to all other applications except yours. You do this with the Windows function SetCapture().

The cursor can still move about all over the display, but no messages are sent to other applications, so they cannot be activated with the mouse until your application either terminates or relinquishes the scope back to other applications. To relinquish the scope to other applications, use the Windows function ReleaseCursor().

The function SetCapture() should be used sparingly, if at all. It can render the mouse dead in a very short period of time. Use the SetCapture() function when you write routines that capture screen images, or something similar where the user cannot be allowed to "flip" between applications. The following illustrates what the code fragment for this operation might look like:

```
if (Do_Screen_Capture)
    {
    SetCapture(hWnd);
    Get_Screen();
    Write_Screen_To_Disk();
    ReleaseCapture();
    }
```

If you do not relinquish control back to other applications with ReleaseCapture(), the mouse is rendered dead for all intents and purposes.

WM_NCHITTEST

The Windows Message WM_NCHITTEST is sent to the window containing the cursor, or a window that used the SetCapture() command, and is sent every time the mouse moves. WM_NCHITTEST is sent by Windows in order to determine the current cursor position. Most programs will bypass this message on to the default Windows procedure, which examines the cursor location, and provides a hit-test code as a return value (See Chapters 23 and 24 regarding hit-test codes). If the hit-test code is HTCLIENT, the cursor is in the client area; otherwise the cursor is in the nonclient area

After WM_NCHITTEST is sent, WM_SETCURSOR is sent for the application to process and set the cursor. Again, most applications bypass this message and let Windows take control. If you trap the message WM_NCHITTEST or WM_SETCURSOR, it is *your* responsibility to check the cursor position and take appropriate action.

Both WM_NCHITTEST and WM_SETCURSOR precede any other mouse messages. The reason is because Windows needs to know where the cursor is, and once it does, it makes sure that the user knows by changing the cursor shape when appropriate.

Part *IV*

Appendixes

Appendix A

The 50 Documented Mouse Functions

This appendix contains a detailed reference to all 50 documented Microsoft mouse functions.

Conventions

To better utilize the appendix, here are some helpful tips.

Programming Examples in the Appendix

Every mouse function listed in this appendix contains a small example to demonstrate using the function. It should be pointed out that these examples are *not* stand-alone programs, but code fragments. However, each code fragment has been tested in a stand-alone program to ensure that it works as specified.

Chapter References

When a mouse function has been used in the mouse function library or a programming example from the previous chapters, the chapter reference is given as:

Chapter reference: 3

Multiple chapter references appear as:

Chapter reference: 3, 4

If the function was not used in an actual programming example, but was discussed in a chapter, the reference appears as:

Chapter reference: 3 (discussion)

Version Numbers

Microsoft began releasing mouse functions 37 through 52 (the advanced mouse functions) in their mouse driver version 6.26. In this appendix, mouse functions 37 and higher include the Microsoft version number in which they became available.

The Logitech mouse driver 6.1 and later, and the Kraft mouse driver 8.2 and later support all available Microsoft mouse functions. However, the majority of other OEM mouse manufacturers have not implemented the advanced mouse functions. For details regarding function availability, consult the documentation supplied with your mouse. Do not assume a mouse driver supports the advanced mouse functions because it states "100% Microsoft compatible" on the packaging.

Three-Button Mice

References to three-button mice are based on the Logitech three-button standards.

Mouse Function 0: Mouse Reset and Status

Mouse function 0 resets the mouse hardware and software (if installed) to the default settings. It also determines if a mouse is present in the system, and the number of mouse buttons.

Input Values

ax = 0

Return Values

ax = mouse status (–1 if mouse hardware is present, and
software installed, otherwise 0)

bx = number of mouse buttons if mouse hardware and software
is installed

Mouse function 0 resets the following values as shown here:

Meaning	Default Value
Cursor location	Center of display
Internal cursor flag	–1 (invisible)
Graphics cursor	Arrow
Text cursor	Reverse video block
Event handler call mask	0 (no event handler)*
Light-pen emulation mode	Enabled
Horizontal mickey-to-pixel ratio	8 to 8
Vertical mickey-to-pixel ratio	16 to 8
Double speed	64 mickeys per second
Minimum horizontal cursor location	0
Maximum horizontal cursor location	Current display mode maximum –1
Minimum vertical cursor location	0
Maximum vertical cursor location	Current display mode maximum –1
Video display page number	0

* Only event handlers not set by function 24

Example

The following resets the mouse and retrieves the mouse status and number of mouse
buttons:

```
mregs.x.ax=0;
int86(0x33,&mregs,&mregs);
mstat=mregs.x.ax;
num_buttons=mregs.x.bx;
```

*Interrupt 0x33 must point to a valid interrupt vector before mouse function 0 can
be called.*

Chapter reference: 1, 3

Mouse Function 1: Show Cursor

Mouse function 1 increments the value of the internal cursor flag. If the value is 0 after calling mouse function 1, the mouse cursor becomes (or remains) visible. If the value is less than 0, the mouse cursor remains invisible. Additionally, mouse function 1 destroys any exclusion area previously set with mouse function 16.

Input Values

ax = 1

Return Values

None.

Example

The following makes the mouse cursor visible if the internal cursor flag is currently –1:

```
mregs.x.ax=1;
int86(0x33,&mregs,&mregs);
```

Chapter reference: 3, 4, 19

Mouse Function 2: Hide Cursor

Mouse function 2 decreases the value of the internal cursor flag. If the value is –1 or less, the mouse cursor becomes (or remains) invisible. For every consecutive call to mouse function 2, a value of 1 is subtracted from the internal cursor flag. Therefore, if you call mouse function 2 five consecutive times, you *must* call mouse function 1 (show cursor) five consecutive times to make the mouse cursor visible.

Input Values

ax = 2

Return Values

None.

Example

The following makes the mouse cursor invisible:

```
mregs.x.ax=2;
int86(0x33,&mregs,&mregs);
```

Chapter reference: 3, 4, 19

Mouse Function 3: Get Button Status and Cursor Position

Mouse function 3 returns the state of the right, left, and middle (if present) buttons. The mouse cursor's current display coordinates are also returned.

Input Values

ax = 3

Return Values

bx = button status

Value	Meaning
0	No button pressed
1	Left button pressed
2	Right button pressed
3	Both buttons pressed
4	Middle OEM button pressed

cx = horizontal mouse cursor coordinate

dx = vertical mouse cursor coordinate

Example

The following retrieves the button status and mouse cursor coordinates:

```
mregs.x.ax=3;
int86(0x33,&mregs,&mregs);
bstat=mregs.x.bx;
x=mregs.x.cx;
y=mregs.x.dx;
```

 The coordinates are returned in graphics coordinates regardless of the actual display mode.

Chapter reference: 5, 6

Mouse Function 4: Set Mouse Cursor Position

Mouse function 4 sets the mouse cursor's current display location. If the mouse cursor is currently visible, it is moved to the new location and remains visible. If the mouse cursor is currently invisible, the position is updated, but the cursor remains invisible.

Input Values

ax = 4

cx = horizontal mouse cursor location

dx = vertical mouse cursor location

Return Values

None.

Example

The following sets the mouse cursor's location to 100,200:

```
mregs.x.ax=4;
mregs.x.cx=100;
mregs.x.dx=200;
int86(0x33,&mregs,&mregs);
```

The coordinates used must be graphics coordinates, regardless of the actual display mode.

Chapter reference: 5

Mouse Function 5: Get Button Press Information

Mouse function 5 returns the number of times a specific button has been pressed since the last time the function was called. Additionally, the cursor's display location when the button was last pressed is returned.

Input Values

ax = 5

bx = button to check (0 = left 1 = right, 2 = OEM middle)

Return Values

ax = button status

Bit	Meaning	Decimal Value
0	1 if left button pressed	1
1	1 if right button pressed	2
2	1 if OEM middle button pressed	4

bx = number of button presses

cx = horizontal mouse cursor location at last button press

dx = vertical mouse cursor location at last button press

Example

The following retrieves the status of the left mouse button, and the coordinates when the button was last pressed:

```
mregs.x.ax=5;
mregs.x.bx=0;
int86(0x33,&mregs,&mregs);
bstat=mregs.x.ax;
num_press=mregs.x.bx;
x=mregs.x.cx;
y=mregs.x.dx;
```

 Once the number of button presses reaches 65,535 it is reset to 0. Additionally, the coordinates returned are graphics coordinates, regardless of the actual display mode.

Chapter reference: 6 (discussion)

Mouse Function 6: Get Button Release Information

Mouse function 6 returns the number of times a specific button has been released since the last time the function was called. Additionally, the cursor's display location when the button was last released is returned.

Input Values

ax = 6

bx = button to check (0 = left, 1 = right, 2 = OEM middle)

Return Values

ax = button status

Bit	Meaning
0	1 if left button released
1	1 if right button released
2	1 if OEM middle button released

bx = number of button releases

cx = horizontal display location at last button release

dx = vertical display location at last button release

Example

The following retrieves the status of the left mouse button, and the coordinates when the button was last released:

```
mregs.x.ax=6;
mregs.x.bx=0;
int86(0x33,&mregs,&mregs);
bstat=mregs.x.ax;
num_rls=mregs.x.bx;
x=mregs.x.cx;
y=mregs.x.dx;
```

Once the number of button releases reaches 65,535, it is reset to 0. Additionally, the coordinates returned are graphics coordinates, regardless of the actual display mode.

Chapter reference: 6

Mouse Function 7: Set Min/Max Horizontal Cursor Position

Mouse function 7 sets the minimum and maximum horizontal display locations the mouse cursor can move within.

Input Values

ax = 7

cx = minimum position

dx = maximum position

Return Values

None.

Example

The following limits mouse cursor movement to the left-hand portion of the display, where **MAXX** is the maximum horizontal display location:

```
mregs.x.ax=7;
mregs.x.cx=0;
mregs.x.dx=MAXX/2;
int86(0x33,&mregs,&mregs);
```

 The coordinates used must be graphics coordinates regardless of the actual display mode.

Chapter reference: 3, 6, 9

Mouse Function 8: Set Min/Max Vertical Cursor Position

Mouse function 8 sets the minimum and maximum vertical display locations the mouse cursor can move within.

Input Values

ax = 8

cx = minimum position

dx = maximum position

Return Values

None.

Example

The following limits mouse movement to the upper portion of the display, where MAXY is the maximum vertical display location:

```
mregs.x.ax=8;
mregs.x.cx=0;
mregs.x.dx=MAXY/2;
int86(0x33,&mregs,&mregs);
```

The coordinates used must be graphics coordinates, regardless of the actual display mode.

Chapter reference: 3, 6, 9

Mouse Function 9: Set Graphics Cursor

Mouse function 9 sets the graphics mouse cursor to a specified graphics image. Additionally, you can change the cursor's hot spot and the type of logical operations performed on the background the cursor is moving over.

Input Values

ax = 9

bx = horizontal mouse cursor hot spot

cx = vertical mouse cursor hot spot

es:dx = address of screen and cursor mask

Return Values

None.

Example

The following sets the cursor mask(s) to the image defined in the array hourglass[].
The cursor's hot spot will be set to the upper-left corner of the graphics image.

```
mregs.x.ax=9;
mregs.x.bx=0;
mregs.x.cx=0;
mregs.x.dx=FP_OFF(hourglass);
segregs.es=FP_SEG(hourglass);
int86x(0x33,&mregs,&mregs,&segregs);
```

 The default hot spot for the graphics mouse cursor is 0,–1.

Chapter reference: 14

Mouse Function 10: Set Text Cursor

Mouse function 10 sets the hardware or software mouse text cursor. If the hardware
cursor is chosen, the cursor's first and last scan lines are specified. If the software
cursor is chosen, the display and cursor mask are specified.

Input Values

ax = 10

bx = type of cursor (0 for software cursor; 1 for hardware cursor)

cx = display mask for software cursor; first scan line for hardware cursor

dx = cursor mask for software cursor; last scan line for hardware cursor.
The maximum number of available scan lines is dependent on the
video display type.

Return Values

None.

Example

The following sets the mouse's software cursor to the default mouse text cursor:

```
mregs.x.ax=10;
mregs.x.bx=0;
mregs.x.cx=0x7FFF;
mregs.x.dx=0x7700;
int86(0x33,&mregs,&mregs);
```

The next example sets the mouse hardware cursor. The scan lines are set to 7 and 8:

```
mregs.x.ax=10;
mregs.x.bx=1;
mregs.x.cx=7;
mregs.x.dx=8;
int86(0x33,&mregs,&mregs);
```

Chapter reference: 15

Mouse Function 11: Read Mouse Motion Counters

Mouse function 11 returns the horizontal and vertical mickey count since the last time the function was called. The mickey count can range from −32,768 to 32,767. The function ignores overflow, and the counts are reset to 0 when the call is finished.

Input Values

ax = 11

Return Values

cx = horizontal mickey count

dx = vertical mickey count

Example

The following retrieves the horizontal and vertical motion counters:

```
mregs.x.ax=11;
int86(0x33,&mregs,&mregs);
hmick=mregs.x.cx;
vmick=mregs.x.dx;
```

Mouse Function 12: Set Event Handler

Mouse function 12 sets an event handler call mask and address. The call mask defines which conditions cause the mouse driver to call the specified event handler.

Input Values

ax = 12

cx = call mask

The following table defines which activity causes the mouse driver to call the event handler. The conditions are specified in the individual bits of the call mask:

Bit	Meaning
0	Cursor position changed
1	Left button pressed
2	Left button released
3	Right button pressed
4	Right button released
5	OEM middle button pressed
6	OEM middle button released
5-15	Not used by Microsoft and two-button mice
7-15	Not used by three-button mouse

es:dx = event handler address

Return Values

None.

Example

The following tells the mouse driver to call the function ehandler() whenever the left button is pressed:

```
mregs.x.ax=12;
mregs.x.cx=2;
mregs.x.dx=FP_OFF(ehandler);
segregs.es=FP_SEG(ehandler);
int86x(0x33,&mregs,&mregs,&segregs);
```

To disable the event handler, you must call function 12 again with the call mask set to 0 or call mouse function 0 or 33 to reset the mouse software.

Chapter reference: 7, 8, 19, 21

Mouse Function 13: Light-Pen Emulation Mode On

Mouse function 13 allows the mouse to emulate a light pen. After calling this function, any calls to PEN functions return the mouse cursor's position at the last pen down.

Input Values

ax = 13

Return Values

None.

Example

The following turns light-pen emulation on:

```
mregs.x.ax=13;
int86(0x33,&mregs,&mregs);
```

When in light-pen emulation, the mouse buttons control the pen state. PEN-DOWN is triggered by pressing both buttons. PEN-UP is triggered by releasing either button.

Mouse Function 14: Light-Pen Emulation Mode Off

Mouse function 14 disables the light-pen emulation mode. After a call to this function, any pen statements will return information about the light-pen only.

Input Values

ax = 14

Return Values

None.

Example

The following disables light-pen emulation:

```
mregs.x.ax=14;
int86(0x33,&mregs,&mregs);
```

Mouse Function 15: Set Mickey-to-Pixel Ratio

Mouse function 15 sets the mickey-to-pixel ratio for both horizontal and vertical movement. Each ratio specifies the number of mickeys for every eight virtual screen pixels.

Input Values

ax = 15

cx = horizontal mickey-to-pixel ratio

dx = vertical mickey-to-pixel ratio

Return Values

None.

Example

The following sets the horizontal ratio to 24/8 and the vertical ratio to 32/8:

```
mregs.x.ax=15;
mregs.x.cx=24;
mregs.x.dx=32;
int86(0x33,&mregs,&mregs);
```

The default horizontal ratio is 8/8, and the default vertical ratio is 16/8.

Chapter reference: 13 (discussion)

Mouse Function 16: Set Exclusion Area

Mouse function 16 allows you to specify a rectangular area of the display about to be updated. If the mouse cursor is in the defined region or moves into it during the update, it becomes invisible. When the display update is complete, you *must* call mouse function 1, show cursor, to guarantee that the cursor is visible.

Input Values

ax = 16

cx = left X coordinate

dx = upper Y coordinate

si = right X coordinate

di = lower Y coordinate

Return Values

None.

Example

The following sets an exclusion area defined with boundaries of 100,100,200,200:

```
mregs.x.ax=16;
mregs.x.cx=100;
mregs.x.dx=100;
mregs.x.si=200;
mregs.x.di=200;
int86(0x33,&mregs,&mregs);
```

Chapter reference: 4, 19, 21

Any call made to Mouse Function 1 (show cursor) will destroy the exclusion area set with Mouse Function 16.

Mouse Functions 17 and 18: Undocumented

Mouse Function 19: Set Double-Speed Threshold

Mouse function 19 sets the double-speed threshold, above which the mouse doubles the rate of cursor travel for the same physical movement from the mouse. The default threshold is 64 mickeys per second.

Input Values

ax = 19

dx = double-speed threshold in mickeys per second (0 for default)

Return Values

None.

Example

The following sets the double-speed threshold to 80 mickeys per second:

```
mregs.x.ax=19;
mregs.x.dx=80;
int86(0x33,&mregs,&mregs);
```

The values for the double-speed threshold remain active until:

- A call to mouse function 0, reset and status, or 33, software reset, is made. This sets the double speed threshold to its default value.

- Mouse function 19 is called with a value of 0 passed into dx. This sets the double-speed threshold to its default value.

- Mouse function 19 is called with an unobtainable value passed into dx, for example, 20000. This effectively kills the double-speed effects.

Logitech has stopped implementing the double-speed threshold in their mouse driver versions 6.1 and later. Logitech now uses the acceleration curves (ballistic speed) instead of the double-speed threshold. See mouse functions 43-45 regarding acceleration curves.

Chapter reference: 13 (discussion)

Mouse Function 20: Swap Event Handlers

Mouse function 20 sets an event handler call mask and address. Additionally, mouse function 20 returns the call mask and address of the previously active event handler (if any), making it possible to reinstall the old event handler. The call mask used to set the event handler defines the conditions that cause the mouse driver to call the event handler.

Input Values

ax = 20

cx = call mask

The following table defines which activity causes the mouse driver to call the event handler. The conditions are specified in the individual bits of the call mask.

Bit	Meaning
0	Cursor position changed
1	Left button pressed
2	Left button released
3	Right button pressed
4	Right button released
5	OEM middle button pressed
6	OEM middle button released
5-15	Not used by Microsoft and two-button mice
7-15	Not used by three-button mouse

es:dx = event handler address

Return Values

cx = old call mask

es:dx = address of old event handler

Example

The following tells the mouse driver to call the event handler ehandler() whenever the left button is pressed, and retrieves the call mask and address of the previous event handler:

```
mregs.x.ax=20;
mregs.x.cx=2;
mregs.x.dx=FP_OFF(ehandler);
segregs.es=FP_SEG(ehandler);
int86x(0x33,&mregs,&mregs,&segregs);
old_mask=mregs.x.cx;
old_seg=segregs.es;
old_off=mregs.x.dx;
```

You can re-enable the old event handler with mouse function 12 or mouse function 20. To disable the current event handler without restoring the old event handler, you must call function 20 again with the call mask set to 0 or call mouse function 0 or 33 to reset the mouse software.

Chapter reference: 8 (discussion)

Mouse Function 21: Get Mouse Driver State Buffer Size

Mouse function 21 returns the size of a buffer needed to hold the mouse driver's current state. Use this function in conjunction with mouse functions 22 and 23 to save and restore the mouse driver's current state. See the discussion in Chapter 8 regarding TSR programming and child processes.

Input Values

ax = 21

Return Values

bx = size of buffer needed

Example

The following retrieves the size of the buffer needed to save the mouse driver's current state:

```
mregs.x.ax=21;
int86(0x33,&mregs,&mregs);
buffsize=mregs.x.bx;
```

Chapter reference: 8 (discussion)

Mouse Function 22: Save Mouse Driver State

Mouse function 22 saves the current state of the mouse driver into a preallocated buffer. Prior to calling function 22, you must:

- Use function 21 to determine the required size of the buffer.
- Allocate the buffer.

- Hide the mouse cursor; otherwise the background image behind the mouse cursor is saved as well.

Input Values

ax = 22

es:dx = pointer to buffer

Return Values

None.

Example

The following saves the mouse driver's current state to buffer:

```
mregs.x.ax=22;
mregs.x.dx=FP_OFF(buffer);
segregs.es=FP_SEG(buffer);
int86x(0x33,&mregs,&mregs,&segregs);
```

Chapter reference: 8 (discussion)

Mouse Function 23: Restore Mouse Driver State

Mouse function 23 restores the mouse driver to the state it was in prior to calling mouse function 22, save mouse driver state. The buffer must have been previously allocated and the mouse driver state previously saved, or unpredictable results will occur. Immediately after calling mouse function 23, the cursor should be made visible by calling mouse function 1, show cursor.

Input Values

ax = 23

es:dx = pointer to buffer

Return Values

None.

Example

The following restores the state of the mouse driver prior to calling mouse function 22:

```
mregs.x.ax=23;
mregs.x.dx=FP_OFF(buffer);
segregs.es=FP_SEG(buffer);
int86x(0x33,&mregs,&mregs,&segregs);
```

Chapter reference: 8 (discussion)

Mouse Function 24: Set Alternate Event Handler

Mouse function 24 sets an alternate event handler call mask and address. The call mask defines which condition causes the mouse driver to call the alternate event handler. Additionally, mouse function 24 allows you to set up to three alternate event handlers, and a variety of key combinations can be specified in the call mask.

Input Values

ax = 24

cx = call mask

The following table defines which activity causes the mouse driver to call the alternate event handler. The conditions are specified in the individual bits of the call mask.

Bit	Meaning
0	Cursor position changed
1	Left button pressed
2	Left button released
3	Right button pressed
4	Right button released
5	SHIFT key pressed

Bit	Meaning
6	CTRL key pressed
7	ALT key pressed
13	OEM middle button pressed
14	OEM middle button released
8-15	Not used by the Microsoft driver
8-12, 15	Not used by OEM driver

es:dx = subroutine address

You must set either bit 5, 6, or 7 of the call mask to 1. If you do not, the mouse driver will not call the alternate event handler. Additionally, when the application is running the appropriate key must be down in conjunction with other mouse events for the handler to be called.

Return Values

ax = error status (–1 if error occurred)

Example

The following tells the mouse driver to call the alternate event handler alt_ehandler() whenever the left button is pressed and the CTRL key is down:

```
mregs.x.ax=24;
mregs.x.cx=66;
mregs.x.dx=FP_OFF(alt_ehandler);
segregs.es=FP_SEG(alt_ehandler);
int86x(0x33,&mregs,&mregs,&segregs);
error_code=mregs.x.ax;
```

The only method to properly disable an alternate event handler set with mouse function 24 is to call function 24 again, and set the handler's call mask bit(s) to 0, or by installing a new alternate event handler for the call mask.

Chapter reference: 8 (discussion)

Mouse Function 25: Get Alternate Event Handler

Mouse function 25 returns the address of an alternate event handler installed with a specific call mask. Use this function prior to installing a new alternate event handler with mouse function 24, to determine if an alternate event handler already exists for the call mask you plan on using. If one does, save its call mask and address so you can restore it (if desired) when the new alternate event handler is no longer needed.

Input Values

ax = 25

cx = specified alternate event handler call mask (see mouse
function 24 regarding the call mask's possible values)

Return Values

ax = error status (−1 if no existing alternate event handler)

cx = alternate event handler call mask (0 if none)

bx:dx = alternate event handler address (0 if none)

Example

The following retrieves the event handler currently set for simultaneous left-button and CTRL keypresses:

```
mregs.x.ax=25;
mregs.x.cx=66;
int86(0x33,&mregs,&mregs);
error_code=mregs.x.ax;
old_mask=mregs.x.cx;
old_seg=mregs.x.bx;
old_off=mregs.x.dx;
```

Mouse Function 26: Set Sensitivity Rate

Mouse function 26 sets the mouse's cursor speed by modifying the internal multiplication factors for horizontal and vertical mickey-to-pixel ratios and the double-speed threshold. The multiplication factors are modified by a sensitivity rate, which can range from 0 to 100. 50 specifies the default multiplication factor of 1.0 for sensitivity and threshold.

Input Values

ax = 26

bx = horizontal speed sensitivity (0-100)

cx = vertical speed sensitivity (0-100)

dx = double-speed threshold (0-100)

Return Values

None.

Example

The following sets horizontal and vertical speed sensitivity rate to 25 and the double-speed threshold sensitivity rate to 75:

```
mregs.x.ax=26;
mregs.x.bx=25;
mregs.x.cx=25;
mregs.x.dx=75;
int86(0x33,&mregs,&mregs);
```

The multiplication factor is applied to the mickeys before the mickey-to-pixel conversion. Additionally, Logitech has stopped implementing the double-speed threshold in their mouse driver versions 6.1 and later. Logitech now uses the acceleration curves (ballistic speed) instead of the double-speed threshold. See mouse functions 43-45 regarding acceleration curves.

Chapter reference: 13

Mouse Function 27: Get Sensitivity Rate

Mouse function 27 returns the mouse's horizontal and vertical speed sensitivity settings and the double-speed threshold.

Input Values

ax = 27

Return Values

bx = horizontal speed sensitivity (0-100)

cx = vertical speed sensitivity (0-100)

dx = double-speed threshold (0-100)

Example

The following retrieves the current speed sensitivity rates:

```
mregs.x.ax=27;
int86(0x33,&mregs,&mregs);
hspeed=mregs.x.bx;
vspeed=mregs.x.cx;
threshold=mregs.x.dx;
```

Some lower-quality OEM manufacturers do not support this function at all, and unpredictable values are returned.

Chapter reference: 12, 13

Mouse Function 28: Set Mouse Interrupt Rate

• Mouse function 28 sets the rate at which the mouse InPort chip generates interrupts. Use this function only with an InPort mouse. Faster rates provide better resolution of the mouse cursor; slower rates allow the application to run faster. The mouse driver has a TSR that services the interrupts generated by the InPort mouse.

Input Values

ax = 28

bx = interrupt rate

Value	Rate
0	No interrupts generated
1	30 interrupts per second
2	50 interrupts per second
3	100 interrupts per second
4	200 interrupts per second

Return Values

None.

Example

The following sets the InPort mouse interrupt rate to 100 interrupts per second:

```
mregs.x.ax=28;
mregs.x.bx=3;
int86(0x33,&mregs,&mregs);
```

 Setting the interrupt rate to a value greater than 4 (200 interrupts per second) could cause the InPort mouse to behave unpredictably.

Mouse Function 29: Set CRT Page Number

Mouse function 29 sets the current CRT page the mouse cursor is displayed on. Your graphics card and the amount of memory installed on the card determine the number of pages available. See your graphics card documentation for specific details.

Input Values

ax = 29

bx = CRT page number

Return Values

None.

Example

The following sets the CRT page to page 2:

```
mregs.x.ax=29;
mregs.x.bx=2;
int86(0x33,&mregs,&mregs);
```

Chapter reference: 12 (discussion)

Mouse Function 30: Get CRT Page Number

Mouse function 30 returns the current CRT page the mouse cursor is displayed on.

Input Values

ax = 30

Return Values

bx = CRT page number

Example

The following retrieves the mouse cursor's current display page:

```
mregs.x.ax=30;
int86(0x33,&mregs,&mregs);
crt_page=mregs.x.bx;
```

Chapter reference: 12

Mouse Function 31: Disable Mouse Driver

Mouse function 31 disables the mouse driver and returns the address of the interrupt 0x33 handler installed prior to the mouse driver. All other mouse driver vectors are removed.

Input Values

ax = 31

Return Values

ax = error status (–1 if unable to remove all vectors)

es:bx = address of previous interrupt 0x33 handler

Example

The following disables the mouse driver and retrieves the address of the previous interrupt 0x33 handler:

```
mregs.x.ax=31;
int86x(0x33,&mregs,&mregs,&segregs);
error_stat=mregs.x.ax;
old_off=mregs.x.bx;
old_seg=segregs.es;
```

Mouse Function 32: Enable Mouse Driver

Mouse function 32 enables the mouse driver and installs all mouse driver vectors. Use this function after disabling the mouse with function 31.

Input Values

ax = 32

Return Values

None.

Example

The following enables the mouse driver:

```
mregs.x.ax=32;
int86(0x33,&mregs,&mregs);
```

In Microsoft mouse driver versions 7.0 and later, the error status flags are the same as in mouse function 0. Prior to version 7.0 it returns nothing.

Mouse Function 33: Software Reset

Mouse function 33 resets all internal mouse variables that are not dependent on the mouse or display hardware. The function does not initialize the mouse hardware.

Input Values

ax = 33

Return Values

ax = −1 (if mouse driver installed, else 33)

bx = number of buttons.

Mouse Function 33 resets the internal values to their defaults.

Meaning	Default Value
Cursor location	Center of display
Internal cursor flag	−1 (invisible)
Graphics cursor	Arrow
Text cursor	Reverse video block
Event handler call mask	All 0 (no event handler)*
Light-pen emulation mode	Enabled
Horizontal mickey-to-pixel ratio	8 to 8
Vertical mickey-to-pixel ratio	16 to 8
Double-speed threshold	64 mickeys per second
Minimum horizontal cursor location	0
Maximum horizontal cursor location	Current display mode maximum −1
Minimum vertical cursor location	0
Maximum vertical cursor location	Current display mode maximum −1
Video display page number	0

* Only event handlers not set by function 24

Example

The following resets the mouse software and retrieves the mouse status and number of mouse buttons:

```
mregs.x.ax=33;
int86(0x33,&mregs,&mregs);
mstat=mregs.x.ax;
num_buttons=mregs.x.bx;
```

Mouse Function 34: Set Language for Messages

Mouse function 34 sets the language in which messages and prompts from the mouse driver are displayed. This function works only with the international mouse driver version and has no effect on domestic-only versions.

Input Values

ax = 34

bx = language number

Value	Language
0	English
1	French
2	Dutch
3	German
4	Swedish
5	Finnish
6	Spanish
7	Portuguese
8	Italian

Return Values

None.

Example

The following sets the mouse driver language to Italian:

```
mregs.x.ax=34;
mregs.x.bx=8;
int86(0x33,&mregs,&mregs);
```

Many OEM mice do not support this function.

Mouse Function 35: Get Language Number

Mouse function 35 returns the current language in which messages and prompts from the mouse driver are displayed. Domestic versions of the mouse driver will always return 0, and international versions will return the actual language number.

Input Values

ax = 35

Return Values

bx = language number

Value	Language
0	English
1	French
2	Dutch
3	German
4	Swedish
5	Finnish
6	Spanish
7	Portuguese
8	Italian

Example

The following retrieves the current language number:

```
mregs.x.ax=35;
int86(0x33,&mregs,&mregs);
language=mregs.x.bx;
```

 Many OEM mice do not support this function.

Mouse Function 36: Get Driver Version, Type, and IRQ

Mouse function 36 returns the mouse driver version, the mouse type, and the IRQ number used by the mouse driver.

Input Values

ax = 36

Return Values

bh = major version number

bl = minor version number

ch = mouse type

Value	Type
1	Bus mouse
2	Serial mouse
3	InPort mouse
4	PS/2 mouse
5	Hewlett-Packard mouse

cl = IRQ number

Value	IRQ
0	PS/2
2-5, 7	Mouse interrupt

Example

The following retrieves the mouse driver version numbers, mouse type, and the IRQ number:

```
mregs.x.ax=36;
int86(0x33,&mregs,&mregs);
maj_ver=mregs.h.bh;
min_ver=mregs.h.bl;
mtype=mregs.h.ch;
irq_num=mregs.h.cl;
```

Chapter reference: 12

Mouse Function 37: Get General Driver Information

Mouse function 37 returns general information about the mouse driver.

Input Values

ax = 37

Return Values

ax = general information

The information contained within ax, and the bits the information resides in are as follows:

- Bits 0-7 contain the count of currently active mouse device drivers. This information is used only by the integrated mouse driver.

- Bits 8 through 11 contain the current interrupt rate as an integer value.

- Bits 12 and 13 contain the current cursor type.

Bit 12	Bit 13	Cursor Type
0	0	Software text cursor
1	0	Hardware text cursor
0	1	Graphics cursor
1	1	Graphics cursor

- Bits 14 and 15 contain the mouse driver type.

Bit #	Value	Driver Type
14	0	Original nonintegrated type
	1	Newer integrated type
15	0	Driver loaded as COM file
	1	Driver loaded as SYS file

bx = in video cursor function flag—0 if not inside mouse cursor drawing code; otherwise the cursor is being displayed, moved, hidden, and so on.

cx = far call flag—reports whether the mouse driver made a far call or interrupt call to the BIOS, DOS, or interrupt handler. The value is decremented when a function has been executed, and incremented when the function terminates.

dx = mouse busy flag—the mouse driver decrements this flag when one of its interrupt handlers is entered and increments it upon the handler's termination. When dx=0, the driver is in an idle state. Use in conjunction with cx to determine if an interrupt handler and BIOS function have been called or just an interrupt handler.

Example

The following retrieves the general mouse driver information:

```
mregs.x.ax=37;
int86(0x33,&mregs,&mregs);
ginfo=mregs.h.ax;
IVFF=mregs.x.bx;
FCF=mregs.x.cx;
MBF=mregs.x.dx;
```

Version availability: 6.26 and later

Mouse Function 38: Get Maximum Virtual Coordinates

Mouse function 38 returns the maximum allowable display coordinates for mouse virtual coordinates. The coordinates returned are the absolute maximum coordinates of the display, regardless of the virtual coordinates set by mouse functions 7 and 8 (use mouse function 49 to retrieve the values set by function 7 and 8). Additionally, function 38 returns if the mouse has been disabled using mouse function 31.

Input Values

ax = 38

Return Values

bx = mouse disabled flag (0 if driver currently enabled,
nonzero if driver has been disabled)

cx = maximum virtual x coordinate

dx = maximum virtual y coordinate

Example

The following retrieves the maximum allowable virtual display coordinates:

```
mregs.x.ax=38;
int86(0x33,&mregs,&mregs);
mflag=mregs.x.bx;
max_x=mregs.x.cx;
max_y=mregs.x.dx;
```

Version availability: 6.26 and later

Chapter reference: 3 (discussion)

Mouse Function 39: Get Screen and Cursor Mask Values and Mickey Count

Mouse function 39 returns the screen and cursor mask values if a software text cursor is being used, or the first and last scan lines if a hardware text cursor is being used. (See mouse function 10 regarding setting the values). Mouse function 39 also returns the horizontal and vertical mickey count. The mickey counters are reset to 0 after the mouse is polled for movement.

Input Values

ax = 39

Return Values

ax = screen mask value or starting scan line number

bx = cursor mask value or ending scan line number

cx = horizontal mickey count

dx = vertical mickey count

Example

Assuming a software cursor is in use, the following retrieves the current values:

```
mregs.x.ax=39;
int86(0x33,&mregs,&mregs);
smask=mregs.x.ax;
cmask=mregs.x.bx;
hmick=mregs.x.cx;
vmick=mregs.x.dx;
```

The mickey counts returned are RAW counts, and are unaffected by any ratios previously set.

Version availability: 7.01 and later

Mouse Function 40: Set Video Mode

Mouse function 40 sets the mouse driver's current video mode and font size. The function ignores modes not supported by your video hardware. To retrieve a list of valid modes, use mouse function 41, enumerate video modes.

Input Values

ax = 40

cx = video mode number

dh = vertical font size (0 for default)

dl = horizontal font size (0 for default)

Return Values

cx = success flag (0 when mode selected is valid. If the mode is not valid, the
success flag contains the value sent as the video mode number.)

Example

The following sets the mouse driver's video mode to 0x12(VGA 640 × 480 16-color),
and the font size to 8 × 14:

```
mregs.x.ax=40;
mregs.x.cx=0x12;
mregs.h.dh=14;
mregs.h.dl=8;
int86(0x33,&mregs,&mregs);
```

Version availability: 7.0 and later

Chapter reference: 17 (discussion)

Mouse Function 41: Enumerate Video Modes

Mouse function 41 returns a list of video modes supported by the mouse driver. The
video modes returned are the same used to set the video mode via function 40. The
string description of the mode may also be available.

Input Values

ax = 41

cx = operation (0 to find first mode; nonzero to find next mode)

Return Values

cx = video mode number

es:dx = pointer to string (if available)

Example

The following finds the first video mode available, then the next. The string infor-mation is ignored as it is *rarely* supported.

```
/* Find First Mode */
/*-----------------*/
mregs.x.ax=41;
mregs.x.cx=0;
int86x(0x33,&mregs,&mregs,&segregs);
vmode[0]=mregs.x.cx;

/* Find Next Mode */
/*----------------*/
mregs.x.ax=41;
mregs.x.cx=1;
int86x(0x33,&mregs,&mregs,&segregs);
vmode[1]=mregs.x.cx;
```

Version availability: 7.0 and later

Mouse Function 42: Get Cursor Hot Spot

Mouse function 42 returns the cursor's current hot spot (see Chapter 14 regarding the hot spot), the mouse type, and the internal cursor flag used to determine if the mouse is visible or invisible (see Chapter 4 regarding the internal cursor flag).

Input Values

ax = 42

Return Values

ax = internal cursor flag (0 if the cursor is visible; –1 or less if the mouse cursor is invisible. The flag is incremented when mouse function 1, show cursor is called and decremented when mouse function 2, hide cursor, is called.)

bx = horizontal cursor hot spot

cx = vertical cursor hot spot

dx = mouse type

The mouse type is returned as:

Value	Mouse Type
1	Bus mouse
2	Serial mouse
3	InPort mouse
4	PS/2 mouse
5	Hewlett-Packard mouse

Example

The following retrieves all information returned by mouse function 42:

```
mregs.x.ax=42;
int86(0x33,&mregs,&mregs);
fcur=mregs.x.ax;
hhot=mregs.x.bx;
vhot=mregs.x.cx;
mtype=mregs.x.dx;
```

Version availability: 7.02 and later

Chapter reference: 4 (discussion)

Mouse Function 43: Load Acceleration Curves

Mouse function 43 sets the acceleration curve data or restores it to the defaults.

Input Values

ax = 43

bx = curve number (set to –1 for default reset or a value of 1-4 to select curve)

es:si = pointer to curve data

Return Values

ax = error flag (0 on success; otherwise nonzero)

The curve data es:si points to is contained within a 324-byte array, which is defined as the following:

Curve Length

Offset in Array	Number of Bytes Used	Description
0	1	Number of mouse counts and factors, curve 1
1	1	Number of mouse counts and factors, curve 2
2	1	Number of mouse counts and factors, curve 3
3	1	Number of mouse counts and factors, curve 4

Mouse Count Table

Offset in Array	Number of Bytes Used	Description
4	32	Array of ascending mouse count threshold, curve 1
36	32	Array of ascending mouse count threshold, curve 2
68	32	Array of ascending mouse count threshold, curve 3
100	32	array of ascending mouse count threshold, curve 4

Scale Factor Table

Offset in Array	Number of Bytes Used	Description
132	32	Array of scale factors at each threshold, curve 1
164	32	Array of scale factors at each threshold, curve 2
196	32	Array of scale factors at each threshold, curve 3
228	32	Array of scale factors at each threshold, curve 4

Curve Name Table

Offset in Array	Number of Bytes Used	Description
260	16	Name of curve 1, 16-character ASCII array
276	16	Name of curve 2, 16-character ASCII array
292	16	Name of curve 3, 16-character ASCII array
308	16	Name of curve 4, 16-character ASCII array

Example

The following sets the acceleration curves to the values contained in c_buff:

```
mregs.x.ax=43;
mregs.x.bx=1;
segregs.es=FP_SEG(c_buff);
mregs.x.si=FP_OFF(c_buff);
int86x(0x33,&mregs,&mregs,&segregs);
error_flag=mregs.x.ax;
```

Version availability: 7.0 and later

Mouse Function 44: Read Acceleration Curves

Mouse function 44 returns the acceleration curve data. See function 43 regarding detailed information on the curve data.

Input Values

ax = 44

Return Values

ax = error code (0 if successful; nonzero on error)

bx = curve number

es:si = pointer to curve data

Example

The following retrieves the acceleration curve data:

```
mregs.x.ax=44;
int86x(0x33,&mregs,&mregs,&segregs);
error_code=mregs.x.ax;
curve_num=mregs.x.bx;
curve_data_seg=segregs.es;
curve_data_ofs=mregs.x.si;
```

Version availability: 7.0 and later

Mouse Function 45: Set/Get Acceleration Curve

Mouse function 45 sets the acceleration curve data or restores it to the defaults. Additionally, the currently active curve data is returned. See functions 43 and 44 for details regarding the curve data.

Input Values

ax = 45

bx = set/get curve number (−1 to return active curve; 1-4 to set active curve)

Return Values

ax = error code (0 on success; otherwise nonzero)

bx = curve number

es:si = pointer to curve string name

Example

The following retrieves the active curve number and name, and prints the curve name to the display:

```
char far *curve_name;
mregs.x.ax=45;
mregs.x.bx=-1;
int86x(0x33,&mregs,&mregs,&segregs);
error_code=mregs.x.ax;
curve_num=mregs.x.bx;
curve_name=(void far *)(((unsigned long)(segregs.es)<<16)|
(unsigned)(mregs.x.si));
while (*curve_name!=0)
    {
    printf("%c",*curve_name);
    ++curve_name;
    }
```

Version availability: 7.0 and later

Mouse Function 46: Undocumented

Mouse Function 47: Mouse Hardware Reset

Mouse function 47 resets the mouse hardware and all mouse driver variables dependent on the display hardware. This function does not reset any software values.

Input Values

ax = 47

Return Values

ax = error flag (−1 on success; 0 on failure)

Example

The following resets the mouse hardware:

```
mregs.x.ax=47;
int86(0x33,&mregs,&mregs);
error=mregs.x.ax;
```

Version availability: 7.02 and later

Mouse Function 48: Set/Get BallPoint Information

Mouse function 48 sets either the BallPoint orientation or button mask information.

Input Values

ax = 48

bx = rotation angle (range: −32,769 to 32,767 degrees relative to internal device orientation)

cx = command (0 to return information; nonzero to set button mask)

Return Values

ax = status: −1 if BallPoint device is not present. If present, the bits in ax contain the state of the buttons. For example:

0 0 0 0 0 0 0 0 0 0 B1 B3 B2 B4

Indicator	Meaning
B1	Set if button 1 is pressed
B3	Set if button 3 is pressed

Indicator	Meaning
B2	Set if button 2 is pressed
B4	Set if button 4 is pressed

bx = rotation angle (range: 0 to 359)

ch = primary button mask: Mask 1 thru 4 is located within the mask bits
as 0 0 B1 B3 B2 B4 0 0 (see previous table)

cl = secondary button mask: Mask 1 thru 4 is located within the mask bits
as 0 0 B1 B3 B2 B4 0 0 (see previous table)

Example

The following retrieves the BallPoint information:

```
mregs.x.ax=48;
mregs.x.cx=0;
int86(0x33,&mregs,&mregs);
bstat=mregs.x.ax;
rangle=mregs.x.bx;
pbmask=mregs.h.ch;
sbmask=mregs.h.cl;
```

The next example sets the rotation angle to 180:

```
mregs.x.ax=48;
mregs.x.bx=180;
mregs.x.cx=0x3C;
int86(0x33,&mregs,&mregs);
```

Version availability: 7.04 and later

Mouse Function 49: Get Min/Max Virtual Coordinates

Mouse function 49 returns the minimum and maximum virtual coordinates of the current display. The coordinates returned are those set by mouse functions 7 and 8.

If not set by these functions, the minimum values are 0, and the maximum values equal the maximum absolute display coordinates.

Input Values

ax = 49

Return Values

ax = minimum virtual x coordinate

bx = minimum virtual y coordinate

cx = maximum virtual x coordinate

dx = maximum virtual y coordinate

Example

The following retrieves the current virtual coordinate settings:

```
mregs.x.ax=49;
int86(0x33,&mregs,&mregs);
min_x=mregs.x.ax;
min_y=mregs.x.bx;
max_x=mregs.x.cx;
max_y=mregs.x.dx;
```

Version availability: 7.05 and later

Mouse Function 50: Get Active Advanced Function

Mouse function 50 returns the availability status of the advanced mouse functions.

Input Values

ax = 50

Return Values

ax = active function flags

Bit	Meaning
15	1 if function 37 active; 0 if not
14	1 if function 38 active; 0 if not
13	1 if function 39 active; 0 if not
0	1 if function 52 active; 0 if not

Example

The following retrieves function 37 availability status:

```
mregs.x.ax=50;
int86(0x33,&mregs,&mregs);
f37_stat=mregs.x.ax >> 15;
```

Version availability: 7.05 and later

Chapter reference: 12 (discussion)

Mouse Function 51: Get Switch Settings

Mouse function 51 returns the current setting of the mouse driver's internal variables into a buffer. The buffer's maximum size is 340 bytes.

Input Values

ax = 51

cx = length of buffer

es:dx = pointer to buffer

Return Values

ax = 0

cx = number of bytes returned to buffer

es:dx = pointer to buffer

The following table defines where the variables are stored in the buffer, and the range of their values:

Byte	Meaning	Range
0	Mouse type (high 8 bits)	0-5
	Mouse port (low 8 bits)	0-4
1	Language	0-10
2	Horizontal sensitivity	0-100
3	Vertical sensitivity	0-100
4	Double-speed threshold	0-100
5	Ballistic curve	1-4 *
6	Interrupt rate	1-4 *
7	Cursor override mask	0-255
8	Laptop adjustment	0-255
9	Memory type	0-2
10	Super VGA support	0-1
11	Rotation angle	0-359
13	Primary button	1-4
14	Secondary button	1-4
15	Drag lock enabled	0-1
16-339	Contain acceleration curve data	

* Range for the Logitech mouse driver is 0-4

Example

The following retrieves the internal variables:

```
mregs.x.ax=51;
mregs.x.cx=340;
mregs.x.dx=FP_OFF(s_buff);
segregs.es=FP_SEG(s_buff);
int86x(0x33,&mregs,&mregs,&segregs);
num_bytes=mregs.x.cx;
```

Version availability: 7.05 and later

Mouse Function 52: Get MOUSE.INI

Mouse function 52 returns a pointer to a string buffer containing the full path of the MOUSE.INI. If MOUSE.INI does not exist, the pointer contains a null string.

Input Values

ax = 52

Return Values

ax = 0

es:dx = pointer to buffer

Example

The following retrieves and prints the path to MOUSE.INI:

```
char far *ini_path;
mregs.x.ax=52;
int86x(0x33,&mregs,&mregs,&segregs);
ini_path=(void far *)(((unsigned long)(segregs.es)<<16)|
(unsigned)(mregs.x.dx));
while (*ini_path!=0)
    {
    printf("%c",*ini_path);
    ++ini_path;
    }
```

Version availability: 8.00 and later

Appendix B

Windows Mouse and Cursor Functions

This appendix contains a reference to all Windows 3.1 API mouse and cursor functions. Please be aware of the fact that many 3.1 API functions, the parameters sent to the functions, and the types of those parameters may be different than their predecessors in Windows 3.0. This appendix assumes you use the STRICT keyword before WINDOWS.H and therefore use 3.1 function prototypes.

The following table is a quick reference to the actions of the individual functions:

Function Name	Description
ClipCursor	Confines the cursor to a rectangular region
CreateCursor	Creates a cursor from two bit masks
DestroyCursor	Destroys a cursor previously created with CreateCursor()
GetCapture	Retrieves a handle to the window that has captured mouse input
GetClipCursor	Determines the region the cursor was last bound to
GetCursorPos	Gets the screen coordinates of the cursor
GetDoubleClickTime	Retrieves the double-click time value
LoadCursor	Loads a cursor from a resource file or a default windows cursor
ReleaseCapture	Releases capture of the mouse

Function Name	Description
SetCapture	Captures the mouse focus so that only a specified windows receives mouse input
SetCursor	Changes the cursor
SetCursorPos	Moves the cursor to the specified position
SetDoubleClickTime	Changes the double-click time value
ShowCursor	Increases or decreases the cursor display count (hide, show)
SwapMouseButton	Reverses left and right buttons

ClipCursor

```
void ClipCursor(const RECT FAR* lprc) /* lprc=address of RECT  */
                                      /* structure.            */
```

This function restricts cursor movement to the rectangular region defined by lprc. If lprc is NULL, the cursor can move about the entire display.

Since the cursor is a shared resource, an application that confines the cursor must also free it before the application terminates or loses focus.

The RECT structure used to set the region is defined as:

```
typedef struct tagRECT
   {
   int left;      /* Upper-left x coordinate  */
   int top;       /* Upper-left y coordinate  */
   int right;     /* Lower-right x coordinate */
   int bottom;    /* Lower-right y coordinate */
   }RECT;
```

Return Values

None.

Chapter reference: 25

CreateCursor

```
HCURSOR CreateCursor(HINSTANCE hinst,
                     int xHotSpot,int yHotSpot,
                     int nWidth,int nHeight,
                     const void FAR* lpvANDbitPlane,
                     const void FAR* lpvXORbitPlane)
```

where

Parameter	Meaning
hinst	Module creating cursor
xHotSpot	Horizontal hot spot
yHotSpot	Vertical hot spot
nWidth	Width of cursor in pixels
nHeight	Height of cursor in pixels
lpvANDbitPlane	Pointer to array containing AND mask
lpvXORbitPlane	Pointer to array containing XOR mask

This function creates a cursor specified by the input parameters. The application must destroy the cursor before termination with the function DestroyCursor().

Return Values

Handle to the cursor if successful; otherwise NULL.

Chapter reference: 24

DestroyCursor

```
BOOL DestroyCursor(HCURSOR hCursor) /* hCursor=cursor to be   */
                                    /* destroyed.            */
```

This function destroys a cursor previously created with CreateCursor().

Return Values

Nonzero if destroyed; 0 if not destroyed.

Chapter reference: 24

GetCapture

```
HWND GetCapture(void)
```

This function retrieves the handle of the window that has the mouse capture (if any).

Return Values

Handle to the window that has the mouse capture if successful; otherwise NULL.

GetClipCursor

```
void GetClipCursor(RECT FAR* lprc) /* lprc=address of RECT    */
                                   /* structure.              */
```

This function retrieves the coordinates the cursor was bound to by the last ClipCursor() function call.

The RECT structure used to store the cursor limits is defined as:

```
typedef struct tagRECT
   {
   int left;      /* Upper-left x coordinate  */
   int top;       /* Upper-left y coordinate  */
   int right;     /* Lower-right x coordinate */
   int bottom;    /* Lower-right y coordinate */
   }RECT;
```

Return Values

None.

GetCursorPos

```
void GetCursorPos(POINT FAR* lppt) /* lppt=address of POINT   */
                                   /* structure.              */
```

This function retrieves the cursor's current coordinates in screen coordinates. The POINT structure is defined as:

```
typedef struct tagPOINT
    {
    int x;     /* Horizontal cursor position */
    int y;     /* Vertical cursor position   */
    }POINT;
```

Return Values

None.

Chapter reference: 25

GetDoubleClickTime

```
UINT GetDoubleClickTime(void)
```

This function retrieves the value of the current double-click time. Double-click time is the maximum amount of milliseconds allowed between button presses for a double-click message to be registered.

Return Values

Current double-click time.

Chapter reference: 23

LoadCursor

```
HCURSOR LoadCursor(HINSTANCE hinst,LPCSTR pszCursor)
```

where

Parameter	Meaning
hinst	Handle of application instance
pszCursor	Cursor name string or resource identifier

This function loads a cursor resource only if it has not been previously loaded. If it has been loaded, it retrieves the handle of the existing cursor.

To load the predefined Windows cursor(s), set hinst to NULL and use one of the predefined values for pszCursor. The possible values are:

Cursor Name	Shape
IDC_ARROW	Arrow cursor
IDC_UPARROW	Big vertical arrow
IDC_CROSS	Cross hair cursor
IDC_IBEAM	I-beam text cursor
IDC_ICON	Square with small square in middle
IDC_SIZE	Cursor with arrows pointing north, south east, and west
IDC_SIZENESW	Cursor with arrows pointing northeast and southwest
IDC_SIZENS	Cursor with arrows pointing north and south
IDC_SIZENWSE	Cursor with arrows pointing northwest and southeast
IDC_SIZEWE	Cursor with arrows pointing west and south
IDC_WAIT	Hourglass cursor

Return Values

The function returns the handle of the loaded cursor. A NULL value indicates failure. If pszCursor specifies a resource other than a cursor resource, the return value will be invalid.

Chapter reference: 24

ReleaseCapture

```
void ReleaseCapture(void)
```

This function releases the mouse capture set with the function SetCapture(), and restores mouse processing to normal.

Return Values

None.

Chapter reference: 25 (discussion)

SetCapture

```
HWND SetCapture(HWND hwnd)    /* hwnd=handle of window that   */
                             /* will receive all mouse       */
                             /* messages.                     */
```

This function sets the mouse capture to the specified window. Once captured, this window receives all mouse input whether or not the cursor is inside the window. Only one window can have the mouse capture at any given time.

When the applications no longer needs all mouse input, use the function ReleaseCapture() to return mouse processing to normal.

Return Values

Handle to the window that previously received the mouse capture.

Chapter reference: 25 (discussion)

SetCursor

```
HCURSOR SetCursor(HCURSOR hCursor) /* hCursor=handle of cursor*/
```

This function changes the current cursor to the cursor resource specified by hCursor. If hCursor is NULL, the cursor is removed from the display.

Return Values

Handle identifying the previous cursor, or a NULL value if no previous cursor existed.

 The cursor specified must have been previously loaded with the function LoadCursor().

Chapter reference: 24

SetCursorPos

```
void SetCursorPos(int x,int y) /* x=horizontal coordinate   */
                               /* y=vertical coordinate      */
```

This function positions the cursor at the location specified by x,y. Use only screen coordinates to position the cursor.

Return Values

None.

Chapter reference: 25

SetDoubleClickTime

```
void SetDoubleClickTime(UINT uInterval) /* uInterval=double-  */
                                        /* click time in      */
                                        /* milliseconds.      */
```

This function sets the value of the current double-click time. The double-click time is the maximum amount of milliseconds allowed between button presses for a double-click message to be registered. The default is 500 milliseconds.

Return Values

None.

Chapter reference: 23

ShowCursor

```
int ShowCursor(BOOL fShow)    /* fShow=effect on display count */
```

This function hides or shows the cursor, depending on the current cursor display count. The cursor display count is maintained internally and can only by modified with the function ShowCursor().

The display count is initialized to 0 when the mouse is installed and −1 if no mouse is installed.

If fShow is TRUE, the display count is incremented. The cursor is visible when the cursor counter is 0 or greater.

If fShow is FALSE the cursor counter is decremented. The cursor is invisible when the counter is less than 0.

Return Values

Current value of the cursor display count.

Chapter reference: 25

SwapMouseButton

```
BOOL SwapMouseButton(BOOL fSwap) /* fSwap=reverse or normalize*/
                                 /* mouse buttons.           */
```

This function allows you to swap the right and left mouse buttons. This is a nifty feature for left-handed people who prefer to use the right button instead of the left.

If fSwap is TRUE, the left button generates right button messages and the right button generates left button messages. If fSwap is FALSE, the buttons are restored to normal operation.

Since the mouse is a shared resource, swapping the buttons will affect operations in all Windows applications.

Return Values

Returns the meaning of the mouse buttons prior to the function being called. If 0, the buttons were normal, and if nonzero, they were reversed.

Windows Mouse Messages

This appendix contains detailed reference to all Windows mouse and cursor messages.

HIWORD( ) and LOWORD( )

In this appendix the functions HIWORD() and LOWORD() are used to signify the high-order word and low-order word of an additional parameter. For instance, HIWORD(lParam) signifies that the parameter is located in the high-order word of lParam.

Client Area Button Messages

The following button messages are sent from Windows when the cursor is in the client area and a mouse button(s) has been pressed, released, or double-clicked:

Message	Meaning
WM_LBUTTONDOWN	Left mouse button pressed
WM_MBUTTONDOWN	Middle mouse button pressed
WM_RBUTTONDOWN	Right mouse button pressed

Message	Meaning
WM_LBUTTONUP	Left mouse button released
WM_MBUTTONUP	Middle mouse button released
WM_RBUTTONUP	Right mouse button released
WM_LBUTTONDBLCLK	Left mouse button double-clicked
WM_MBUTTONDBLCLK	Middle mouse button double-clicked
WM_RBUTTONDBLCLK	Right mouse button double-clicked

Additional Parameters

wParam specifies which various virtual keys and other buttons are down (if any). The possible values can be one or any combination of the following:

Constant	Meaning
MK_CONTROL	CTRL key is down
MK_SHIFT	SHIFT key is down
MK_LBUTTON	Left button is down
MK_RBUTTON	Right button is down
MK_MBUTTON	Middle button is down

LOWORD(lParam) is the horizontal cursor location relative to the upper-left corner of the client area.

HIWORD(lParam) is the vertical cursor location relative to the upper-left corner of the client area.

Return Values

Applications should return 0 after processing any of the previous messages.

Chapter reference: 23

Nonclient Area Button Messages

The following button messages are sent from Windows when the cursor is in the nonclient area and a mouse button(s) has been pressed, released, or double-clicked:

Message	Meaning
WM_NCLBUTTONDOWN	Left mouse button pressed
WM_NCMBUTTONDOWN	Middle mouse button pressed
WM_NCRBUTTONDOWN	Right mouse button pressed
WM_NCLBUTTONUP	Left mouse button released
WM_NCMBUTTONUP	Middle mouse button released
WM_NCRBUTTONUP	Right mouse button released
WM_NCLBUTTONDBLCLK	Left mouse button double-clicked
WM_NCMBUTTONDBLCLK	Middle mouse button double-clicked
WM_NCRBUTTONDBLCLK	Right mouse button double-clicked

Additional Parameters

wParam is the hit-test code (see WM_NCHITTEST).

LOWORD(lParam) is the horizontal cursor location as a screen coordinate.

HIWORD(lParam) is the vertical cursor location as a screen coordinate.

Return Values

Applications should return 0 after processing any of the previous messages.

Chapter reference: 23

WM_MOUSEACTIVATE

This message is sent from Windows when a mouse button is pressed and the cursor is in an inactive window. The message is received by the parent window only if the child passes it to the function DefWindowProc().

Additional Parameters

wParam is the parent window of the window being activated.

LOWORD(lParam) is the hit test code (see WM_NCHITTEST).

HIWORD(lParam) is the identifier of the mouse message.

Return Values

An application processing this message should pass the message on to the function DefWindowProc(), or return a value specifying if the window should be activated, and if the mouse event should be discarded. The value sent must be one of the following:

Value	Meaning
MA_ACTIVATE	Activate the window
MA_NOACTIVE	Do not activate window
MA_ACTIVATEANDEAT	Activate the window and discard the mouse event (rat snack)
MA_NOACTIVATEANDEAT	Do not activate the window; discard the mouse event

WM_MOUSEMOVE

This message is sent from Windows when the mouse moves and the cursor is in the client area. If the mouse is not captured, the message is sent to the window containing the cursor. If the mouse has been captured, the message is sent to the window having mouse capture.

Additional Parameters

wParam specifies which virtual keys and other buttons are down (if any). The possible values can be one or any combination of the following:

Constant	Meaning
MK_CONTROL	CTRL key is down
MK_SHIFT	SHIFT key is down
MK_LBUTTON	Left button is down
MK_RBUTTON	Right button is down
MK_MBUTTON	Middle button is down

LOWORD(lParam) is the horizontal cursor location as a screen coordinate.

HIWORD(lParam) is the vertical cursor location as a screen coordinate.

Return Values

Applications should return 0 after processing this messages.

Chapter reference: 24

WM_NCHITTEST

This message is sent whenever the mouse moves. It is sent to the window where the cursor is located or to a window that used the function SetCapture().

Additional Parameters

LOWORD(lParam) indicates the horizontal cursor location as a screen coordinate.

HIWORD(lParam) indicates the vertical cursor location as a screen coordinate.

Return Values

The return value of DefWindowProc() indicates the cursor's location and is one of the following:

Constant	Meaning
HTBORDER	In the border of a window with no sizing border
HTBOTTOM	In lower horizontal border of window
HTBOTTOMLEFT	In lower-left corner of window border
HTBOTTOMRIGHT	In lower-right corner of window border
HTCAPTION	In the title area
HTCLIENT	In the client area
HTERROR	On a screen background or dividing line between windows (same as HTNOWHERE, but is accompanied with a system 'beep')
HTGROWBOX	In a size box (same as HTSIZE)
HTHSCROLL	In the horizontal scroll bar
HTLEFT	In the left border
HTMENU	In a menu area
HTREDUCE	In a minimize box (button)

Constant	Meaning
HTRIGHT	In the right hand border
HTSYSMENU	In a system menu or close button of child window
HTTOP	In the upper horizontal border
HTTOPLEFT	In upper-left corner of window border
HTTOPRIGHT	In upper-right corner of window border
HTTRANSPARENT	In a window currently covered by another window
HTVSCROLL	In a vertical scroll bar
HTZOOM	In a maximize box (button)

Chapter reference: 25

WM_NCMOUSEMOVE

This message is sent from Windows whenever the mouse moves and the cursor is in the nonclient area.

Additional Parameters

wParam indicates the hit-test code (see WM_NCHITTEST).

LOWORD(lParam) indicates the horizontal cursor location as a screen coordinate.

HIWORD(lParam) indicates the vertical cursor location as a screen coordinate.

Return Values

Applications should return 0 after processing this message.

WM_SETCURSOR

This message is sent from Windows when the mouse cursor moves and the mouse has not been captured. If an application traps this message, it is responsible for handling the cursor within the nonclient area.

Additional Parameters

wParam indicates the handle of the window that contains the cursor.

LOWORD(lParam) indicates the hit test code (see WM_NCHITTEST).

HIWORD(lParam) indicates the number of mouse messages.

If LOWORD(lParam) is HTERROR, and HIWORD(lParam) is a mouse button down message, the function MessageBeep() is called.

Return Values

Applications should return TRUE to halt further cursor processing or FALSE to continue.

Chapter reference: 24, 25

Index

A

Acceleration curves
    setting, 506-508, 509-510
    retrieving, 508-509
Advanced mouse functions, 513-514. *See also*
    Mouse functions 36-52
Alternate event handler, 97, 124, 487-489
    call mask, 124, 487-488
Anchors
    in CAD operations, 166-167
    in crosshairs operations, 163
    event handler, using with, 123
AND
    logical operations, 201, 230
    write mode, 14
Applications Programming Interface (API), 377,
    517
Assembly
    event handler, 100-103
    inline, 263
    /MX compiler option, 108
ATI Graphics Ultra, 257
AUTOEXEC.BAT, 4

B

Background image. *See* Image
Ballistic speed, 195. *See also* Acceleration curves
BallPoint mouse, 511-512
BBUTTON_DOWN, 35, 37, 105, 121, 244, 294,
    303
BBUTTON_UP, 35, 37, 105, 121, 244, 294, 303
.BGI files, 29
BIGARROW, 427, 430-432, 432

BIOS. *See* ROM BIOS
Bit mask. *See* CreateCursor(); Cursor mask;
    Screen mask; Write mode 0
BITMAP_SIZE, 267, 274, 279-282, 285
Borland
    .BGI files, 29
    compiler, 7, 112-113, 243, 245, 287-289,
        304-306, 372-373
    graphics library, 29, 113
    run menu, in Windows, 374
    video function library, 10, 15
Boundaries
    cursor. *See* Cursor range
    even byte, 260-262
BSTATE, 36, 37, 104, 107, 120, 244, 294, 303
Buffer
    acceleration curve, 507-509
    mouse state, 485-487
    MOUSE.INI, 516
    switch settings, 514-516
Bus mouse, 182, 499, 506
Buttons, 33
    number of, 39, 46, 107, 295, 466-467,
        495-496
    presses in DOS, 81-90, 95, 106-107,
        115-121, 469-472, 511-512
    presses in Windows, 383-391, 527-529
    releases in DOS, 81-90, 95, 106-107,
        115-121, 472-473, 511-512
    releases in Windows, 383-391, 527-529
    reverse trap, 86
    status, determining, 81-90, 106-107,
        115-121, 469-470
    swapping, 525

C

CAD. *See* Computer Aided Design
Call mask
    of alternate event handler, 124, 487-488
    of event handler, 96-97, 292, 350, 478,
        483-484
Calling mouse functions, 6-7, 34-35, 37-44,
    174-178, 295-304, 466-516
Capture, of mouse, 461, 520, 523
Cell sizes, text mode, 35, 46
change_background(), 13, 19, 25, 134, 139
change_color(), 13, 18-19, 25, 31
change_sprite_color(), 266, 285-286, 310, 337, 341
change_sprite_line_color(), 266, 285, 310, 337,
    340
Character
    attributes, 230
    cell sizes, 35, 46
Child process, 124
clear_line_from(), 13, 18, 24, 30, 31, 67
Client area
    button messages, 383-398, 527-528
    coordinates, 391, 445-450
    default registered cursor, 414
    detailed information, 391-396
ClientToScreen(), 454, 458
ClipCursor(), 452, 454, 458, 461, 517, 518
Clock speed, 87
cm_or_el, 178, 231
CMX, 36, 37, 104, 106-107, 116, 120, 123, 149,
    163, 244, 294, 303, 350
CMY, 36, 37, 104, 106-107, 116, 120, 123, 149,
    163, 244, 294, 303
CODE keyword, 381
Compiler options, 108, 112-114, 288-290, 305-306,
    372-373
        /AC, 114, 290, 305
        /AH, 114, 289-290, 305
        /AL, 114, 290, 305
        /AM, 114, 290, 305
        /AS, 114, 290, 305
        /Au, 100, 288-290
        /B, 288-289
        /c, 373, 288-290, 305
        /Fe, 114
        /Gs, 114, 289-290, 305
        /Gw, 373
        -mc, 113, 289, 305
        -mh, 113, 288-289, 305
        -ml, 113, 289, 305
        -mm, 113, 289, 305

        -ms, 113, 289, 305
        /MX, 108
        /Oe, 114
        -W, 372-373
        /Zp, 373
COMPILER.H, 7-10, 30, 248
    modifying, 9, 248
Compilers. *See* Borland; Microsoft
Compiling
    in integrated environment, 112-113, 245,
        288, 304, 372
    from command line, 113-114, 245,
        288-290, 305-306, 372-373
Computer Aided Design (CAD)
    coordinates, anchoring, 166-167, 169-170
    techniques for, 165-178, 348-363
Conditional hide. *See* Exclusion area
Conditional off. *See* Exclusion area
CONFIG.SYS, 4, 69
CONIO.H, 249
COPYPUT write mode, 14, 167, 172, 263, 336-337
COPY_PUT, 9, 167, 172, 267, 307, 337
COURB.FON, 29
CreateBitmap(), 442
CreateCompatibleDC(), 442
CreateCursor(), 434, 438, 443, 517, 519
Crosshairs, 151-164
    anchoring coordinates, 157-158, 163
    defining coordinates, 156, 162
CRT page
    retrieving, 174, 176, 180, 182, 493-494
    setting, 182, 492-493
CS_DBLCLKS, 390
CS_HREDRAW, 390
CS_VREDRAW, 390
ctype, 178, 231
Cursor. *See* Graphics cursor; Text cursor;
    Windows cursor
Cursor coordinates
    converting, in DOS, 36, 74, 76
    converting, in Windows, 396, 445, 454
    in DOS, 71-79, 104, 107, 116, 123, 292,
        467, 469-473, 501-502
    in Windows, 391, 395-396, 398, 445-450,
        454, 521, 528, 530-532
Cursor flag
    in DOS, 60-62, 468, 505-506
    in Windows, 452-454
Cursor flicker, 60, 420, 438
Cursor mask
    in graphics cursor, 200-201, 475-476
    in sprite cursor, 314, 342-344

in text software cursor, 230, 476-477, 502-503
in Windows cursor, 434-439, 519
Cursor position. *See* Cursor coordinates
Cursor range
limiting in DOS, 41-42, 49-52, 90-94, 129-130, 473-475, 501-502
limiting in Windows, 454-455, 461, 518, 520
limiting sprite, 334
restoring in DOS, 143
restoring in Windows, 454-455, 461
Cursor visibility, 53-66
CURSOR_MOVED, 35, 37, 104, 116, 118, 120, 122, 190, 244, 294, 303, 349-350
CURSORS.RES, 427-428
Curve name table, 508
Curve length, 507

D

DATA keyword, 381
Data segment
in event handler, 100
in sprite driver, 287-288
DBL_CLICK_TIME, 87, 90
Default registered cursor, 414, 420
#define statement, 7
DefWindowProc(), 371, 380, 384, 529-531
delay(), 27-28, 87, 89
DeleteObject(), 443
DeleteDC(), 443
DESCRIPTION keyword, 381
DestroyCursor(), 432, 438, 443, 517, 519-520
destroy_sprite(), 266, 281, 310-313, 316, 336, 347
Detection of mouse
in DOS, 6, 34, 38, 45, 295, 466-467
in Windows, 452, 459
Device driver, 3-4
Device-dependent cursor, 434-439
Device-independent cursor, 434, 439-444
Disable Mouse Driver, 494
Display
disruption, 53-68, 326
updating, 53-68, 326, 334
variable frequency, 258, 317
Domestic mice, 496-498
DOS, 4
DOS.H, 4, 249
do_sprite(), 266, 281-282
Double-click time, 405, 409-410, 521, 524
Double-clicking
in DOS, 82, 86-90
in Windows, 390, 405-410, 521, 524

Double-speed threshold, 176, 190, 194-198, 482-483, 490-491
draw_rectangle(), 13, 19-20, 26, 28, 171
draw_sprite(), 266, 268, 282-285, 292, 294, 299, 310, 355, 347-348
Dual cursors, 348-363
Dynamic cursor, 434

E

EGA. *See* Enhanced Graphics Adapter
EGA_REG_READ, 36, 38, 68-69, 244, 294
EGA.SYS, 68-69
ellipse(), 9, 14, 166, 176
Enable Mouse Driver, 494-495
Enhanced Graphics Adapter (EGA)
display, 67-69, 254-256
display modes. *See* Graphic modes
registers, 66-69, 264-265
write modes, 260
Enumerate Video Modes, 504-505
Event driven platforms, 90, 368
Event handler, 96-109, 111-125, 478-479, 483-484, 487-490
address, 97, 478-479
alternate, 97, 124, 487-489
alternate call mask, 487-488
call mask, 96, 478
compiling, 107-108, 242
disabling, 292, 350
installing, 96, 98, 105, 119, 304
sprite driver, keeping active, 335
status variables, defined, 35-36
status variables, resetting, 105, 118, 145
swapping, 123, 483-484
terminating, 117
Event processing, 96, 100-101, 302-303. *See also* Buttons; Cursor coordinates
Event processor, 100, 104, 302
EVENT.ASM, 101-103, 107, 242, 306
EVENTC.OBJ, 242, 108
EVENTH.OBJ, 242, 108
EVENTL.OBJ, 242, 108
EVENTM.OBJ, 242, 108
event_processor(), 104-107, 245, 292, 302-303, 309
EVENTS.OBJ, 108
event_status, 104, 106
evp_type, 8, 287
Exclusion area, 58, 62-68, 481-482
EGA, problems with, 66-69
possible bug, 65
setting, 62, 481-482
sprite driver, 334-335

exec(), 124
EXETYPE keyword, 381
EXPORTS keyword, 382

F ——————————————————

Far call flag, 501
Far functions, 101, 288
Floating menus, 127. *See also* Menus
Focus, 455
.FON files, 30
Font size, 29, 503-504. *See also* HFONT_SIZE,
    VFONT_SIZE
FP_OFF(), 97
FP_SEG(), 97
Functions. *See* Mouse driver functions; Mouse
    functions 1-52; Mouse function library; Video
    function library; Sprite driver functions

G ——————————————————

GDI. *See* Graphics Device Interface
GENERIC.C, 369-371, 414
GENERIC.DEF, 371
Get Active Advanced Function, 182, 513-514
Get Alternate Event Handler, 489
Get Button Press Information, 82, 471-472
Get Button Release Information, 35, 43, 82, 301,
    472-473
Get Button Status and Cursor Position, 35, 42, 71,
    82, 300, 469-470
Get CRT Page Number, 174, 176, 180, 493-494
Get Cursor Hot Spot, 60, 505-506
Get Driver Version, Type, and IRQ#, 174-176,
    498-499
Get General Driver Information, 500-501
Get Language Number, 497-498
Get Maximum Virtual Coordinates, 52, 501-502
Get Min/Max Virtual Coordinates, 512-513
Get Mouse Driver State Buffer Size, 125, 485
Get MOUSE.INI, 516
Get Screen and Cursor Mask Values and Mickey
    Count, 502-503
Get Sensitivity Rate, 177, 191, 491
Get Switch Settings, 514-516
GetBitmapBits(), 443
get_button_rls_info(), 35, 43-44, 82, 89, 244,
    301-302, 309
GetCapture(), 517, 520
GetClientRect(), 454, 458
GetClipCursor(), 517, 520
get_crt_page(), 174, 176, 180, 245, 309
GetCursorPos(), 445, 449-450, 460, 517, 521

GetDoubleClickTime(), 405, 409, 517, 521
GetMessage(), 380
get_mouse_button(), 35, 42-43, 71, 73, 82, 244,
    300-301, 309
get_mouse_sensitivity(), 175, 176-177, 191, 192,
    245, 309
get_mouse_type(), 174, 175-176, 180, 245, 309
get_new_cursor(), 418-419, 424-426, 431-432
GetSystemMetrics(), 442, 452, 459
gInstance, 369, 378
GlobalAlloc(), 442
GlobalFree(), 444
GlobalLock(), 443
GlobalUnlock(), 443
GMODE, 12, 21, 32, 316
GRAPH.H, 249
Graphical User Interface (GUI), 208, 227, 367
Graphics cursor, 199-228, 475-476, 500. *See also*
    Cursor coordinates; Cursor flag; Cursor
    flicker; Cursor mask; Cursor range; Cursor
    visibility
      bit expansion, 201-202
      coordinates, 71-79, 104, 107, 116, 123
      cursor mask, 200-201, 475-476
      cursor size, 47, 51
      defined, 200, 262
      hot spot, 203, 475-476, 505-506
      keyboard, moving with, 76-79
      modifying, 203-207, 209-227, 475-476
      screen mask, 200-201, 475-476
      Windows shapes in DOS, 208-227
Graphics Device Interface (GDI), 439
Graphics library
    Borland, 29, 114
    Microsoft, 30, 114
Graphics modes
    320X200 4-color, 202
    320x200 16-color, 202
    320x200 256-color, 202
    640x200 16-color, 254, 264, 315
    640x350 1-color, 254, 264
    640x350 16-color, 254-256, 264, 315, 322,
      326
    640x480 1-color, 254, 264
    640x480 16-color, 254-256, 264, 315, 322,
      504
    800x600 16-color, 253-258, 264, 315,
      317-331
    1024x768 256-color, 264
    mode 0x04, 202
    mode 0x0D, 202
    mode 0x13, 202

retrieving, 504-505

setting, 12-13, 15, 22, 318-319, 326, 503-504

vs. text mode, 11-12, 32, 36

GRAPHICS.H, 249

GRAPHICS.LIB, 29, 113

GUI. *See* Graphical User Interface

H

Hardware cursor

in mouse driver, 229-230, 234-237, 476-477

in Video hardware, 256

HCELL_SIZE, 35, 37, 39-43, 46, 243, 293, 295-303

HCURSOR, 438, 442

header(), 13, 20, 27

Header files, 47, 115, 178

HEADER1.H, 47

HEADER2.H, 115

HEADER3.H, 178-179

HEAPSIZE keyword, 381

Hewlett-Packard mouse, 182, 499, 506

HFONT_SIZE, 12, 14-18, 28

Hide Cursor, 34, 40, 58, 61-62, 297, 468-469

hide_mouse_cursor(), 34, 39-40, 58-59, 61-62, 244, 291-292, 297-298, 309, 335, 350

hide_sprite(), 266, 286, 292, 297, 310, 348, 361-362

hInstance, 369, 377-378

HIWORD(), 391, 395-396, 399, 527, 533

HORIZ_OFFSET, 268, 282, 308, 312, 315, 326, 333

Horizontal offset, 255-256

Hot spot

default mouse cursor, 203, 475-476, 505-506

sprite cursor, 315, 334

Windows cursor, 434, 519

hPrevInstance, 369, 377-378

HTBORDER, 531

HTBOTTOM, 398, 403, 424, 531

HTBOTTOMLEFT, 398, 403, 425, 531

HTBOTTOMRIGHT, 398, 403, 425, 531

HTCAPTION, 398, 403, 425, 531

HTCLIENT, 424, 462, 531

HTERROR, 398, 403, 531, 533

HTGROWBOX, 398, 403, 531

HTHSCROLL, 398, 403, 425, 531

HTLEFT, 399, 403, 425, 531

HTMENU, 399, 403, 425, 531

HTREDUCE, 399, 403, 425, 531

HTRIGHT, 399, 404, 425, 532

HTSYSMENU, 399, 404, 425, 532

HTTOP, 399, 404, 425, 532

HTTOPLEFT, 399, 404, 425, 532

HTTOPRIGHT, 399, 404, 426, 532

HTTRANSPARENT, 532

HTVSCROLL, 399, 404, 426, 532

HTZOOM, 399, 404, 426, 532

Huge functions, 287-288

hWnd, 369, 377-380

I

IBM Enhanced Graphics Adapter. *See* Enhanced Graphics Adapter

IBM Video Graphics Array. *See* Video Graphics Array

Icon, 374, 455

IDC_ARROW, 414, 415, 522

IDC_CROSS, 415, 522

IDC_IBEAM, 415, 522

IDC_ICON, 415, 522

IDC_SIZE, 414, 415, 522

IDC_SIZENESW, 415, 522

IDC_SIZENS, 415, 522

IDC_SIZENWSE, 415, 522

IDC_SIZEWE, 415, 522

IDC_UPARROW, 415, 522

IDC_WAIT, 415, 522

Image

restoring, 53-55, 57, 260

saving, 53-55, 57, 260

iMessage, 371, 380

IN_GMODE, 14, 14-27, 30, 35-37, 39-43, 244, 293, 295-303, 333

Initializing

mouse driver, 3-4, 6, 34, 38-39, 44, 295-296, 466-467

sprite driver, 313-316, 333

init_sprite(), 311-312, 314, 324, 329, 338-339, 345-346, 352-353

#include statement, 47

InPort mouse, 182, 257, 491-492, 499, 506

*inregs, 5

install_event_handler(), 105, 116, 119, 245, 292, 304, 310, 316, 336

install_video(), 12, 13, 15-16, 21-22, 31-32

int86(), 4-6

int86x(), 5

Integrated mouse driver, 500

Internal cursor flag, 60-62. *See also* Cursor flag

Internal display count, 452-454, 525

International mice, 496-498

Interrupt

rate, 491-492, 500

services, 4, 100-101

subroutine. *See* Event handler

vectors, 45, 467, 494-495
Interrupt 0x10, 47, 257, 317
Interrupt 0x33, 4, 6, 45, 368
INTNO, 5
IRET, 45, 100
IRQ number, 181, 498-499

K

KBMENU.INC, 146-149
Keyboard
    moving cursor with, in DOS, 76-79
    moving cursor with, in Windows, 450-452,
       455-461
    input, 146
Keepers loop, 72
Kraft mouse driver, available functions, 466

L

Language, of mouse driver, 496-498
LBUTTON_DOWN, 35, 37, 99, 104, 116, 118,
    120, 244, 294, 303
LBUTTON_UP, 35, 37, 105, 121, 244, 294, 303
left_arrow, 349, 351-352
LIB.EXE, 243, 306
Library files, 239-249
    Additional Global, 30, 240, 245, 310
    creating, 240-243,306
    graphics libraries, 29-30, 113-114
    using, 245-249, 310
LIBRARY keyword, 381
Light-Pen Emulation Mode Off, 480
Light-Pen Emulation Mode On, 479-480
Limiting cursor range. *See* Cursor range
limit_to_client_area(), 457-458, 461
line(), 9, 14, 18-19, 169-170
Linker options, 243, 306, 373
LL_bitmask(), 265, 269
LL_clrscr(), 318, 320
LL_esetres(), 264, 268
LL_gotoxy(), 318, 320-321
LL_mapmask(), 264, 268
LL_modereg(), 264, 268
LL_outch(), 318, 321
LL_planerd(), 265, 272
LL_planewr(), 265, 272-273
LL_rdgwin(), 265, 269-270
LL_readmap(), 264, 269
LL_readwin(), 265, 273
LL_setfunction, 265, 269
LL_setmode(), 318-319, 326
LL_setres(), 264, 268

LL_setvideo7mode, 318-319, 326
LL_wrgwin(), 265, 270-271
LL_write3byte(), 265, 276-278
LL_writewin(), 265, 275-276
Load Acceleration Curves, 506-508
LoadCursor(), 414, 416, 418, 423, 430, 517,
    521-522
load_sprite(), 266, 279-281, 310, 312, 314-315, 347
Logical operations, 201, 230
Logitech
    3-button standard, 466
    ballistic speed, 195
    double-speed threshold, 195, 483, 490
    mouse driver, available functions, 466,
       513-514
    Video Cursor Interface (VCI), 257
LOWORD(), 391, 395-396, 399, 527, 533
lParam, 371, 380, 391, 395-396, 421, 424, 528-533
lpPoint, 449-450, 521
lpszcmdparam, 369, 377-378
lpvANDbitPlane, 519
lpvXORbitPlane, 519

M

MA_ACTIVATE, 530
MA_ACTIVATEANDEAT, 530
Macro Assembler, 107
Macro definition, 7
MainWndProc(), 371, 377, 380, 382, 391
Make files,112. *See also* Project files
manage_window_cursor(), 209, 222-224
MA_NOACTIVE, 530
MA_NOACTIVATEANDEAT, 530
MASM.EXE, 108
MAX_COLOR, 14, 18-19, 21, 25
Maximize button, 374
Memory
    models, 108, 113-114, 241-242, 288-290,
      305
    planar, 255
Menus, 127-150
    coordinates, 129-130,
    keyboard input, 146-150
    types, 127-131
Message processing
    in DOS,
    in Windows, 368, 379
Message, 369, 378
MessageBeep(), 533
MEVENT.INC, 104-105
Mickey, 189, 477-477, 502-503

Mickey-to-pixel ratio, 190, 480
Microsoft
    compiler, 7-9, 112-114, 242, 245, 288-290,
        304-306, 373
    .FON files, 30
    graphics library, 30, 114
    mouse, 3
    stack checking, 112, 242, 288, 290, 304-305
    video function library, 10, 21
Minimize button, 374
mirror image, 348
mirror operations, 348
mirror_cursor, 349, 351
MK_CONTROL, 391, 394, 397-398, 528, 530
MK_LBUTTON, 391, 394, 397-398, 528, 530
MK_MBUTTON, 391, 394, 397, 528, 530
MK_RBUTTON, 391, 394, 397-398, 528, 530
MK_SHIFT, 391, 394, 397-398, 528, 530
MODE_NUMBER, 268, 308, 312, 315, 319, 333
Module definition files, 371, 380-382
Mouse
    buffer. *See* Buffer
    buttons. *See* Buttons
    cursor. *See* Cursor coordinates; Cursor flag;
        Cursor flicker; Cursor mask; Cursor
        range; Cursor visibility; Graphics
        cursor; Text cursor; Windows cursor
    detection. *See* Detection of mouse
    driver. *See* Mouse driver
    scope, 461
    sensitivity. *See* Sensitivity
    speed. *See* Speed
    status. *See* Status
    supported video modes, 255-256
    type, determining, 174-176, 180-181,
        498-499, 505-506
Mouse busy flag, 501
Mouse count table, 507
Mouse cursor. *See* Cursor coordinates; Cursor
    flag; Cursor flicker; Cursor mask; Cursor
    range; Cursor visibility; Graphics mouse
    cursor; Text mouse cursor; Windows cursor
Mouse driver
    default values, 467, 496
    disabling, 494
    general information, 500-501
    initializing, 3-4, 6, 34, 38-39, 44, 295-296,
        466-467
    installing, 3-4
    language, 496-498
    resetting, 6, 34, 38-39, 44, 61, 117, 466-467,
        494-495, 510-511

restoring driver state, 486-487
saving driver state, 485-486
switch settings, 514-516
type, 500
vectors, 45, 467, 494-495
version number, identifying, 174-176, 180,
    182, 498-499
version number, of mouse functions, 466
Mouse driver functions
    Calling from C program, 6-7, 34-35, 37-44,
        174-178, 295-304, 466-516
    Disable Mouse Driver, 494
    Enable Mouse Driver, 494-495
    Enumerate Video Modes, 504-505
    Get Active Advanced Function, 182,
        513-514
    Get Alternate Event Handler, 489
    Get Button Press Information, 82, 471-472
    Get Button Release Information, 35, 43,
        81-82, 301, 472-473
    Get Button Status and Cursor Position, 35,
        42, 71, 82, 300, 469-470
    Get CRT Page Number, 174, 176, 493-494
    Get Cursor Hot Spot, 60, 505-506
    Get Driver Version, Type, and IRQ#,
        174-176, 498-499
    Get General Driver Information, 500-501
    Get Language Number, 497-498
    Get Maximum Virtual Coordinates, 52,
        501-502
    Get Min/Max Virtual Coordinates, 512-513
    Get Mouse Driver State Buffer Size, 125,
        485
    Get MOUSE.INI, 516
    Get Screen and Cursor Mask Values and
        Mickey Count, 502-503
    Get Sensitivity Rate, 177, 191, 491
    Get Switch Settings, 514-516
    Hide Cursor, 34, 40, 58, 61-62, 297, 468-469
    Light-Pen Emulation Mode Off, 480
    Light-Pen Emulation Mode On, 479-480
    Load Acceleration Curves, 506-508
    Mouse Hardware Reset, 510-511
    Mouse Reset and Status, 6, 34, 38, 44, 61,
        117, 295, 466-467
    Read Acceleration Curves, 508-509
    Read Mouse Motion Counters, 477-478
    Restore Mouse Driver State, 125, 486-487
    Save Mouse Driver State, 125, 485-486
    Set Alternate Event Handler, 97, 124,
        487-488
    Set CRT Page Number, 182, 492-493

Set Double-Speed Threshold, 190, 482-483
Set Event Handler, 35, 44, 97-98, 302, 335, 478-479
Set Exclusion Area, 34, 40, 62, 298, 468, 481-482
Set/Get Acceleration Curve, 509-510
Set/Get BallPoint Information, 511-512
Set Graphics Cursor, 175, 178, 203, 475-476
Set Language for Messages, 496-497
Set Mickey-to-Pixel Ratio, 190, 480-481
Set Min/Max Horizontal Cursor Position, 34, 41, 49, 299, 473-474
Set Min/Max Vertical Cursor Position, 34, 41, 49, 300, 474-475
Set Mouse Cursor Position, 34, 41, 77, 298, 470-471
Set Mouse Interrupt Rate, 491-492
Set Sensitivity Rate, 175, 177, 191, 490
Set Text Cursor, 175, 178, 231, 476-477
Set Video Mode, 256, 503-504
Show Cursor, 34, 39, 58, 61-62, 296, 468
Software Reset, 495-496
Swap Event Handlers, 97, 123, 125, 335, 483-484
Mouse function 0, 6, 34, 38, 44, 61, 117, 295, 466-467
Mouse function 1, 34, 39, 58, 61-62, 296, 468
Mouse function 2, 34, 40, 58, 60-62, 297, 468-469
Mouse function 3, 35, 42, 71, 81-82, 300, 469-470
Mouse function 4, 34, 41, 77, 298, 470-471
Mouse function 5 81-82, 471-468
Mouse function 6, 35, 43, 81-82, 301, 472-473
Mouse function 7, 34, 41, 49, 299, 473-474
Mouse function 8, 34, 42, 49, 300, 474-475
Mouse function 9, 175, 178, 203, 475-476
Mouse function 10, 175, 178, 231, 476-477
Mouse function 11, 477-478
Mouse function 12, 35, 44, 97-98, 335, 302, 478-479
Mouse function 13, 479-480
Mouse function 14, 480
Mouse function 15, 190, 480-481
Mouse function 16, 34, 40, 62, 468, 298, 481-482
Mouse function 17, 482
Mouse function 18, 482
Mouse function 19, 190, 482-483
Mouse function 20, 97, 123, 125, 335, 483-484
Mouse function 21, 125, 485
Mouse function 22, 125, 485-486
Mouse function 23, 125, 486-487
Mouse function 24, 97, 124, 487-488
Mouse function 25, 489

Mouse function 26, 175, 177, 191, 490
Mouse function 27, 175, 177, 191, 491
Mouse function 28, 491-492
Mouse function 29, 182, 492-493
Mouse function 30, 174, 176, 493-494
Mouse function 31, 494
Mouse function 32, 494-495
Mouse function 33, 495-496
Mouse function 34, 496-497
Mouse function 35, 497-498
Mouse function 36, 174, 176, 498-499
Mouse function 37, 500-501
Mouse function 38, 52, 501-502
Mouse function 39, 502-503
Mouse function 40, 256, 503-504
Mouse function 41, 504-505
Mouse function 42, 60, 505-506
Mouse function 43, 506-508
Mouse function 44, 508-509
Mouse function 45, 509-510
Mouse function 46, 510
Mouse function 47, 510-511
Mouse function 48, 511-512
Mouse function 49, 512-513
Mouse function 50, 182, 513-514
Mouse function 51, 514-516
Mouse function 52, 516
Mouse function library, 34-44, 293-304
    event_processor(), 104-106, 245, 292, 302-303
    get_button_rls_info(), 35, 43-44, 82, 89, 254, 301-302, 309
    get_crt_page(), 174, 176, 180, 245, 309
    get_mouse_button(), 35, 42-43, 71, 73, 82, 244, 300-301, 309
    get_mouse_sensitivity(), 175-176, 191-192, 245, 309
    get_mouse_type(), 174-175, 180, 245, 299
    hide_mouse_cursor(), 34, 39-40, 58-59, 61-62, 244, 291, 297-298, 309, 335, 350
    install_event_handler(), 105, 116, 119, 245, 292, 304, 310, 316, 336
    reset_event_status(), 105, 118, 136, 145-146, 245, 304, 310
    reset_mouse(), 34, 38-40, 44, 61, 117, 244, 295-296, 309
    set_event_handler(), 35, 44, 97-98, 105, 117, 245, 302, 309, 335
    set_graphics_cursor(), 175, 177-178, 203, 206-207, 221-222, 245, 309
    set_hide_bounds(), 34, 40, 62, 64-65, 73, 244, 292, 297-298, 309, 334

set_mouse_hlimits(), 34, 41, 49-51, 90, 92, 143, 244, 299, 309, 334

set_mouse_position(), 34, 40-41, 77, 122, 244, 292, 298-299, 309

set_mouse_sensitivity(), 175, 177, 191, 245, 309

set_mouse_vlimits(), 34, 41-42, 49-50, 90, 92, 143, 244, 299-300, 309, 334

set_text_cursor(), 175, 178, 231, 233, 236, 245, 309

show_mouse_cursor(), 34, 39, 48, 58-59, 61-62, 244, 291, 296, 309, 335, 350

Mouse Hardware Reset, 510-511

Mouse motion counters, 477-478. *See also* Speed; Mickey

Mouse Reset and Status, 6, 34, 38, 44, 61, 117, 295, 466-467

MOUSE1.C, 48

MOUSE2.C, 50

MOUSE3.C, 55-56

MOUSE4.C, 58-60

MOUSE5.C, 63-65

MOUSE6.C, 72-73

MOUSE7.C, 75-76

MOUSE8.C, 77-78

MOUSE9.C, 83-85

MOUSE10.C, 88-89

MOUSE11.C, 91-94

MOUSE12.C, 111, 115-117, 245

MOUSE13.C, 119-122

MOUSE14.C, 131-142

MOUSE15.C, 155-159

MOUSE16.C, 168-171

MOUSE17.C, 173-176

MOUSE18.C, 179-181

MOUSE19.C, 192-194

MOUSE20.C, 195-198

MOUSE21.C, 204-207

MOUSE22.C, 210-227

MOUSE23.C, 231-234

MOUSE24.C, 234-237

MOUSE25.C, 246-247

MOUSE26.C, 311-313

MOUSE27.C, 322-326

MOUSE28.C, 327-331

MOUSE29.C, 337-342

MOUSE30.C, 344-348

MOUSE31.C, 351-358

MOUSE.COM, 3, 500

MOUSEDRV.C, 293-304

MOUSEDRV.H, 307-310

MOUSEDRV.LIB, 306

mouse_error(), 13, 21, 27, 48

MOUSE.H, 37-38

MOUSE.INC, 38-44

MOUSE.INI, 516

MOUSELIB.C, 241-242, 248

MOUSELIB.H, 243-245, 249

MOUSELIB.LIB, 241-245

MOUSE_SIZE, 35, 37, 51, 244, 293, 350

MOUSE.SYS, 3, 500

MOUSE_THERE, 35, 37-45, 244, 293, 295-302, 452, 456, 459

MOUSE_VISIBLE, 35, 37, 39-40, 61, 244, 293, 296-297

MOVEABLE keyword, 381

mregs, 36, 38-45, 244, 294

MS_ARROW, 208, 211

MS_CROSS, 208, 212

msegregs, 36, 38, 44, 178, 244, 294, 302

MS_IBEAM, 208, 211

MS_ICON, 208, 213

MS_SIZE, 208, 215

MS_SIZENESW, 208, 217

MS_SIZENS, 208, 216

MS_SIZENWSE, 208, 218

MS_SIZEWE, 208, 215

MS_UPARROW, 208, 214

MSVIDLIB.INC, 10, 11, 21-28, 248

MS_WAIT, 208, 219

MULTIPLE keyword, 381

Multiplication factor, 190, 490-491

MV_BBUTTON, 35, 37, 120, 243, 293

MV_LBUTTON, 35, 37, 120, 243, 293

MV_RBUTTON, 35, 37, 120, 243, 293

/MX compiler option, 108

N

NAME keyword, 381

nCmdShow, 369, 377-378

Near function, 101

NEC Multisynch, 258, 317

new_sprite(), 266, 278-279, 310, 312, 347

nHeight, 519

Non-Client area
    button messages, 383-390, 398-405, 528-529
    coordinates, 398, 402, 445
    detailed information, 398-405

Nonintegrated mouse driver, 500

NOREGS, 69

NUMBER_BUTTONS, 37, 39, 105, 243, 293, 295-297

nWidth, 519

O

OEM08.FON, 29
OLDC, 9, 248
Optional mouse functions, 174-182. *See also*
    Mouse function library
OPTIONAL.INC, 175-178
Origin, in text and graphics, 28
out_int_xy(), 13, 17, 23-24, 31
*outregs, 5
out_text(), 386
out_text_xy(), 13, 17, 23, 318, 321, 31

P

PAGE, 268, 286-287, 315, 321
Parent program, 124
PatBlt(), 443
PEN-DOWN, 480
PEN-UP, 480
Pixel
        compression, 201-202
        expansion, 201-202
        coordinates, mouse, 71-79, 107
        coordinates, hot spot, 203
        in cursor image, 201
        masking, 260-262
        to mickey ratio, 190
Planar memory, 255
POINT structure, 449, 458, 521
Polling, 95. *See also* Button presses; Button
    releases; Cursor coordinates
PostQuitMessage(), 380
PRELOAD keyword, 381
Procedure declaration, WinMain(), 377-378
Program initialization, WinMain(), 378-379
Program termination, WinMain(), 380
Project files
        Borland and Microsoft, differences, 112
        in DOS, 112, 245, 310
        in Windows, 372
PS/2 mouse, 182, 499, 506
pszCursor, 522

R

R6000 runtime error, 112
RBUTTON_DOWN, 35, 37, 99, 104, 116, 121,
    244, 294, 303
RBUTTON_UP, 35, 37, 105, 119, 244, 294, 303
Read Acceleration Curves, 508-509
Read mode 0, 260
Read Mouse Motion Counters, 477-478
RECT structure, 454, 458, 518, 520

Recursion, 103
Reference cursor, 350, 358
Registers
        AX, 6, 45, 106
        BX, 6, 46, 106
        CX, 6, 106
        DX, 6, 106
        EGA, 66-69, 264-265
        general, 6
        status, 103
        working, 5
        VGA, 68, 264-265
REGS, 5, 38, 244, 294, 308
ReleaseCapture(), 462, 517, 523
reset_event_status(), 105, 118, 136-137, 141, 245,
    145-146, 304, 309
reset_mouse(), 34, 38, 40, 44, 61, 117, 244, 295,
    309
Resource cursors, 427-432
Resource Workshop, 427
Restore Mouse Driver State, 125, 486-487
Reverse button trap, 86
REV_REF.INC, 359-363
right_arrow, 349, 351
ROM BIOS
        functions calls, 4, 100
        Interrupt 0x10, 47, 257, 317
        Interrupt 0x33, 4, 6, 45, 368
Rotation angle, BallPoint, 512
Runtime error R6000, 112

S

Save Mouse Driver State, 125, 485-486
Scale factor table, acceleration curve, 508
Scan lines, 230, 476-477, 502-503
Scope, 461
Screen mask
        in graphics cursor, 200-201, 475-476
        in text software cursor, 230, 476-477,
            502-503
Screen modes. *See* Graphics modes; Text modes
ScreenToClient(), 445, 450
*segregs, 5
SelectObject(), 442
Sensitivity,
        mouse, retrieving, 175-177, 191-194, 491
        mouse, setting, 175, 177, 191-194, 490
Sequential platforms, 90, 130, 368
Serial mouse, 182, 499, 506
Serial port, determining, 181
Set Alternate Event Handler, 97, 124, 487-488
Set CRT Page Number, 182, 492-493

Set Double-Speed Threshold, 190, 482-483
Set Event Handler, 35, 44, 97-98, 335, 478-479
Set Exclusion Area, 34, 40, 62, 468, 298, 481-482
Set/Get Acceleration Curve, 509-510
Set/Get BallPoint Information, 511-512
Set Graphics Cursor, 175, 178, 203, 475-476
Set Language for Messages, 496-497
Set Mickey-to-Pixel Ratio, 190, 480-481
Set Min/Max Horizontal Cursor Position, 34, 41,
    49, 299, 473-474
Set Min/Max Vertical Cursor Position, 34, 41, 49,
    474-475
Set Mouse Cursor Position, 34, 41, 77, 298,
    470-471
Set Mouse Interrupt Rate, 491-492
Set Sensitivity Rate, 175, 177, 191, 490
Set Text Cursor, 175, 178, 231, 476-477
Set Video Mode, 256, 503-504
SetCapture(), 461-462, 518, 523, 531
SetCursor(), 416, 432, 438, 443, 518, 523-524
SetCursorPos(), 451, 452, 460, 518, 524
SetDoubleClickTime(), 405, 409, 518, 524
set_event_handler(), 35, 44, 97-98, 105, 117, 245,
    302, 304, 309, 335
set_graphics_cursor(), 175, 177, 203, 206-207,
    221-222, 245, 309
set_hide_bounds(), 34, 40, 62, 64-65, 73, 292,
    244, 297, 309, 334
setlinestyle(), 9, 14, 174-176
set_mouse_hlimits(), 34, 41, 49, 51, 90, 92, 143,
    244, 299, 309, 334
set_mouse_position(), 34, 40-41, 77, 122, 244,
    292, 298-299, 309
set_mouse_sensitivity(), 175, 177, 191, 245, 309
set_mouse_vlimits(), 34, 41-42, 49, 90, 92, 143,
    244, 299-300, 309, 334
set_sprite_mode, 266, 286, 310, 337
set_text_cursor(), 175, 178, 231, 233, 236, 244,
    309
setwritemode(), 9, 14, 154, 157
Shadow map, 68, 292
Show Cursor, 34, 39, 58, 61-62, 296, 468
ShowCursor(), 451, 453-454, 460, 518, 525
show_mouse_cursor(), 34, 39, 48, 58, 61-62, 244,
    291, 296, 309, 335, 350
show_sprite(), 266, 287, 292, 296, 310, 348,
    361-362
ShowWindow(), 379
shut_down_video(), 13, 16, 23, 32
SIZEICONIC, 461
SIZEZOOMHIDE, 461
Sizing arrows

in DOS, 208-209
in Windows, 376, 383, 414-415
SMALLVID.INC, 318-321
SM_MOUSEPRESENT, 452, 459
sm_or_sl, 178, 231
Software Reset, 495-496
Software cursor, 229-234, 476-477
spawn(), 124
Speed, mouse, 189-198, 477-478, 490-492
    maximum obtainable, 198
    retrieving, 491
    sensitivity rates, 191, 490-491
    setting, 190-194, 490
    threshold, 176, 190, 194-198, 490-491
Sprite, 259
Sprite cursor, 259
    destroying, 316
    hot spot, 315, 334
    initializing, 313-316, 363
    limiting range, 334
    mask, 314
Sprite driver
    compiling, 288-290
    data segment, 287-288
    usage rules, 333-336
Sprite driver functions
    change_sprite_color(), 266, 285-286, 310,
        337, 341
    change_sprite_line_color(), 266, 285, 310,
        337, 340
    destroy_sprite(), 266, 281, 310, 313, 316,
        336, 347
    do_sprite(), 266, 281-285
    draw_sprite(), 266, 268, 282-285, 292, 294,
        299, 310, 348, 361-362
    hide_sprite(), 266, 286, 292, 297, 310, 348,
        361-362
    init_sprite(), 311-312, 314, 324, 329,
        338-339, 345-346, 352-353
    LL_bitmask(), 265, 269
    LL_esetres(), 264, 268
    LL_mapmask(), 264, 268
    LL_modereg(), 264, 268
    LL_planerd(), 265, 272
    LL_planewr(), 265, 272-273
    LL_rdgwin(), 265, 269
    LL_readmap(), 264, 269
    LL_readwin(), 265, 273-275
    LL_setfunction, 265, 269
    LL_setres(), 264, 268
    LL_wrgwin(), 265, 270-271
    LL_write3byte(), 265, 276-277

LL_writewin(), 265, 275-276
load_sprite(), 266, 279-281, 310, 312,
    314-315, 347
new_sprite(), 266, 278, 310, 312, 347
set_sprite_mode(), 266, 286, 310, 337
show_sprite(), 266, 287, 292, 296, 310,
    348, 361-362
sprite_imagesize(), 266, 278, 280
sprite_cursor, 294, 308, 312, 315, 349, 347
sprite_imagesize(), 266, 278, 280
SPRITELL.C, 267-287
sprite_type(), 266-267, 304, 308
SPRITLLH.OBJ, 289
SPRITLLL.OBJ, 289
SPRITLLC.OBJ, 289
SPRITLLS.OBJ, 289
SREGS, 5, 38, 244, 294, 308
Stack checking, 112, 242, 288, 290, 304-305
STACKSIZE keyword, 382
Static cursors, 434
Status, mouse
    in DOS, 6, 34, 38, 45, 295, 466-467
    in Windows, 452, 459
STDIO.H, 249
Stretching
    ellipses, 172-176
    lines, 166, 168-171
    rectangles, 171
STRICT keyword, 377, 369, 517
STUB keyword, 381
Super VGA. *See also* Video Graphics Array (VGA)
    800x600 16-color, 253-258, 264, 315,
        317-331
    1024x768 256-color, 264
    ATI Graphics Ultra, 257
    OEM Video modes, 254-255, 317-318, 326
    problems with, 253-255
    Video7 VRAMII Ergo, 49, 256
Swap Event Handlers, 97, 123, 125, 335, 483-484
SwapMouseButtons(), 518, 525
Switch settings, 514-515

T ————————————————

tagPOINT structure type, 521
tagRECT structure type, 518, 520
TASM.EXE, 107
TCVIDLIB.INC, 10, 11, 15-21, 249
Terminate-stay-resident (TSR), 125
Termination, Windows application, 455
Text cursor, 229-237, 476-477, 500, 502-503; *See
    also* Cursor coordinates; Cursor flag; Cursor

flicker; Cursor mask; Cursor range; Cursor
visibility
    coordinates, 71-73, 76-79, 107, 123
    defined, 229-231
    hardware cursor, 229-230, 234-237, 476-477
    keyboard, moving with, 76-79
    software cursor, 229-234, 476-477
_TEXT fixup errors, 108
Text modes
    disruption, 57
    retrieving, 504-505
    setting, 12, 15, 22, 32, 503-504
    vs. graphics mode, 11-12, 32, 36
Text scrolling, 28
Timing. *See* Double-clicking
TLIB.EXE, 243, 306
TMODE, 12, 32, 21, 316
touch_cursor(), 66, 122
Triple-click, 90
Turbo Assembler, 107
turn_off_move_event(), 350, 353

U ————————————————

Undo, 167
Union, 5
UpdateWindow(), 379
USING_SPRITE, 291-292, 294, 296-297, 299, 303,
    308, 312, 315-316, 333, 335

V ————————————————

Variable frequency display, 258, 317
VCELL_SIZE, 35, 37, 39-43, 243, 293, 295-303
Vectors, 45, 467, 494-495
Version number
    mouse driver, identifying, 174-176, 180,
        182, 498-499
    mouse functions, 466
VFONT_SIZE, 12, 14-18, 28
VGA. *See* Video Graphics Array
Video cursor function flag, 500
Video Cursor Interface (VCI), 257
Video Electronics Standards Association (VESA),
    257
Video function library, 11-32
    change_background(), 13, 19, 25, 134, 139
    change_color(), 13, 18-19, 25, 31
    clear_line_from(), 13, 18, 24-25, 30, 31, 67
    delay(), 27-28, 87, 89
    draw_rectangle(), 13, 19-20, 26, 28, 171
    ellipse(), 9, 12, 176
    header(), 13, 20, 27, 31

install_video( ), 12, 13, 15-16, 21-22, 31-32
line( ), 9, 14, 158-159, 169-170
mouse_error( ), 13, 21, 27, 48
out_int_xy( ), 13, 17, 23-24, 31
out_text_xy( ), 13, 17, 23, 318, 321, 31
setlinestyle( ), 9, 14, 174, 176
setwritemode( ), 9, 14, 154, 157
shut_down_video( ), 13, 16, 23, 32
testing, 30
Video Graphics Array (VGA)
display, 67-68, 254-258
modes. *See* Graphics modes
registers, 68, 264-265
write modes, 260
Video hardware cursor, 256
Video modes. *See* Graphics modes; Text modes
Video7 VRAMII Ergo, 49, 256
videolib, 10
VID_MAXX, 14-16, 21-22, 27, 50, 315, 318-320, 350
VID_MAXY, 14-16, 21-22, 27, 50, 315, 318-320, 350
VIDTEST.C, 30-32
Virtual coordinates, 501-502, 512-513
Virtual keys, 391, 397-398
Virtual screen, 47, 52
VK_DOWN, 460
VK_LEFT, 460
VK_RIGHT, 460
VK_UP, 460

W

WA_ACTIVE, 459
WAND1, 427-428, 432
Window resizing, 455
Windows
3.1, 377
control menu, 374
Control Panel, 405
event processing, 368
file menu, 374
generic program, 369-382
icon, 374, 455
message processing, WinMain( ), 379
module definition files, 371
mouse driver, 368
procedure declaration, WinMain( ), 377-378
program initialization, WinMain( ), 378-379
program termination, WinMain( ), 380
restore option, 376

sizing functions, 376, 383
system menu, 374
Windows cursor, 413-444. *See also* Cursor
coordinates; Cursor flag; Cursor flicker;
Cursor mask; Cursor range; Cursor visibility
bitmap cursor mask, 434, 519
coordinates, 391, 395-396, 398, 445, 454
cursor size, 434
default, management, 414-426
destroying, 432
device-dependent, 434-439
device-independent, 434, 439-444
dynamic, 434
hot spot, 434, 519
keyboard, moving with, 452-461
modifying, 413-444
resources, 427
static, 434
WINDOWS.H, 377, 517
WinMain( ), 369, 377, 382, 432
WINSTUB.EXE, 381
WM_ACTIVATE, 454, 459
WM_CREATE, 409, 442, 459
WM_DESTROY, 371, 380, 455
WM_KEYDOWN, 452, 460
WM_KILLFOCUS, 455, 461
WM_LBUTTONDBLCLK, 390, 387, 528
WM_LBUTTONDOWN, 383, 387, 390, 395, 397-398, 409, 527
WM_LBUTTONUP, 391, 387, 395, 528
WM_MBUTTONDBLCLK, 388, 528
WM_MBUTTONDOWN, 388, 527
WM_MBUTTONUP, 388, 528
WM_MOUSEACTIVATE, 529-530
WM_MOUSEMOVE, 419, 420, 431, 438, 443, 445, 449, 530-531
WM_MOVE, 455, 461
WM_NCHITTEST, 462, 531-532
WM_NCLBUTTONDBLCLK, 529, 389
WM_NCLBUTTONDOWN, 383-384, 388, 529
WM_NCLBUTTONUP, 384, 388, 529
WM_NCMBUTTONDBLCLK, 389, 529
WM_NCMBUTTONDOWN, 389, 529
WM_NCMBUTTONUP, 389, 529
WM_NCMOUSEMOVE, 445, 450, 532
WM_NCRBUTTONDBLCLK, 529
WM_NCRBUTTONDOWN, 383, 402, 529
WM_NCRBUTTONUP, 529
WMOUSE1.C, 384-389
WMOUSE1.DEF, 384
WMOUSE2.C, 392-396

WMOUSE2.DEF, 391
WMOUSE3.C, 400-404
WMOUSE3.DEF, 399
WMOUSE4.C, 406-410
WMOUSE4.DEF, 406
WMOUSE5.C, 416-420
WMOUSE5.DEF, 416
WMOUSE6.C, 421-426
WMOUSE6.DEF, 421
WMOUSE7.C, 429-432
WMOUSE7.DEF, 428-429
WMOUSE8.C, 434-438
WMOUSE8.DEF, 434
WMOUSE9.C, 440-444
WMOUSE9.DEF, 440
WMOUSE10.C, 446-450
WMOUSE10.DEF, 446
WMOUSE11.C, 456-461
WMOUSE11.DEF, 455
WM_PAINT, 379, 387
WM_QUIT, 380
WM_RBUTTONDBLCLK, 388, 410, 528
WM_RBUTTONDOWN, 383, 388, 395, 398, 410, 527

WM_RBUTTONUP, 383, 388, 396, 528
WM_SETCURSOR, 420-421, 424, 462, 532-533
WM_SETFOCUS, 461
WM_SIZE, 409, 455, 461
WndClass, 369, 378
WndClass.hCursor, 414, 416
wParam, 371, 380, 390-391, 395-398, 403, 528-533
Write mode 0, 260
write_control_key(), 394, 395-397

X

xHotSpot, 519
XOR
      logical operations, 201, 230
      write mode, 14, 57, 154, 167-168, 172, 263, 336
XOR_PUT, 9, 154, 168, 267, 297, 337

Y

yHotSpot, 519

Technical support is available for this book by registering to Jeffrey Donovan's Technical Support BBS. This BBS operates 24 hours a day and runs the GAP Communications BBS system from GAP Development Company.

What You Get   You get a comprehensive BBS dedicated to supporting the works of Jeffrey S. Donovan. You may leave questions and messages to Mr. Donovan, and he will reply back (on the BBS) within a 24-48 hour period. There will be bulletins posted regarding any updates and additions to the book, and from time to time files may be available for downloading. You may feel free to discuss subjects not covered in the book (so long as they relate to the mouse).

What You Don't Get   The BBS is not a shareware house. Few if any files are available for downloading and uploads are not allowed except on a request by request basis.

Because of the time involved in providing comprehensive technical support there is a fee of $20.00 per year. Only readers who mail in the registration form and fee are allowed on the BBS and the public is strictly prohibited from access.

To register, fill out the following form (photocopies are not accepted) and make your check or money order out in the amount of $20.00, payable to Jeffrey Donovan. Send them both to:

Jeffrey Donovan
P.O. Box 23351
Santa Barbara, CA 93102

Be sure to write down and remember your password. You will need it to log on. You will be allowed on the system approximately 24 hours after your registration is received.

The BBS number is (805) 962-0996. Dial in at 1200-9600 baud, no parity, 8 data bits, 1 stop bit.

Registration for Jeffrey Donovan's Technical Support Hotline BBS.

_____

First Name: _____ Last Name: _____

Street Address: _____

City: _____ Zip: _____

Daytime Phone: (   )_____ - _____

Your Password :_____ (12 letters or fewer)